MAKING A NATION,
BREAKING A NATION

Literature and Cultural
Politics in Yugoslavia

For Jurij's
Who else to too
may projects in to
may areas.
With all my admiration,
Andrew
7/6/99

Cultural Memory

in

the

Present

Mieke Bal and Hent de Vries, Editors

MAKING A NATION, BREAKING A NATION

*Literature and Cultural Politics
in Yugoslavia*

Andrew Baruch Wachtel

STANFORD UNIVERSITY PRESS

STANFORD, CALIFORNIA

1998

Stanford University Press
Stanford, California
© 1998 by the Board of Trustees of the
Leland Stanford Junior University

Printed in the United States of America

CIP data appear at the end of the book

Frontispiece: Ivan Meštrović, monument to
Petar Petrović Njegoš, plaster study (1932).
The artist stands alongside the monument.
Meštrović Museum, Zagreb. Photo courtesy
of the University of Notre Dame Archives.

Acknowledgments

This project could not have been completed without help and encouragement from colleagues all over the world. In particular, I would like to acknowledge the suggestions and corrections I received from Marija Mitrović, Bogdan Rakić, Michael Heim, Tomislav Longinović, Ellen Elias-Bursac, Gordana Crnković, and an anonymous reviewer for Stanford University Press. Thanks to their efforts I have avoided countless mistakes and have come to see many facets of the Yugoslav cultural situation that would have otherwise eluded me. I am sure that some errors remain, however, and they bear no responsibility for them. I had illuminating conversations on various aspects of the book with Aleš Debeljak, Ilya Kutik, Jurij Perovšek, and Boris A. Novak. My Northwestern colleague Saul Morson was a constant and sympathetic interlocutor and a keen reader at all stages of the project. I received much bibliographic assistance from the staff of the National and University Library (NUK) in Ljubljana, Slovenia, as well as from the interlibrary loan division of the Northwestern University Libraries. Permission to publish photographs of the work of Ivan Meštrović was graciously granted by the Fondacija Ivana Meštrovića, Zagreb. Financial support for my research and writing came from a variety of sources, including The National Council for Soviet and East European Research, the Fulbright-Hays Faculty Research Abroad Program (United States Department of Education), IREX (funds provided by the National Endowment for the Humanities and the United States Department of State under the Title VIII program), and Northwestern University. None of these organizations is in any way responsible for the views expressed here. My mother, Miriam Wachtel, read the entire manuscript with a sharp editorial eye. The production staff at Stanford University Press was outstanding: thanks, as always, to my editor, Helen Tartar, to Nathan MacBrien, and to Erin M. Milnes. Finally, I would like to express my gratitude to Elizabeth Calihan and Samuel Barnes Wachtel, who were there every step of the way.

A.B.W.

Contents

Figures

MAKING A NATION,
BREAKING A NATION

*Literature and Cultural
Politics in Yugoslavia*

Introduction

This is a book about Yugoslavia. Not Yugoslavia the country, which came into existence in 1918 and exists, in name at least, to this very day. Rather, this book is concerned with the idea of the "Yugoslav nation," the vision of the South Slavic community (in Slavic languages *yug* means "south") as an essential unity despite differences in language, religion, and historical experience. Although its roots can be traced earlier, the idea was first clearly articulated in the 1830s and 1840s among small groups of intellectuals. Having undergone a series of ideological transformations that broadened its appeal, this national ideal competed with various particularist nationalisms (among them Bulgarian, Serbian, Croatian, Slovenian, Macedonian, and Bosnian) for the allegiance of the South Slavs through the rest of the nineteenth and much of the twentieth centuries. Most commentators have been inclined to believe that the Yugoslav national idea gradually gained in popularity throughout much of its existence, although this has always been difficult to prove. It is certain, however, that no one at the turn of the nineteenth century would have identified him- or herself as a Yugoslav, whereas studies in the 1960s showed that the majority of the country's citizens held some form of Yugoslav national identity.[1] Beginning in the late 1960s, however, the idea lost popularity precipitously, and at present it is preserved almost exclusively in the consciousness of émigrés scattered thinly all over the world.

From the foregoing a few presuppositions should be clear. First of all, nation and state are not necessarily one and the same, even if many national movements do aspire to have a state of their own.[2] Following the lead of many theorists, I view the nation not as a political entity but as a state of mind, an "imagined community" in the lapidary terminology of Benedict Anderson, whose members belong to it not because of any objective identifying criteria such as common language, history, or cultural heritage (although in many particular cases such criteria can be and are adduced) but because they think they do. In the case of Yugoslavia, many citizens of the Habsburg and Ottoman empires or the kingdoms of Serbia and Montenegro considered themselves members of a Yugoslav nation well before a Yugoslav state came into existence. Conversely, by the 1980s, many citizens of the country called Yugoslavia did not believe they belonged to a Yugoslav nation.

The second important point is that as a created phenomenon, national identity is always potentially up for grabs. No matter how similar a group of people appears to be on the surface, there is sure to be some level at which difference appears, for each of us "moves in an indefinite number of communities, some more inclusive than others, each making different claims on our allegiance,"[3] and more than one of these might well allow for the kind of communal identification on the basis of which national consciousness is formed. An absurd, but deft, characterization of one pole of this phenomenon is Jonathan Swift's famous parable of the Lilliputians, who divide themselves into two parties solely on the basis of which side of an egg they open.[4] Nevertheless, this is sufficient for them to perceive each other as belonging to distinct groups and leads to their irreconcilable enmity. And even in the real world, the differentiation processes of various population groups seem to follow not logic so much as Freud's principle of the narcissism of small differences. Conversely, no matter how heterogeneous a group of people might appear to an observer, there is a level at which its members could choose to see each other as belonging to one nation. Indeed, in principle at least, the concept of nation does not require an "other" in opposition to which it defines itself, as Liah Greenfeld notes: "A nation coextensive with humanity is in no way a contradiction in terms."[5] Any actual nation, as opposed to Swift's dystopian and Greenfeld's utopian versions, contains people with a broad range of both similarities and differences. Insofar as it is a nation, its members have agreed to overlook the differences and view the similarities as essential.

And who decides whether a given group is one nation or many? This is perhaps the most complex question of all. It is, after all, a fiction to think that most people independently choose their national identity.[6] Rather, people have to be taught what a nation is in the first place (for the very concept of a nation is modern, dating back at the earliest to the seventeenth century) and then how to identify with "their own nation." Given that this is so, they can also be retaught, and their national identity and ways of viewing it can change. As Paul R. Brass puts it in the introduction to his excellent study of nationalism in India, "It follows, finally, from all these points that the process of ethnic identity formation and its transformation into nationalism is reversible. It is reversible because of both the dynamics of external competition and the internal divisions and contradictions that exist within all groups of people, however defined."[7] In Brass's view, and in the view of many other theorists of nationalism, elites in a given population make the decisions that define a nation, which then "trickle down" to the population at large.

But, paradoxically, because national identity is, as Anderson puts it, "conceived as a deep, horizontal comradeship" (16), the elites who forge a nation must always assert that *their* nation is not a created object but rather the expression of an already existing unity. In this respect, the nation functions as a myth, which "has the task of giving an historical intention a natural justification, and making contingency appear eternal. . . . In passing from history to nature, myth acts economically: it abolishes the complexity of human acts, it gives them the simplicity of essences, it does away with all dialectics, with any going back beyond what is immediately visible, it organizes a world which is without contradictions because it is without depth, a world wide open and wallowing in the evident, it establishes a blissful clarity: things appear to mean something by themselves."[8] As a result, elites cannot merely impose national consciousness; rather, they propose a national definition, basing it on existing and invented traditions, and the chosen population accepts, modifies, or rejects the definition. Ultimately, those nations will form whose elites present well-articulated, well-chosen national visions. And they will continue to succeed until either some other group provides a better-articulated and better-chosen vision or the initial vision discredits itself.

Of what do these national visions consist? Naturally, a common language or common traditions and ways of life turn out to be the easiest material to use in forging a nation. These have been yoked, in certain cases, to some basic political ideals, but the essential building blocks of national identity are undoubtedly cultural ones. As Anderson emphasizes: "Nationality, or, as one might prefer to put it in view of that word's multiple significations, nation-ness, as well as nationalism, are cultural artifacts of a particular kind."[9] In his painful study of Nigeria, Wole Soyinka states this even more bluntly: "Before politics, there was clearly culture. . . . This hierarchy of evolution also explains why man resorts to his cultural affiliations when politics appear to have failed him, never the other way around."[10] The preeminence of culture in the formation of national identity would suggest that in studies of nationalism, both theoretical and empirical, the emphasis should be placed squarely on an exploration of the development of national culture. What aspects of existing cultural traditions do elites use in order to forge a national identity? How do they go about doing so? When do they succeed, and when do they fail? The goal of this book will be to provide some answers to these questions by focusing on a single, highly complex test case: Yugoslavia from the 1830s through the 1980s.

In particular, I will concentrate on the cultural processes by which the idea of a Yugoslav nation was developed and on the reasons for the ultimate failure of that idea to bind the South Slavs into a viable nation and state. My premise is simple: the collapse of multinational Yugoslavia and the establishment of separate uninational states—or, even worse, states that have strived to become so despite the inconvenient presence of members of other national groups on their territory—were not the result of the breakdown of the political or economic fabric of the Yugoslav state; rather, these breakdowns, which manifestly occurred and have been copiously documented, themselves sprang from the gradual destruction of the concept of a Yugoslav nation. Had a viable concept of the nation existed, the collapse of political authority would have been followed by the eventual reconstitution of a Yugoslav state, as was the case after World War II (and as has happened frequently enough over the past two centuries in, say, Germany or France), rather than to the creation of separate nation states for the various South Slavic groups.

Because I will focus on nation building and its failures in Yugoslavia rather than on state building, the causes I cite and the evidence I adduce for Yugoslavia's collapse differ markedly from those that most others have considered. I concentrate on culture and cultural politics in the South

Slavic lands from the mid–nineteenth century to the present in order to delineate those ideological mechanisms that helped lay the foundation for the formation of a Yugoslav nation and a Yugoslav state in the first place, sustained this state during its approximately seventy-year existence, and led to its dissolution. Agreeing with Benedict Anderson that "nationality . . . as well as nationalism, are cultural artifacts" (13), I examine the relatively long-term processes by which both governments and independent cultural leaders attempted to create in the potential and actual citizens of a political Yugoslavia a sense of Yugoslav national identity that would overarch and connect the existing South Slavic cultures.

My study is organized chronologically and focuses on the four most important ways that partisans of Yugoslavia attempted to advance their ideas of national unity: (1) linguistic policies that functioned to create a shared national language, and, when this proved impossible, at least a unified Serbo-Croatian language; (2) the promulgation of a Yugoslav literary and artistic canon that was interpreted as embodying desired traits of national unity; (3) educational policy, particularly relating to the teaching of literature and history in schools; and (4) the production of new literary and artistic works that incorporated a Yugoslav view variously defined. In an attempt to avoid a schematic view of these complicated cultural and political processes, I will eschew an encyclopedic treatment of the subject, focusing instead on key debates or figures in the areas of educational policy, cultural canonization, and literary creation.

Certainly there was in Yugoslavia considerable disagreement, tension, and evolution in how the relationship between the various South Slavic cultures and the national culture and state was to be conceived. Still, it is my contention that some version of Yugoslavism—some powerfully fostered ideological defense of an overarching culture whose centripetal force would balance the centrifugal force exerted by the many separate local cultures—was both an essential part of what sustained Yugoslavia in the first place and in the end a necessary condition of its survival as a state.

Attempts at nation building in Yugoslavia can be divided into three basic categories differentiated on the issue of how a national culture should be created and on what it should be based. According to the earliest Yugoslav view, one that, as we will see in Chapter 1, captivated not only Serbs but many Croats and even some Slovenes as well, the South Slavs would, for all intents and purposes, have eventually adopted a slightly modified form of Serbian culture. The allure of such an approach was understandable. The Serbs were the largest South Slav group, and they were the first in modern times to throw off external rule and create an autonomous state. What is more, they had preserved a viable folk culture that had drawn the admiration of major European cultural figures. Although they did not all see it exactly this way, the men of the first Yugoslavizing generation tended to take cultural and linguistic practices identified with Serbia as the norm and to create a uniform standard based on them. Had this approach to the creation of a Yugoslav nation triumphed, Yugoslavia might have eventually become a uninational and unicultural state, such as France, for example. As occurred in France with Parisian culture, the culture of one group of the population would have become dominant, and that of the others would have been relegated to marginal status. Regional differences would have continued to exist, but ultimately there would have been a single culture, called Yugoslav but for the most part actually Serbian, in a united Yugoslav state. There were, however, significant obstacles in the way of such a solution. These had to do primarily with the fact that Croats and particularly Slovenes already had separate, although not always well-articulated, cultural traditions that they were unwilling to abandon, at least not in favor of Serbian cultural norms. What is more, as they were not under Serbian political sway in the nineteenth century, they could and did continue to develop their own traditions in this period. By the time political union came, these separate traditions were even better entrenched than they had been in the 1830s and 1840s.

It is highly significant that this initial Yugoslav view derived from German romanticism, at base a synthetic ideology, which on Yugoslav soil encouraged attempts at pan–South Slavic unity. In his description of Russia, a country whose national views were also highly influenced by the German model, Andrzej Walicki characterizes Germanic-influenced romantic nationalism as a concept of "the nation as *a whole transcending its individual parts,* a unique collective individuality evolving historically by its own 'distinctive' principles."[11] It was precisely the romantic idea that the South Slavs could indeed overcome the differences manifest in their individual parts to create a collective Yugoslav nation that underlay the thinking of such men as Petar Petrović Njegoš and the Croatian Illyrians. Speaking generally, it can be said that all forms of Yugoslav nationalism retained this synthetic character, which tended to become broader over time.

In addition to its synthetic bias, the German romantic view left one other crucial trace on national thinking among the South Slavs. In her study of German national thought, Greenfeld characterizes the romantic attitude as follows:

> The Romantics had no understanding and no taste for the liberty of the individual—namely personal independence and freedom from coercion and arbitrary government. . . . The real freedom . . . which mercilessly underscored the pettiness and insignificance of all other notions of freedom was the freedom to fulfill the purpose of nature, to become "whole," that is, true to and fully conscious of one's individuality. . . . The achievement of such full consciousness of individuality, for men, was possible only through fusion with the state, and thus freedom resulted from and was only possible because of the unconditional subjugation of the individual to collective authority and the virtual dissolution of the individual personality within the state.[12]

In the German lands, such views produced a collectivistic-authoritarian model of the nation rather than an individualistic-libertarian one. The difference between the two is simple but telling. Whereas the latter (characteristic of national thought in Great Britain and most of its former colonies) views the individual members of a nation as sovereign and is directly linked to democracy, the former sees individuals as important only insofar as they are part of a unique and sovereign national group to which their individuality is subordinated.[13] Thus it was that Yugoslav nationalism (as well as the South Slavic particularist nationalisms that appeared at approximately the same time) was oriented to a collectivistic-authoritarian model, and with very few exceptions this model of the nation has remained central to all South Slavic national views.

In the period that stretched from the 1850s to the 1890s, support for the idea of Yugoslavia diminished. Although there were major exceptions, most important among them the tireless Josip Juraj Strossmayer, Catholic Bishop of Djakovo, who devoted the majority of his considerable resources to propagating the Yugoslav ideal, for the most part the period saw little cooperation among the South Slavs. This, I would argue, is no accident, for the resistance to pan–South Slavic ideas reflects cultural and philosophical processes broader than but related to the Yugoslav experience. When idealist romantic ideologies gave way to materialist and positivist ideas, a diminution in interest in the Yugoslav idea was inevitable. For realism, the literary movement that embodies these philosophical ideas, is concerned with nothing if not a careful consideration of particularity, and among the South Slavs such a focus tended to reveal the yawning gulf separating the various groups on the ground. Thus, during this period there was no cultural imperative toward synthesis and therefore little interest in the Yugoslav option. The relative importance of cultural, as opposed to political, factors in forming the Yugoslav identity can be seen in the fact that interest in Yugoslavism declined precipitously in this period even though political conditions for its realization were no less propitious than they had been in the 1830s or 1840s.

When the Yugoslav idea again came to prominence at about the turn of the century, it did so under the aegis of a new, synthetic vision of the nation—what I call a multicultural model. The reappearance of the Yugoslav ideal at this point is again no accident; it coincided almost exactly with the beginning of modernism, which as a cultural worldview has strong ties to romanticism. In particular, modernist philosophical thought rehabilitates idealist views, and modernist literary practice is more open to synthetic borrowing than is realism. Thus it was that a new synthetic view of Yugoslav culture arose triumphant well before the country itself became a reality. Like their predecessors in the 1840s, partisans of this model hoped for the eventual creation of a single Yugoslav culture, but this one would not merely have been Serbian culture renamed. Rather, it would have borrowed the best elements—although there was disagreement as to what these might be—from each of the separate South Slavic cultures to create an overarching Yugoslav culture, one that had never existed before but that could be shared by all. This new culture would not necessarily have required the disappearance of the separate national cultures, even if many cultural theorists thought they would wither away in the very long run. In the short run, at least, they would have continued to exist, but they would have been balanced and made less relevant by the new supranational culture. Had such a plan succeeded, Yugoslavia might have come to look something like the United States, whose national culture is a synthesis of recognizable elements drawn from many separate cultures. These arguments, which will be discussed in detail in the latter part of Chapter 1 and in Chapter 2, were quite powerful. They helped create a great rebirth of enthusiasm for the Yugoslav ideal before World War I, and laid the groundwork for the agreements to create a Yugoslav state after the war. Interestingly enough, despite Serbianizing tendencies in most other areas, successive interwar Yugoslav governments did not promote a return to the romantic Serbianizing program of the 1830s and 1840s, but generally supported a version of synthetic culture. Unfortunately, however, this cultural vision was overwhelmed by political developments in interwar Yugoslavia, which generally worked to impose Serbian domination on the rest of the country, thereby helping to undercut successes in the nation-building arena.

That there must have been some success in inculcating a Yugoslav ideal in the population at large can be seen by the triumph of a reconstituted Yugoslavia after the bloodbath of World War II. In the period immediately following the war, the idea of a common Yugoslav culture was resurrected; now, however, the goal was to create it not by combining various national cultures but rather by ignoring them as much as possible—I consider this supranational culture in Chapter 3. This was the only time in Yugoslav history that the government was centrally involved in cultural policy making; in the first fifteen postwar years party authorities played a central role in defining a new Yugoslav culture. The separate national cultures were allowed to exist at the harmless level of folk culture, and the great variety of these among the nations of Yugoslavia was emphasized "probably in order that it should not occur to those same nations to seek anything other than folklore, their own state or geographical identity, for instance."[14] In the more important realm of cultural creation, however, works could be "national in form" only if they were "socialist in content"; that is, if they expressed the party line on Yugoslav socialism and on the ideals of "brotherhood and unity" among the various Yugoslav nations. The problem, however, was that the state-sponsored supranational model, derived as it was from Soviet socialist realism, was almost devoid of content. Once themes of the partisan war had played themselves out, supranational Yugoslav culture was unable to renew itself, particularly because the authorities, steeped as they were in collectivistic thinking that derived both from the Yugoslav and the communist tradition, remained cool to a supranational culture built on individualistic Western lines.

Ultimately, under pressure from the resurgent national cultures, in the early 1960s it was decided that political and economic forces (Titoism and the Yugoslav version of socialism) would be sufficient to hold the state together, and attempts to create a unified national culture of any kind were more or less abandoned—an analysis of the results of this policy is at the center of Chapter 4. Again, although local factors played a role in this decision, broader cultural patterns should not be ignored. By the 1960s, modernism and its synthetic bias were on the wane, and the postmodern trends that replaced it, with their distrust for synthesizing metanarratives and their embrace of relativist thinking and of the particular, were hostile to any version of synthesis. It was in this cultural atmosphere that, for the first time, Yugoslavia pursued what might be called a multinational policy guaranteeing separate but equal rights to all the national cultures and allowing each to develop as it chose. Had this worked, Yugoslavia would have developed into a multinational country, such as India. But unlike India, Yugoslavia had been formed on collectivist bases. In the absence of any unifying cultural glue, more homogenous collectivities could and did easily challenge the Yugoslav idea, which had lost its raison d'être. Once the credibility of that vision was effectively destroyed, I argue, the violent collapse of the country was almost unavoidable. It is possible that Yugoslavia could have survived as a multinational state had its leaders moved to a multinational cultural policy while simultaneously democratizing the country and transforming the basis of Yugoslav identity to an individualistic-libertarian model. But this would have entailed a cultural shift of monumental proportions, and it was not attempted in Yugoslavia. As more and more people saw themselves with less and less of a connection to people outside of their own ethnic group, the possibilities for economic and political compromise diminished.

The Yugoslav Background

For those who are not already expert on Yugoslav affairs, the following historical sketch may prove helpful as background to the discussion of Yugoslav nationalist thought of the nineteenth and twentieth centuries that is presented in the rest of the book. Those who do know the background are encouraged to skip this section, which has been made as short as possible.[15]

Yugoslavia presents a particularly complicated but unusually rewarding case study of nation building. As the result of a spectacularly tangled web of historical and geopolitical factors, the central section of the Balkan peninsula contains a mix of people and cultures as heterogeneous as anywhere on earth. It was not always this way. In pre-Roman times, the region is thought to have been populated exclusively by Illyrians (probably the ancestors of today's Albanians). At the height of the Roman Empire, the territories of the future Yugoslavia, particularly the Pannonian Plain and the Adriatic Coast, were thoroughly Romanized. By the sixth and seventh centuries, however, in the wake of the barbarian invasions that destroyed Rome, the area became somewhat depopulated. It was repeopled by Slavs, among others, who migrated into the area from their ancestral homes, presumably somewhere to the north of the Black Sea. When these Slavs, the ancestors of today's Serbs, Croats, and Slovenes, moved into the Balkans they may well have already been divided into separate tribal groups, but it is likely that they spoke the same language and shared the vast majority of customs. Thus, and this fact would be of cardinal importance in modern times, the South Slavs were at one time almost certainly a unified tribe.

The Balkans have always been at a geographical crossroads, however, and the Slavic tribes were not fated to be left alone in their new lands for long. Most important, the region lay at the fault line dividing Christendom between Catholicism and Orthodoxy. Although the official split between Eastern and Western branches of the church did not occur until 1054, differences were already apparent by the time Christian missionaries first appeared among the South Slavs in the ninth century. And when the dust had settled after approximately two centuries of alliances, compromises, and conversions, the ancestors of today's Serbs and Macedonians had ended up firmly in the embrace of Byzantine Christianity, whereas the Croats and Slovenes professed the Roman Catholic faith. This doctrinal division would ultimately have vital consequences, for it split the formerly unified South Slavs down the middle into separate and frequently adversarial spheres of cultural influence.

In the course of the Middle Ages a number of South Slavic kingdoms waxed and waned on the Balkan peninsula. None was fated to be long lasting, but at various times between the ninth and fourteenth centuries, Bulgarian, Macedonian, Serbian, Croatian, and Bosnian kingdoms controlled much of the territory that would one day become Yugoslavia.[16] Of course, we must realize that the national designations are being used anachronistically here. Insofar as these names were employed at all in this period, they designated the affiliations of political and dynastic leaders. The common people almost certainly had no notion of belonging to a Serbian, Croatian, Macedonian, or Bosnian nation, nor were rulers averse to considering any inhabitants of territories they controlled as their proper subjects. The long-term significance of these sundry kingdoms was not in any political legacy, but rather in their overlapping claims to the same land.[17] For depending on which period one chooses to consider, it is possible for any South Slavic group to claim that its ancestors had once held sway over most of the Balkans, opening up possible claims for a Greater Serbia, Bulgaria, Croatia, and so forth.

The cultural and geopolitical situation in the Balkans became even more complex in the second half of the fourteenth century with the arrival of the Ottoman Empire. Just as they had been located squarely on the fault line separating the Roman and Byzantine worlds, the territories of the South Slavs now became the locus of the ever-shifting border between Christianity and Islam. The Ottomans would ultimately control the southern parts of the future Yugoslavia for some five hundred years, leaving an indelible imprint on the cultural and linguistic practices even of those Slavs who chose not to convert to Islam. And those who did choose to convert, a substantial portion especially in Bosnia, added a third religion with its concomitant cultural practices to the South Slavic mix. What is more, although the various South Slav groups had lived in relatively stable and distinct communities before the Ottoman invasion, in its aftermath great migrations occurred that led to a thorough mixing of the various groups. Successive waves of Serbs fled north from territories under the suzerainty of the Turks to those controlled by the Habsburgs or the Hungarians. Promised religious liberty in exchange for the thankless task of guarding the Habsburgs' southern border, these Serbs settled in a crescent of land on the Croatian border called the Military Border or "Krajina," where they remained until they were driven out by the Croatians in 1995. South Slavic Moslems and Christians both lived on Bosnian territory, with the former dominant in the cities and the latter forming the rural labor force. Simultaneously, the southern regions that had formed the center of the Serbian medieval patrimony became increasingly Islamicized, and non-Slavic Albanians (the majority of whom had converted to Islam) replaced migrating Serbs. Of the South Slavic groups, only the Slovenes remained more or less untouched by these great migrations, but their small numbers and proximity to the seat of Habsburg power left them highly vulnerable to Germanization.

One of the most important results of the invasions and migrations of this period was that cultural life, particularly secular cultural life, among the South Slavs stagnated. For the vast majority of Serbs and Croats, mere survival was in question, and there was neither the stability nor the leisure for cultural production. Among the Serbs, the autocephalous Orthodox Church was the only pre-Ottoman institution to survive, and it ultimately played a major role not so much in preserving as in defining the Serbian national identity. Among the Croats, secular culture developed in this period only along the Adriatic littoral in the cities loyal to and protected by Venice. Ragusa (Dubrovnik) in particular became an important center of Renaissance culture. Literary and cultural life in the vernacular flourished among the Slovenes for a brief period during the Reformation in the sixteenth century, but the Counter Reformation of the seventeenth century put an abrupt end to these tendencies.

Thus, by the end of the eighteenth century, the once unified and relatively stable South Slavic groups presented a very different picture. They now professed three different faiths, lived under the governmental systems of three separate societies, and had adopted cultural practices that differed widely in the various parts of the Balkans. Secular culture was weak or absent in almost all areas, and their lands remained a battleground. At the same time, they now lived intermingled in many border areas. This was the situation that obtained when ideas of national awakening and revival, imported primarily from the German lands, made their appearance in the Balkans.

This book will concentrate on one national view, the Yugoslav or pan–South Slavic view, in its various manifestations. As we have noted in our whirlwind historical survey, it was easy to find fundamental bases for discord among the various South Slav national groups. Nevertheless, there were strong arguments available for those intellectuals beginning in the 1830s who wished to create a Yugoslav nation. In addition to shared ethnic background, they could and did point to linguistic similarity (if not identity), to shared cultural traditions (folk song in particular), as well as to the wisdom of a larger national grouping as a defense against demonstrably rapacious neighbors, and to the impracticality and danger of separating closely related peoples who, in many regions, lived side by side. Using arguments such as these as a springboard, they tried to convince the various South Slavic peoples that they would be best off viewing each other as essentially the same. Although they generally did not downplay the existence of significant differences among the groups, most of them felt that these were diminishing and hoped that in time they would disappear, ultimately making Yugoslav as unproblematic an adjective as British or French. It should never be forgotten, however, that these Yugoslav views always competed with those of particularist nationalisms, dominating them at some times and being dominated by them at others.

I pay relatively little attention to particularist nationalisms for a couple of reasons. First of all, this book focuses primarily on cultural processes, and except for the contemporary period, in which particularist nationalist views are treated in depth, most major cultural figures among the South Slavs tended to hold some form of Yugoslav ideology.[18] Equally important, however, is the fact that most recent work on the area has concentrated on particularist nationalisms, for obvious reasons, with the result that the rich tradition of Yugoslav thought is being obliterated.

Explaining the Collapse

In general, attempts to explain the current catastrophic situation in the former Yugoslavia have ignored the cultural bases of the problem; rather they tend to fall into two categories, which can roughly, if somewhat whimsically, be called "deterministic-historical" and "fiendish-political." Proponents of the former type, primarily members of the media who have too often obtained their information from people already caught up in the maelstrom of conflict, usually point to "age-old" religious hatreds and rivalries.[19] Those preferring the latter, including almost all who have studied the region in depth, blame the more recent actions of some individual or group: Tito, the Yugoslav Communists and their economic policies, Germany, Slobodan Milošević, or the leaders of militant Islam.

Undoubtedly, both these explanation types contain elements of truth, but I believe that both are fundamentally flawed. The trouble with arguments of the former type—which might also be called inevitability arguments—is both historical and theoretical. Ancient hatreds were undoubtedly present, but they are not sufficient for understanding systematic, large-scale violence in the Balkans, or elsewhere for that matter. To be sure, there was always a certain amount of tension present among the various South Slav groups, but there were few instances of widespread violent conflict among them in Yugoslavia's history or pre-history. Indeed, at least as far as Serbs and Croats are concerned (and it is their inability to get along that was ultimately fatal), there is little evidence of such hatred before the second half of the nineteenth century.[20] And, as the evidence presented in this book will make abundantly clear, even in later periods one finds at least as much evidence of Serb-Croat cooperation as of animosity.

Had these ancient hatreds really been as deep-seated and intractable as is claimed, it is hard to imagine how Yugoslavia would ever have been constituted after World War I, let alone reconstituted after the bloodbath of World War II (in comparison to which, by the way, the recent violence has been tame). Those commentators who tout this explanation will usually claim that Yugoslavia was an artificial country, created not because of but despite the wishes of its citizens.[21] Yet the historical and cultural record shows that the vast majority of leading South Slav figures supported some sort of Yugoslav ideology rather than more narrow nationalist ones, and the promulgation of the first and the second Yugoslavia was greeted with widespread joy. Even after this joy turned rather more bitter, many men and women continued, despite frequent setbacks, to support the idea of Yugoslavia. Indeed, a surprising number support it to this day, despite its seemingly irreversible demise.

There are theoretical problems with the inevitability argument as well, and they are bound up with the mistaken impression of clarity provided by hindsight. If South Slavic Serbs, Croats, and Bosnians are presently fighting each other, it proves easy enough to show that they had deep historical reasons for doing so; but, if one goes deep enough below the surface (and one does not usually have to go very deep), it is possible to discover the potential for equally divisive rifts in practically any nation. For example, German Protestants from the North and German Catholics from the South now live in harmony, but were they, for whatever reasons, to begin fighting, the same commentators who tell us about the inevitability of conflict in Yugoslavia would recall the bitter religious wars of the seventeenth century, the "artificial" way in which Bismarck constructed modern Germany, German behavior during World War II, and so forth. We would be told that, from the days of the Teutons, the Germans have been barbarians, and we would be provided with a genealogy of conflict that would pronounce it the inevitable result of deep-seated hatreds that had only been temporarily papered over by unconvincing ideologies. The point is that if potentials for mutual enmity can be found in almost any country, they have little or no explanatory power in and of themselves. Whether they lead to conflict or compromise depends on a host of factors, the most important of which center on the way they are used or abused in culture and cultural politics. Thus, the inevitability argument is dangerous not just because it gives us license to ignore the sufferings of millions of innocent victims in the former Yugoslavia (it is this aspect of the problem that has drawn the despairing attention of most responsible observers), but because it allows us to assume in advance that Yugoslavia is somehow completely different from supposedly more civilized nations. As I will argue in the Conclusion of this book, it is precisely because the Yugoslavs are not so very different from any other group of people that we need to pay careful attention to their failures of nation building, recognizing that the potential for violent collapse is present in all heterogeneous societies.

Most better-informed observers have rightly skewered the inevitability argument, but they replace it by pointing to relatively recent political or economic factors. Typical is this observation by the Slovenian Slavoj Žižek: "Old ethnic hatreds, of course, are far from being simply imagined: they are a historical legacy. Nevertheless, the key question is why they exploded at precisely this moment, not earlier or later. There is one simple answer to it: the political crisis in Serbia."[22] Yet although it is relatively easy to demonstrate that specific political actions of Slobodan Milošević and/or Franjo Tudjman, the German government, the European Union, and the United Nations, as well as the economic collapse spawned by failed Communist policies, contributed to the breakdown of and spread of violence in the former Yugoslavia, such observations do not lead to any "simple" answers to the important questions. After all, economic collapse accompanied by the rise of dictatorial regimes is a common enough phenomenon, but it does not always lead normal citizens to murder and rape their neighbors or destroy the few economic goods they possess. Somehow, we must account for passions far deeper than those produced by the political process (although not so deep as to be "inevitable"). Thus, although I have great respect for the care with which Branka Magaš, Sabrina Ramet, Misha Glenny, Susan Woodward, and others have described Yugoslavia's death agonies, I am unconvinced by their various causal arguments. At their strongest, such arguments focus on the harnessing of nationalism by Serbian and Croatian postcommunist leaders (all of whom, by the way, are former communists themselves), but, because they tend to view nationalism in a narrow political context, they are mostly unable to explain why it could have been marshaled so effectively and easily.

In the end, both explanation types are equally unconvincing, although for opposite reasons. Inevitability arguments assume that the outlooks of individuals and groups are immutable. They implicitly or explicitly claim, without in any way proving, that national affiliations (at least in the Balkans and other supposedly "primitive," "tribal," and "barbaric" areas) are based on principles of ethnic, religious, or, less frequently, linguistic similarity and that any cultural or political formation that attempts to bridge them is doomed to failure. Explanations that focus on recent political and economic factors, though effective at discrediting inevitability arguments, do not seem able to explain the deep passion, violence, and hatred that have marked the Yugoslav conflicts. All claim that their chosen crucial factor explains the appearance of violent nationalism (usually Serbian), but it is hard to see from their explanations why this should inevitably have been so; after all, the causes they adduce can be discovered elsewhere not to have produced the same effects. As far as I am concerned, and as I will argue in this book, the various causes that have been cited for the collapse of Yugoslavia were secondary to the disintegration of the very concept of the Yugoslav nation, and it is to that *cultural* process we must turn if we wish to see how existing deep-seated rivalries and hatreds were at various times overcome or encouraged and how they reemerged triumphant. It was, to my mind, the successful challenge to any supranational Yugoslav vision by particularist national ideals that drove the country to destruction and led to the rise of figures such as Milošević and Tudjman, rather than the other way around. We need to see Yugoslavia for what it was: the quintessential battleground between collectivistic national visions based on ideals of synthesis versus those based on particularity. And it is only in this process that we will find the anything but simple answers to the questions that interest us.

The history of Yugoslavia's rise and fall inevitably brings up the question of whether the Yugoslav case has relevance for other parts of the world. Considering the quantity of existing multinational states, and the number of them that appear to be under severe entropic pressure—Rwanda, Burundi, Sri Lanka, India, and Russia, to name just a few—this is not an idle question. Regarding the Austrian Empire, A. J. P. Taylor has said: "The conflict between a super-national dynastic state and the national principle had to be fought to the finish; and so, too, had the conflict between master and subject nations. Inevitably, any concession came too late and was too little; and equally inevitably every concession provoked more violent discontent. The national principle, once launched, had to work itself out to a conclusion."[23] If Yugoslavia's experience is typical, exactly the same can be said of the multinational postdynastic state.[24] Although it is true, as Ernest Gellner has pointed out,[25] that by no means does every potential national group experience nationalist urges, in the time since he wrote his book (1983) the number that has experienced such urges has increased exponentially, and it would behoove us to think seriously about the reasons for this. Thus, in my conclusion I ask, is the triumph of particularist nationalisms inevitable in multinational states? If it is not, should we and can we do anything to prevent it?

Inevitably, a similar question comes up in relation to the United States. In this regard, it is my belief that certain versions of what is sometimes called the multicultural (but what I think is more accurately called the multinational) view of the United States and which is generally, and I think properly, seen as a challenge to the melting-pot ideal, has the potential to reproduce in that country the conditions that led to the violent collapse of Yugoslavia. Although the United States was constructed on entirely different bases than was Yugoslavia, a process of parallel cultural evolution is leading the citizens of that nation to replay, albeit at a slower and less dramatic pace, the sequence of moves that destroyed Yugoslavia. In the conclusion to this book, by pointing out the unexpected analogies between racial policy in the United States and national/ethnic policy in Yugoslavia, I hope to be able to add a new urgency to the debate surrounding the so-called culture wars in the United States.

1

The Rise of the Yugoslav National Idea

At the beginning of the nineteenth century, the Austrian branch of the Habsburg family controlled territories inhabited by a heterogeneous array of national groups, including Hungarians, Italians, Romanians, Czechs, Slovaks, Poles, Ruthenians, Slovenes, Serbs, and Croats. Although the empire was not particularly brutal toward these minority peoples (at least not by twentieth-century standards), neither did it treat them as equal partners. Local society was highly stratified, with German-speaking landlords atop a pyramid whose base was formed of peasants from the above groups.[1] In between were merchants and craftspeople, mostly German speakers, who congregated in the local capitals. Decisions of importance were made in Vienna, high administrators were generally Austrian, or, if they came from the ranks of the other nations, fully Austrianized. The language of commerce and day-to-day business was German, whereas Latin was still the political lingua franca. Before the eighteenth century, this type of social and political organization did not pose insurmountable problems. In what was still a traditional society, individuals were inclined to identify themselves either on a purely local basis (as members of a certain village or town) or by their class, occupation, or religion. Although they were, to be sure, under the ultimate political jurisdiction of some central government, their contacts with and allegiance to it were at best nominal.

By the beginning of the nineteenth century, however, a new mode of identification arose, one that eventually came to have catastrophic effects on the stability of the Habsburg Empire. Specifically, cultural and political leaders discovered the power of nationalism as a mobilizing force. Using political models that had been developed primarily in France and cultural models borrowed from Germany, these leaders successfully convinced many individuals (perhaps even a majority) to self-identify not on the basis of occupational, class, or religious ties, but on national ones. The nationalist movements that destabilized the Habsburg Empire in the course of the nineteenth century illustrate with particular clarity the ways in which belief in a shared national destiny arose and developed, for the patterns by which each of the above-mentioned national groups "discovered" its nationality were very similar.

The first step was a linguistic and cultural awakening. Small groups of intellectuals, inspired by German romantic idealizations of the common folk, began to recognize their own people as a repository of national traditions. Most importantly, they rediscovered their native languages; although these languages had, in most cases, never been used for high cultural purposes and had in the past been little more than a source of amusement for the Germanized gentry and the Latinized intellectuals, they had been stubbornly preserved by the rural peasantry. Naturally, peasant tongues lacked the niceties demanded by a modern European literature; but they could serve as a foundation on which to create a vernacular literary language. Simultaneously, nationally conscious intellectuals came to recognize the value of other types of folk customs and traditions, raising to cult status folk music, dancing, costume, and customs.[2] Again, as they had with language, intellectuals felt a need to clean up, to systematize—in general to Europeanize—the traditions they discovered among the common people. But be that as it may, by the 1840s most of the minority nations of the Habsburg Empire had experienced, or were beginning to experience, a full-scale cultural renaissance defined in national terms.

At first, the nationalists were a tiny minority—one Czech intellectual at an early meeting of nationalist-inclined intellectuals quipped: "If the ceiling were to fall on us now, that would be the end of the national revival."[3] Initial numerical weakness, however, proved to be unimportant. Rather quickly, among each of the nations a dedicated (and self-interested) larger group appeared that was able to transform the simmering cultural and intellectual awakening into a roiling mass movement. In some cases, the leaders were drawn from the intellectual classes themselves, but the local bourgeoisie or even the gentry could and did take over the leadership of national movements. Cleverly exploiting the symbols of national unity that had been rediscovered (sometimes invented out of whole cloth) by the intellectuals, they built political movements that functioned to instill in the masses a horizontal sense of belonging to a single nation, posited as more essential than the vertical divisions that had hitherto separated peasants, bourgeoisie, and aristocrats. Still, the glue that held these movements together was cultural and linguistic rather than political, and it is the cultural basis for these movements that explains why, even today, those nineteenth-century writers, composers, and artists who dipped into the wellsprings of the national folk culture for their inspiration are treated as national heroes throughout Eastern and Central Europe—Petöfi, Mickiewicz, Mácha, Prešeren, Smetana, and Dvořák are the George Washingtons and Thomas Jeffersons of the former subject peoples of the Austro-Hungarian Empire.[4]

As national movements gathered strength, the empire became increasingly unstable. A nationalist-inspired revolt in Hungary in 1848 was put down only with the help of Russia. In order to stave off collapse, the Habsburgs reached a power-sharing compromise with the Hungarians in 1867, raising them to more or less equal status in the empire.[5] This compromise, however, did nothing to appease other national groups in "the prison house of nationalities"—as the Austro-Hungarian Empire came to be known—particularly since, having had their own national aspirations satisfied, the Hungarians immediately began aggressive campaigns to Magyarize the smaller national groups in the territory under their control.

In the South Slavic lands under Habsburg rule, the national situation was perhaps more chaotic than anywhere else in the empire. Three distinct, albeit closely related, South Slavic groups lived on these territories in the first half of the nineteenth century. Inhabiting a rather compact territory south and west of Vienna were the Slovenes, by far the smallest group of South Slavs. The Catholic Slovenes spoke a distinctive language, one whose literary tradition stretched back to the sixteenth century, a period in which most of them had temporarily converted to Protestantism. By the nineteenth century, however, most lived as illiterate peasants in lands economically dominated by German-speaking populations. In an arc stretching from the Adriatic Sea in the southwest to the Hungarian border were the Croats. They, too, were Catholic and spoke three separate dialects, one of which resembled some dialects of Slovene and the largest of which bled imperceptibly into dialects of Serbian. Finally, on the empire's southern fringes were substantial numbers of Orthodox Serbs whose ancestors had been invited into the Habsburg lands in the seventeenth century to serve as buffers against the Ottoman Turks. Although the three groups kept to themselves for the most part, in many places, particularly along the borders of their territories, they intermingled, sometimes even living side-by-side in the same villages and towns.

For the Habsburg South Slavs, three basic options for national revival were available. One was for intellectual leaders from each group to develop separate national movements on the bases of the unique linguistic, religious, and quotidian traditions of their respective common folk. This was the approach taken by most of the potential national groups—Poles, Hungarians, Romanians, Czechs, Slovaks—within the Habsburg Empire in this period.[6] It was also chosen by many Slovenes as well as some Croats and Serbs.

Other cultural leaders, however, particularly among the Croats, put their hope in the creation of a pan–South Slavic (Yugoslav) national identity. They recognized that there were significant differences among Serbs, Croats, Slovenes, and Bulgarians but, like the forgers of Italian and German unity (and for many of the same reasons), they felt that with time and effort these differences would come to seem inessential.[7] It needs to be emphasized that modern Serb, Croat, and Slovene national identification, although based on certain historical identities, were themselves only just coming into existence at this time. Yugoslav partisans recognized that the majority of the common people still did not possess a well-developed national identity, so there was no prima facie reason for assuming that they could not be brought to self-identify on the basis of broad similarities. And, in fact, it was and remains true that for all that separates them these groups do share a great deal, particularly in the area of language, which was generally considered the primary national unifying factor in German nationalist thought.

The logic for attempting to convince the folk to identify themselves as Yugoslavs rather than as Serbs, Croats, or Slovenes was both cultural and political. On the one hand, intellectually and culturally this period developed under the eminently synthetic ideology of romanticism, German in particular.[8] Schemes for overcoming traditional divisions between spirit and matter, god and human beings, were in the air, and in such an atmosphere the belief that the differences separating closely related peoples could be overcome seemed quite natural. The strength of the Habsburg Empire added to the political attraction of synthesis. It appeared unlikely that any of these peoples could achieve autonomy on their own, but perhaps they could do so were they united. Finally, even in the nineteenth century it was obvious, at least to some, that unless similarity triumphed over difference, intra–South Slav bloodletting would be the inevitable result.

The third option for achieving "national" consciousness was to galvanize the populace around pan-Slavic feeling. It is true that few, if any, intellectuals of the mid–nineteenth century thought it would be possible or desirable to create a single Slav culture and a single Slavic state, but many were drawn to schemes of cooperation with their "Slavic brothers," even before the creation of an official pan-Slavic movement (led by Russia) in the 1860s. The appeal of the pan-Slavic approach was all the stronger because many of the intellectual leaders of the various Slavic peoples (at least those who were subjects of the Habsburgs) had studied together in Vienna or at the Charles University in Prague. But despite the sentimental allure of pan-Slavic feeling, no major group of South Slav intellectuals appropriated pan-Slavic ideology as a serious model for the national liberation of their people(s). Nevertheless, all three forms of "national" consciousness existed simultaneously during the course of the nineteenth century in the Habsburg-controlled South Slavic lands, and it is the coexistence of these three ideologies (particularly the first two) that is the most significant culturopolitical fact in the history of the Yugoslav lands from the mid–nineteenth century until today.

Nor were the Serbs, Croats, and Slovenes in the Habsburg Empire the only groups of South Slavs to experience the pull of nationalism at this time. For it must also be recalled that not all of the South Slavs lived in the territory of the Austrian Empire. All the Bulgarians and Macedonians, as well as the great majority of the Serbs and many Croats, lived in lands controlled by the Ottoman Empire.[9] The Montenegrins were, for all intents and purposes, independent at this point, as were some of the Serbs after the successful rebellion of 1815. Through the nineteenth century, what had begun as a small autonomous Serbian enclave gradually expanded, and Serbs in Serbia developed a national ideology of their own, sometimes in concert with but usually independent of the parallel efforts of the Habsburg South Slavs. Because this national movement was driven by prior political independence, it differed in many respects from the patterns typical of the nationalisms of the Habsburg minorities. What the Serbians shared with Habsburg South Slavic groups, however, was a tendency to imagine the nation in collectivist terms (borrowed from the font of their respective national views: Germany) rather than in individualistic ones. The inclination to imagine the nation as composed of groups, rather than as an aggregation of otherwise unattached individuals remained a constant in all versions of South Slavic nationalism, and it is a prominent feature of those literary and cultural works that shaped South Slavic national thought as well.

Language and Nationalism Among the South Slavs: 1814–1918

Although modern thought on nationalism rejects the belief that a single language is a necessary component of national existence,[10] this notion, expressed most succinctly by von Humboldt ("Die wahre Heimat ist eigentlich die Sprache"), was generally accepted in the nineteenth century. In any case, the majority of nineteenth-century nationalisms in Eastern and Central Europe began with the revival and codification of the national language, and the South Slav lands were no exception. But the specifics of South Slav linguistic thought cannot be discussed without clearing up two general misconceptions regarding this topic. The first is the frequently held belief that the process of linguistic codification, as with most others connected to nationalism, occurs in some natural or organic way. Such beliefs are often encouraged by nationalist leaders, whose goal is to make their movements seem both natural and inevitable, but they have little relation to reality. Linguistic codification is pursued quite consciously, usually by a small group of writers and intellectuals, and their choices are eventually imposed on the population as a whole through standardized systems of education and the influence of the media. This is true even when the literary standard is adopted from "the language of the people."

The second, equally common misconception is that states such as Italy and Germany were easier to create and are more stable because all Italians and Germans speak the same language, whereas one of the reasons for Yugoslavia's difficulties was that its inhabitants spoke various languages. To believe this is to misunderstand completely the ways in which languages

were codified in the nineteenth century and the ways in which they work
at any point. To this day, the dialectical differences that separate the various
speakers of what is called Italian are so large that, without special training,
a Milanese can barely understand the conversation of two Sicilians. In the
nineteenth century, before the advent of mass communication, these differences would have been even more marked. Italian became Italian because Italian intellectuals agreed on a standardized literary language based
primarily on Northern Italian dialects, and the use of this standardized language was generally encouraged: taught in schools, used by the state bu-
reaucracy, and so forth. The South Slavic lands in the early nineteenth century were not dissimilar to Italy in this regard. Indeed, if anything, the
South Slavs would have probably understood each other better than the
erstwhile Italians. At the very least, even given the nineteenth-century conviction that linguistic unity was a sine qua non for national unity, there was
no reason to believe it could not be achieved in the South Slavic lands.

The belief in the necessity for a single national literary language coupled with the conviction that such a language could be achieved in the
South Slavic lands led, in the course of the nineteenth century, to a series
of linguistic reforms that functioned both to codify and modernize the various South Slavic languages and to bring them (particularly Serbian and
Croatian) together. Linguistic reform among the Serbs began in the first
decades of the nineteenth century with the work of Vuk Stefanović Karadžić. Until this time, the Serbian written language (usually called
Slaveno-Serbian) had been based on the liturgical language of the Serbian
Orthodox Church. The choice was by no means surprising, since the
church was the only Serbian institution to have survived the Ottoman invasions and occupation, thus preserving a high-cultural tie (however tenuous) with the Serbian kingdoms of the middle ages. This written language
retained many archaic features from the Old Bulgarian dialects from which
it had originated, and it had added many Russian features as a result of
Russian Orthodox influences during the years of the Ottoman occupation.[11] As a result, it differed markedly from the language spoken by Serbian peasants, such as the Karadžić family. Karadžić himself was born in
Šumadija (the region in which the first Serbian uprising began in 1804) in
1787. A self-educated man, he served in Karadjordje's staff as a scribe. After
the collapse of the Karadjordje uprising, Vuk fled to Vienna, where, with
the encouragement of the Slovenian Slavist Jernej Kopitar,[12] he published a

Serbian grammar (1814) and dictionary (1818). For the next thirty years, Vuk would work, often in highly adverse circumstances, to direct the Serbian literary language away from the Slaveno-Serbian favored by the church and many intellectuals to a regularized version of the peasant-based dialect spoken in Herzegovina but understood throughout most of the Serbian and Croatian lands. Ultimately Vuk's work laid the groundwork for a Serbian and Croatian linguistic rapprochement and provided a powerful symbol of potential Yugoslav unity.

As far as Vuk himself was concerned, however, his reforms were not pan–South Slavic in nature but exclusively Serbian. Nevertheless, because in his view a Serb was not a South Slavic Orthodox Christian who spoke the so-called Štokavian dialect on which he based his norm but rather any speaker of this dialect regardless of religious affiliation or self-definition, Serbdom included many people who considered themselves Croats as well as all the inhabitants of Bosnia and Herzegovina. In a limited sense, then, Vuk can be considered a conscious partisan of South Slav unity, because his linguistic national definition encouraged greater emphasis on what linked various South Slav groups that had traditionally been separated on the basis of religious or political affiliation.

While Vuk was pursuing linguistic reform and cultural revival among the Serbs, parallel efforts were being undertaken in the Croatian lands, where the historical and political situation was quite different from that of Serbia. Unlike the Serbs, who spent most of the period from the fifteenth to the nineteenth century trying merely to survive under the difficult conditions of Ottoman rule, some of the Croat cities, those lying along the Adriatic littoral, had been prosperous Venetian outposts during the Renaissance. In these Dalmatian cities, particularly Dubrovnik (Ragusa), an active cultural life had been possible, and the achievements of Italian Renaissance literature found Croatian propagators as well. By the early nineteenth century, however, these traditions were no more than a distant memory. The Croatian lands themselves were divided, with part administered by Vienna and part by Budapest. As the cultural influence of Latin waned, pressures to Germanize or to Magyarize waxed correspondingly. Croatian resistance to these pressures took the form of cultural revival under the aegis of a group that called itself the Illyrians. In the late 1830s and 1840s, under the leadership of a young lawyer, Ljudevit Gaj, the Illyrians called for a series of linguistic reforms in order to revive the Croatian language.[13]

The linguistic situation in Croatia at this time was at least as complicated as it was in Serbia, although the complications were of a completely
different order. Rather than growing out of a split between the language of
the church and that of the peasants, the obstacles to linguistic standardiza-
tion in Croatia were the result of the existence of three distinct dialects—
the so-called Štokavian, Čakavian, and Kajkavian—each with its own literary and popular tradition.[14] In Zagreb, Croatia's administrative and cultural
capital, the Kajkavian dialect is traditionally spoken. This was the dialect
that Gaj and most of his followers spoke,[15] and it possessed a flourishing literary tradition at this time. Although one might therefore have predicted
that the Croatian reformers would have picked Kajkavian as the literary
standard for modern Croatian, they chose instead to adopt a language based
on Štokavian. The choice was dictated by two powerful factors. First, the
Štokavian dialect had been the norm of the Dubrovnik Renaissance writers.
In choosing Štokavian, the reformers thereby drew a direct line to the most
cosmopolitan and polished cultural traditions. Another, equally powerful
incentive for the choice of Štokavian, however, was that, of the three Croatian dialects, it was closest to the literary language Vuk had codified in
neighboring Serbia. Thus, the choice of Štokavian created the potential for
the eventual development of a unified Serbo-Croatian literary language.

The "Illyrian" language that Gaj and his collaborators created was de-
ployed in the course of 1835 and 1836 in the newspaper *Novine horvatzke*
(Croatian News) and, most importantly, in its literary supplement *Danica*
(The Morning Star). These papers served not only as vehicles for the propagation of a new literary language, but also as carriers of pan–South Slavic
ideology. "*Danica* ordinarily began with one or two poems, generally more
distinguished for their patriotism than artistic qualities. These would be
followed by several short articles of a mixed nature: information about
other Southern Slavs, biographical notes on Russian or Serbian rulers, brief
stories and anecdotes from the Slavic world, and letters from subscribers."[16]
Gaj's "Proglas za 1836 godinu" (Proclamation for the Year 1836) serves as an
excellent illustration of the pan–South Slavic beliefs of the Illyrian movement: "The discordant strings of this lyre are Carniola, Carinthia, Istria,
Kranj, Styria, Croatia, Slavonia, Dalmatia, Dubrovnik, Bosnia, Montenegro, Herzegovina, Serbia, Bulgaria, and Lower Hungary [i.e., all the lands
inhabited by Southern Slavs]. . . . Let's stop each strumming on his own
string, and tune the lyre to a single harmony."[17]

Nevertheless, despite their Yugoslav sympathies, through the 1840s most of the Illyrians' linguistic efforts were focused on Croatia. The next major concrete step toward Croatian and Serbian linguistic union was not taken until 1850, when a conference on the subject was held in Vienna. The parties to the conference, who included major Croatian writers such as Ivan Mažuranić, Dimitrije Demeter, Ivan Kukuljević, the Serbian philologists Vuk Karadžić and Djura Daničić, and the Slovenian Slavist France Miklošič, declared "that the Serbs and Croats were one people, and, therefore, should have a single literature, which also requires a common literary language."[18] They agreed on a five-point program designed to reduce the differences in the literary idioms used by Croatian and Serbian writers. Most important, they resolved to use a single dialect (the so-called Ijekavian dialect spoken in Eastern Herzegovina, and in parts of Bosnia, Montenegro, and Western Serbia) as the basis for the national standard rather than creating a new, synthetic language from various existing dialects.[19]

Not all writers in Serbia and Croatia (not even all the signatories of the document) actually switched to the proposed standard, but the very fact of their meeting indicated a recognition that the creation of a single literary language for Serbs and Croats was possible.[20] What is more, and this is extremely significant, among Croats who did not subscribe to the Vienna Agreement, the most sizable and influential group dissented not because they rejected the idea of a joint Serbo-Croatian, but rather because they preferred a different path to the creation of a common literary language. Instead of choosing a single dialect as the basis for the unified language, they believed it would be preferable to "achieve linguistic and national unity by a gradual fusion of što dialects into a common language."[21] In their view, such a synthetic language would be far richer because it would draw on a wider linguistic base and would reflect the linguistic and practical experience of a larger subset of the population.

Further efforts in bringing the languages closer together were undertaken by Serbian linguist Djura Daničić in his capacity as first secretary of the Yugoslav Academy of Arts and Sciences. Before discussing Daničić's work, a few words about the academy itself are in order. Proposed in 1861 (although it did not officially open until 1866) and backed by the financial and moral support of the Catholic bishop from Djakovo, Josip Jurij Strossmayer, the Yugoslav Academy of Sciences reflected the Yugoslav ideal in its very name and charter. In Strossmayer's vision, the academy was to be a rallying point for the eventual unity of all the South Slavs, not merely Serbs and Croats but Slovenes and Bulgarians as well. In keeping with the preferred strategy of nineteenth-century nationalism, the academy's efforts were purely cultural, with pride of place given to literary and linguistic development, particularly of the Serbs and Croats. The ethnic makeup of its original officers reflected the desire for Serbian and Croatian cooperation. The academy's first president was the Croatian historian Franjo Rački.[22]

To Daničić was entrusted the academy's most important task—the preparation of a comprehensive *Dictionary of the Croatian or Serbian Language.* This monumental project was, with numerous interruptions, to occupy the academy for almost its entire existence: the first volume of the *Dictionary* appeared in 1880–82 and the last was not published until 1975! The academy *Dictionary* was far more than a lexicon; it also provided "a grammar, an accentology, a stylistics, and a model of the new literary language."[23] What is more, the *Dictionary* marked a victory for Vuk's conception of a unified literary language based primarily on a single dialect—interestingly enough, this dialect was not the one spoken by Daničić. As had been the case with Gaj and the Illyrians, Daničić was willing to sacrifice his own linguistic habits for what he saw as the common good.[24]

Other proposals for the further unification of Serbo-Croatian took shape in the period of Yugoslav agitation just before World War I.[25] These centered around the questions of dialect (again) and alphabet. In 1913, a number of people, including Jovan Skerlić, perhaps the most important and certainly the most prolific Serbian proponent of Yugoslav cultural and political integration in the pre–World War I period, proposed a new linguistic compromise between Serbs and Croats under the terms of which the Ijekavian dialect (the one that had been favored by Vuk but that was not employed by most Serbs) would be replaced by the Ekavian dialect, and, in return, the Latin alphabet would be used exclusively for the written language.[26] The war put an end to any immediate possibility of implementing the compromise, however, and Skerlić's premature death ensured that there would be no one with sufficient prestige in Serbia after the war to push it through. As a result, the Serbo-Croatian language continued to exist "written in either the Latin alphabet or in Cyrillic, in either the *je-* or *e-* variety of the *što* dialect."[27]

If the developmental pattern of Serbian and Croatian in the course of the nineteenth century seemed to almost all observers to be leading, inevitably, toward the creation of a single language, the situation vis-à-vis Slovenian was a great deal more complicated. The literary standard for both Serbian and Croatian was still in flux in the late 1830s, which allowed linguistic reform to coincide with increased pan–South Slavic contact, thereby encouraging work toward a common language. Efforts at codifying a unified modern Slovenian language, however, had begun significantly earlier and were all but finished by the time that increased intra-Slavic contact raised recognition of the desirability of a single literary language for all the South Slavs. As early as 1808–9, the linguist Jernej Kopitar (whom we have already met in connection with Vuk Karadžić) had written what amounted to a Slovenian normative grammar, "to eliminate particularisms in the literary language and to unite all the Slovenian regions through a literary Slovenian."[28] Although by no means were all of Kopitar's suggestions ultimately incorporated into modern Slovenian, his work gave "later writers, including Prešeren, a stable linguistic framework within which to work."[29] By the mid-1830s, with the publication of Prešeren's sonnets and his epic *Krst pri Savici* (The Baptism on the Savica), modern literary Slovenian had essentially been fully formed. As a result, by the time proposals for a unified South Slavic language were seriously floated, the Slovenes had their national poet and his language, and most Slovene intellectuals were, understandably enough, not enthusiastic at the prospect of giving these up for the sake of potential future glory.[30]

Nevertheless, a number Slovenes attempted, with varying degrees of success, to orient the Slovene literary language toward Croatian (or, Illyrian, as it was often called in the late 1830s and 1840s). For the most part, they did so in the belief that the Slovenes were too small a nation to survive in the modern world and that they would inevitably have to give up their native language despite their attachment to it. The most radical of these was the poet Stanko Vraz, who eventually became so convinced of the need for a unified South Slavic language that he gave up Slovene entirely and wrote his poetry in Gaj's new Croatian. In abandoning his native language, however, he gave up any attempt at redirecting it toward the other South Slavic languages, and thus, although his example was cited by some (mostly not Slovenian) commentators as a way toward a single South Slavic language, it proved a dead end. Still, debates about the role and place of Slovenian continued throughout the nineteenth century. Indeed, as late as 1913 the editors of one of Slovenia's cultural periodicals, *Veda*, surveyed readers and selected intellectuals on the subject of whether or not the Slovenes should give up their language. Not surprisingly, the only contributors who thought this was necessary were non-Slovenes, although some Slovenes were willing to consider such proposals as the adoption of a single technical language for all the South Slavs.[31]

In parallel with the either/or debate, and of far more consequence for Slovenian in the long term, were the linguistic reforms undertaken by Matija Majar-Ziljski and his followers. These included Luka Svetec and the Slavist France Miklošič (a participant in the Vienna Agreement of 1850, which tried to define a unified Serbo-Croatian). They concentrated on orienting literary Slovenian toward those of its own dialectal forms that were closest to Croatian or Serbian. Their goal was not the abandonment of Slovenian in favor of any other existing language, but its fusion with incipient Serbo-Croatian to create a pan–South Slavic idiom. Although this never happened, many of their reforms were accepted, with the result that modern standard Slovenian became much more similar to Serbo-Croatian than it might otherwise have been.

Canonizing a "Yugoslav" Literature: The Folk Tradition

For those who believed that the South Slavs could or should be a single nation the issue of language was primary. It was almost equally important, however, to discover common cultural practices that could be seen to bind the various groups of South Slavs into a single community. After all, the recognition of a shared culture, like that of a shared language, helps make possible the broad horizontal sense of kinship that has been identified as the key component of national identity. As with a common language, the existence of a common culture allows promoters of national ideology to discover the nation's foundations deep in the mysterious past, predating any present political arrangements that may hinder contemporary national unification. Of course, given a sufficiently heterogeneous population (such as that possessed by almost any modern potential nation), the only way to find such a culture is to select specific works or practices that are shared by large numbers of people and to ignore others.

In the realm of culture, it has been suggested that one of the key

X

NB

~

*not =
oral vs.
print
but oral
vs. hur.*

driving forces for nationalism was the rise of mass print culture.[32] Perhaps this is best illustrated by South Slavic nationalism, in which the recognition of an existing common culture was effected through the publication of what had been, until the early nineteenth century, an almost exclusively oral culture. What is more, and this, too, parallels the situation with the South Slavic language(s), orally transmitted folk songs became a bone of contention between those who were propagating separate South Slav nationalisms and those who strove for South Slavic integration.

The first extensive efforts to collect and publish the South Slavic oral tradition were carried out by Vuk Karadžić. We have already noted Vuk's importance in the area of linguistic reform, but of at least equal importance was his work in setting to paper the sung poetry he had heard as a boy (and consciously collected as an adult) from wandering minstrels—called *guslari* in Serbian after the one-stringed instrument, the *gusle*, with which they accompanied their singing. Although the church had been the sole source of institutionalized and high-cultural continuity in the Serbian lands during almost five centuries of Ottoman rule, folk songs had remained a mass cultural reservoir of traditional language, imagery, and themes. In 1814 and 1815, with the help of the Slovene Jernej Kopitar, Vuk published two collections of oral poetry.[33] The first contained mostly lyric songs ("women's songs" as Vuk called them), whereas the second contained some of the most stirring heroic songs that Vuk would collect. Kopitar, who occupied the influential position of censor of South Slavic and modern Greek materials at the Viennese court, caused Vuk's work to be known among those German intellectuals who believed in the creative and nation-building potential of the simple folk. The freshness and vitality of the poetry in Vuk's collection caused a sensation in Western Europe, where the oral folk poetry tradition, although revered, was for the most part merely a memory. The songs brought Serbia onto the world cultural scene for the first time and spurred translations by such luminaries as Goethe, Walter Scott, Mérimée, and Pushkin.[34] Equally important, the prosody as well as the themes and images of the folk poetry Vuk published provided the basis for a contemporary Yugoslav literature.

As far as Vuk himself was concerned, sung poetry was basically a Serbian tradition. He called his collections "Serbian Folk Songs," even though his collecting trips took him to Montenegro, Bosnia, Herzegovina, and the Croatian littoral. Vuk's national designation of the folk songs he collected was, however, questioned almost from the very beginning. The Croatian "Illyrians" were also quite interested in folk songs, hoping to use them, as well as the language itself, as a unifying force. Indeed, their desires to demonstrate South Slav cultural unity through folk song sometimes went well beyond the bounds of mere collection, as an epistolary dispute between Prešeren and Stanko Vraz indicates. Prešeren worked with a Polish émigré, Emil Korytko, collecting Slovenian folk songs in 1837 and 1838. Korytko wished to publish the songs through the office of Ljudevit Gaj. As Prešeren wrote Vraz: "It was indicated to him that Dr. Gaj's office was prepared to undertake the printing only under the condition that the songs exhibited a purely Illyrian, not *Carniolan* tendency."[35]

Even without bending the truth too far, however, it was possible to demonstrate that sung poetry, particularly oral epic, was the shared property of many South Slavs whom even Vuk would never have considered Serbs. One significant work that demonstrated this was the Čakavian collection published by the Croatian scholar Stjepan Mažuranić in 1876. This slim volume includes many unique poems, but it also contains a large quantity of epic songs that double those published by Karadžić, including many devoted to Marko Kraljević. This personage could even be found as far afield as Slovenia, where he seems, in the Slovenian cultural imagination, to have blurred together with the legendary King Matjaž.[36] Ultimately, the fact that similar songs were traditionally sung by people living throughout the South Slavic lands provided a powerful argument for the essential unity of the South Slavs, one that was to be used frequently by Serbs and Croats of Yugoslav orientation particularly just before and after World War I.[37]

Although Vuk collected scores of oral epic poems, many in multiple variants, I will limit my discussion to three that, taken together, illustrate all the themes and tropes that would come to be seen as fundamental for Yugoslav culture: "Propast Carstva Srpskoga" (The Downfall of the Serbian Empire), "Smrt Majke Jugovića" (The Mother of the Yugoviches), and "Marko Kraljević poznaje očinu sablju" (Prince Marko Recognizes His Father's Saber).[38] The first two are taken from what has come to be known as the Kosovo cycle, for they deal directly with a mythologized version of the events surrounding the fateful 1389 battle that, by tradition, marked the collapse of the medieval Serbian Empire and the beginning of five centuries of Turkish domination. The last is one of many poems dealing with

the life and adventures of Marko Kraljević, who in real life was an ambiguous figure, the ruler of a quasi-autonomous Christian kingdom but a
vassal to the Turkish sultan. All of these poems were transcribed from oral
performance, and they all employ the traditional ten-syllable heroic line
with a caesura after the fourth syllable (the *deseterac*).[39] The opening lines
of "The Downfall of the Serbian Empire" serve as a veritable encyclopedia
of South Slavic oral tropes, as well as a terse catalogue of some themes central to the tradition:

> Poletio soko tica siva
> Od Svetinje od Jerusalima,
> I on nosi ticu lastavicu.
> To ne bio soko tica siva,
> Veće bio svetitelj Ilija;
> On ne nosi tice lastavice,
> Veće knjigu od Bogorodice,
> Odnese je caru na Kosovo,
> Spušta knjigu caru na koleno
> Sama knjiga caru besedila:
> "Care Lazo, čestito koleno!
> Kome ćeš se privoleti carstvu?
> Ili voliš carstvu nebeskome,
> Ili voliš carstvu zemaljskome?"

> Flying hawk, grey bird,
> out of the holy place, out of Jerusalem,
> holding a swallow, holding a bird.
> That is no hawk, grey bird,
> that is Elijah, holy one;
> holding no swallow, no bird,
> but writing from the Mother of God
> to the Emperor at Kosovo.
> He drops that writing on his knee,
> it is speaking to the Emperor:
> "Lazar, glorious Emperor,
> which is the empire of your choice?
> Is it the empire of heaven?
> Is it the empire of the earth?"[40]

Besides the decasyllabic line, other notable tropes on display in this
opening section are fixed noun-adjective combinations (grey falcon [mis-
translated as hawk, for some reason]), antithetical constructions (not this,

but that), and repetition ("is it the empire . . . "). Poetic virtuosity is on display as well in the "rhyming" of the word *koleno* in two completely different meanings (it can mean either "knee" or "family"—this is unfortunately lost in translation). Most of these techniques would be borrowed and adapted by writers and artists who wished to create a new high Yugoslav culture on the basis of folk poetry.

Thematically this poem is remarkable for the choice offered Tsar Lazar. As the poem unfolds, he is told that if he wishes for an earthly kingdom he need do nothing more than go out and fight the Turks. He will be victorious, but his empire, being earthly, will be brief. If he chooses the empire of heaven, he must

> weave a church on Kosovo, build its foundation not with
>   marble stones,
> build it with pure silk and with crimson cloth, take the
>   Sacrament, marshal the men,
> they shall all die.[41]

Lazar's choice of the heavenly kingdom not only "explains" the Serbian loss; it provides a paradigm for seeing the Serbs (and the South Slavs in general) as a people of God, who choose honor over mere victory, physical suffering over easy glory, martyrdom over conquest. Many later works would address these same themes implicitly or explicitly, sometimes repeating, sometimes reversing them, in a bid to provide a cultural definition for the Yugoslav nation.

"The Mother of the Yugoviches" is one of the more unusual poems collected by Vuk. As opposed to the almost exclusively martial and male focus of the majority of epic songs, this one is more lyrical and focuses on the grieving women left behind when their husbands and sons fight. The different focus could be attributed to the fact that the singer from whom the poem was recorded was a woman (female singers of heroic songs were by no means unknown, but they were the exception rather than the rule), or it may reflect a somewhat more lyrical Croatian epic tradition (in the original edition the song bears the unusual note "from Croatia," indicating that Vuk at least felt its geographical provenance to be significant). The poet begins by saying that the Yugoviches were one of the families that served in Tsar Lazar's army at Kosovo, providing a father and nine sons. But instead of cataloguing the heroic actions of the males, the poet focuses on the clan's matriarch.

Boga moli Jugovića majka,
Da joj Bog da oči sokolove
I bijela krila labudova,
Da odleti nad Kosovo ravno,
I da vidi devet Jugovića
I desetog star-Juga Bogdana.

The mother of the Yugoviches prayed
for God to give her a hawk's eyes
and give her a swan's white wings,
to fly above flat Kosovo,
to see the nine, the Yugoviches,
and the tenth one, Yug Bogdan the old.[42]

As she flies over the field, however, she sees her husband and sons lying dead. In the remainder of the poem, the mother is depicted as trying to rein in her grief, to cope with her personal loss, which is at the same time a metonym for the loss of an entire way of life. She is able to hold herself together until, in one of the most effective and gruesome scenes in the tradition, two black ravens drop a severed hand wearing a gold ring into her lap. The amputated hand, a metonym of a metonym, concentrates the catastrophe to such an extent that she is quite literally no longer able to hold herself together, and in her grief she repeats the fate of her family. As the poet puts it in her characteristically terse fashion: "Nadula se Jugovića majka, / Nadula se, pa se i raspade" (The Mother of the Yugoviches swelled, / she swelled, she broke into pieces). This poem, with its personal and lyrical focus, would prove to be of central importance to a number of Croatian figures at the beginning of the twentieth century as they attempted to create a synthetic Yugoslav culture, a marriage of what they saw as the best of the Serbian and Croatian national traditions.

Marko Kraljević was the only epic hero to appear in songs belonging to Serbs, Croats, and Slovenes. As Svetozar Koljević describes him:

Marko the Prince—or Marko Kraljevich—is the most popular and the most controversial Serbian epic hero. He is the greatest champion of the helpless, ready to die for justice and honour, but ready also to kill or maim in revenge or even out of spite. He has a magic sword and an extraordinary horse; his hand can squeeze water out of wood which has been drying for nine years in a garret. But he also sometimes has to run for his life or to win by fraud because some of his enemies are stouter than he is. He is ferocious but tender-hearted, and, above all, so prone to drinking that a little money for wine can sometimes cool off his heroic rage.[43]

"Prince Marko Recognizes His Father's Saber" resembles a legend that exists in any number of cultures; that of the sword that, after many adventures and much treachery, finds its proper owner. In this variant, a Serbian soldier escaping after the Battle of Maritsa (this battle, fought in 1371, was a prelude to the devastating Kosovo defeat) asks for safe conduct from a Turkish family. Although the girl who finds him grants it, her brother kills him, thereby breaking one of the greatest Slavic taboos—against harming a guest. When this young man later goes to serve in the sultan's army he carries the sword he took from the stranger, a sword no one can draw from its scabbard. Marko, who as the sultan's vassal is also with the army, draws the sword, recognizes it, and asks how the young man acquired it. When he hears the story he cuts the man's head off with it.

It is the ending of the song that provides us with a most typical picture of Marko. Here, the emperor, who is presumably disturbed by the spectacle of one of his vassals killing another, sends his men to arrest Marko. In a scene reminiscent of Achilles sulking in his tent, they pass on their summons to Marko, who is drinking wine and in a black mood:

> A uzima tešku topuzinu,
> Pa otide caru pod čadora;
> Koliko se ražljutio Marko,
> U čizmama sjede na serdžadu,
> Pa pogleda cara poprijeko,
> Krvave mu suze iz očiju.
> Kad je care sagledao Marka
> I pred njime tešku topuzinu,
> Car s' odmiče, a Marko primiče,
> Dok doćera cara do duvara:
> Car se maši u džepove rukom,
> Te izvadi stotinu dukata,
> Pa ih daje Kraljeviću Marku:
> "Idi, Marko, napij mi se vina:
> Što su mi te tako ražljutili?"
> "Ne pitaj me, care poočime!
> Poznao sam sablju baba moga;
> Da sam Bog d'o u tvojim rukama,
> I ti bi me 'vako ražljutio."
> Pa on usta i ode čadoru.

> He took up his heavy club,
> he went down to the Emperor in his tent.

And Marko was so very angry,
he sat down on the praying-rug in boots.
Marko glances at the Emperor,
the blood and the tears stream from his eyes.
And the Emperor sees Marko,
he sees the weight of his club,
he moves away. Marko comes closer,
he presses the Emperor to the wall.
The Emperor's hand fumbles in his pocket,
he takes out a hundred ducats,
he gives them to Marko the Prince.
"Go, Marko, drink wine,
why did they make you so very angry?"
"Never ask, Emperor, father in God.
I found my father's sword,
and if God had put it in your hands
I would have been as angry with you."
And he rose and went to his own tent.[44]

For the exploited Christian peasants who listened to this tale, the image of Marko (who was able to commit such sacrileges as walking in shoes on a Moslem prayer rug and threatening the sultan himself) must have been ineffably sweet, albeit vicarious, revenge. At the same time, Marko's vulnerability made him a character to whom these same peasants could relate. He was, in a sense, a larger-than-life extension of themselves, a hero who, despite his inferior position in the hierarchy, embodied a stubborn resistance that would eventually triumph.

Yugoslav Literary and Artistic Creation: The Romantic Unitarist Synthesis

The crowning achievement in each of the East and Central European lands that underwent a nationalist revival in the nineteenth century was the production of original creative work that exploited the newly systematized national language and incorporated the traditional cultural heritage. Poets like Sándor Petőfi in Hungary, Adam Mickiewicz in Poland, and Alexander Pushkin in Russia were prized by critics of taste and discernment for their exquisite verse. But what eventually earned them large bronze statues in the streets and squares of their respective countries was not so much the quality of their literary output, as their ability to express the nation's collective self (or so, at least, claimed the nation-building intellectuals who pushed the candidacy of these "national poets"). The existence of a national poet was seen as proof that a given people had attained a level of cultural development sufficient for its pretensions to nationhood to be taken seriously. For a future nation's potential citizens, the work of the national poet provided both a source of pride and a rallying point for future cultural development. If high culture was previously seen as something borrowed from other nations, now the Poles, Hungarians, or Russians could imagine beginning their own tradition, and future generations of writers would inevitably trace their genealogy back to Petöfi, Mickiewicz, or Pushkin rather than to Shakespeare, Homer, Dante, or Goethe.

In the South Slavic lands, the situation was no different. Here, too, with almost miraculous alacrity poets appeared to take advantage of the reformed language that Vuk, Gaj, and their followers had provided. As was the case in linguistics, there was general agreement among South Slavic (at least Serb and Croat) intellectuals about the desirability of creating a common Yugoslav culture. As had happened in the area of language, however, when it came time to discuss what such a common culture should look like and how it should be created, strong disagreements surfaced. Among linguists, the debate centered on whether the best method for creating a unified Serbo-Croatian language was to choose one existing dialect (the "purest" or the one used by the largest number of speakers) or, rather, to create a new dialect that would enfold the existing ones. In the case of culture, the question was whether Yugoslav culture should be derived, primarily, from one of the existing cultures, or whether it should be formed by amalgamating bits and pieces of all of them into a previously unknown synthesis. Roughly speaking, during the first, romantic, stage of Yugoslav cultural development, the former method was chosen by most, and the unitary culture proposed leaned heavily toward Serbian cultural practices. In the period just before World War I, however, a multicultural synthesis that would borrow from each of the separate South Slavic traditions became more popular.

Two basic types of literary work competed to build the foundations for "Yugoslav" literature in the initial, romantic period. The first comprises relatively brief lyrics whose subject matter is precisely a call for South Slav unity. In terms of form, these poems may or may not use the meters of folk poetry (although they often do), and their language may be more or less at-tuned to that of the common folk. Ultimately, however, they display their Yugoslav sentiment first and foremost in their subject matter, with formal and linguistic Yugoslavism secondary. Such works were clearly of great symbolic importance to "Yugoslavizers," but their brevity and the fact that no one individual produced a body of high-quality work of this kind mil-itated against their forming the basis for a proposed Yugoslav literature. The other, and ultimately more important, group consists of longer works that employ an updated version of traditional oral heroic verse to create a modern national epic. Two major works of this type, Ivan Mažuranić's *Smrt Smail-age Čengića* (The Death of Smail-Aga Čengić) and Petar Petro-vić Njegoš's *Gorski vijenac* (The Mountain Wreath), eventually became the leading candidates for canonization as the national epic of the South Slavs.

To give an idea of the kind of lyric verse that would later be canon-ized as part of the Yugoslav poetic tradition, let us consider the poetry of the Croatian Petar Preradović. Preradović (1818–72) followed a rather sur-prising career path for a future Yugoslav national poet. The son of a mili-tary officer, he himself joined the Austrian army, rising eventually to the rank of general. Most of his education was in German, as was his first po-etry, and he claimed almost to have completely forgotten his native lan-guage. During the early 1840s, however, Preradović became interested in the literary situation of his native land, and he began to write "Illyrian" po-etry that was immediately acclaimed by the burgeoning Croatian cultural establishment. Preradović himself continued to doubt his talent, fearing that the development of his poetic voice had been forever hampered by his loss of feeling for his native tongue. As he wrote to fellow Illyrian Stanko Vraz: "Everything that I write is as if seen through a dream, the dream of the first years of my life when I heard no other voices than my mother's. I have been overgrown with too many foreign customs, feelings, and thoughts to become a true native writer."[45] Despite his fears, however, Pre-radović came to be recognized as perhaps the most talented lyric poet the Illyrian movement produced.

Preradović's poem "Rodu o jeziku" (To the Nation Regarding Lan-guage) is a typical example of the poetry of national revival. The poem's epigraph is von Humboldt's phrase "Die wahre Heimat ist eigentlich die Sprache," about which we have had occasion to speak earlier. This is fol-lowed by nine elegant ten-line stanzas exhibiting a regular pattern of rhyme (aabccbdeed) and meter (trochaic, the first couplet pentameter [a deseterac, in fact], followed by eight lines of tetrameter). Such a strict form was, of course, unknown to folk poetry. The poem itself is a dithyramb to the concept of one's native language in general (a subject that was clearly of personal as well as social concern to the poet), and a hymn to a unified Illyrian tongue in particular. From the point of view of future Yugoslav canonizers, the most significant stanzas are the sixth and seventh, in which Preradović lays out his view of the speakers of his nation's language, their heroes, and their ethos.

> Od Stambula grada do Kotora,
> Od Crnoga do Jadranskog mora
>   Njegvu carstvu prostor puče.
>   Tuj po gorah i dolinah
>   Preko devet pokrajina
>   Svud ga majke djecu uče,
>   Sokolova, sokolića
>   Njegovijeh gniezdo tu je,
>   Svuda tud se pjevat čuje,
>   Pjesan Marka Kraljevića.
>
> Junačkijem glasom u njem poje
> Junak narod uspomene svoje.
>   Uz gusle se u njem ore
>   Kroz sve vieke nama doli
>   Sve radosti i sve boli
>   Našeg svieta—pjesni tvore
>   Utrnulih naših plama
>   Osvjetlanih naših lica,
>   Sva je naša povjestnica
>   Velik samo sbor pjesama![46]

> From Istanbul to Kotor
> From the Black Sea to the Adriatic
>   The expanse of its kingdom stretches.
>   Through mountains and valleys,
>   Over nine regions
>   Mothers teach it to their children.
>   Falcons, falcons,
>   Their nests are everywhere
>   That one can hear songs
>   About Marko Kraljević.

They are sung in a heroic voice.
A heroic nation's memories.
   One can hear to the sound of the gusle
   Throughout the ages down to us
   All the joys and sorrows of
   Our people—are created in song.
   From our dying flames
   To our illuminated faces.
   Our entire history
   Is a great collection of songs.

The nation that Preradović is imagining, it appears, is an ultra-inclusive South Slavic one that contains, linguistically at least, the Bulgarians (who live in the proximity of Istanbul) as well as Serbs and Croats. The national ethos Preradović proposes is the traditional Serbian attribute of heroism, which appears somewhat out of place in this lyrical genre. Nevertheless, its identification as a, if not the, national trait is highly significant. Not only does Preradović share this belief with his contemporaries Njegoš and Mažuranić, but, as we will see in the course of this book, the idea that all Yugoslavs are united by a heroic attitude toward life will remain more or less a constant throughout the nineteenth and twentieth centuries, even as it undergoes a complicated evolutionary development. In terms of literary and cultural traditions, the nation is conceived as a singer of songs, about Marko Kraljević in particular.

Preradović would expand this latter focus in an unfinished drama about Marko Kraljević. This play, based on a folk legend that Marko Kraljević will rise again to lead his people to final victory over their oppressors, shows even more "foreign" influence than his lyric poetry and is set for the most part in contemporary Bosnia, although it also includes a host of allegorical spirits and demons. According to the legend, Marko's rebirth will be prepared by the appearance of a person who can organize today's South Slavs and convince them to follow the risen Marko. In this play it is the Bosnian peasant Stevan (who speaks primarily in the heroic deseterac), who convinces his followers to fan out through all the South Slavic lands to prepare the people. My summary sounds messianic, of course, and there is no doubt that Marko's appearance is meant as a kind of substitute for the second coming and that national revival stands in here as the local equivalent of the establishment of the kingdom of heaven on earth. The play ends with the risen Marko and the peasant Stevan on the field at Kosovo awaiting the arrival of all the South Slavs, who will, by uniting, avenge the five-century-old defeat. Insofar as he presents such events as Kosovo and such characters as Marko not as Serbian but rather as South Slavic in general, Preradović can be seen as a forerunner of a whole series of (mostly Croatian) authors who would attempt to build a synthetic South Slavic culture by employing traditionally Serbian themes in an untraditional (basically Western European) artistic form.

Ljudevit Gaj may have been the organizer and propagator of the Illyrian Yugoslav ideal, and Preradović its leading lyric poet, but Ivan Mažuranić was the most talented writer to join the movement. Born in a peasant family in 1814, Mažuranić, like Gaj, earned a law degree and became active in all facets of Croatian intellectual and political life. Unlike Gaj, whose political career was cut short by a combination of his Yugoslav militancy and his own questionable judgment, Mažuranić rose quickly in post-1848 Croatian society. Indeed, from 1873 to 1880 he occupied the position of *ban*, the highest political and administrative office in Croatia. Mažuranić's literary output was small and was produced almost exclusively in the period 1835–47. Nevertheless, *The Death of Smail-Aga Čengić*, his relatively brief epic (just over one thousand lines) was recognized from the time of its publication as a fundamental work for any future Yugoslav literary canon.[47]

Mažuranić took as his theme an incident from contemporary history. In 1840, a small group of Montenegrins had killed Čengić, a Turkish official, while he was on a tax-collecting mission. Mažuranić does not so much tell the story as provide five highly condensed pictures focusing first on Smail-Aga and his suite ("Agovanje" [Smail-Aga's Lordship]) and then on the solitary nocturnal journey from the Aga's camp to the Montenegrin capital of Cetinje embarked on by the Turkish renegade who will betray Smail-Aga's whereabouts ("Noćnik" [The Night Fugitive]). This is mirrored in part 3 by a wonderfully atmospheric description of the reverse journey taken by the Montenegrins who will ambush the Aga ("Četa" [The Band]). The longest section of the work ("Harač" [Tax Collecting]) begins with a lengthy description of the exploitation by the Turks of their Christian subjects and ends with the attack of the Montenegrins. The brief final chapter ("Kob" [Fate]) forms a kind of coda characterizing the remains of the once-feared and now-dead Aga.

The fact that Mažuranić, a Croat, chose an episode from Montenegrin rather than Croatian history for his epic was obviously significant. In their attempts to induce readers to imagine the Yugoslav nation as a single entity, writers such as Preradović and Vraz had overtly linked the Croats with the other South Slavs. Mažuranić never mentions any South Slavic group besides the Montenegrins in his epic, but it was immediately clear to his readers that he considered them to be exemplary South Slavs and that the story as a whole is meant to be read as a kind of synecdoche; the victorious struggle against Smail-Aga Čengić stands in for an entire five-hundred–year history of resistance on the part of the South Slavs to the Turks (and, by extension, to other imperial powers). This cycle, it is implied, is now reaching its climax with the revival of South Slavic independence. Like Preradović, Mažuranić identifies martial heroism and defiance as the defining characteristics of the South Slavs. These are embodied not in any individual, but in the band as a collective entity. This latter fact is important because it makes Mažuranić's work a strong expression of the collectivistic mentality that has remained paramount for South Slavic national thinking.

Equally significant for Mažuranić's attempts to create a Yugoslav national literature was the verse form he used in the epic. As noted earlier, although Preradović had employed some of the inflections of folk poetry in his verse, it was formally closer to the European models he had learned in German schools. Mažuranić, on the other hand, wrote the majority of his epic in the deseterac, that is, a written imitation of the most common oral heroic poetic form. Again, his technique was in some sense just the opposite of Preradović's. Preradović mentioned the names of characters derived from the oral tradition, but he employed them, for the most part, in an untraditional literary form.[48] In *The Death of Smail-Aga Čengić*, on the contrary, there is no mention of folkloric characters; the verse form alone recalls the entire context of the folk epic. Nor is it merely the rhythm of the verse line that calls the oral epic to mind: Mažuranić also employs the entire panoply of "oral" tropes, including stock formulas, repetition, and negative characterization. Indeed, Mažuranić's work was so close in spirit to the work of his Montenegrin contemporary Njegoš (see below) that there were consistent rumors claiming that the epic had actually been written by the latter. Although these can undoubtedly be discounted, their existence shows the extent to which Mažuranić participated in the Serbianizing of Yugoslav culture in this period.[49]

A year after the appearance of *The Death of Smail-Aga Čengić* came the publication of what ultimately became the single most important work of "Yugoslav" literature, Petar Petrović Njegoš's epic in dramatic form entitled *Gorski vijenac* (The Mountain Wreath). Njegoš was in many respects the outstanding figure produced by the South Slavs in the nineteenth century. He was born in 1813 to the Njegoši tribe in Montenegro, perhaps the most primitive and poorest European land of its day. As it happened, Njegoš's uncle was both the spiritual and the political leader of this mountain principality (his title, prince-bishop, indicated his combined clerical and lay powers). Upon his uncle's death in 1830, Njegoš was appointed in his stead, and he spent the rest of his short life (he died of tuberculosis in 1851) attempting to improve the situation of his homeland. He strengthened the power of central authority, opened Montenegro's first schools, built its first roads, and defended his tiny land against Turkish onslaughts. Simultaneously, he wrote some of the finest poetry that has ever been produced in his language. Unlike Mažuranić, who was specifically attempting to advance the creation of a single South Slavic nation through his work, Njegoš saw himself as an exclusively Serbian writer. Nevertheless, as we will see at various points throughout this book, his work ultimately came to be canonized as *the* major work of Yugoslav literature.

The Mountain Wreath opens with the dedication "prahu oca Srbije" (to the ashes of the father of Serbia),[50] that is, to Karadjordje who led the Serbian uprising against Turkish rule in 1804. He subsequently declared himself commander of Serbia, but after the Turks crushed his rebellion in 1813 he was forced to flee to Austria. When he returned to his homeland in 1817 he was assassinated by a rival claimant for Serbian leadership, Miloš Obrenović, thus beginning a feud between the two dynasties that would last into the twentieth century. In Njegoš's dedication, Karadjordje is extolled as a military leader of equal stature to Napoleon, Suvorov, and Kutuzov, a man who "diže narod, krsti zemlju, a varvarski lance sruši, / iz mrtvijeh Srba dozva, dunu život srpskoj duši" (roused people, christened the land, and broke the barbarous fetters, / summoned the Serbs back from the dead and breathed life into their souls). This attempt to elevate a character from Serbian history to a more general, at least pan-European pedestal, is part of Njegoš's overall epic strategy to imbue a relatively minor event in Montenegrin history with universal significance.[51] In a move that will be typical for the work as a whole, recollections of glory are immediately tempered by tragedy: "Da, viteza sustopice tragičeski konac prati: /

tvojoj glavi bi sudjeno za v'jenac se svoj prodati!" (Yes, a hero's life is always haunted by a tragic ending. / It was destiny that your head had to pay the price for its wreath [1]). The introduction ends with an invocation of the legendary Serbian medieval hero of the battle of Kosovo, Miloš Obilić, as well as the battle's traditional villain, the traitor Vuk Branković, thereby tying the rebirth of Serbia to its legendary demise in 1389.

With the beginning of the main body of the text, Njegoš switches to the ten-syllable line of the folk epic and introduces his central character, the brooding Bishop Danilo. Although Danilo's historical prototype was the prince-bishop of Montenegro at the turn of the eighteenth century, his psychology is that of Njegoš himself, and he is best understood as an autobiographical character. Danilo contemplates and curses the conquests that have been made by Islam and thinks about how they can be rolled back. True, Montenegro itself is still free, but Danilo believes that this freedom, hard-won on the battlefield, is threatened, not by arms but by slow conversion to Islam. Danilo curses those Slavs who have gone over to Islam, employing the characters of the oral epic for the sake of comparison:

> Bog vas kleo, pogani izrodi,
> što će turska vjera medju nama?
> Kuda ćete s kletvom pradjedovskom?
> Su čim ćete izać pred Miloša
> i pred druge srpske vitezove,
> koji žive doklen sunce grije?

> May God strike you, loathsome degenerates,
> why do we need the Turk's faith among us?
> What will you do with your ancestor's curse?
> With what will you appear before Miloš and before
>   all other Serbian heroes,
> Whose names will live as long as the sun shines? (7)

In Danilo's mind, however, the desire to rid his land of converts to Islam is tempered by a recognition that although they may be traitors to the nation, these men and women are blood relations. Although he has summoned a council of the Montenegrin tribes to plan the destruction of these "Turks," he recognizes full-well the tragedy of the situation.

> Kad današnju premislim viječu,
> raspale me užasa plamovi:
> isklati se brača medju sobom

When I think of today's council meeting,
flames of horror flare up deep inside me.
A brother will slaughter his own brother. (7)

It is Danilo's personal tragedy to be paralyzed by contradictory desires: on the one hand, he believes that only a "religious cleansing" of his land can effect its eventual rebirth; yet on the other, he is aware of the horrors that such a civil war would bring. In this respect, Danilo's prototype is no real person, but the romantic incarnation of Hamlet, always trapped between the need to act and the inability to do so. Danilo can thus be considered a kind of generic refugee, a character from a romantic drama who has been forced to inhabit the world of traditional epic. The rest of the Christian Montenegrins, more standard epic characters all, lack any trace of Danilo's Hamlet complex. The straightforward response of one of the clan leaders to Danilo's brooding is typical:

Da li ovo svetkovanje nije
na komu si sabra Crnogorce
da čistimo zemlju od nekrsti

Is today not a festive occasion
on which you have gathered Montenegrins
to rid our land of loathsome infidels? (7)

This split between the tragically conflicted individual and the confident group also embodies the collectivistic basis of South Slavic national thought. For, ultimately, the epic's plot revolves at least as much around how and whether Danilo can join himself to the collective will as it does around the massacre of the converts that forms the work's ostensible subject.

The collectivistic bias of *The Mountain Wreath* is further emphasized by the intermittent presence of an updated version of a Greek chorus. The role of the chorus, here called a *Kolo* (the Serbian word for the national round dance), is to open up the historical level of the epic by making connections between the events of the drama and past moments in Serbian history. In its first appearance, the Kolo singers link the Christian-Moslem split among the Montenegrins to the conflict between Miloš Obilić and Vuk Branković.[52] These overt connections, in addition to the formal qualities of the verse lines, tie Njegoš's masterpiece directly to the national oral epic. Indeed, one noteworthy aspect both of this work and of Serbian historical consciousness in general, is the way in which time tends to collapse, with the interval between events of the Battle of Kosovo and the present (whenever that may be) reduced almost to nothing.[53] The chorus expresses the perspective of the collective and presents the Montenegrin myth more forthrightly than do any of the "historical" characters:

> Što uteče ispod sablje turske,
> što na vjeru pravu ne pohuli,
> što se ne hče u lance vezati,
> to se zbježa u ove planine
> da ginemo i krv prolivamo,
> da junački amanet čuvamo,
> divno ime i svetu slobodu.

> Those who escaped before the Turkish sword,
> those who did not blaspheme the True Faith,
> those who refused to be thrown in chains,
> took refuge here in these lofty mountains
> to shed their blood together and to die,
> heroically to keep the sacred oath,
> their lovely name, and their holy freedom. (12–13)

When the Montenegrin leaders have gathered, it is clear that all are in favor of destroying their Islamicized kin. They implore Danilo to stop his endless ruminations and to give the order to begin. Yet Danilo still hesitates:

> Slušaj, Vuče, i ostala braćo!
> Ništa mi se nemojte čuditi
> što me crne rastezaju misli,
> što mi prsa kipe sa užasom.
> Ko na brdo, ak' i malo, stoji
> više vidi no onaj pod brdom;
> ja poviše nešto od vas vidim—
> to je sreča dala al' nesreča.
> Ne bojim se od vražjega kota,
> neka ga je ka na gori lista,
> no se bojim od zla domaćega. . . .
> Zlo se trpi od straha gorega.

> Now listen, Vuk and my brothers!
> At what you see in me do not wonder,
> that dark thoughts are tearing my soul apart
> and that my chest is heaving with horror.

Who stands on a hill ever so briefly,
sees so much more than the one in foothills.
Some things I see more clearly than you do—
That is either our luck or misfortune.
I fear them not, this brood of the devil,
may they be as many as forest leaves,
but I do fear the evil at our home. . . .
One bears evil for fear of a greater one! (21)

Still in the grip of doubt, Bishop Danilo calls for talks with the converts to Islam, hoping they can be brought to see the light without violence, although well aware that this will not happen. The talks themselves are noteworthy because it is the "Turks" who propose sharing the land, whereas the Christians refuse. One of the former proposes:

Iako je zemlja pouzana,
dvije vjere mogu se složiti
ka u sahan što se čorbe slažu.
Mi živimo kao dosad bratski,
pa ljubovi više ne trebuje.

Though this country is a bit too narrow,
two faiths can live together side by side,
just as two soups can be cooked in one pot.[54]
Let us live together like brothers,
and we will need no additional love. (36)

He is answered immediately with "Bismo, Turci, ali se ne može!" (We would like to, Turks, but it cannot be!) Presumably, the reader is supposed to recognize that the converts to Islam sound more humane because they are hypocrites; that is, they believe that time is on their side and that the sultan's minions will eventually conquer the rest of Montenegro. They never say this, however, and if we look at *The Mountain Wreath* through the prism of the 1990s, the conversations between the Montenegrin Moslems and their Orthodox brothers look chillingly prophetic.

Even these unproductive talks do not cure Danilo of his inability to act, and the whole middle section of the work is a long pause during which Njegoš builds tension by moving the central question into the background (although it reappears continually). He provides in its stead a series of vignettes of Montenegrin life, which many commentators have taken as a kind of encyclopedia of Serbian folk customs. Along the way, Njegoš man-

ages to interpolate almost every genre of folk poetry into his text, providing a prayer, a wedding song, a lament, and a fragment of a typical epic. A
number of purely comic episodes, including a wildly estranged description
of Venice by a Montenegrin who clearly understood not a bit of what he
saw there, a description of an illiterate priest attempting to read, and the
capture of a "witch," similarly serve to retard the action and build expectations for the inevitable clash to come.

In the course of *The Mountain Wreath*, Danilo's ambivalence is
raised to a basic principle of world organization. As the chorus puts it at
one point: "Čašu meda još niko ne popi / što je čašom žuči ne zagrči" (No
one has yet drunk a cup of honey / without mixing it with a cup of gall
[22]). By far the strongest expression of this dualist philosophy, however,
appears at the end of the work in the remarkable speech of the old Abbot
Stefan:

> Sv'jet je ovaj tiran tiraninu,
> a kamoli duši blagorodnoj!
> On je sostav paklene nesloge:
> u nj ratuje duša sa tijelom,
> u nj ratuje more s bregovima,
> u nj ratuje zima i toplina,
> u nj ratuju vjetri s vjetrovima,
> u nj ratuje živina s živinom,
> u nj ratuje narod sa narodom,
> u nj ratuje čovjek sa čovjekom,
> u nj ratuju dnevi sa noćima,
> u nj ratuju dusi s nebesima.

> This world is a tyrant to the tyrant,
> let alone to a truly noble soul!
> It is work of infernal discord:
> in it the soul is at war with the flesh;
> in it the sea is at war with the shores;
> in it cold is at war with the heat;
> in it the winds are at war with the winds;
> in it creature is at war with creature;
> in it nation is at war with nation;
> in it man is at war with others;
> in it the days are at war with the nights;
> in it spirits are at war with heaven. (91)

Although this speech obviously has something to do with a dualism typical of European romanticism, it also has a home-grown antecedent: the dualistic Bogomil heresy, which gripped much of the Balkans in the thirteenth and fourteenth centuries. Traces of Bogomil philosophy unquestionably remained among the South Slavs, and they appear to be at the foundations of Njegoš's text as well. Unlike Bishop Danilo, however, the Abbot Stefan is not paralyzed by his recognition of the world's essential duality. Instead, he exhorts the Montenegrin Christians to purge the country of its Islamic element, arguing that resurrection can only come through death.[55] The specific resurrection he has in mind is that of the Serbian people. Thus, as in the case with many epics, the direction of this work is circular (the form of the round dance that plays such a crucial role here), with events in the poem's present forging a tie to the medieval Serbian kingdom. Like the *Odyssey*, *The Mountain Wreath* will end with the hero's return to the home that had seemingly been lost; in this case, however, the home is the unity of national life that was lost on Kosovo, and the hero is a collective rather than an individual.

Ultimately, even the wavering Bishop Danilo is won over, although he never gives an overt order for the massacre. Still, when he is told by a local leader that, at least in one area, the "Turks" who did not run away were killed, their houses burned, and their mosques destroyed, he rejoices:

> Blago meni, moji sokolovi,
> blago meni, junačka svobodo!
> Jutros si mi divno voskresnula
> iz grobovah našijeh djedovah!
>
> You have brought me great gladness, my falcons,
> great joy for me. Heroic liberty!
> This bright morning you've been resurrected
> from every tomb of our dear forefathers! (95)

The final scenes of the work are somewhat deflationary, and consist merely of the delivery of reports of the successful anti-Moslem campaign to Bishop Danilo and the Abbot Stefan. The difference in their characters is highlighted one last time in one of the final "stage directions": "Bishop Danilo cries and Abbot Stefan laughs" (100).

The above analysis of the linguistic and literary trends characteristic for the romantic period of the 1830s and 1840s allows us to risk a general definition of the Yugoslav culture (as well as the concomitant Yugoslav nation) that was imagined by South Slavic intellectuals at this time: it was, we can say, Yugoslavism with a decidedly Serbian cast. Certainly as far as figures such as Vuk and Njegoš were concerned, sympathy for other South Slavs was not accompanied by a desire to create a culture that would synthesize their various cultural traditions. And although most of the Illyrians did not wish to see the disappearance of Croatian culture, their efforts unquestionably led to its Serbianization. Thus, a writer such as Mažuranić specifically used Serbian themes and folk verse forms in a literary language that was chosen for its compatibility with modern Serbian. Nevertheless, although the romantic period produced wonderful literary works that were destined to become cornerstones of the later Yugoslav literary canon, the attempt to transform Serbian culture into Yugoslav culture turned out to be a dead end. Although it was not theoretically inconceivable that such a policy could have worked in the long run (particularly had Serbian political domination accompanied it), it seems that the cultural specificity of the Croats and Slovenes was too well established by this period for them to be easily swallowed up by an encompassing Serbian identity.

In any case, when new attempts at constituting a Yugoslav nation at the beginning of the twentieth century took place, they were based on a rather different synthesis, one that promised to create a national identity that would be far more sensitive to the variety of the South Slavic traditions. This new conception of the nation was spurred, in part, by the manifest failure of the Romantic period to create successful, popular Yugoslav nationalism. Indeed, for a number of reasons, the period that stretched from the 1860s to the beginning of the twentieth century was a low point for any vision of Yugoslav cooperation and synthesis, even despite the constant efforts of Bishop Strossmayer and his Yugoslav Academy. In part it was a question of simple cultural exhaustion after the great romantic upsurge. What is more, the concerns of realism, which supplanted romanticism as the central literary tendency, were antithetical to the kind of synthetic thinking that drove the pan–South Slavic project. Descriptions of "life as it is" as called for by influential figures such as the Serbian Svetozar Marković and the Croatian August Šenoa led to an emphasis on particularities and masked the broad cultural similarities that had been favored by the romantics. Equally important, however, were the conscious efforts of Austrian and Hungarian politicians, who, following a policy of divide and rule, did their best to set Serb against Croat within the Habsburg lands. Simultaneously, in Serbia proper, consolidation was the order of the day, and few politicians or cultural figures concerned themselves with further plans to unite the South Slavs.

Creating and Canonizing Yugoslav Culture: 1903–1918

At the beginning of the twentieth century, however, the political and cultural climate regarding Yugoslavism changed rather suddenly. A 1903 palace coup in Belgrade brought Petar Karadjordjević to the Serbian throne, replacing the Austrophilic Aleksandar Obrenović. Although Petar had been known for his strong Serbian nationalist leanings, Yugoslav sentiment experienced a gigantic resurgence during his reign. In his much later novel *Timor mortis*, the Serbian writer Slobodan Selenić sets the scene in Belgrade at about the turn of the century: "Those were the days of the sudden flowering of the Yugoslav idea, and Belgrade was, through a series of royal celebrations, transformed into a true South Slavic stage of fiery patriots. In the city one could find many literati, journalists, and politicians of Yugoslav orientation. At the same time the first Yugoslav student congress was held. Ideas of reciprocity permeated the loud declarations that issued from both the excitable youth and the stable adults who flocked to Belgrade from all the Yugoslav regions, from Slovenia all the way to Bulgaria."[56] Selenić's hero, a Serb who had been born on the territory of the Habsburg Empire, and a man who does not believe in the possibility of Yugoslav unity, feels completely alien in the city: "Amidst the unanimous shouting of brotherhood, liberation of the people from the Austro-Hungarian prison, Yugoslavism, old Stojan, who never stopped cursing Starčević and the rightists, Mažuranić and the obzoraši, Frank and the clericals, seemed to many to be senilely stubborn, perhaps even a bit crazy."

The new Yugoslavism embraced by the post-1903 generation of Serbs, Croats, and Slovenes differed from its predecessor in that it was far more devoted to multicultural synthesis than to Serbianization. There was a general willingness to allow Serbia to play the role of Piedmont politically, but only on the condition that it did not demand that role in the cultural sphere. Jovan Skerlić, who was perhaps the most outstanding Serbian proponent of a new type of Yugoslavism in this period, described his position as follows: "Religious divisions and political life have made their mark, and the Slavic South is today divided into four national groups and three religions. Religious and national proselytizing are not possible, nor are cultural or political hegemony."[57] Two different approaches to the creation of a national culture came to the fore in the immediate prewar period. The first continued to emphasize the use of themes and figures drawn from traditional folk poetry. However, instead of embodying these themes in folkloric forms, a new generation of artists and writers attempted to express them in the most up-to-date European genres. The result was a series of works that appeared to contemporaries to be "Serbian" in form and European (i.e., Croatian) in content. The work of such writers and artists can be seen as an evolutionary outgrowth of the heroic epic mode of Mažuranić and Njegoš. At the same time, another group of writers and artists proposed abandoning the folk tradition entirely and expressed their Yugoslav solidarity in their willingness to collaborate with fellow Yugoslavs to create a modern European culture for their nation, one not based specifically on the national past; these writers were, in a sense, continuing in the more lyrical vein that Preradović had pioneered.

Yugoslavizing efforts that combined themes traditionally perceived as Serbian with European genres were most apparent among Croatian writers and artists. One of the more famous examples of literary work of this kind was the tragedy *Smrt majke Jugovića* (The Death of the Mother of the Yugoviches) by Ivo Vojnović.[58] Although its title clearly refers to the sung poetry we quoted earlier and Vojnović frequently does employ the decasyllabic line, the play's lexical and syntactic texture and its overall composition invoke a modernism that decisively distances it from the folk tradition.

The most crucial cultural figure of this inclination, however, was not a writer but rather the Croatian sculptor Ivan Meštrović. In the period before and during World War I, Meštrović became one of the world's most famous artists, and the leading spokesman for a new kind of Yugoslav culture. As it happened, sculpture was an ideal choice for the expression of the new Yugoslav synthesis. First of all, sculpture was practically unknown in Serbian culture, which, like other Orthodox traditions, permits painted icons but prohibits three-dimensional figures. It had, however, been quite well developed in the Dalmatian cities, especially on the exteriors of the region's Venetian-inspired churches. As a result, when he chose to carve the figures of epic poetry, Meštrović automatically achieved a bold melding of cultural traditions. Furthermore, figurative sculpture is much more easily accessible than high literature, particularly because it does not depend on translation to reach an international audience. Considering that, by the early twentieth century, even the most ardent Yugoslav-inclined intellectuals recognized that South Slavic political integration would only come about with the support of at least some of the European powers, this aspect was crucial.

Meštrović's life story is almost as compelling as Njegoš's. He was born in 1883 the son of a farmer in the Croatian uplands, at that time one of the poorest and most desolate regions of Europe. His early schooling was minimal, although he was exposed to a vibrant oral poetic tradition. He started to sculpt on his own and eventually made his way first to the Dalmatian coast and then to Vienna, where, after great financial difficulties, he was accepted as a student at the academy in Vienna. He exhibited together with other artists of the Viennese "secession" beginning in 1902. In 1907 he moved to Paris, where his exhibition drew praise from none other than Auguste Rodin.

Meštrović burst onto the Yugoslav national scene with his controversial exhibition at the Rome Exposition of 1911. He had been expected to show his work at the pavilion of the Habsburg Empire, but he refused to do so unless a separate pavilion was provided for South Slavic artists. When this was denied, he and his compatriots offered to exhibit their work at the Serbian pavilion.[59] The mere fact of a Viennese-trained, already well-respected artist turning his back on Central European culture to throw in his lot with the Serbian "barbarians" was sensational enough. But the work he exhibited in Rome, fragments from his so-called Kosovo or St. Vitus Day temple (the Battle of Kosovo was fought on St. Vitus Day), was even more sensational. Despite the fact that Meštrović had completed only a wooden model of the building, viewers were impressed by its monumental, classical feel, embellished by such typical secessionist touches as caryatids and sphinxes. In form, it combined Catholic and Orthodox elements (it was built on the pattern of a Roman Catholic cross, but the dome looked more like that of a Byzantine rather than a Catholic church; see Figure 1). Scattered around the hall were Meštrović's figures inspired by the heroes of South Slavic oral poetry: Marko Kraljević, Miloš Obilić, the mother of the

FIGURE 1. Ivan Meštrović, Kosovo temple, wooden scale model, 1912. Narodni muzej, Belgrade. Photo courtesy of The University of Notre Dame Archives.

Yugoviches, a guslar, and many others. Even today these sculptures retain their monumental presence and, in the case of the male figures, the pent-up strength that seems about to spring from sculpture directly into life. (See Figures 2 and 3.)

For many of Meštrović's contemporaries, for whom these figures also symbolized the entire spirit of the Yugoslav awakening, they seemed nothing short of miraculous. As one contemporary put it:

Meštrović's temple has deep national significance. In this sense it towers above all previously existing artistic monuments from ancient times until today. What the pyramids were for the Egyptians, pagodas for the Indians, the Parthenon for the Greeks, the Colosseum for the Romans, what the Gothic cathedrals were for the Middle Ages, the luxurious palaces for the Renaissance, what the National Gallery is for today's Englishmen and the Louvre is for the French, that is what Meštrović's temple is for the Southern Slavs. But it must be pointed out: not a sin-

FIGURE 2. Ivan Meštrović, *Miloš Obilić*, 1909. Narodni muzej, Belgrade. Photo courtesy of Northwestern University Libraries.

FIGURE 3. Ivan Meštrović, *Marko Kraljević*, plaster study, 1909. Narodni muzej, Belgrade. Photo courtesy of Northwestern University Libraries.

gle one of the monuments mentioned above is in as close touch with the national soul as the Temple is with our soul, the Yugoslav soul.[60]

Meštrović himself made no secret of his Yugoslav views: "I tried to give a single synthesis of the popular folk ideals and their development, to express in stone and architecture how deeply rooted in all of us are the memories of the greatest moments and most significant events of our history. . . . The temple cannot be dedicated to any one confession or separate sect, rather to all of them together, to all who believe in the ideals expressed in our folk songs."[61]

The evolutionary connection between the vision of Yugoslav culture proposed by Meštrović and that which had been propagated by the romantics of the 1840s, based as it was on a shared heroic vision and a reliance on traditionally Serbian themes, was transparent at this time. For a compelling, albeit post facto, account of the continued relevance of the romantic Yugoslav tradition in this period, we can turn to descriptions taken from Miroslav Krleža's monumental novel *Zastave* (Banners). As opposed to the Serbian hero of Selenić's *Timor mortis*, Krleža's main character, Kamilo Emerički, Junior, is at first intensely fascinated by the prospect of Yugoslav unity. Eventually, however, Emerički comes to realize the speciousness of much of what passes for Yugoslavism (without necessarily rejecting all versions of the idea, however). In this respect, he is clearly an autobiographical stand-in for the writer himself, whose life-long support for Yugoslavism was unquestioned, but whose uncompromising dissent from the forms that life in Yugoslavia actually took was equally clear. Emerički's skepticism reaches its climax when he listens to a lecture given by one Mitar Mitrović to the Yugoslav student club in Vienna, just before the war: "And what is our national task? To create cultural monuments for Ourselves, attesting to the True Purpose of Our Appearance on this Balkan earth. And what are these great and eternal values for which it is worthwhile to place one's head on the altar of the fatherland if not oral folk poetry, Njegoš, and Meštrović?"[62] Mitrović's speech reflects what had, by the immediate prewar period, become an article of faith among a reasonably broad group of young intellectuals, both Serb and Croat. The bases for a Yugoslav culture were held to exist, and these bases were to be found in folk culture and in its high-cultural incorporations by romantic and modernist artists.

At the same time that Croatian intellectuals were combining traditional themes with the forms and genres of high modernism to synthesize an up-to-date Yugoslav culture, other figures, both Serbian and Croatian, began to propose a rather different approach. Relying on irony and humor, which were generally in extremely short supply among the Croatian Yugoslavists, some of these writers attempted to employ traditional themes and images while simultaneously subverting their traditional message. Perhaps the most successful work of this type is Radoje Domanović's 1901 story "Marko Kraljević po drugi put medju Srbima" (The Return of Marko Kraljević). In this story Marko tells God that the Serbs have been calling for him to return and help them avenge the defeat at Kosovo for some five hundred years and that he would like to do so. Although God knows that this will lead to no good, he grants Marko's wish. What ensues is a major case of culture shock, as Marko, the modern Serbs, and Domanović's readers eventually come to realize that the ethos of heroism represented in folk song and preserved at least in theory in modern Serbian culture (and certainly in the work of modern figures like Meštrović) is not an appropriate foundation for a twentieth-century Yugoslav culture and society.

In place of the traditional and heroic, groups of writers attempted to discover new bases for synthesis, turning their attention to modernist trends in European culture. They reasoned that a new Yugoslav synthesis would be best achieved not by dwelling on the past, but rather by placing their hopes in a future linked indissolubly with the latest developments in world culture. Almanacs, journals, and miscellanies that supported this version of Yugoslavism became relatively common in the immediate prewar period. A glance at one such work, *Almanah srpskih i hrvatskih pjesnika i pripovijedača* (The Almanac of Serbian and Croatian Poets and Prosaists) published in 1910, gives a good feeling for the genre. The almanac, which was published simultaneously in Belgrade and Zagreb, employs both Cyrillic and Latin alphabets. Contributors include many of the best-known and most talented Serbian and Croatian writers of the day, among them Jovan Dučić (who would later in life become a Serbian nationalist), Milan Rakić, Aleksa Šantić, Vladimir Nazor, and Ksaver Šandor-Djalski. It opens with a one-page introduction by its editor, Milan Ćurčin, which explains that all the contributors are "active supporters of the idea of national unity, in which they see the salvation and future of our tribe."[63] Rather than emphasizing a shared cultural past, however, the authors exhibit their solidarity in a (tacit) mutual agreement to orient their work toward the most up-to-date European cultural trends. Indeed, in its layout and overall appearance, the almanac echoes contemporary modernist journals of France, Germany, and Russia, and many of the texts display clear influences of European decadence and modernism as well.

As was typically the case, the cultural situation in Slovenia vis-à-vis the Yugoslav synthesis was somewhat more complicated. Indeed, the Slovenes were somewhat late to embrace the idea of Yugoslav unity, but by the immediate prewar period

all parties, including the Social Democrats, who were already on record (at Tivoli) as standing for a "Yugoslav" culture, promoted a program for the cultural and linguistic union of Southern Slavs. The youth organizations, *Preporod, Omladina,* and the National Catholic Youth sponsored lectures in other Yugoslav tongues; they traveled to the Balkans; they invited Serb, Croat, and Bulgar students to Slovenia and provided complementary housing for them. Yugoslavs exchanged professors; and Slovene students enrolled at Zagreb University (which Illyrists proposed as a center for Slovene-Croat cultural activity). Slovenes studied the Croat and Serb languages and cultures. Some sent volunteers, military and medical, to the Balkan wars to help liberate their Yugoslav brethren from Ottoman oppression.[64]

What is more, some Slovenian writers began not merely to agitate for Yugoslav union, but to incorporate an overt Yugoslav message into their literary work. As was the case with their Croatian and Serbian counterparts, the basis for a new Yugoslavism was synthetic. One novel that captured this feeling was Fran Maselj Podlimbarski's *Gospodin Franjo* (Mr. Franjo, 1913). The book was published by Slovenska matica, the leading Slovenian cultural society, and it reflects the Yugoslav orientation of that organization as well as the author's point of view. Podlimbarski's main character is an earnest and idealistic Slovenian engineer, France Vilar, who takes a job in Bosnia in the period immediately after the Austro-Hungarian occupation. Living in and around the city of Tuzla, Vilar quickly becomes aware that the Austrian claim to be bringing Bosnia into the modern world (which was the purported justification for their occupation) is nothing more than a sham. Practically without exception the Austrian administrators and military personnel are shown to be rapacious, boorish, and lacking in any morality or culture of their own. Vilar comes to hate almost all of them and spends his time instead with the local population (mostly the Orthodox, including a nationalist monk named Jovica Milošević). It is the simple Bosnian folk who rechristen him with the local honorific "gospodin" and the Serbo-Croatian "Franjo." He listens in fascination to the singers of folk epics and their gusles, and watches the folk dances. They provide for him a way to rediscover his own national identity (and, by extension, that of any Slovenian), which, he recognizes, has been almost lost under layers of Germanized accretions. Watching a Bosnian kolo "Vilar looked thoughtfully at the long line [of dancers] and he almost envied these people their simple entertainment. He recalled similar entertainments in Slovenia. How forced and fake they were, because there was nothing popular or national in them. What had been national had long ago been covered over by foreigners."[65]

Vilar's colleagues believe he has simply "gone native," and, if their view were correct, it would be easy for the reader to conclude that Podlimbarski is advocating a new version of Yugoslav (i.e., Serbianizing) romanticism. Nothing could be farther from the truth, however. Vilar never rejects the need to "civilize" the natives. What he wants is for them to preserve the valuable aspects of their culture while taking the best that civilization has to offer. And, in fact, the story of his life provides a perfect synecdoche for this new version of Yugoslavism. At the end of the novel the Austrian-educated, western-trained Slovenian Vilar leaves Austrian territory for Serbia and marries Danica, the spontaneous, "uncivilized" sister of the monk Milošević. Their symbolic union points the way to a future of national cooperation, which is further cemented by Vilar's new job: constructing a railroad through newly captured Macedonia.

This same period also saw the appearance of Slovenian journals with a synthetic Yugoslav perspective. Typical was *Glas juga* (Voice of the South), edited by V. M. Zalar, who succeeded in publishing two issues in Ljubljana before the outbreak of World War I shelved it and all other overtly Yugoslav proselytizing for a number of years.[66] The journal's manifesto, attributed to one A. Jenko, provides an excellent summary of the main points found in most prewar Yugoslavizing propaganda. One nation is being built, it is claimed, and the journal is designed to help: "We will present in this regard all the material necessary for the creation of a strong national culture, built on new foundations of national individuality, independence, and optimism. . . . The creation of a Yugoslav nation is for us the logical conclusion to a long historical process, which leads unavoidably to the unification of groups related by blood, and which share common interests, in particular a common struggle for existence and for the preservation of their individuality."[67] Articles were printed in Slovenian as well as Ser-

bian and Croatian, both Cyrillic and Latin alphabets were used, although
the journal came out strongly in favor of Skerlić's proposal for a single literary language in which Cyrillic would be abandoned and the Ekavian
dialect used exclusively. The journal is uncommitted regarding the future
of Slovenian, but a review of the discussion of the question of linguistic
unification in *Veda* (which, it will be recalled, had surveyed its readers
in 1913 on the topic of whether Slovenian should be abandoned) leaves little doubt that its eventual disappearance is foreseen, in the long run at least.

Cultural Yugoslavism During World War I

The years 1914–18 should have been most unpropitious for Yugoslav-
oriented culture for any number of reasons.[68] Most obviously, by a deliber-
ate policy on the part of the Austro-Hungarian military, Croat and Slovene
battalions were frequently used to fight against their "brother" Serbs. Under wartime conditions severe censorship became the order of the day, particularly in the Slovene provinces, where many prewar advocates of Yugoslavism were arrested and their publishing or performing venues
closed.[69] Those organs that were allowed to continue publishing in the
Habsburg South Slavic lands were either completely apolitical (and heavily
censored when they forgot to be) or overtly in support of the empire's war
aims.[70] Serbia was occupied by Austrian, German, and Bulgarian forces,
and the active pro-Yugoslav cultural life that had characterized Belgrade in
the prewar years evaporated.

Nevertheless, Yugoslav cultural agitation continued, and, especially
by 1917, became stronger than ever. In the early war years, the focus of Yugoslav cultural propaganda shifted from the South Slavic lands themselves
to the émigré communities. Of particular importance in this regard were
the activities of the Yugoslav Committee headquartered in London. This
group, whose members were Yugoslav-inclined South Slavs from the Habsburg lands, dedicated itself to influencing public opinion and convincing
policy makers in England of the desirability of a postwar Yugoslav state.
One way they did so was through the sponsorship of a major exhibition of
Meštrović's sculpture at London's Victoria and Albert Museum.[71] The introduction to the monograph dedicated to the exhibition illustrates just
how highly Meštrović was regarded as a messenger of Yugoslav culture by
many South Slavic and European intellectuals:

Both the exhibition of the sculpture and the publication of this book form part of an attempted scheme to supplement the military reputation of the Serbocroats by demonstrating the civilising capacities of the race. The heroes of Meštrović's imagination in the halls of the Victoria and Albert Museum in 1915 probably amazed the British public not much less than the deeds of the Serbian soldiers amazed the world at that period of the war. And these two, the Serbian soldier and the Dalmatian sculptor, best represent to-day the positive qualities of the Southern Slavs.[72]

The most influential British supporter of the Yugoslav committee was the well-known scholar R. W. Seton-Watson. It was Seton-Watson who gave an international imprimatur to Meštrović as the national artist of Yugoslavia, and his essay in the monograph on Meštrović (an article entitled "Meštrović and the Jugoslav Idea") illustrates what an important influence cultural expression had on shaping political views. Seton-Watson concluded his contribution with the following stirring lines: "Meštrović the artist is an elemental force, and as such he typifies, and has given voice to, the yearnings and aspirations of a nation long despised but indomitable. His work is immortal, and with him shall triumph the Jugoslav Idea."[73]

Yugoslav-oriented newspapers, almanacs, and other publishing ventures sprouted all over the European diaspora.[74] Although it is hard to know exactly who published and who consumed Yugoslav propaganda during the war, one way to measure the extent of Yugoslav feeling in the exiled Serbian community is by tracking publications in Cyrillic of Mažuranić's *Death of Smail-Aga Čengić*. This work, of course, had been identified with Yugoslavism from the very beginning, but it had always been more popular among Croats. Nevertheless, in 1916, two organizations of Serbian students put out hand-copied and lithographed versions of the work. Excerpts were published in an anthology that was put together in Nice in 1917, the Serbian Ministry of Education and Religious Affairs on Corfu published another edition in early 1918, as did an émigré organization in Geneva.[75]

By 1917, even in the South Slav lands under Habsburg control, demonstrations of Yugoslav cultural identity became more and more frequent and increasingly difficult to suppress. Among the major cultural events of that year in Zagreb, for example, were festivities to celebrate the fiftieth anniversary of the Yugoslav Academy of Arts and Sciences in July and Ivo Vojnović's sixtieth birthday. This latter event was marked on October 9 with a special performance in the Croatian National Theater of his "Ekvinocij" (The Equinox). The day was an unofficial national holiday, and tributes to Vojnović emphasizing his Yugoslav nature appeared in all the newspapers. "Vojnović's success is our national success," exclaimed *Savremenik* (The Contemporary) the organ of the Croatian Writers' Association, "even more because he is equally Croat and Serb. There is no Croat who is more Serbian than Vojnović and no Serb who is more Croatian. He is the expression of the entire people, the artistic incarnation of the folk epic combined with antique culture (like Mažuranić), a European and a guslar, an orator and—recently—the comrade of all who, endure, struggle and keep quiet."[76]

March 19, 1918, was the one hundredth anniversary of the birth of Petar Preradović. According to the March 20 edition of Ljubljana's *Tedenske slike* (The Week in Pictures) massive celebrations had been prepared in Zagreb for the event, but these had been forbidden by the authorities. In particular, there was supposed to have been a performance of Preradović's play "Kraljević Marko," but it was banned and the theater remained dark. The March 27 issue, however, reported that, despite the ban, masses of people celebrated in their own way. "Stores in Zagreb were closed and many roofs displayed Yugoslav banners. People flocked to the poet's grave to leave flowers. They placed Serbian, Croatian, and Slovenian ribbons at the feet of his monument (these were quickly removed by the police), and sang Yugoslav patriotic songs."[77]

The entire April issue of *Savremenik* was devoted to Preradović, as was the March 16 issue of the biweekly journal *Književni jug* (The Literary South). The latter opened with a poem by the Bosnian Serb poet Aleksa Šantić (published, significantly, in Latin letters) called "Prolog," and dedicated to "Pesniku Narodnog Jedinstva" (the Poet of National Unity, i.e., Preradović).

> Na vrelu bratstva oprasmo očiju vid,
> I više mi nismo slepi . . .
> Oprasmo mrlje, i krv, i greh, i stid,
> I sad smo k'o bogovi lepi!
>
> Gle duše, što ih vekovni točio crv,
> U jedan splele se venac—:
> Jedna je loza i jedna kraljevska krv
> Srb, Hrvat i Slovenac.[78]
>
> We have fixed our eyes on the heat of brotherhood,
> And we are no longer blind . . .

> We have seen blots, and blood, and sin, and shame
> And now we are beautiful as gods!
>
> Look, the souls that a worm has been gnawing forever
> Have twined into a single crown—:
> We are of one family, and one royal blood
> Serb, Croat and Slovene.

According to Niko Bartulović, one of the journal's editors, "Petar Preradović was in his lyrics a national poet par excellence. . . . In Preradović's time the loftiest political activity revolved around the motives of his poetry, around Slavdom and Yugoslavdom, the questions of Dalmatia and national unification. The idea of Yugoslavdom, not merely cultural, but also political is developed so powerfully that it speaks to us even today, after so many decades" (240).

By late 1917 it had become difficult to find a printed organ that was not in favor of Yugoslav unity. Even semiofficial papers such as *Tedenske slike* propounded Yugoslav views. In an article in the monthly cultural journal *Slovan*, Anton Loboda agitated for full national (i.e., Yugoslav) integration in the following words: "That is our ultimate aim; we are well aware that it will not be achieved overnight, that our generation will not live to see it, but rather the next, or the third or fourth. We will achieve it through a longer or shorter transitional stage, whose first phase we see as the most intensive possible cultural cooperation of Slovenes, Serbs, and Croats."[79] Many organs appear simply to have assumed that Yugoslav unity had been achieved by the conclusion of the war. Thus, an article in the leading Slovene newspaper, *Slovenski narod*, described a conference of Slavic youth held in Zagreb in August 1918 as bringing together participants representing the "young Polish, Czecho-slovak, and Yugoslav intelligentsia."[80] That is, it did not occur to the paper to say, Serb, Croat, and Slovene intelligentsia, although it is certain that there were participants from all three groups present.

Thus, by the time the Great War ended, the South Slav elites had achieved a fair degree of consensus as to how a Yugoslav culture could be created. Rather than following a unitarist model based primarily on Serbian cultural practices, they proposed a multicultural model that would draw on the traditions of all three of the South Slavic tribes that were fated to be joined in the Kingdom of the Serbs, Croats, and Slovenes.

Creating a Synthetic Yugoslav Culture

The disintegration of the Austro-Hungarian Empire at the end of World War I allowed for the creation of a united South Slavic state, a dream that had fed the activities of many leading Serbian, Croatian, and Slovenian cultural and political figures throughout the nineteenth century. The new Yugoslav state (it was officially called the Kingdom of the Serbs, Croats, and Slovenes until its name was changed to Yugoslavia in 1929) was, however, dogged with serious problems almost from its very beginnings, as the utopian prewar ideals of brotherhood and integrationism ran into the realities of significant cultural, political, and economic differences. Although various attempts at compromise were effected during its twenty-three-year lifespan, the first Yugoslav state was unable to achieve real stability, and it collapsed in a matter of days under the Nazi onslaught of 1941. In this respect, of course, it did not differ substantially from most of the other interwar European polities. What is more, despite the short life and ultimate failure of this first Yugoslav state, a number of conflicting and in some cases constructive political and cultural views regarding potential strategies for creating a Yugoslav nation were articulated during its existence. Finally, the legacy of the first Yugoslavia left indelible marks on the cultural and political landscape of the South Slavic lands. Indeed, it would not be an exaggeration to say that the foundations for all of Serbian, Croatian, and Slovenian history in the twentieth century were laid during the cultural and political debates of the 1920s.

The central issue facing the new state was how to integrate a wildly diverse group of peoples of varying religious, linguistic, ethnic, political, and economic backgrounds. As we have seen in the previous chapter, some work in this direction had already been accomplished in the prewar period, but much remained to be done. As one prescient observer put it a few months after the new state was created: "The problem of our revolution is not one of destruction, but of building. . . . We need to build our new country, to build a new citizen and person. The basic problem of our revolution is not state-building, social or economic development. It is—for on this rests the possibility of a satisfactory answer to the aforementioned questions—to a much greater extent national and cultural."[1]

There were, naturally, quite a number of nation-building possibilities open to the fledgling state, ranging from centralization to some form of federalism. In the minds of most contemporaries, however, some form of centralism appeared inevitable. After all, Italy and Germany, the most recent models available in Europe, were centralized states, as were the always influential England and France. And although some of the former citizens of the Habsburg Empire were in favor of a federalist model, the experience of dual power centers during the empire's final years would not have disposed a dispassionate observer to a sanguine view of the merits of a federal system. Centralization, it is true, has generally taken the blame for the failure of interwar Yugoslavia, but it must be noted that the type of political centralization chosen, one in which Serbian hegemony was imposed on the state's other inhabitants, was not the only available option. What I will attempt to illustrate in this chapter is that there were other, more equitable forms of centralization potentially available in interwar Yugoslavia, forms that had or could have had the support of substantial numbers of at least the better-educated Yugoslavs. I will concentrate on the ways in which responsible Serbs, Croats, and Slovenes attempted to create a synthetic culture based on elements taken from all three national cultures in order to foster a viable Yugoslav national idea. I will argue that although political and social disagreements threatened the stability of the first Yugoslav state, its real failure was its inability to create a consensus regarding the twin concepts of the Yugoslav nation and its culture.

Creating a Yugoslav Nation: 1918–1939

No understanding of the problems faced by the first Yugoslavia or the solutions proposed to them can proceed without a recognition of the crucial ethnocultural belief that underpinned the country: that the Serbs, Croats, and Slovenes formed a single nation. At the present time, when each of these groups is aggressively asserting its independent national identity, it is hard to remember that for the vast majority of educated South Slavs just before and after World War I, the Serbian, Croatian, and Slovenian appellations were seen as "tribal." Although few would have questioned the existence of religious, cultural, and linguistic differences separating the three, they were seen as surface phenomena. At the same time, the Yugoslav-oriented elites recognized that the national solidarity they felt was in short supply among the less well educated. Their goal, then, became the creation and fostering of a coherent Yugoslav national identity in the mass of the inhabitants of the new state. For their inspiration, Yugoslav intellectuals turned to models borrowed not from the experience of the empires of which they had been a historical part (Ottoman or Habsburg), but rather from such newly unified and centralized nation-states as Italy and Germany. Although the analogies they drew may seem far-fetched in the wake of Yugoslavia's subsequent failure and the apparent nation-building successes of Germany and Italy, they did not seem unreasonable at the time. As one proponent of Yugoslav integration put it, "Cultured Tuscans hated the Piedmontese like their worst enemies! Sicilians and Neapolitans were born foes. How many conflicts, how much hatred and mutual distrust there was. North and South were two worlds, two different understandings of honor and morality, with completely different ways of life, traditions, temperaments, and daily habits."[2] His point was that if the Italians had nevertheless managed to overcome their regional differences to create a strong national state with a unified national culture (at least a unified high culture, which was of central concern to the nation-building elites), so could the Yugoslavs.

As we noted in the previous chapter, the national unity of the South Slavs had come to be widely accepted among the educated youth in the immediate prewar period. During the war, this position animated the propaganda of the London-based Yugoslav Committee. They published a series of pamphlets meant to sway public opinion on the subject, and the very first page of their programmatic "Southern Slav Programme" states: "The Southern Slavs or Jugoslavs [*jug* in Slav means *the south*] who include Serbs, Croats, and Slovenes, are one and the same people, known under three different names."[3]

Contemporary racial theory had played a major role in developing ideas about which groups could and should participate in the Yugoslav nation-building project. Such theories, which often sound uncomfortably close to the exclusionary doctrines that undergirded the Nazi racial project, have today been discredited. But the creators of these studies believed in their validity, and rather than castigate them for scientific naiveté (which, in any event, was no greater than that exhibited by their colleagues in Europe and the United States) we should rather recognize their attempts at nation building. Indeed, in examining their theoretical work in the context of what is now generally believed about the need to create or invent any national tradition, we can see that the ethnographers and anthropologists who tried to prove that the Serbs, Croats, and Slovenes were a single people were merely playing their role in the general project of nation building.

While the war was still raging and its outcome in doubt, the ethnographer Jovan Cvijić, perhaps the best-respected Serbian scholar of his day, produced a book in which he argued that most Serbs and Croats belonged to a "Dinaric" type.[4] He believed that a Yugoslav nation could and would be created as an amalgamation of this with other closely related South Slavic racial types (the "Central" [primarily Macedonians] and the "Pannonian" [Slovenians as well as most inhabitants of Slavonia, Srem, and Banat]). Although he saw the Bulgarians (the "East Balkan type") as closely related to other Yugoslavs, he recognized that recent historical experience militated against their becoming part of the Yugoslav amalgam, at least in the short-term.

Theories such as Cvijić's clearly played a role in the formation of the political ideology of Yugoslavia's first monarch. Thus, in his speech agreeing to the unification of the fledgling state of the Slovenes, Croats, and Serbs with the Kingdom of Serbia, the then Prince-Regent Aleksandar proclaimed: "In accepting this communication I am convinced that by this act I am fulfilling my Royal duty and that I am thereby only finally realising what the best sons of our *race—of all creeds and of all three names* from both sides of the Danube, the Sava and the Drina—began to prepare already under the reign of my grand-father."[5]

Throughout the interwar period, in most official contexts the existence of the three separate nations was recognized only within the formulation "the three-named people."[6] In effect, the relationship of the Serbs, Croats, and Slovenes was seen as Trinitarian, analogous to Christian views of the relationship of God the Father, God the Son, and the Holy Spirit, who were, according to both Eastern Orthodox and Catholic dogma, simultaneously three and one. This formulation must have seemed a stroke of genius to those who coined it, for whatever the doctrinal differences that separated Orthodox and Catholic Christians, the concept of the Trinity was familiar to all. Even the most backward peasant could be expected to understand his relationship to his compatriots under this formulation (which left comfortingly ambiguous the question of which group should play which specific role in the Trinity). What is most important, however, is that the formulation emphasized the basic theoretical equality of the three parts. Whatever might have been the case in practice, therefore, the unitary synthesis as a cultural principle did not imply the Serbianization of Yugoslavia. At the same time, the sleight of hand that found unity in difference allowed worrisome questions about exactly how a unified Yugoslav nation should be constructed to be pushed to the side.

Although it might seem that reconciling the historical and cultural differences separating three peoples should have been difficult enough, the situation in Yugoslavia was complicated by the fact that at least 20 percent of the country's total population consisted of people who were not Serb, Croat, or Slovene.[7] But, as the country's official name—the Kingdom of the Serbs, Croats, and Slovenes—indicated, only these three groups were viewed as constitutive populations of the new nation. Although the 1921 constitution did not formally discriminate against the minorities who made up almost two million of the country's twelve million inhabitants, they were, at least as far as the nation-building program goes, persona non grata.[8] Furthermore, although universal manhood suffrage was introduced in 1920, women never received the right to vote and were in an officially subordinate position throughout the country. In this respect Yugoslavia did not differ from most of its neighbors, but the exclusion of women from the political process meant that they were not seen as full participants in the nation-building process. Thus, as is the case with most other so-called nation states, the Yugoslav nation did not include the entire population by any means.

Even the category of adult male South Slavs was more diverse than the census figures imply. This is because Macedonians and Moslem speakers of Serbo-Croatian were lumped into the Serbian or Croatian population, although neither group could be fit comfortably into those categories.[9] Macedonians, despite the fact that their language is quite distinct from Serbo-Croatian, were considered South Serbians, a classification that in effect forced them to assimilate with the Serbian population if they wanted to become part of the nation-building process. Macedonian dissatisfaction with this state of affairs helped strengthen clandestine parties favoring autonomous status for the region, in particular the terrorist group IMRO (Internal Macedonian Revolutionary Organization), whose public declaration stated that they would struggle "against both the Serbian and Greek governments and against the Bulgarian government, which are or may become instruments of their own or foreign imperialist designs on Macedonia."[10]

Bosnian and Herzegovinian Moslems were another and even more complicated case. Descendants of Serbs and Croats who converted to Islam during the long period of Turkish rule, they were ethnically identical to their neighbors. As we have seen in the previous chapter in the discussion of *The Mountain Wreath*, in the nineteenth century the existence of Islamicized Slavs was seen as a barrier to South Slavic unity. In the interwar period, with the disappearance of the Ottoman threat, the Serbo-Croatian speaking Moslems seemed far less dangerous. Instead, both Serbs and Croats attempted to claim their Moslem brothers for their own and were eager to include them in the nation-building project, provided they were willing to be assimilated into the broader nation, conceived in modern European terms.[11] And many Moslems, particularly among the younger educated elite, were willing to assimilate, providing they did not have to give up their religion and with the understanding that some of their cultural practices would become part of the grand Yugoslav cultural synthesis.[12]

Thus, in sum, the ethnocultural ideal of the Kingdom of the Serbs, Croats, and Slovenes was male and South Slavic. And throughout the existence of the first Yugoslavia, the national goal was the creation of a fully fledged Yugoslav people and a unified Yugoslav culture on the basis of a national unity theorized as essentially already present. The question, how-ever, was how fast to move in reconciling "tribal" differences and how to go about doing so. In the political arena, as we will see below, the domi-nant Serbian political parties generally took positions quite similar to what we have called the romantic national ideology characteristic of the mid–nineteenth century. That is, they insisted that the other South Slavs could and should essentially be folded into the existing Serbian state and its institutions.

In the cultural sphere, however, cooperation and compromise were more the order of the day. In part this was because the Serbian political elite generally stayed out of the country's culture wars. In their view, a supranational Yugoslav culture was unnecessary; the creation and nurtur-ing of strong state institutions were seen as adequate to the nation-building task. This left culture to the country's intellectuals, and here the three "tribes" were on a far more equal footing. The Serbs, after all, had been the military victors in World War I, and it was entirely logical, although ulti-mately destructive, for them to impose their political will on their "broth-ers" from the defeated Habsburg Empire.[13] In the areas of high culture and cultural theorizing, however, the Serbs were no more advanced than the Croats or the Slovenes. As a result, attempts at the cultural Serbianization of Slovene and Croat culture were far less frequent than the political situ-ation might have led one to expect. Instead, cultural theorizing was domi-nated by figures who strove to create a multicultural Yugoslav nation, one whose culture would synthesize the best elements of each of the separate South Slavic "tribes."

The New State

World War I ended with the Kingdom of Serbia in possession of im-mense political capital within the South Slavic lands. After years of heroic suffering, its armies had defeated and helped to destroy the once mighty Austro-Hungarian Empire, and they had liberated practically all the terri-tories on which the South Slavs lived. The promulgation of the Kingdom of the Serbs, Croats, and Slovenes, on December 1, 1918, was greeted by waves of celebrations all over the territory of Yugoslavia, as the kingdom came to be popularly known. For example, on December 3, 1918, banner headlines in *Slovenski narod* (The Slovenian Nation), the most important Slovenian newspaper, announced "Proclamation of Union with Serbia." Commentary on the subject was unanimously favorable: "They [the Serbs] want full union with us. All will be absorbed in a new creation. The first step of the heir to the throne Aleksandar, his first speech, is the best guarantee for the peaceful evolution of our new state." Articles in the same paper filed from Zagreb described large crowds in the streets of the Croatian capital. They were singing national hymns and marching in favor of union. An important demonstration took place in the National Theater as well. "The actors and audience sang national songs together."

Yugoslav nationalist euphoria did not last long, however, because the various constituent groups that made up the new state held contradictory ideas regarding the political form the new kingdom should take. Politicians from the former Kingdom of Serbia as well as the de facto monarch, Prince-Regent Aleksandar, believed that the Serbs, by virtue of their greater numbers and their military victory, should control the new state, which would be a centralized constitutional monarchy. On the other hand, the majority of Croats and Slovenes, who despite whatever hatred they may have felt for their former rulers still wished to retain much of their traditional political culture, favored some greater or lesser degree of federation. They worried, quite reasonably as it turned out, that in joining with Serbia they might merely be exchanging one form of political subordination for another.

The conflict between a centralist, Serb-dominated view of Yugoslavia and some form of federalism had been brewing behind the scenes throughout World War I. In 1914 the Serbians were able to defend themselves effectively against the Austro-Hungarian attacks that marked the beginning of the Great War. In 1915, however, the Serbian army was effectively crushed by the combination of renewed attacks from the north (by Austrian and German forces) and the southeast (by Bulgarian troops) together with a raging typhus epidemic. What remained of the army, together with the country's political leadership, escaped over the mountains to Albania and then on to the safe haven of Corfu. From Corfu, Serbian political leaders—including primarily the prince-regent and Nikola Pašić, leader of the powerful Radical party—attempted to convince the Entente to support a postwar solution that would leave Serbia firmly in control of the northern Balkans. "'Liberation' and 'unification' of the Serbs, Croats, and Slovenes meant essentially Serb unification, which, as a secondary aim ('great solution'), did not exclude a wider program of 'incorporating the Croats and Slovenes within a Great Serbia.'"[14] Thus, the primary Serbian objective was unquestionably the unification of all Serbs into a single state, and Pašić was prepared to bargain away large numbers of non-Serb South Slavs in exchange for the realization of this goal.[15] In this respect, Pašić and his followers were worthy heirs to Ilija Garašanin, whose policy "outline" of 1844 laid the foundations of the great-Serbian policy of unification.

Opposition to great-Serbian views came, not from Croatian or Slovenian nationalists—who were few in number and without influence at this point—but from Yugoslav-oriented politicians and intellectuals from the Habsburg territories. Although many men of this stripe were arrested and interned at the beginning of the war, many others escaped, and they formed the so-called Yugoslav Committee (Jugoslavenski odbor), which was headquartered in London. The Yugoslav Committee lobbied hard for a postwar Yugoslavia that would include all South Slavs (except the Bulgarians) as well as all the territories in which they lived. In a series of pamphlets published in 1915–16 as well as through the sponsorship of cultural exhibitions (that of Meštrović described in the previous chapter being the most substantial), the Yugoslav Committee tried to make its case to the British influential public.[16]

Eventually, the exigencies of the war forced at least a nominal agreement and compromise between the Serbian government and the Yugoslav Committee, which was hammered out on Corfu in July 1917. The so-called Corfu Declaration proclaimed that the Serbs, Croats, and Slovenes wished to live in a united state that would be "a constitutional, democratic and parliamentary monarchy headed by the Karadjordjević dynasty."[17] Despite this agreement, however, the Yugoslav state that was ultimately created after the war was rather close if not identical to that desired by great-Serbian idealists. Its creation was a complicated process that stretched from the formation of the first postwar Yugoslav cabinet in December 1918 to the adoption by a narrow margin of the so-called Vidovdan Constitution on June 28, 1921.

The political infighting during this period has been copiously detailed by Ivo Banac in his indispensable book *The National Question in Yugoslavia.* What happened, in a nutshell, was that no political party was able to attract significant support from all regions of the country; instead, parties appealed almost exclusively to particular "tribal" sentiments.[18] In this situation, Serbian politicians took advantage of the relative weakness and disunity of their Croatian and Slovenian counterparts to promulgate a centralist Yugoslav state. A tragic factor, and one not generally recognized, is the generational and demographic background to this solution. Nikola Pašić (born 1845), the leading architect of Serbian policy before, during, and after the war, came of age during the period when Yugoslav cooperation was at a low ebb. Thus, he and his contemporaries gravitated quite naturally to a great-Serbian policy. The twenty-year period preceding World War I had, however, seen a gigantic rise in Yugoslav feeling among younger Serbs, many of whom would and should have become leaders by the 1920s. But precisely this generation was decimated during the war (indeed, by some estimates, 90 percent of young college-educated Serbian males were killed). As a result, Serbian politics remained the province of the older generation. Be that as it may, as Banac puts it in his conclusion: "The Vidovdan Constitution sanctioned the untenable centralist solution of Yugoslavia's national question. Reached without the participation—and against the will—of most of the non-Serb parties, it bore the seeds of further rancor."[19]

Although Banac's view is generally considered authoritative on this point, it is not entirely unproblematic. The issue is not merely centralization, but centralization with a strong Serbian accent. Certainly, during the war and in its immediate aftermath the majority of Croatian and Slovenian politicians and cultural leaders believed in the desirability of a Yugoslav state. Indeed, in the negotiations on integration that took place during the war, Croatian and Slovenian leaders insisted on using the name Yugoslavia as a symbol of the future country's unity, whereas it was the Serbs who balked, fearing the symbolic loss of their national identity in the new state. What is more, the recent models of state building to which the Yugoslavs looked provided evidence that centralization did not have to lead to the monopolization of political power by a single group or region. After all, although the Piedmontese had provided much of the political leadership for Italian unification, the centralized Italian state was by no means Piedmont writ large. Had a version of centralism less favorable to Serbian interests been worked out in the immediate postwar period, "tribal nationalism," particularly in Croatia, would have had much less hold. Such a model of *cultural* unitarism was, in fact, the prevailing one in the first Yugoslavia. Thus, it is not exactly correct to say that centralization itself was the key problem. Rather, the way in which political centralization was carried out led to the political gridlock that plagued Yugoslavia in the interwar period.

Be that as it may, the period from 1921 to 1929 saw a gradual worsening of the political situation. Although there was a parliament and elections were held regularly, effective power was in the hands of Serbian politicians who pursued centralizing policies that increasingly alienated the other "tribes." As a result, in this period the most influential Croatian political parties, Stjepan Radić's Croatian Peasant Party and the Frankists, came out in favor of Croatian autonomy at a minimum and complete independence at maximum. An article in the liberal Zagreb journal *Nova Evropa* (The New Europe), a publication that found Serbian hegemony and tribal separatism equally distasteful, compared the political situation to a seesaw. Serbian hegemonic tendencies led to Croatian counterreaction, and both together eliminated the possibility of effective compromise.[20]

In Slovenia, the political climate was tempered by the fact that independence was clearly an unviable alternative, considering the fact that Italy was occupying almost one-third of the Slovene lands and overtly hankering for more. Slovene politicians, therefore, tended to be more cooperationist than their Croatian counterparts. What is more, their separate language and greater distance from Belgrade meant that they were less affected on a day-to-day basis by Serbianizing political trends. Still, throughout the existence of interwar Yugoslavia there were Slovenian political leaders from a wide spectrum of parties who demanded a federalization of the country as a means to greater local autonomy.[21] They were, however, opposed by the most powerful political grouping in Slovenia: the Liberals, who took as an article of faith that the Serbs, Croats, and Slovenes were "ethnically a single people . . . no unit of which could live a free and separate life." Therefore, what was needed was a unitary state in which "the separate parts of the nation could develop their own culture and preserve their own traditions, linking them with the traditions of the nation as a whole."[22]

The political situation in the country reached a point of true crisis in the wake of the June 1928 murder of Stjepan Radić, shot on the floor of the national assembly by a Montenegrin delegate of the Radical party. In the six months that followed, King Aleksandar attempted to broker an agreement as to the future of Yugoslavia, proposing first the political separation of Croatia and Slovenia from Serbia and later some form of federalism. When the latter was rejected by the leading Serbian political parties, the king dissolved parliament and declared a royal dictatorship. The first days of the dictatorship were unquestionably a success. Croats and Slovenes hoped that the king would curb Serbian power, and he certainly did make a number of symbolic gestures toward the creation of a non-Serbian centralization. Chief among these were changing the official name of the country to Yugoslavia, the requirement that Serbian military regiments display Yugoslav and not "tribal" flags, and the creation of a neutral day for military displays rather than the Serbian national holiday of Vidovdan.

Nevertheless, the king was ultimately unsuccessful in his attempts to recruit prominent Croatian political leaders to cooperate in the Yugoslavization of Yugoslavia. The result was that by the early 1930s, in the revised parliament power was again almost exclusively in the hands of Serbian parties. "Tribal" distrust was the order of the day, and the situation was not made any easier by the assassination of Aleksandar in 1934 at the hands of a Macedonian terrorist in the pay of the Ustashas, an émigré separatist Croatian organization. The Kafkaesque political situation by the late 1930s was captured nicely by Rebecca West in her 1937 account *Black Lamb and Grey Falcon*. In her chapters on Croatia, West describes her interaction with three men, the Serbian Jew Constantine (in fact the Serbian Jewish writer Stanislav Vinaver), the Dalmatian Croat Valletta, and the Zagreb Croat Gregorievich. Constantine believes in the necessity of the existing Yugoslavia, Gregorievich believes in an ideal Yugoslavia in which equality, not Serbian dominance, would be the order of the day, whereas Valletta is a federalist. In a conversation about corruption, Constantine admits that Valletta's complaints regarding dishonest Serbian officials are not without foundation but says that these individuals remain employed because of a shortage of competent people to take on administrative tasks. "'Then why do you not draw on us Croats for officials?' asked Valletta. . . . 'But how can we let you Croats be officials?' spluttered Constantine, 'You are not loyal!' 'And how,' asked Valletta, white to the lips, 'can we be expected to be loyal if you always treat us like this?' 'But I am telling you,' grieved Constantine, 'how can we treat you differently until you are loyal.'"[23]

Ultimately, political centralization as it was carried out in the first Yugoslavia was a failure. Serbs, who made up some 39 percent of the state's population were neither numerous nor strong enough to impose their political will on the rest of the country without provoking endless conflict, yet they were unable or unwilling to entertain any other form of political interaction. By the time King Aleksandar attempted to convince the country to accept non-Serbian centralization, it was too late. Most Croats and Slovenes were already so alienated that efforts to woo them into agreeing to a new version of unitarism came to naught. Indeed, suspicions that unitarism was always and only another name for Serbian domination in Yugoslavia were perhaps the most enduring political legacy of the interwar period, one that would ultimately cause insoluble problems for Tito and his associates after World War II.

The political failure of Serb-dominated centralism in Yugoslavia was unfortunate in another regard as well. Because the political arena tended to dominate public discussion, other areas of public life, particularly ones relating to the creation of a Yugoslav national culture were pushed to the background. This was tragic, because cultural unitarism proceeded in far more creative ways than did its political counterpart. The ideas proposed in the cultural arena could have provided a basis for a non-Serbian Yugoslav culture, one that would have been strong enough to resist both Serbian hegemony and the "tribal" nationalist hatreds that arose in reaction to it.

Cultural Models in the First Yugoslavia: 1918–1939

In the euphoria immediately following the war, the unification of the three "tribes" was often believed to have been accomplished merely by their political amalgamation. A poem published on the front page of the December 13, 1918, issue of the leading Slovenian newspaper *Slovenski narod* (The Slovenian Nation) captures the atmosphere of those heady days:

Z. L Mozirski
  Pozdravljen Kralj

Živel Peter, kralj svobode,
živel nam junaški car.
Složil v jeden tri si rode,—
bodi veren mu vladar!

Jug slovanski Te pozdravlja,
car—spasitelj naših muk
in prisego Ti ponavlja,—
venca Te slovanski jug!

    vstal je narod troedin:
Slava naj Ti večna klije,
kralja Marka vernik sin!

V kolo slavsko pobratimi,
Srb, Slovenac, in Hrvat!—
Domovina poljub primi,
srce bratsko primi brat.

Složil v jeden tri si rode,
car—spasitelj naših muk:
Živel Peter, kralj svobode,
venca Te slovanski jug!

Hail Peter, king of freedom,
Long live our heroic tsar.
You have fused three peoples into one,—
be a worthy ruler to them!

The Slavic South salutes you,
O Tsar, the salvation of our suffering,
and we repeat our oath to You,—
The Slavic South crowns you!

Our three in one nation has arisen
Let them glorify you always,
The true ancestor of Marko the King!

Let us be brothers in a glorious dance,
Serb, Croat, and Slovene!—
Accept a native kiss,
and a brotherly heart.

You have fused three peoples into one,—
O Tsar, the salvation of our suffering
Hail Peter, king of freedom,
The Slavic South crowns you!

In time, as the three peoples got to know each other better and as political differences began to drive the country apart, the difficulty of reconciling the "surface" differences separating the three tribes was recognized.

    The question of what sort of culture the new state should encourage was a complicated one, and in the period after 1918, a number of attitudes toward the creation of a national culture coexisted in Yugoslavia. They can be summed up by three words: unification, cooperation, and toleration. Each of these approaches had the backing of powerful cultural interests in the country, and it is the waxing and waning of their relative degrees of influence that tells the story, not merely of interwar Yugoslavia but of postwar Yugoslavia as well. By unification, I mean active efforts to create a culture that would be the same for all Yugoslavs, regardless of their religion or ethnic origin. Partisans of the most extreme forms of such a program called for a uniform system of education and the more or less immediate creation of a single national literary language as well as a synthetic culture to replace the existing national cultures. Their underlying belief was that, without a shared culture, the country could not survive.[24] As it turned out, they appear to have been correct, although it is not obvious that such a policy, even if it had been embraced by all of Yugoslavia's cultural and political figures, would have succeeded.

Three forms of cultural unification were possible: (1) an existing culture (most likely Serbian) could be chosen as the standard—in the context of Yugoslavia, I have called this the romantic model; or (2) a new culture could be created that would combine elements of the existing "tribal" cultures—this will be called the multicultural model; or (3) a culture could be created that was not based on existing tribal cultures at all—the supranational model. In the interwar period, all three models coexisted, but the latter two were dominant.[25]

Backers of cultural cooperation believed that the cultures of the various Yugoslav nations should interact as much as possible, should borrow themes, techniques, and approaches from each other, but that no immediate efforts should be made to eliminate national differences. Holding that the members of each tribe had a responsibility to know and understand the cultures of the others, they felt that in time it was likely that tribal cultural peculiarities would become less extreme and might even disappear, but they did not feel it advisable or necessary to rush the process along. Indeed, the variety that characterized Yugoslav culture was, in their view, one of its strengths.[26]

Finally, supporters of toleration believed that it was neither necessary nor advisable to meld the separate tribal cultures in any way; rather, all that was required for a successful state was that the separate cultures tolerate each other's existence. The process of nation building, in their view, was exclusively social and political, rather than cultural.

These cultural positions should, however, be seen as lying on a continuum. That is to say, believers in unitarism could and often did slide toward cooperation. This became more and more true as time went on, given both the disastrous consequences of forced political unitarism as well as the ever-greater realization that, despite having much in common, the various Yugoslav groups were also quite different. Cooperationists could support greater or lesser degrees of collaborative work. And believers in tolerance were rarely against all forms of collaboration. The far poles of this continuum were, on the unitarist side, national chauvinism—that is, the belief that the cultures of Yugoslavia should all meld into one's own culture—whereas tolerance could always slide toward separatism. Since the result of thinking at either of the poles tended toward intolerance, one can even see this continuum as a kind of circle in which the two extremes met.

The cultural situation was further complicated by the fact that the opinions of the cultural and political leaders within each of the three main groups in the country differed significantly. As a result, no group came into the new state with a unified set of cultural and political demands. If we examine the cultural problem region by region, we can appreciate just how complicated the balance of cultural and political forces in the new country was. As we have already seen, Serbian leaders on the political front, particularly the governing Radical party, were strong unitarists, and theirs was a unitarism that leaned heavily toward Serbian dominance. But in the first decade of Yugoslavia's existence one is hard pressed to find major Serbian intellectuals or writers who showed a strong preference for a unitary culture, much less for one based on the nineteenth-century romantic vision of synthesis on Serbian terms. Rather, in the first Yugoslavia Serbs generally followed a policy of cultural cooperation. Serbian intellectuals were quite willing to interact with Croatians and Slovenians, many of whom moved to Belgrade in the aftermath of the war, as well as to publish their works and articles about them in Serbian journals and newspapers, but they saw no need for any further steps toward integration. There were, however, Serbian writers who worked, at least implicitly, for a supranational culture, including Miloš Crnjanski and, later, Marko Ristić.

The basic Serbian attitude toward culture in the interwar years can be seen most clearly through an examination of the most prestigious Ser-

bian cultural periodicals, *Letopis Matice srpske* (The Chronicle of the Serbian Cultural Society [Novi Sad]) and *Srpski književni glasnik* (The Serbian Literary Gazette [Belgrade]). The latter, under the leadership of Jovan
Skerlić, had been a strong voice for unitary culture in the immediate prewar years. During the war, both periodicals were closed down, and when
they were revived they showed little interest in unitarist culture. To be sure,
the first issue of the new series of *Srpski književni glasnik* began with an editorial stating that the journal would continue the Yugoslavizing policies
that had distinguished it in the prewar period.[27] But in fact the journal itself showed little flexibility, as one could note by the retention of its former
name. Although Zagreb journals frequently published articles using the
Cyrillic as well as Latin alphabet, the Belgrade journal published only in
Cyrillic. And the writers and artists of Yugoslav bent whom the Croatian
journals celebrated (the Illyrians, Vojnović, Meštrović) were barely mentioned in the pages of *Srpski književni glasnik*. This is not to say that the
journal ignored Croatian and Slovenian literature. One can find reviews
and articles devoted to both subjects, and the journal was willing to publish the work of such Croatian writers as Vladimir Nazor and Tin Ujević.
Nevertheless, we can see here a spirit of cultural cooperation, rather than
an enthusiasm for a unified multicultural or supranational culture.

In Croatia, the political scene quickly came to be dominated by nationalists who believed in tolerance at best and separatism at worst. It is a
much disputed question of the chicken and egg variety as to whether their
separatist tendencies arose in response to Serbian hegemony or the other
way around, but whatever the answer, the struggle between Croat attempts
at national self-assertion and Serb refusals to assent to these eventually became the central and most damaging political problem in the country. Surprisingly enough, however, few of Croatia's leading intellectuals favored nationalism or separatism in the cultural sphere; rather, they were the primary proponents of national unification. In the immediate prewar period
Croatia had been the center of pan-Yugoslav agitation, and these tendencies continued during and after the war. Although such ideas could be expressed only with care in wartime conditions, they were nevertheless present in most of the major nonclerical Croatian cultural journals (most
clearly in *Savremenik* (The Contemporary, the journal of the Croatian
Writers' Association) and in *Hrvatska njiva* (Croatian Field). Thus, for example, well before the end of the war, in April 1917, *Savremenik* devoted a

long article to the first performance of Petar Konjović's "Vilin veo" (The Vila's Veil), a new opera in three acts that had recently been performed at the National Theater. Billed as a highly "national" (read Yugoslav) opera, it incorporated such Serbian folk heroes as Kraljević Marko, Miloš Obilić and the mythological Vila (fairy) Ravijojla in a seamless, Wagnerian operatic texture.[28] The use of traditionally Serbian folk characters in a Wagnerian-style opera was, of course, the musical equivalent of Meštrović's cultural synthesis in sculpture, and the praise lavished on the production was an indication of the journal's embrace of a multicultural synthesis.

The most radical experiment in creating a multicultural Yugoslav culture was provided by the journal *Književni jug*, which began appearing in January 1918 and continued to publish until the end of 1919. Its contributors included practically every major writer from Serbia, Croatia, and Slovenia. Each issue published literary work in Serbo-Croatian and Slovenian and employed both the Cyrillic and Latin alphabets. The journal's first number, January 1, 1918, left no doubt as to the goals and strategies of the editorial board. It opens with a photograph of a sculpture by Ivan Meštrović entitled "Hrist" (Christ). Meštrović was, of course, the best-known purveyor of multicultural Yugoslav culture in the period, so the inclusion of his work was more than appropriate. The lead article, by one of the journal's editors, Niko Bartulović, is entitled "Zadaci vremena" (Tasks of the Time) and sets out the basic objectives of the publication:

We now see hundreds of practical tasks: the question of a unified literature, of a unified language with a single literary language and orthography. . . . If we get to know one another through the popularization of Slovenian writing among the Croats and Serbs and vice versa; if we accustom our people truly to look at our literature as a single whole; all of that would be a great deed. In this way, greater assimilation would occur all by itself, as would the purification of our language and our pride in a great literature which has Prešeren alongside Njegoš and Kranjčević alongside Zupančič. (3–4)

Given its editors' belief that a unified multicultural national culture was the sine qua non of a stable Yugoslavia, it is not surprising that one of the central tasks *Književni jug* set itself was the canonization of past writers worthy to be included in the ranks of Yugoslav literature. In addition to the figures mentioned above, other artists advanced as candidates for Yugoslav canonization included Petar Preradović and the Slovene Ivan Cankar. And though the original literary work the journal published did not necessarily deal with Yugoslav national themes, the editors do seem to have gone out of their way to find such works. Thus, volume 1, number 2, contains a patriotic sonnet by Aleksa Šantić called "Naš apostol" (Our Apostle), which ends with the lines

> Lepa deca Juga tvojim vatrom gore,
> Tvojim letom lete, da te svake zore
> Zagrle na visu tvojih zlatnih dela.

> The beautiful children of the South burn with your fire,
> They fly with your flight, so that at every morn
> They can embrace your golden deeds on the heights.[29]

Književni jug survived only until 1919, but two other journals of strong Yugoslav orientation continued to publish in Zagreb. One was the newspaper *Jugoslavenska njiva* (Yugoslav Field) and the other was *Nova Evropa* (The New Europe).[30] Founded in March 1917 as *Hrvatska njiva*, *Yugoslav Field* changed its name after the creation of the Kingdom of the Serbs, Croats, and Slovenes, and took as its program "the national consolidation of Yugoslavia," a notion that, in the opinion of the editors of the tenth anniversary edition in 1926, was "becoming an ever greater factor, because a consciousness of unity and the strength of democratic ideals grows ever greater."[31] The unitarist nature of their Yugoslav program can be seen from the cultural texts they mention as supporting it:

And Yugoslavism? Is it not a postulate of popular thought? Take a short look at everything great that we have ever created! Our epic and lyric folk poetry . . . are those not a part of all of our people, are they not an expression of the people's soul? Did not that spirit inspire and give wings to our greatest artistic works—Čengić-Aga and The Mountain Wreath? Does it not breathe from the stone sculptures of Meštrović?[32]

Even more influential was the journal *Nova Evropa*, which appeared in 1920 and continued to promulgate a Yugoslav message until the beginning of World War II. This journal was affiliated with the English journal *New Europe* (founded by the indefatigable R. W. Seton-Watson), although it had its own editorial board and published materials primarily relating to Yugoslavia. Its board of founding editors and contributors included practically every intellectual and writer of consequence from Belgrade and Zagreb, as well as a smattering of Slovenes.[33] Initially, the journal's editors seemed sure that national cultural unification had been achieved. As time wore on, and inter-"tribal" disputes came to dominate the Yugoslav scene, they realized that much work still needed to be accomplished. But they never gave up the vision of a unified, synthetic Yugoslav culture.

At the same time, Croatia was also a hotbed for leftist intellectuals enamored of communist internationalism. As opposed to the intellectuals grouped around the multiculturally oriented journals mentioned above, figures such as Miroslav Krleža and August Cesarec imagined a rather different kind of synthesis. Their preference was for the creation of a supranational culture of internationalist bent, but had their vision been implemented, it would have also led to the creation of a unified Yugoslav culture, albeit of a very different kind. Krleža in particular was extremely active as a publicist and cultural commentator in the interwar period and founded a series of journals that attacked multicultural solutions to Yugoslavia's national question and fended off attempts by more orthodox Marxists to force culture into Stalinist modes.

In Slovenia, the situation was altogether different. There, political leaders recognized that given the geopolitical situation, surrounded by voracious neighbors, Slovenia had no choice but to work with the other Yugoslav tribes. They tended, therefore, to be inclined to cooperation, even though they were frequently unhappy with Serbian political high-handedness. But whereas most Slovenian intellectuals were willing to recognize the need for political cooperation, their governing cultural attitude was tolerance. The strongest statement of such views before the creation of the Kingdom of the Serbs, Croats, and Slovenes was made by none other than Slovenia's greatest modern writer, the politically pro-Yugoslav Ivan Cankar, in a 1917 article entitled "Slovenes and Yugoslavs." "As you can see," Cankar summed up, "I have looked at the Yugoslav problem for what it is: that is, as an exclusively *political* problem. . . . Some kind of Yugoslav question in the cultural or overall linguistic sense does not exist for me at all. Maybe it once existed, but it was solved when the Yugoslav tribes separated into four peoples with four completely clear and independent cultural lives."[34]

This position was refined as the new state was forming in a declaration by leading Slovenian *Kulturträger*: "After the formation of a state of the Slovenes, Croats, and Serbs, the cultural section expects that this *new completely politically unified state*, no matter how organized, *will* insofar as possible and with all the means at its disposal *speed the development of the intellectual life of all three peoples on the basis of cultural autonomy.*"[35] In particular, Slovenian intellectuals were almost always opposed to plans for cultural unification because they believed that these would inevitably lead to the disappearance of the Slovenian language and, ultimately, to the Serbo-Croatization of the Slovenians. At the same time, they were willing to mandate the teaching of the Serbo-Croatian language and of "Yugoslav" history in the schools, particularly because in so doing they weakened the influence of the Catholic Church and its Slovene allies.[36]

Unlike Croatians, many of whom migrated to Belgrade in the immediate postwar period, Slovenian intellectuals tended to remain in Ljubljana. *Ljubljanski zvon* (The Ljubljana Bell), the leading cultural periodical in Slovenia in the pre- and interwar periods, reflected Slovenia's more or less isolationist attitude well. Even during the short period of postwar euphoria, the journal published almost nothing that was not by Slovenian authors. And although books and journals from the other Yugoslav capitals were reviewed, it is difficult to discern that they had much influence on the Slovenian cultural scene in the interwar period.

Language and Yugoslav Nationalism: 1918–1939

In the nineteenth century, the central cultural task of the Yugoslav-oriented intelligentsia was the creation of a unified Serbo-Croatian literary language. As we noted in the previous chapter, a final step toward unification was proposed in 1913; this would have been a grand compromise in which the Ekavian dialect (used by most Serbs and all Slovenes and Macedonians) would have been declared the single basis for a literary language that would have been written exclusively in the Latin alphabet. Immediately after the war, this compromise was proposed again by Nikola Andrić at a meeting of the Croatian Writers' Association, but it appears to have garnered little support among Serbian cultural figures and was not adopted.[37] Even so, the governing assumption shared by practically all linguists and intellectuals in the interwar period was that Serbo-Croatian was a single language, albeit not yet uniform. True, the 1930s saw a renaissance of Croatian dialect (Kajkavian) poetry—the most famous instance is Miroslav Krleža's *Balade Petrice Kerempuha* (The Ballads of Pete Kerempuh)—but such works were more or less isolated and did not challenge the basic unity of literary Serbo-Croatian so much as extend its poetic potential. In his prose essays or his novels, for example, Krleža would never have dreamed of employing the Kajkavian dialect except for emphasis or in dialogue.

The belief in the essential unity of Serbo-Croatian was expressed most explicitly in the preface to the first number of a journal entitled *Naš jezik* (Our Language), which began publishing in 1930 under the control of an editorial board consisting of distinguished linguists from both Serbia and Croatia. Although the journal's title implies that the language was indeed one, the editors prefaced the initial number with a somewhat ambiguous statement, now endorsing, now questioning the extent of achieved unity. Their belief in the desirability of a unified language was certain, however:

> Our nation has liberated itself and united, and thus has brought together that which had been separated for centuries. It is our belief that our unification in the area of the literary language will produce positive results, although there have been some difficulties which must be overcome. It is in order to make the task easier for all those who love our literary language that we launch this journal. It [the journal] is predicated on the belief that our modern literary language, among the various groups of our people, has wonderful elements which could be developed into a wonderful literary language for our whole national community. Indeed, the best guarantee of our unification is the literary language which was the predecessor of our national unity. From here it happened that practically every group of our people has literati who write in the same way. . . . We simply wish to take that which is the best and most accurate in the language of all these writers and extend it to the rest of our people.[38]

But if the issue of Serbo-Croat linguistic unity was considered essentially solved, the question of the relationship between that language and Slovenian came to the fore. Although, in the early days of the Illyrian movement some Slovenes supported abandoning their language and writing in Serbo-Croatian (the most illustrious of these was the poet Stanko Vraz), Slovenian already existed as a fully formed literary language before Serbo-Croatian was modernized. And though various reforms did bring Slovenian closer to Serbo-Croatian in the course of the nineteenth century, most Slovenes were not interested in Yugoslavism if it required giving up their own cultural and linguistic identity, as the 1913 survey on the subject conducted by the journal *Veda* (Science) proved. Nevertheless, the issue arose again in the context of the new state. Some proponents of Yugoslavism (and not, by the way, Serbian politicians) insisted that a national culture simply could not be created if the entire nation did not employ a single literary language. The most measured were willing to admit that this did not necessarily mean unaltered Serbo-Croatian, but one language it would have to be. In response to Slovenian assertions of the inviolability of their cultural heritage, one of the editors of *Nova Evropa* replied:

> If we truly want something new and something united, can we and do we dare leave everything as it was and continue on as we have always done? The answer must be, obviously, negative. . . . If we want to and will become a single people and to have a single state—we have to have one literary language in the future . . . perhaps that could even be today's Slovenian. But it has to be a single one. . . . There is, however, one thing that must be said in connection with the above. The Slovenes must recognize, in their own interest, the fact that those who speak Slovenian are in a tiny minority compared with those whose language is Serbo-Croatian. It would not be at all unnatural and unfair if it were their literary language that has to accept more sacrifices than does Serbo-Croatian.[39]

The final, categorical rejection of the invitation to give up their language on the part of Slovenes did not come until 1932 in a book entitled *Kulturni problem slovenstva* (The Cultural Problem of Slovenia), by the critic and cultural historian Josip Vidmar.[40] Vidmar carefully brings up the arguments of those Slovenes who felt that full cultural amalgamation with the Serbo-Croat majority (which is seen here as a unified nation) was inevitable or necessary only to demolish them. In particular, he tries to show that although the Slovenes are small in number, the nation is no smaller than other European groups who have successfully built their own cultures. What is more, he argues, forcing the Slovenes to write and work in a language different from the one they speak would eliminate the possibility of true creativity among them, thereby contributing to a net loss for Yugoslavia.

But while debate simmered among the cultural elite, on the ground no active attempts to coerce the Slovenes into giving up their language were made. Although the Serbo-Croatian language and the Cyrillic alphabet became required components of the school program as early as 1921, these reforms were carried out in the context of the Sloveniazation of the public school system and with the enthusiastic support of Slovenia's most powerful political party, the Liberals.[41] The extent to which the national language continued to dominate the educational system in the traditional

Slovenian lands can be seen from the contents of a reader meant to be used in the fourth grade of Slovenian schools: of some 131 texts in that reader, all but 11 are in Slovenian.[42]

Although linguistic coercion was not employed to any great extent in Slovenia, it was pursued vigorously in Macedonia. Macedonia had been a bone of contention between Serbia, Greece, and Bulgaria throughout the second half of the nineteenth century, with each side making historical and/or linguistic claims to the area. The Second Balkan War (1913) was fought over these issues, and Bulgaria's decision to support the Central Powers during World War I was made in the hopes of annexing Macedonia. As a result, perhaps unsurprisingly, the Yugoslav government did everything possible to assert that the inhabitants of Macedonia were in fact "Southern Serbs" whose culture had been corrupted by Bulgarian influences over the years. In part because of the uncomfortable nearness of Macedonian and Bulgarian, neither a Macedonian language nor nationality was recognized in the first Yugoslavia and all education in the region was conducted in Serbo-Croatian.

Defining a Multicultural Yugoslav Culture: 1918–1941

Let us, for the moment, concentrate our attention on those intellectual and cultural figures who believed in the necessity of a single multicultural Yugoslav culture, one that would synthesize the best that each of the constituent national groups had to offer. This group included all of those we have labeled unitarists as well as most cooperationists (for the two differed most on the question of how aggressively to pursue a single multi-stranded national culture). From the country's inception, these people, whatever their place on the continuum, recognized the existence and dangers of the split between their view of what a successful Yugoslav state would require and that of the country's political leaders. Concerns on this score were voiced even before the ink had dried on the proclamation announcing the formation of the Kingdom of the Serbs, Croats, and Slovenes, as a long editorial in the mid-December 1918 issue of *Književni jug* attests. Entitled "Political Freedom and Culture," the article, written by one of the journal's editors, Niko Bartulović, is remarkable both for what in retrospect seems its overly optimistic tone regarding the amount of cultural unity that Yugoslavia had achieved before and during the war, and for the accuracy of its prophetic fears for the future. Bartulović begins with the claim that in ancient civilizations the attainment of political unity and power preceded cultural successes, while in the modern period the reverse has been true. Focusing on Eastern and Central Europe, he continues: "All the political and economic powers that have arisen in our period trace their origins to purely cultural revivals and movements that only later developed politically and economically. The two newest European powers, Italy and Germany, are essentially of purely literary origin."[43] Yugoslavia, in Bartulović's view, had come into existence in the same fashion.

The unity of Yugoslav culture was an accomplished fact the very moment that the culture became self-conscious. And feeling itself to be one, it simultaneously came to the conclusion of complete national unity, from which the conclusions of political and social unity arose naturally. Thus we see the remarkable fact that all of our intellectuals, all of our best poets, whether they were Serbs, Croats, or Slovenes, from the beginning of our cultural revival, were the most enthusiastic and committed Yugoslavs. It is sufficient merely to mention the names Daničić, Strossmayer, Kopitar, Gaj, Zmaj, Vraz, Preradović, Stojan Novaković, and Vojnović; and we can say for certain that there was not a single even less-well-known cultural figure in the Slavic South who was a separatist. (356)

Bartulović's list, which includes figures active from the 1830s through his own day—Serbs, Croats, and Slovenes—is indeed impressive, and it underscores the reasons that Yugoslav integrationists had for optimism.

A belief in the idea of the multicultural unity of Yugoslav culture was what united the contributors to *Književni jug*. Even at this very early stage, however, they recognized that the kind of cultural unity they envisioned would need to be nurtured and developed. What is more, they were not so naive as to think that every Yugoslav citizen recognized the existence of a Yugoslav culture. This was not seen as a critical problem, however. After all, in Germany and Italy national unification had also begun as the utopian dream of a few intellectuals. Even after political unification had been achieved, it took many years and great effort on the part of cultural leaders and the state to create German or Italian citizens out of the less-educated elements of the population. This was the work that the editors of and contributors to *Književni jug* took upon themselves in Yugoslavia.

What worried Bartulović, however, and what in retrospect indeed became the undoing of the first Yugoslavia, was not the national or cultural identification of the masses, but the ideas and plans of the country's political leaders.

While our intellectuals and writers were creating the foundations not only of our cultural but also of our political unity and freedom, the political representatives of all three parts of our people were those who, in the great majority of cases, were completely deaf to culture. Our cultural leaders understood quite well the axiom that national unity implied national freedom, at least potentially. The politicians, on the contrary and despite the examples of Germany and Italy, wanted to achieve freedom without unity. (356)

This split between the best and the brightest, who were working for the spread of ideas of cultural unity among the Yugoslav "tribes," and political figures, who were unable to recognize the need for such work—either because they thought it would simply happen on its own or because they did not want it—was to become Yugoslavia's curse and its tragedy. Bartulović was prescient enough to recognize the dangers from the beginning: "After these political days, during which, understandably enough, everything including culture became politicized, it is necessary, as soon as possible, to concentrate again on spiritual and cultural work so as not to bring our freedom and our human tasks to decay and destruction as happened in Germany" (357).

In this early period a number of influential figures stepped up to describe what a synthetic multistranded Yugoslav culture would look like and what its elements would be. In an article entitled "The Bases of Yugoslav Civilization," Jovan Cvijić described the future unified culture by identifying the contributions that could be made by each of the separate tribal cultures. Cvijić attributed to the Serbs boundless idealism and an ethic of self-sacrifice whose exemplars were Tsar Lazar, Miloš Obilić, and Saint Sava. In Cvijić's view, the Serbs would contribute their observational gift, as well as their capacity for fantasy and intuition to Yugoslav civilization. At the same time, Cvijić identified certain deficiencies in Serbian culture that could be corrected only by hybridization with other South Slavs. In particular, he felt that Serbs lacked the discipline to express their gifts in concrete forms. Croats, according to Cvijić, had shown a particular talent for cultural and scientific work. They were believed to share many of the qualities of Serbs in an attenuated form but to make up for this by possessing more self-discipline. The Slovenes, although they were the smallest group, were expected to inject their capacity for hard work and their rationalism into the South Slavic mix. Borrowing metaphors from popular genetics, Cvijić concluded optimistically: "New qualities that until now have been expressed but weakly will appear. An amalgamation of the most fertile qualities of our three tribes will come forth ever more strongly, and thus will be constructed the type of a single Yugoslav civilization—the final and most important goal of our country."[44]

Cvijić's ideas would be developed further in the course of the 1920s and 1930s. In the view of some Yugoslav thinkers, the state's goal should have been the creation of a perfect Yugoslav type who would be "not merely a new person, but a person of better physical quality, with more stamina, healthier, economically more progressive, with more material goods, and even more important, spiritually higher, marked by more noble motives and sensations, with better habits, a stronger will and ability to act, greater intelligence and enlightenment."[45] This type would only be created through the combination of all the Yugoslav elements. And though no forced program of eugenics was proposed, Yugoslav intellectuals were called upon to set an example and put this program into action for the good of the country as a whole.

The most thorough-going attempt to demonstrate the existence of a single Yugoslav race as well to define its culture was made in a curious book entitled *Karakterologija jugoslovena* (The Characterology of the Yugoslavs), published in 1939 by Vladimir Dvorniković. Drawing on a mind-boggling array of sources, ranging from skull and skeleton size, folk customs, crafts, music, and poetry to the creations of contemporary literature and sculpture, as well as the ethnographic and racial theories of his predecessor Cvijić, Dvorniković set out to demonstrate "scientifically" the existence of a Yugoslav race.[46] Although his thousand-page tome pretends to originality, it is in fact nothing more than an amplification of Cvijić's theses. Still, it is valuable as a eulogy for and encyclopedia of interwar unitarist anthropological and cultural Yugoslav mythology.

Dvorniković naturally does not deny that differences among the peoples inhabiting Yugoslavia exist. But he claims that these differences are contingent and temporary and that they mask a deeper and more profound racial unity. The Yugoslavs, in Dvorniković's view, are the prime exemplars of the Dinaric race, the ideal physical characteristics of which were captured in the sculpture of Ivan Meštrović (206). The Dinaric race, in Dvornikovićʼs view, is the prototype of a male warrior (208), but, unlike the warriors of the German or Turanian races, whom they superficially resemble,[47] the Yugoslavs share with their brother Slavs a purely peace-loving spirit (280, 333). Like Cvijić before him, Dvornikovićʼ believes that a primary trait of the Yugoslavs is their ability to sacrifice themselves for a higher goal (323). In the end, Dvornikovićʼ identifies as primary traits of his Yugoslav characterology "dynamism, rhythm, strong temperament, strong expressivity, and the constructive ability of fantasy" (514), combined with a capacity for struggle and patience (652).

Creating a Multicultural Genealogy

Perhaps the most important way in which national traditions are created is through the canonization of predecessors. Activities of this sort can be carried out by private individuals and groups as well as by the state through its educational system. In the first Yugoslavia, independent intellectuals were of primary importance in this regard, although the government's ministries of culture and education, particularly the latter, played a role as well. Overall, however, the central government was rather inactive in the area of cultural policy, reflecting its political leaders' general belief that state building should take priority over nation building. The absence of state support for the creation and nurturing of a unified culture was frequently lamented. Witness, for example, the following statement from the Croatian poet Gustav Krklec:

We have neither a unified strong cultural activity inside the country, nor do we have a unified, healthy well-organized cultural propaganda abroad. That is, in other words, a definite lack in the cultural atmosphere without which there is no initiative, no pride, and no desire for serious work. Private initiatives, which in our country often occur in nice forms and with a great deal of good will and illusions, have still not disappeared, but they are far from able to provide what a well-organized government initiative could.[48]

In the private sphere, however, a number of important and influential attempts were made to demonstrate the existence of a unified Yugoslav culture on a historical and theoretical level. Perhaps the most far-reaching of these was a longish article by the Croatian literary historian, Antun Barac.[49] Barac takes issue with the views of the majority of his predecessors, who had argued that the literary traditions of the Serbs, Croats, and Slovenes were unrelated.[50] He claims that they had merely been observing surface phenomena, all the while failing to see the fundamental unity of Yugoslav literature, which he characterizes using geographical ("underground river that flows all together even when it is unseen") and biological ("beating of a single heart") metaphors (152). Barac asserts that only secondary and tertiary figures of the nineteenth century had been separatist in outlook and proposes a list of "Yugoslav" writers that includes practically every big name in the three national traditions. He does note that the Slovenes had traditionally been somewhat outside of the Serbo-Croatian literary orbit, but adds that "all in the national soul that is tenderest, finest, most sensitive that was expressed in folk poetry has not been truly expressed in high literature by the Serbs or Croats, but rather by the Slovenes—Prešeren, Vraz, Zupančič, Cankar, Novačan, etc." (152). Thus, Barac's view of the relationship between the literatures of the Yugoslav people mirrored the anthropological outlook Cvijić had expressed at the same time. Although in Barac's view the high literatures of the Serbs, Croats, and Slovenes were not identical, taken together they served to express all facets of the national spirit; they were three and one simultaneously.

The belief that a multistranded Yugoslav literary culture had in many respects already come into existence was echoed in a book published by the major Serbian literary historian Pavle Popović.[51] Popović admitted that before the middle of the eighteenth century, the literatures of the three nations had little in common. But in his opinion, the situation had changed completely in the nineteenth century. "Two particularities characterize this new Yugoslav literature. The first is its national unity; the other is its national [*narodni*] character. Serbian, Croatian, and Slovenian literature, which until this time were separated and without mutual contact, now became closer, linked up, and became an indivisible whole" (48). As had Barac, Popović believed that the primary impetus for unity had been the reorientation of high culture throughout the South Slavic lands away from religion and toward folk poetry.

A few years later, Popović made his view of the evolutionary process characteristic of Yugoslav literature even clearer.

Our history of literature has not yet taken *the idea of national unity* into account, but I believe that this is an error. Our literature unquestionably strives toward unity. From the beginning it is only a collection of various, separate, regional literatures; later, particularly in the new period, they all begin to come together, intermingle, unite; today we already have many elements of unity in our collective literature of the Serbs, Croats, and Slovenes; soon there will be more, and eventually this literature will become one in the fullest sense of the word. That is its process, its course of development, and perhaps its central character.[52]

Whereas Popović and Barac were relatively conservative in their assertions regarding the amount of unity that had actually been achieved, others were less circumspect. A pamphlet called *Jugoslav Culture*, published in English some time in the 1920s by Milan Marjanović and clearly meant for Western consumption, is the most extreme statement of achieved Yugoslav cultural unity. Marjanović, a tireless popularizer of the brand of unity expressed in Meštrović's heroic prewar synthesis, proclaimed:

The Jugoslavs—that is to say, the Serbs, Croats, and Slovenes—are a virile, gifted nation, full of temperament, and with strong leanings towards culture. . . . The artistic spirit of the nation, which found expression in poetry, ornamental design, and traditional customs, has at all times and throughout Jugoslavia been identical in form and style, and all efforts at higher intellectual achievements on the part of the educated classes have show[n] a persistent tendency toward national unification. (1–2)

And he ended his pamphlet with the following optimistic peroration: "At the close of the XIXth and the beginning of the XXth century the younger generation of Jugoslavs have succeeded in obliterating all traces of particularism between the three great groups of Southern Slav literature and art. The Jugoslav culture of today appears as a unified whole, animated by a deep racial patriotism, and thoroughly in sympathy with all that is best in modern enlightenment and true human progress" (15).

By the mid-1920s, optimistic pronouncements of achieved cultural unity had become tempered by the realities of the intranational bickering that was such a characteristic feature of the first Yugoslavia. Nevertheless one finds them all over the liberal periodical press, particularly in the journal *Nova Evropa*, which, despite a basic political focus, frequently published materials about Yugoslav culture. Contributors to *Nova Evropa* were apt to say that a true Yugoslav culture was coming into being rather than that it had already been attained, but they, too, saw the evolutionary process of its creation as inevitable: "When the Balkan wars again strengthened the general position of Yugoslavdom and opened better perspectives for the future, the Yugoslavs again turned to their unresolved internal problems, without fear and with the best intentions of solving and explaining them. Among the most important problems was that of a unified culture that would be expressed in a single language and literature."[53] Despite this author's admission that Serbo-Croatian and Slovenian literature are not identical (neither this nor any other author from this period expressed any doubt that modern Serbian and Croatian literature formed an organic whole), he still calls for them to be considered together. His reasons for so doing are based not on the similarities of the literatures themselves, but rather on their shared relationship to external forces, and he exploits a biological metaphor (in general, the vocabulary of evolutionary biology was a favorite among Yugoslav cultural critics of this period) to make his point: "The basic indication of an organism is the unity of its reaction to anything external, and the concentration of those of its own elements that exhibit a unifying tendency. Yugoslav literature is such an organism."[54]

The views of literary historians were echoed and amplified for the reading public by the editors of a number of new literary anthologies that appeared in the first Yugoslavia. The earliest such work appears to have been *Antologija savremene jugoslavenske lirike* (Anthology of Contemporary Yugoslav Lyric Poetry), edited by Dr. Mirko Deanović and Ante Petravić. This collection attempts to mirror in its composition the latest views on Yugoslav culture, organizing poems through the late nineteenth century in separate Serbian, Croatian, and Slovenian sections while presenting modern poetry without regard to "tribal" affiliation. In the introduction the editors explicitly justify their choice:

One of the most difficult tasks in compiling this first attempt to gather together in a single anthology the three facets of our lyric poetry was that we still do not have a single literary history that would cover and treat together all of our three-named literature [here they provide a footnote to Popović's literary history as a first step in this direction]. We have arranged separate Serbian, Croatian, and Slovenian groups in parallel, since they developed separately and in parallel despite the fact that they were linked together. It was impossible otherwise to show earlier Yugoslav literature, since it is only in its newest phase that one can see it as a single whole in spite of linguistic and other differences between its separate parts. Thus it was only in the third section of the anthology that we could group together all those poets who speak the same language. In this sense one should understand the title of our book, for we wished to cover with a single rubric all three branches of our literature, which despite the fact that they have separate names nevertheless comprise a single Yugoslav lyric tradition.[55]

Yugoslav literary theory even trickled down to the readers that were issued to children in the Yugoslav school system, particularly in the higher grades.[56] This system was under the supervision of a centralized Ministry of Education in Belgrade, which approved textbooks for use in schools throughout the country.[57] Let us look, for example, at the excellent reader dating from 1928 compiled for the third level of middle schools. It includes representative selections from Serbian, Croatian, and Slovenian literature, and its multicultural Yugoslav orientation is clear from the fact that texts are grouped thematically rather than by the author's nationality. Furthermore, the authors are identified by their region of origin rather than by their "tribal" affiliation, thereby allowing the compiler to avoid the whole question of whether a given text belongs to Serbian or Croatian literature. Should anyone have wanted to do so, however, they would have discovered that the percentage of authors of a given nationality mirrored almost exactly the population percentages of the country as a whole, although there is no overt indication that any form of affirmative action criteria were applied to the selection process.[58]

The texts themselves include a large number of folk songs, riddles, and poems, and although the majority date from the nineteenth century, the compiler also provides excerpts from the work of such living authors as Krleža, Andrić, and Zupančič. Whereas it seems that no effort has been made to instill Yugoslav patriotism directly through this anthology (that is, it does not contain poems thematically devoted to South Slav unity), quite frequently the compiler places texts on the same theme by Serbian, Croatian, and Slovene authors side by side, creating an impression of commonality and difference simultaneously.[59] All texts are presented in the alphabet and language in which they were originally published. Slovenian-language selections are glossed heavily below, but Serbian and Croatian students would have at least become familiar with the Slovenian language in this fashion. There are, however, two relatively minor ways in which the text is Serbo-centric. The first is the clear expectation that the reader will not need glosses for standard Serbian words, whereas he or she will for standard Croatian or older Serbian texts. Thus, a Croatian or Slovene reader would be at a disadvantage since purely Serbian words in modern texts are not glossed. Additionally, the capsule biographies provided at the end of the text are all in Cyrillic. Still in all, the anthology does give a strong impression of the unity of Yugoslav literature.

Other readers provided students with schematic descriptions of Yugoslav literary history in its relation to politics. The following characterization of the Illyrian movement gives an idea of the ideology that marked the treatment of cultural history:

Although the Illyrian movement was of short duration, it nevertheless reached all strata of the people and built the foundations for Yugoslav cultural and literary unity. First of all, the people became aware of the relatedness of all the Yugoslav tribes, and they saw that the Serbs, Croatians, and Slovenes were a single nation, of a single blood and language. The Illyrian efforts made possible in all the regions—except Slovenia—a united literary language, that same one that Vuk Karadžić had brought into literature. In this way the basis for a united Serbian and Croatian literature was created, and this later led to the political and cultural union of the Serbs, Croats, and Slovenes.[60]

Although the question of a unified national literature received the lion's share of attention because of its traditional central role in the creation of national consciousness in European countries, textbooks did not ignore other areas of integration in the attempt to build a Yugoslav national consciousness (or to prove that it already existed). In addition to folk poetry, the Illyrian movement, and the writings of Njegoš and other poets of the nineteenth century who were deemed to have been inclined toward Yugoslavdom, a series of national myths that would serve to bind the state together were provided. One particularly popular source of such mythology was the volunteer movement during World War I. It was in fact true that after the crushing defeat of the Serbian army in 1915, a fairly large number of émigrés to such far-off places as the United States and Australia, along with young Croats and Slovenes from the Habsburg lands had joined volunteer brigades that eventually played a modest role in the liberation of the South Slavic lands. Their activity loomed large in the new national mythology, however, not so much for any actual military prowess but because it belied the conviction held by many Serbs that they alone should get the credit for the liberation of the nation. *Nova Evropa*, ever on the lookout for unifying features, devoted a whole issue to the volunteer movement in 1927 and called for greater publicity for the efforts of the volunteers, while noting, "Even though more than 10,000 Yugoslavs from all our regions participated in the volunteer movement in Russia . . . it is hard to gather information on it."[61]

Again, the mythology of the volunteer movement trickled down to school textbooks. The following patriotic snippet had the advantage of combining information about the multinational character of the volunteers with the mythology of the ruling dynasty as all-Yugoslav rather than merely Serbian. It is taken from the memoirs of a Slovene who had served as a volunteer and was included in a reader designed for Slovenian school children. "The king spoke with us and asked us about our homelands. When I told him that I was a Slovene volunteer he turned to me and said: 'You too, my son, will return to the home for which you have sacrificed so much.' His conversation was so calm, sure, and convincing, that the fear that had overtaken us when we began our thorny path all but disappeared. We saw that here was an old man who wanted to be among his people in these fateful days, who wanted to share every evil with his people."[62]

Another set of Yugoslav myths revolved around the organization "Union or Death" (a.k.a. "Black Hand"). Among other things, this group of officers in the Serbian army provided the weapons for the assassination of Archduke Franz Ferdinand. Again, *Nova Evropa* was quite concerned to demonstrate that they were not merely a Serbian, but an all-Yugoslav group (a couple of articles were published on the group in 1927 in commemoration of the tenth anniversary of the show trial at which the group's leader, "Apis" (Dragutin Dimitrijević), was condemned to death by a Serbian military court (July 26, 1927, 67–74; Sept. 11, 1927, 139–151).

The Young Bosnia movement, too, was treated intensively, with great care taken to emphasize its all-Yugoslav cultural leanings. *Nova Evropa* published excerpts from the trial records of the group, including the following from the testimony of Lazar Djukić:

> JUDGE. Did you have any kind of society?
> DJUKIĆ. We did, we had the society "Serbo-Croatian Nationalist Youth."
> J. What was the tendency of that society?
> DJ. Literary.
> J. And political?
> DJ. No, only literary.
> J. Your other colleagues who were in this society spoke differently about it.

DJ. Political only in the sense that we were for the unity of the Serbs
and Croats.[63]

This testimony is just a sample, but it demonstrates that the members of
the group thought of themselves as Yugoslav nationalists, cultural primarily, although political as well.

By far the most frequently canonized "Yugoslav" cultural phenomena, however, were oral folk poetry and the literary work of Petar Petrović Njegoš. As we noted in the previous chapter, it was through folk poetry that the Southern Slavs first burst onto the European cultural scene.
And as we have seen earlier in this chapter, unitary-minded literary historians pointed to the rapprochement between high literature and oral poetry (particularly in the works of Njegoš and Mažuranić) as the starting
point for a unified Yugoslav literature. In time, the deseterac became almost an object of sacred veneration among Yugoslav nation builders.
Dvorniković, for example, called the Yugoslav decasyllabic line the expression of the patriarchal-epic soul of the Yugoslav race and stated:
"There is no more direct key to the collective Yugoslav temperament,
both historical and modern, than folk song and music."[64] No Yugoslav-
oriented literary anthology, textbook, or history was without a large section devoted to folkloric texts.

There were, however, some problems for interwar Yugoslav multiculturalists who wished to canonize oral folk poetry as a foundation of Yugoslav culture. Most important was that this same body of work had served as
a central building block of exclusively Serbian nationalism in the nineteenth century. It had, therefore, to be reinterpreted in a Yugoslav rather
than in a Serbian key if it was to serve the new multicultural ideology. The
key to such a reinterpretation lay in moving the center of interest away
from the purely epic songs of the Kosovo cycle and toward poems that in-
tersected more directly with the traditions of the other Yugoslav tribes.
Dvorniković's treatment of folk poetry illustrates quite clearly how this
could be done: turning away from purely epic and heroic visions of Yugoslav culture (both of which characteristics were deemed too close to purely
Serbian views of their own tradition), Dvorniković claimed instead that
"the lyric and epic soul do battle in the Yugoslav; they do battle but both
are melancholy."[65] In this equation it is clear that the epic comes from the
Serbian side, the lyric from the Croatian and Slovenian. For Dvorniković,

the most characteristic figure in Yugoslav folk poetry is Marko Kraljević because Marko's battles were not so much with the Turks as within himself. What is more, Marko could serve as an exemplary figure because, as Dvorniković also noted, he was not an uncompromising Serb and therefore had more appeal to the other branches of the Yugoslav people. And indeed, it is probably no coincidence that Marko is the only figure associated with the Serbian epic whose exploits were also traditionally sung by both Croatian and Slovenian oral poets.

The variety and traditional importance of oral culture to all three Yugoslav "tribes" made it relatively easy to canonize a "Yugoslav" interpretation of folk poetry in the interwar years. A more difficult question was what to do about those writers of the nineteenth century who had mined that tradition in high cultural works, particularly Njegoš, whose *Mountain Wreath* had been central to the romantic unitary cultural project of the nineteenth century. Reinterpreting this work in a Yugoslav light, despite its overt dedication "to the ashes of the father of Serbia" and its message of intolerance toward the Moslem Slavs who made up some 10 percent of the new nation's population, required great critical dexterity. It was almost as if intellectuals in the United States had attempted to use D. W. Griffith's *The Birth of a Nation* as a central text of U.S. national identity. And yet, Njegoš did indeed become a posthumous prophet of Yugoslavdom, and throughout the 1910s, 1920s, and 1930s it was standard practice in literary histories of Yugoslavia to say that Njegoš "to this day has remained on the highest poetic pinnacle of our people" and to add that "well-known passages in *The Mountain Wreath* are the most beautiful and greatest that our artistic literature exhibits."[66]

What strategies were used to make Njegoš and his *Mountain Wreath* acceptable, nay, admirable in a Yugoslav context? The most obvious was avoidance of the unpleasant. This was particularly appropriate for the writers of school readers and anthologies. Since they were in any case expected to provide only excerpts from *The Mountain Wreath*, it proved easy to choose inoffensive passages. By far the most popular excerpt for such purposes was the digression in which Vojvoda Draško describes his visit to Venice. Of course, this section has nothing at all to do with the most problematic action of the work. It does not even bring out the central philosophical message of permanent struggle. It is, however, quite funny and was evidently deemed to be the safest passage for student consumption.[67]

Another tack was to shift attention away from the subject matter of *The Mountain Wreath* and turn readers' attention to extratextual information. Here, one could find a veritable treasure trove of Yugoslav-oriented material, primarily drawn from Njegoš's correspondence. In one oft-quoted letter to Osman-Pasha of Skoplje, for example, Njegoš had said: "I would like more than anything on earth to see accord between brothers in whom a single blood flows and who were nursed with the same milk."[68] To be sure, he said this after noting that brother had been fighting brother in Montenegro for hundreds of years and placing the blame for this squarely on the shoulders of "foreigners," that is, the Ottoman Turks. But in the minds of Yugoslav nationalists, and perhaps in Njegoš's as well, this implied that were outside influences to disappear, discord between brothers of different religions would as well.

Njegoš's credentials as a political Yugoslav were bolstered by citation from his letter to the Croatian leader, Ban Jelačić: "Secret fate has placed you at the head of the Southern Slavs. Luck crowns you with amazing advantages. . . . Everyone who loves our nation, our entire nation looks up to you and stretches out their hands to you as to a heaven-sent Messiah."[69] Comments like these, plus the fact that Njegoš was never a stickler for the external regalia of the Orthodox religion despite his high clerical office, allowed commentators to make impossibly extravagant claims: "Inspired by the great thought of the liberation of his nation and its incorporation into a great, free, and enlightened motherland, Njegoš was equally attached to Belgrade, Zagreb, Travnik, Dubrovnik, Skadar, and Mostar. As far as he was concerned, the rebellious Bosnian vizier Gradaščević, Ali-Pasha Rizvanbegović, and Osman-Pasha Skopjak were just as much his brothers as Aleksandar Karadjordjević or Ban Jelačić. It wasn't important to him whether any of them crossed himself or not or what he called himself; what was important was that they were all sons of the some mother, of the same people, that they were brothers."[70]

Equally popular as a method of displaying Njegoš's Yugoslavism was to concentrate not on the plot of his major work, but rather on a more abstract philosophy that was asserted to run through *The Mountain Wreath* as well as his other important epic, *The Ray of the Microcosm*. "His *Mountain Wreath* is a hymn to freedom, a rejection of force and tyranny, a glorification of national and human ideals, the affirmation of moral ideas over brute desires. In our rotten, cowardly, trivial, and ideal-less days, *The*

Mountain Wreath, with its high moral ideals, is a great source of inspiration."[71] Such claims seem today almost comical, a willful misreading of the spirit of Njegoš's work, but in their defense it should be pointed out that a coherent reading of *The Mountain Wreath* is possible using such categories. Through the mouth of Bishop Danilo, Njegoš does indeed deride tyranny, offering in its stead an enlightenment ideal based on abstract human rights. The most famous passage in this regard, and one that was frequently quoted aphoristically, goes as follows:

> Just as every wolf has the right to his sheep,
> so has every tyrant to a weakling.
> But to place foot upon the tyrant's neck,
> to make him know what the Right of men is,
> this is the most sacred of one's duties![72]

The problem, however, and what was skipped by most Yugoslav-inclined commentators on the work, is that the Islamicized Slavs who bear the brunt of the Montenegrins' attempts at "ethnic cleansing" are not identical to the Turks. It may indeed have been true that only a united Montenegro could have kept the Turks at bay, but it is also true that the way in which that unity is achieved in *The Mountain Wreath* is through fratricidal bloodletting. When the global tyranny of Turk against Yugoslav is echoed by the local tyranny of Christian Slav against Moslem, the result is tragic. Njegoš seems to have recognized that his "hymn to freedom" was built on blood and to have agonized over it, but most interwar critics blithely passed over this aspect of the work.

Perhaps the only interwar commentator to capture the essence of Njegoš's position, while still attempting to bring him into the Yugoslav canon, was the writer Ivo Andrić. Andrić was himself a convinced Yugoslav, and we will note the ways in which his description of Njegoš coincides with his own position a bit later in this work. In his essay "Njegoš as Tragic Hero of Kosovo Thought," Andrić does not speak directly about *The Mountain Wreath*. Rather he concentrates on Njegoš's personal situation, seeing him as a synecdoche for Yugoslavia as a whole: "The tragedy of this struggle was sharpened and deepened by the unavoidable fratricidal battles that our difficult history has frequently provided. The tragedy was all the greater for Njegoš in that from his high point of view, like all the great and light-bearing souls of our history, he could capture at a glance the totality of our nation, without differentiating between belief or tribe."[73] But by characterizing Njegoš with a paraphrase taken from Bishop Danilo, Andrić turns *The Mountain Wreath* into a fully autobiographical work. Njegoš (and Bishop Danilo as his literary stand-in) is seen as having been placed in the same position as Prince Lazar, who, according to the oral poems of the Kosovo cycle, was forced to choose between an earthly and a heavenly kingdom. He chose the latter, leading to his inevitable defeat at the Battle of Kosovo, a defeat that produced tragic situations for all who had to deal with its consequences. As prince-bishop, Njegoš combined in himself the earthly and heavenly kingdom, but no angel of the lord came to ask him which he would choose. He had, instead, to try to balance the two, and it was this tragic balancing act that defined him and, by extension, his greatest work.

Although, as we have noted, the Yugoslav state generally stayed out of the cultural sphere, the canonization of Njegoš as national artist was carried out with enthusiastic government support. Official efforts at canonizing Njegoš in the first Yugoslavia culminated in 1925 when the writer's remains were transferred from Cetinje to Mount Lovćen.[74] This three-day ceremony was attended by King Aleksandar, who praised Njegoš as a poet "whose words, planted in the souls of all our millions, sprouted through the generations like the words of our oral poetry."[75] The entire tone of the ceremonies, which were followed zealously in the Yugoslav press, bordered on a piety more appropriate for the treatment of a saint than a writer.[76] Before the transfer, the coffin holding Njegoš's remains was opened to allow the king and queen to have a look. The coffin was again opened on Mount Lovćen in the presence of the entire Orthodox Church hierarchy of Yugoslavia. And the plaque that was placed above his mausoleum by the king called Njegoš "the immortal apostle and herald of the unity of our people."[77]

Not surprisingly, the event was treated most extensively in Serbia. The two major Serbian literary periodicals, *Srpski književni glasnik* and *Letopis Matice srpske* devoted entire issues to Njegoš the man and the poet, extolling him as the greatest star in the Yugoslav cultural crown. They, too, clearly recognized that Njegoš was both a cultural and a political symbol, as the following quote indicates: "The ceremonies in Cetinje from September 20–23 . . . will by all accounts have historical importance from a political and cultural point of view."[78] The solemnity of the reburial was enhanced by the simultaneous, albeit coincidental, announcement that the Austrian government was returning to Yugoslavia the original manuscript of *The Mountain Wreath*, which had been in their possession since Njegoš had submitted it to the Habsburg censorship. Like the transfer of Njegoš's remains, the return of the manuscript was hailed as a historic moment, and it encouraged the conflation of religious, political, and literary canonization.

Nevertheless, not everyone was willing to make of Njegoš and *The Mountain Wreath* exemplars of Yugoslav culture. For some, the whole process was distasteful and distorting. As one critic complained in an article published at the time of the reburial entitled "Let's Return Njegoš to Literature": "National ideologues have created a prophet out of him, a precursor to Yugoslav thought, and they have placed him as a link in the chain with which they avidly connect Gundulić and Kačić, and then through Strossmayer and Prince Michael to our days."[79] Others disputed the validity of seeing Njegoš as the true heir to the oral tradition. For example, the author of a 1935 article commemorating the one hundredth anniversary of Vuk's recording of the folk poet Filip Višnjić, asserted that "Višnjić, in his song about the revolt against the 'dahija' is quite close to Mažuranić," whereas "Njegoš, as opposed to the folk poet Filip Višnjić and a poet in the folk spirit like Mažuranić, conflates the whole problem of revolutionary struggle and success with the problem of putting into motion and action the physical strength of the fighter."[80]

This position was echoed by Dvorniković, who acknowledged Njegoš's importance and the power of his poetry, but refused to see in him either an exemplar for the Yugoslav race as a whole or the true heir to the oral tradition. In Dvorniković's view, Njegoš's celebration of the Kosovo cycle, and of Miloš Obilić in particular, caused him to slight the true center of the oral tradition, Marko Kraljević. For this liberal ideologist of Yugoslav multiculturalism, Njegoš's refusal to contemplate the possibility that Islam could add anything to the Yugoslav mix was a major error, one that the more flexible Marko was believed to have avoided: "Marko is a hero, and individualist, the guardian of his personal honor and arms, yet he is also a defender of the raja, a fighter for national and human rights. Human rights above all—a quality that Njegoš in his apotheosis of nationalism could not forgive him. The Montenegrins never embraced Marko because he was not an uncompromising Serb and Christian, and he got along well with honorable Turks."[81]

Literary and Artistic Creation, 1918–1941: Multicultural Yugoslav Culture and Its Discontents

If the selection of works from the past worthy of being included in the Yugoslav canon was difficult, reaching a consensus on how to produce new works of Yugoslav content was fraught with even greater complication, particularly given the acrimonious political situation in the new country. In the prewar period, when many of the Southern Slavs were still under Habsburg rule, vague statements of cultural similarity had been sufficient, and it was easy to overlook the practical difficulties of combining the "tribal" cultures into a coherent unity. Now, however, despite the seemingly endless debates that had taken place on the Yugoslav idea before, during, and immediately after the war, even the greatest partisans of Yugoslav unity were constrained to note that concepts such as Yugoslav culture, the Yugoslav person, and the Yugoslav nation needed to be sharpened, especially as they pertained to the contemporary situation. As was admitted in a *Nova Evropa* editorial: "First, to this point the Yugoslav idea has not been clearly defined, precisely delineated, and logically laid out—it lacks its own picture. Second, the whole discussion is governed by a single, shared, united, central tone, from which one can easily and beautifully see that the Yugoslav idea is the most sacred, most sovereign, most chaste, greatest, most useful, and best of all the ideas that we have had to this point. When we put these two things together we reach a paradox: that the most essential is that which does not yet exist!"[82]

Despite the unpropitious political climate, many figures from among all three South Slavic tribes continued the work of their predecessors, agitating for increased inter-Yugoslav cross-fertilization and writing works with an overt Yugoslav message. Such figures could be found even in Slovenia—the best example being the poet and translator Alojzij Gradnik. As a translator, Gradnik provided his countrymen with excellent Slovenian-language renderings of the core Yugoslav texts: the sung poetry and stories that had been collected by Vuk Karadžić and Njegoš's epic *The Mountain Wreath*. In his own poetry, Gradnik frequently dealt overtly with cultural and political themes, as in this poem taken from his collection *De profundis* (1926):

> Smo res družina? Enega imena?
> Smo ene vere? Enega plemena?

Ni jezik drug? Ni volja, misli, duh? . . .
O bratje! Hočemo nazaj k propasti?
Spet v prejšnji mrak in mraz? Pustimo rasti
V vseh srcih le ljubezen, vero, up! . . .
Prostrane domovine so dobrave,
Ne glejmo nanje, bratje, iz nižave!
Stopimo na najvišje naše gore!
Samo z gora se vidi vrelo zore
In le z vrhov v bodočnost daljna pot.[83]

Are we truly a family? A single name?
Are we of one faith? A single tribe?
Do not our languages differ? Our wills, thoughts, spirit?
Oh, brothers! Do we wish to go backward into the abyss?
Back to earlier darkness and muck? Let love, hope,
and faith grow in every heart! . . .
The forests of our land are spacious,
Let's not look at them from the canyons!
Step instead into our highest mountains!
The incipient dawn can be seen only from the mountain.
The path into the future is only from the heights.

The opening, of course, is meant to relay as reported poetic speech the opinions of those who doubted the possibility of Yugoslav unity, whereas the thrust to the heights and future points to the unity that will eventually emerge. Poems such as these clearly echoed the "patriotic" tradition of such prewar Yugoslav avatars as Petar Preradović, Silvije Strahimir Kranjčević, and Aleksa Šantić.[84]

Of the great precursors to the multicultural Yugoslav idea, however, only Ivan Meštrović was still active throughout the interwar period, so it makes sense to focus our discussion of interwar attempts to create a multi-cultural Yugoslav culture with a consideration of his work during this time. This effort is complicated by the fact that the sculptor produced a wide range of work in the 1920s and 1930s, by no means all of which could be considered Yugoslav in orientation.[85] Still, throughout the interwar period, Meštrović retained supporters, both Croatian and Serbian, who tried to build his reputation and advance his standing further.[86] Their activities were supported by the artist himself. For although he, like many another Croatian artist, was disappointed with the political directions the Yugoslav state took, Meštrović never stopped producing the kind of multicultural work that had made him the only viable living candidate for the unofficial post of Yugoslav national artist.

It was Meštrović, for example, who received royal commissions to design and build such inherently Yugoslav projects as the mausoleum on Mount Lovćen in which Njegoš's relics were to be housed (the preliminary drawing for this memorial is shown in Figure 4), the monument celebrating the victory in World War I, and the Tomb of the Unknown Soldier.[87] And it was to Meštrović that liberal believers in Yugoslavia turned for comment after King Aleksandar's assassination in 1934. Meštrović recalled:

The last time the King and Queen visited Zagreb, apropos of the famous assassination attempt that the King accidentally escaped, in a long conversation I tried to convince him of the need to take better care, since the enemies of the nation were watching him carefully, seeing in him the personification of Yugoslavia, which they would dearly love to destroy. He said to me, "What do you want, I know that anything could happen to me. I must be prepared for anything. But those who think that in destroying me they will destroy Yugoslavia are wrong. I am just one person, but Yugoslavia was built by many before me, and it will only be stronger if I fall."[88]

It is worth pausing for a moment to consider Meštrović's Tomb of the Unknown Soldier at Avala, some ten miles outside of Belgrade. As Benedict Anderson has noted: "No more arresting emblems of the modern culture of nationalism exist than cenotaphs and tombs of Unknown Soldiers. The public ceremonial reverence accorded these monuments precisely *because* they are either deliberately empty or no one knows who lies inside them, has no true precedents in earlier times. . . . Yet void as these tombs are of identifiable mortal remains or immortal souls, they are nonetheless saturated with ghostly *national* imaginings."[89] By commissioning a tomb to the unknown Yugoslav soldier in the 1930s, King Aleksandar was quite obviously trying to cash in on the unificatory symbolism that such a monument was supposed to provide.[90] And what better way for a Serbian king to show his Yugoslav feeling than by asking the Croatian sculptor Meštrović to plan and build it?

In its very layout, the tomb was meant to symbolize Yugoslavia's role as mediator between East and West, for the monumental portals, supported by gigantic caryatids clad in folk clothing from various regions of

FIGURE 4. Ivan Meštrović, design for Njegoš's mausoleum on Mt. Lovćen. Published in *Nova Europa* 11, no. 1 (Jan. 1, 1925): 9.

Yugoslavia, face in those directions. (See Figure 5.) The diversity of the caryatids' origins not only recalls the variety of the peoples of Yugoslavia but implies that all have contributed their part to the unity symbolized by the presence of a single unknown soldier (rather than one from each part of the country). In its inclusion of avowedly non-Serbian figures, the tomb indicates that Meštrović's multicultural conception of Yugoslav culture had evolved since the days of the Kosovo temple. Whereas then traditionally Serbian themes were rendered in Western form, now non-Serbian material was incorporated on the thematic level as well. At the same time, the monumental figures also clearly invoke the caryatids Meštrović had carved for the Kosovo temple. In both cases, a monument to male heroism is supported and introduced by stiff, gigantic female figures that are given the task of expressing what Ivo Vojnović called "the dumb petrified terror of century upon century."[91] By the time Meštrović finished the tomb in 1938, however, the symbolism would have seemed quite different. In the wake of Aleksandar's assassination and the ominous clouds gathering over the country it must have been tempting to see the completed work not as the grave of some unknown soldier, but rather as a cenotaph for the ideal of a multicultural Yugoslavia.

Despite his continued presence on the Yugoslav cultural scene, however, Meštrović and his art were attacked furiously from many different angles in the interwar period, and his heroic multicultural synthesis ultimately failed as a basis for a contemporary Yugoslav culture. The reasons for this failure are complex, but they are worth looking into because it was through implicit and explicit criticism of Meštrović's work that other, productive versions of Yugoslav culture were advanced.

A number of critics, both Croatian and Serbian, questioned Meštrović's claims to have captured the essence of the Yugoslav nation, however

FIGURE 5. Ivan Meštrović, Tomb of the Unknown Soldier, granite, 1933–38. Avala. Photo courtesy of the University of Notre Dame Archives.

defined. Thus, although not denying the artist's plastic talent, Miroslav Krleža, an astute observer and keen critic of art, could not help but note that whereas Meštrović's themes were Yugoslav enough, his artistic technique had nothing to do with any national traditions, nor was it original.[92] Krleža produced a long and careful formal analysis to prove that Meštrović's sculpture, despite what the artist himself might have thought, had nothing to do with religion, Yugoslav nationalism, or anything other than pure sculptural form. All the rest were merely verbal interpretations that had been grafted onto Meštrović's work by various opportunists, incompetent critics, and foreigners who wanted to see Yugoslavia as an antidote to German civilization. "Meštrović comes from Vienna, that same Vienna against which Meštrović's sculpture is used in the political battle as a symbol of national liberation."[93] Because Meštrović was "a Catholic, a Croatian, a Viennese secessionist, whose work has nothing in common with the Byzantine foundation of the people's character" his art was rejected as a possible basis for a new national art.[94] Of course, it would have been equally possible to say that Meštrović's eclecticism, his ability to combine traditional Serbian themes with an openness to European art that was more characteristic of the Croatian tradition, was precisely the only method of creating a new synthetic Yugoslav art. But what Krleža found objectionable was what we would now call the "fakeloric" aspect of Meštrović's works. In this he was probably a bit unfair, since, as Meštrović and his closest supporters pointed out, the oral epic had been part of his life from childhood. It was his earliest artistic memory and, what is more, in using European techniques to express these themes, Meštrović was not going against any national traditions, since in sculpture there were none for all intents and purposes.

The openly European nature of Meštrović's technique discomfited many Serbian critics as well. As we have seen, King Aleksandar was a Meštrović supporter, and the artist received a number of important commissions to provide monumental works for Belgrade. But these were by no means always acceptable to local officials or to the public, who saw in Meštrović's work the contamination of their own traditions by foreign methods. Such criticisms came to a head in the controversy that surrounded the erection of Meštrović's statue *Victory* in interwar Belgrade. This larger-than-life statue depicts a classically proportioned naked male warrior carrying a sword and an eagle. It was originally commissioned as the central element of a fountain to celebrate Serbia's victories in the Balkan wars of 1912–13. When World War I began, however, Meštrović had finished only this one figure. After the war, the Belgrade municipal government decided not to construct the entire fountain, but merely to place the finished statue in Kalemegdan Park in the center of the city (Figure 6). This decision was greeted with howls of dismay by Belgrade's bourgeoisie, who asked, "Why was the statue naked and should it be, and how is it possible to imagine a victor without peasant shoes and a soldier's cap [the traditional trappings of a Serbian warrior]?"[95] (See Figure 7.) Thus, as Krleža had predicted, Meštrović's European classicism modified by contemporary central European technique proved incomprehensible and unacceptable to large numbers of Serbs. The only art they were willing to accept as truly Yugoslav was one built in all respects on their own traditions.

On the other hand, some Serbian critics, most notably the renowned poet Jovan Dučić, took the opposite tack. Dučić discussed Meštrović in an article whose overall goal was to define what is Serbian about Serbia, and in so doing Dučić pointed to a mystical and religious feeling that he claims is expressed primarily in oral poetry.[96] He asserts that all "guslari" are in fact Serbs, even if they changed their religion so that they now look like others. As opposed to Krleža, Dučić is perfectly happy to admit that the Kosovo temple did indeed capture the spirit of the national epic. But, according to Dučić, Meštrović was able to do this because he, like many Dalmatians, was actually descended from Serbs who escaped from the Turks to Dalmatia. Thus, whatever he may think, he is not a Yugoslav at all, but merely a Serb in disguise. As a result, Meštrović's so-called Yugoslav synthesis is seen as actually Serbian culture.

As if this were not bad enough, Dučić goes on to say that although Meštrović's later work is undeniably talented, it is disappointing and foreign to him because it shows that the artist had succumbed to "Catholic mysticism." Here, he clearly has in mind Meštrović's religious sculpture primarily. Of course, in the Orthodox tradition, there is no free-standing religious sculpture, so Dučić cannot accept this work as something that reflects Meštrović's true nationality (that is, Serbian). It can only be treated as a foreign influence. Thus, as far as Dučić is concerned, the source of Meštrović's style is unimportant. Insofar as he produces sculpture that is related

FIGURE 6. Ivan Meštrović, *Victory* monument, bronze, 1913. Kalamegdan Park, Belgrade. Photo courtesy of the University of Notre Dame Archives.

to Serbian themes he is simply a Serbian, and when he doesn't, he is an antinational Catholic mystic. Dučić separates what Meštrović and the Yugoslav unitarists of his stripe desperately wanted kept together. You can either be a Catholic sculptor or a Serb, he says, but there is no way to combine the two.[97]

Meštrović was also open to attacks from the left in the interwar period: led by the writers Miroslav Krleža and August Cesarec, leftist-oriented critics derided "nationalist" works like the Kosovo temple as examples of passé romanticism. Such works may have had their raison d'être before the war, but, from their point of view, in the new conditions of postwar Yugoslavia, Meštrović's work symbolized nothing more than national false consciousness, an artificial attempt to create the impression of a unified nation. Insofar as it succeeded in fostering such an impression, it masked the fact of class struggle, which they saw as the characteristic feature of the new Yugoslav state. As Cesarec put it in an essay entitled "The Vidovdan of Bats": "Instead of thinking about what 1919 means to us, they [Meštrović and his followers] go back to 1389 and on the ruins of our generation they serve up a funny stew about a resurrected Kosovo, about Tsar Lazar's legacy; all about the past and nothing new."[98] Such criticisms were echoed in other sources. For example, a cartoon that ran in the Belgrade daily *Politika* during the height of the controversy surrounding *Victory* showed, under the caption "A Proposal for the 'Victory'" Monument, a caricatured corpulent capitalist atop a pedestal at whose base were a group of cripples wearing their World War I uniforms.[99] Although this cartoon did

FIGURE 7. Ivan Meštrović, *Victory* monument, bronze, 1913. Kalamegdan Park, Belgrade. Photo courtesy of Northwestern University Libraries.

not have anything to say specifically about Meštrović's sculpture, it certainly implied that the realities of interwar Yugoslav life were nothing like the clean, classical statue the artist had created. (See Figure 8.)

By the late 1930s, it was obvious even to Meštrović's most ardent supporters that Yugoslavs were not going to accept him as their national artist. Even worse from their point of view was that this rejection indicated the failure of the Yugoslav nation-building project in general. For if Meštrović would not serve, then who conceivably could? A certain tone of peevishness can be felt in the admission of this fact by Meštrović's great supporter Milan Ćurčin, the editor of *Nova Evropa*, in an article devoted to complaints about Meštrović's *Crucifixion*, which had been hung in the rededicated St. Mark's Church in Zagreb. Ćurčin expresses amazement that though Meštrović is acclaimed in the advanced countries of Western Eu-

ЈЕДАН ПРОЈЕКТ ЗА СПОМЕНИК „ПОБЕДНИКА"

FIGURE 8. Cartoon from the Belgrade daily *Politika*, May 20, 1927, 1. The caption reads, "A Proposal for the 'Victory' Monument."

rope both as a great artist and a prophet of Yugoslavdom, in Yugoslavia it-self, everyone seems unhappy with his work.

And it is not just his "Christ" or his "Pieta," which, in the opinion of our people "don't fit" with their surroundings, with the environment in which the artist thought them up and in which he placed them. . . . People from Zagreb or central Croatia, even the best educated, cannot forgive Meštrović for his early works in which he celebrates in stone "Serbian Kosovo" and Serbian heroes; and they don't know and don't feel that those heroes and those folk songs are just as Croatian as they are Serbian, and that Meštrović drank in their spirit and meaning with his mother's milk. But, on the other hand, Serbians from Serbia won't accept Meštro-vić's folk heroes and victors in bronze as their own—they aren't wearing soldiers' hats and peasant shoes! [100]

In a word, what happened to Meštrović was the worst fate that can befall a synthesizer. Rather than being accepted by the two sides as a bridge be-tween cultures, he ended up being seen as a foreign body by both.

While literary and cultural critics busied themselves proving that Meštrović's art was either nonnational or nonsynthetic, a new generation of artists, mostly writers, appeared on the scene with fresh ideas about how a Yugoslav culture could be created. Many of them had no quarrel with the basic goal of cultural synthesis, but they did object to the specific synthesis that Meštrović had proposed because of his resolutely unironic approach to the material of folk culture, because of his heroic stance, and/or because he limited the sources of his inspiration primarily to the Serbian Orthodox and Croatian Catholic traditions. Regarding the first two issues, Meštrović was a worthy heir to Njegoš, who had also made use in a straightforward way of the heroic ethos that characterized much of South Slavic traditional poetry. But what had been a reasonable artistic approach in the 1840s was perceived by many as completely passé by the early twentieth century. Al-though this point of view was rarely expressed directly in criticism (except in that of Krleža and Cesarec), it was implicitly present in a whole series of literary works, primarily Serbian, in which the oral epic base was taken not as something to be reproduced in all its antique patriarchal heroics but rather as a springboard to a new kind of art, one that would refer to the epic without reproducing its ethos. This ultimately ironic attitude toward the oral poetic heritage marked a completely different path to creating a Yugoslav art, undermining Meštrović's approach from within, as it were.[101]

Although, as we noted in the previous chapter, some literary works that called into question the heroic model of Yugoslav culture had been produced even before the war, the direct experience of World War I produced a strong antiheroic reaction and changed attitudes of the many writers and artists who had participated in it. After the mindless slaughter they had seen over the course of four years, it was difficult to find solace in the optimistic, heroic, and collective ideals that had fired their minds and hearts in the immediate prewar period. This collective loss of innocence, which was typical not just in Yugoslavia but throughout Europe, helped usher in an artistic era pervaded by an introspective, often pessimistic gloominess and a concern with individual perception, and encouraged parodic treatment of earlier ideals.

Perhaps the best example of the parodic approach to the heroic Yugoslav tradition is Ivo Andrić's first published story "Djerzelez u hanu" (Djerzelez at the Inn) from his triptych "Put Alije Djerzeleza" (Djerzelez Ali's Journey). The central action of the story itself involves the eponymous hero, a legendary figure drawn from Yugoslav Moslem culture, who is known more for his strength than for his intelligence and whose impulsive personality is reminiscent of Marko Kraljević's. Here, he is made a fool of by a number of travelers at the inn, who convince him first of all that a beautiful Venetian woman guest is available for the taking and who devise a sham footrace to demonstrate who among them is most worthy of her. To the delight of all, Djerzelez runs like a madman, his lust and desire to perform a heroic feat having blinded him completely to the reality of the situation. At the end of the story, a dejected Djerzelez is compelled to saddle his own horse and flee the site of his humiliation. As the critic Marija Mitrović convincingly puts it in her analysis of this story: "Andrić begins his prose career with a description of the movement of his hero from sung poetry into the most coarse and severe prosaic reality. It is truly an anti-epic, anti-heroic story that deconstructs the aureole of glory that had been created in poetry,"[102] and, one might add, in the sculptural synthesis of Meštrović.

But the story is significant not merely for its destructive power; in addition to debunking heroic mythology Andrić greatly extends the range of subject matter considered as part of an implied Yugoslav world, depicting an imagined Yugoslavia far broader than the Serbian Orthodox, Croatian, and Slovenian Catholic axis. The story takes place at an inn near the Bosnian town of Višegrad, where a remarkably broad cross-section of individuals has gathered:

Sulaga Dizdar with three tax collectors traveling on business; two Franciscan friars from Kreševo who were going to Istanbul in connection with some kind of suit; an Orthodox monk; three Venetians from Sarajevo with a young and beautiful woman. It was said that they were ambassadors from Venice traveling overland to the Porte—they were carrying a letter from the Pasha in Sarajevo and were accompanied by a bodyguard, but they held themselves aloof and looked dignified and suspicious. There was a trader from Serbia with his son, a tall quiet youth with a sickly red face.[103]

To be sure, Andrić depicts his Moslem hero ironically, but in placing him at the center of his story, he opens for consideration the question of how the Moslem heritage can be incorporated into the Yugoslav synthesis. Andrić's implicit invitation to broaden the perception of the nation to include not merely Serbs, Croats, and Slovenes was taken up by a number of other writers in interwar Yugoslavia, many of whom treated Moslem characters with a great deal of sympathy.[104] One story typical of this trend is "Turčin" (The Turk) by the Croatian writer of Yugoslav inclination, Dinko Šimunović. The story is narrated by an older man who recollects a scene from his childhood. He says that his mother taught him to pray and as part of the prayer asked for him to be defended from "unbelievers and apostates." He continues: "And among the unbelievers and apostates were Turks, Jews, Ristians (Orthodox), Lutherans, and Freemasons. About Turks she knew only that they believed in Mohammed, enslaved, burned, and killed; about the Jews that they had killed Jesus; about the Orthodox that their priests married and they didn't believe in the Pope, while regarding the Lutherans and the Freemasons she knew nothing other than that they were enemies of God."[105] It is clear from the narration that in this part of Croatia such unbelievers were part of the cultural memory but did not live in the immediate vicinity.

The narrator goes on to describe a day when a poor Moslem farmer arrives selling hazelnuts. The boy, who has never been allowed to speak with a "Turk," happens to be outside alone, and they begin to talk. The man seems quite nice, so the boy goes in to ask his mother to buy some nuts. She comes out and begins to talk to the Moslem also, discovering from his conversation that they do indeed believe in God, and in heaven and hell as well. She asks: "If you believe in God and the soul, and in heaven and hell, how can you have several wives? Keep their faces covered and lock them up like livestock." He replies: "My dear woman, who does such things? Only the agas, beys, pashas, and viziers! . . . They can because they are rich and they don't work, their peasants work for them. I have only one wife, like the other peasants. She works with me and the children in the fields, and she has never covered her face. . . . If you want me to tell you the truth, I'll say that I heard in Lebanon that some rich Christians had two or even three wives, they just don't keep them in the same house."[106]

The story ends with the Moslem giving the poor Christian boy a small pocket knife as a present, and he notes: "And as she watched him go my mother thought for a long, long time. . . . That her heart was changed from that day on I could tell from the evenings when we would pray before the icon. . . . There were no more prayers only for those 'under the wing of the one church of salvation,' rather a wish that God would bless and give happiness to all good people."[107] No wonder the writer Vladimir Nazor, in his obituary for the author praised him by calling him a "nationalist" (which, in the context of 1933, meant a Yugoslav nationalist).[108]

At the same time, by no means did every writer in Yugoslavia espouse a multicultural synthesis as the best path of development for Yugoslav literature. For the first time in the cultural history of Yugoslavia, writers appeared who attempted to avoid any traditional "national" themes no matter how defined. Their attitude was forcefully expressed by the great Serbian poet Miloš Crnjanski:

Everywhere today one feels that thousands and thousands have passed by corpses and ruins, that they have gone around the world and returned home looking for ideas, laws, and life as it was. They have searched for the old familiar literature, for well-known comfortable sensations and interpretations of ideas. They want the lyric poetry of eternal, everyday metaphors, that dear mish-mash of verses, images, and chrysanthemums. . . . But new ideas have arrived, new inspirations, new laws, and new morals.[109]

The fact that the political situation in postwar Yugoslavia also failed to correspond to the ideal synthesis that the prewar nationalist youth had desired only exacerbated the general mood of disillusionment and helped create a climate in which a nonnational literature became possible to imagine. The Croatian poet Augustin (Tin) Ujević described the pervasive attitude perfectly in a 1922 interview: "As Augustin I spent my early youth in an idealistic struggle for our national liberation and unification, expending a lot of words and dreams. Liberation and unification have come in a formal sense, but things have remained the same as they were."[110]

But cultural and political disillusionment were not the only factors pushing interwar Yugoslav culture away from homegrown models. A great many of the writers who debuted during and immediately after the war had spent many years living and working in Western Europe. As a result, they were not only in tune with the latest developments in European culture but their self-image differed from that of their older contemporaries. Instead of seeing themselves as provincials who needed to absorb some superior European culture, they came to believe that despite their geographical marginality they could be cultural equals involved in the same project as their European counterparts. They groped toward a new way to create a shared Yugoslav culture, not by combining folk and national elements with Western European formal devices, but rather by producing a true modernist literature in the Serbo-Croatian or Slovenian language. It should be added that none of the writers involved in this effort actually claimed to be proposing a new model for Yugoslav culture as a whole. Nevertheless, a careful examination of the work of the major writers of this period shows that the groundwork for such a culture was indeed in place by the late 1920s. As had been the case with the evolution of Yugoslav culture from the romantic Serbianizing synthesis of the mid–nineteenth century to the heroic multicultural synthetic route exemplified by Meštrović, the appearance of a new cultural model did not mean the disappearance of older ones. Instead, all these cultural models coexisted.

Any number of interwar writers could be examined to illustrate the shift from a multicultural synthetic culture to a purely Western modernist model, but I would like to concentrate on Tin Ujević.[111] Ujević, as noted above, was extremely active in the nationalist youth movement just before World War I. His prewar poetry is marked "by his craftsmanship in the sonnet form and his thorough knowledge of earlier Croatian literature."[112] He spent the war years living in Paris, however, and the poetry he published after his return to Yugoslavia was strongly influenced by Western European trends including, in Ujević's own words "much craziness, dadaism, surrealism."[113] At the same time, readers were quick to recognize that despite foreign influences, Ujević's voice, in his best lyrics, was strikingly personal and original, and his use of the language brilliant.

A poem of 1925 entitled "Desetgodišnjica vlažnoga humka" (The Tenth Anniversary of a Moist Barrow) can serve as an example both of Ujević's original use of Serbo-Croatian as well as his affinities with modernist European poetic trends. In its subject matter the poem records a typically modernist neoromantic hymn to an ambivalent faith in the resurrective power of love and the creative process. As the poem opens, the lyric voice proclaims the violence of its suffering:

> Patnje moga mozga još od malih nogu,
> rezanoga makazama!
> Glava je otpala od tijela, ja čekam smrt na pruzi[114]

> From my earliest youth, the suffering of my brain,
> sliced by scissors!
> My head has fallen from my body, and I wait death by the tracks.

The free verse form immediately signals Ujević's distance from his more traditional contemporaries and his affinity with the European avant-garde. This affinity is underscored as the poem continues by frequent alliterations, unconventional poetic lexicon, references to a wide variety of places and figures drawn from world mythology, as well as "futurist" images of railroads and runaway trains:[115]

> Više je vozova prostrujalo kroz moj mozak
> prepun zemljotresa
> sa zahuktanim lokomotivama

> Many trains have streamed through my brain
> full of earthquakes
> with rushing locomotives.

Although it would be hard to claim that there is anything particularly "Yugoslav" about this text other than the language in which it is written, the poetic "I" does give one indication of his specific location; characteristically, it is at the intersection of East and West. Thus, on the one hand, he hears "echoes of Nordic lyres," whereas on the other he prepares to set off for Teheran and Isfahan. The poem ends with the lyric voice proclaiming his oxymoronic life in death:

> Ja sam već desetljeće mrtav,
> i otada živim u grobu
> sa smislom, i s bolom, i s dušom,
> u grobu moje vatre.

I have been dead for ten years,
and from that time on I've lived in my tomb
with sense, with pain, and with my soul,
in the tomb of my fire.

Ujević also illustrated in his behavioral patterns a new sensibility, bringing with him from Paris a bohemian mentality that often took on grotesque forms in the conventional cultural world of interwar Yugoslavia.[116] His outlandish behavior caused him to be deported several times from Belgrade, where he lived on and off throughout the 1920s. It was of significance that Ujević chose to live in the traditional Serbian capital, and a look at his publication venues in this period shows that he was equally at home sending his work to Serbian or Croatian journals, an indication that he considered his work at the very least pan-Yugoslav.[117] He lived in Sarajevo from 1930 to 1937 and in Split in the years just before World War II, all the while proclaiming himself Yugoslavia's first and only truly European artist.[118]

But however attractive it may have been to some interwar intellectuals, the idea that a new Yugoslav culture could be created solely on the basis of the most up-to-date European models was problematic given the realities of interwar Yugoslavia as well as the mindset typical for South Slavic nationalism. Flaunting one's individuality simply did not fit very well with the collectivistic bent of South Slavic national thought, and no writer, no matter how talented, could create an individualistic culture from scratch. A devastating literary critique of this cultural attitude forms one of the central elements of Miroslav Krleža's 1932 novel *Povratak Filipa Latinovicza* (The Return of Philip Latinovicz). Krleža, who has been described as the great "naysayer" of Yugoslavia, took obvious pleasure in skewering the social and cultural givens of interwar Yugoslavia.[119] The novel, which combines the archmodernist theme of the "portrait of the artist" with a Freudian-inflected return to the origins plot, is clearly allegorical. Through the novelistic depiction of Philip, Krleža takes on the question of whether a European modernist sensibility can provide a coherent cultural program for the country. Although Philip is not a bohemian in the style of Tin Ujević, he shares with him and with many other Croatian and Serbian intellectuals and artists the experience of years of living abroad.

Philip is a successful modernist painter who has been living in Paris for many years. And as his last name indicates, he is the carrier of European cultural values in a generic Central European shell. Just before the action of the novel begins, Philip has had a midlife crisis that expresses itself in a fragmentation of the universe and a collapse of perception: "For quite a while Philip had noticed how all objects and impressions fell apart into details under his gaze. . . . Colours, for instance, the living source of his warmest emotions, were beginning to fade in his eyes."[120] His return home, figured as a search for his real father, is a Freudian-inspired attempt to overcome present psychic dysfunction by coming to understand childhood traumas. Simultaneously, it is an escape from civilization and its discontents to the pastoral beauty of the Croatian countryside.

At first it appears that the combination of a Western European sensitivity with the muck and mire of interwar Yugoslavia will be invigorating. "Everything round Philip was so natural, so real and alive, that it captivated him with its sheer genuineness: he revived in the blue open spaces, full of genuine light and unadulterated scents."[121] As time wears on, however, it becomes clear that the "European" path will not provide a solid basis for a Yugoslav culture. In the first place, Philip recognizes that though the natural world of Pannonia might be invigorating, even a shared native language cannot disguise the fact that he and the uneducated local inhabitants have nothing in common. He comes to this conclusion while sitting with Joe Podravec, a local cabman: "Two men were seated there on that box-seat: one of them an eccentric neurasthenic, a sectarian in painting, a relativist, a fauvist, a colourist, and they spoke the same language, and yet actually they were two languages and two continents!"[122] As incomprehensible as the man on the street may be, however, he is still preferable to the local European-educated elite. These men and women (all friends of his mother, including the man who turns out to be his father) have absorbed all the buzz words of advanced European culture, but they are nothing more than vulgar caricatures. Krleža, one of the great polemicists of the century and a convinced Marxist, draws these individuals in the vilest and blackest colors possible.

Eventually, Philip finds a kindred soul in Bobočka Raday, an equally displaced person in the Croatian wilderness. Initially it appears that their union might provide a fulfilling basis for some kind of Europeanized local culture (or that it will at least allow them both to escape), but this final hope is dashed in the end of the novel with the bloody murder of Bobočka by her former lover, Baločanski. In the final scene, which is in fact a revision of the last scene of Dostoevsky's *The Idiot*, we see Philip as a latter-day Prince Myshkin who, far from being rejuvenated, has been utterly destroyed by the realities of interwar Yugoslav life.[123]

Just because Krleža skewered both Meštrović's heroic multicultural synthesis and Ujević's European-oriented modernism does not mean that he was opposed to Yugoslavism. As Stanko Lasić, one of the most subtle critics of Krleža has put it:

His [Krleža's] Yugoslav orientation is an attempt to create a new foundation for a literary entity that would be a "third way"; that is, a Yugoslav answer to the battle of the Eastern and Western cultural spheres. . . . His thought about Yugoslav literary unity was based first and foremost on Starčević's call for resistance, self-reliance, and the affirmation of native values and strengths. At the same time, the material with which Yugoslav literature was to oppose Europe and its particular myths was not Starčević's idea of [Croatian] national identity but Gaj's idea of national self-abnegation in favor of a Yugoslav literary totality.[124]

Lasić goes on to point out that in the 1920s Krleža proposed an even grander and more untenable synthesis, hoping to graft a "progressive" (that is, proletarian-oriented) point of view onto his version of a Yugoslav literature. In fact, however, in his own literary work, Krleža was too independent, too individualistic, and too idiosyncratic to follow any kind of party line.

The only leftist-oriented Yugoslav writer who did manage to bring his work in line with progressive internationalist (read incipient socialist realist) trends, was Krleža's frequent collaborator August Cesarec. Born in Zagreb in 1893, Cesarec was the son of a leftist carpenter and was himself a convinced Marxist from his youth. His earliest poetry, published just after the war, makes up in youthful internationalist ardor what it lacks in polish and subtlety, as the final lines of his poem "For an Eternal May 1st" attest:

> O braćo moja, o armije crvenih boraca širom čitave kugle,
> sa grebena se smrtnog maknimo u borbu posljednju
> za vječan Prvi Maj, za večan Prvi Maj!
> Za bratimstvo čovječje vječno![125]

> Oh my brothers, oh army of red warriors spanning the
>   entire globe,
> let us go from the deadly mountain into the final battle
> for an eternal May 1st, for an eternal May 1st!
> For the eternal brotherhood of humankind!

However, in his mature fiction of the late 1920s and 1930s, much admired in Communist-era Yugoslavia, Cesarec succeeded in creating a new model for a Yugoslav national literature. Like the work of Tin Ujević and Miloš Crnjanski, it rejected a multicultural model grounded on a synthesis of the traditional South Slavic folk and national cultures in favor of a supranational approach. But rather than basing his supranational cultural vision on Western modernism, Cesarec oriented his toward internationalist socialist realism. In the oft-quoted formulation of Zhdanov, socialist realism has as its task "the true and full depiction of reality in its revolutionary development." Under the conditions of so-called achieved socialism in the USSR, this approach was not conducive to the production of great fiction. In interwar Yugoslavia, however, where the disjunction between reality and ideal could be embodied as that between actual life in the country and some potential revolutionary future, it worked fairly well. As one Communist-era critic describes it, Cesarec's work encompasses "the reality of Yugoslavia under the Karadjordjević sceptor. It is full of violence, elementalism, hopelessness, victimization, insanity, and evil."[126] But this portrait of "life as it really is" is always leavened by the presence of "people worthy of their humanity, antitheses of evil," representatives of "life in its revolutionary development."

Thus, despite the political instability and nationalist posturing that marked the first Yugoslav state, cultural critics, artists, and writers worked hard to devise and implement a culture that could serve the country's nation-building needs. The strength of belief in some form of a Yugoslav nation among South Slavic elites in this period can perhaps best be measured by the fact that despite all the political problems of the interwar period and despite the horrific nationalist excesses that characterized the war years, there was great support for the reconstitution of Yugoslavia after the war.

At least three different models competed for the Yugoslav cultural crown in the interwar period, however. The first, a multicultural synthesis that borrowed from the traditions of all three of the constituent Yugoslav tribes had already been proposed in the prewar period as a substitution for the initial unitarist, essentially Serbian model that had been characteristic of the romantic period. The multicultural model was exemplified in the heroic sculpture of Ivan Meštrović and canonized by his many admirers, and it was a fixture of the Yugoslavizing cultural discourse of the interwar period. At the same time and in reaction to dissatisfaction both with Meštrović's synthesis and political conditions in the country, two new models for a Yugoslav culture appeared. Although neither the Western-oriented modernists nor the Soviet-oriented leftist internationalists overtly proclaimed that their supranational approaches could serve as the basis for a Yugoslav culture, these two models were to compete for dominance after World War II. The latter, with its built-in collectivistic orientation, had a significant advantage given both the inclinations of the Communist leadership and the basic tendencies of South Slavic nationalist thought.

3

Supranational Yugoslav Culture:
Brotherhood and Unity

In the aftermath of the Nazi invasion of Yugoslavia in April 1941 the country collapsed. The Germans and their allies split the country into pieces, and the ease with which they did so was an indication not just of their overwhelmingly superior military force, but also of the fact that constant interethnic political squabbling had at least temporarily overshadowed any strong feelings for the concept of the Yugoslav nation among the populace at large. The Germans kept for themselves parts of Slovenia as well as all of Serbia (where they installed a puppet civilian administration) and gave their Italian allies most of the rest of Slovenia, some of the Adriatic coast, and all of Montenegro, Kosovo, and Western Macedonia. The Hungarians took a small chunk of Slovenia and about half of Vojvodina, and the partition was completed with the award of the rest of Macedonia and some of Southern Serbia to Bulgaria. In addition, the Germans set up the so-called Independent State of Croatia (NDH—whose territory included all of Bosnia and Herzegovina as well as Croatia proper) under the command of the Ustasha terrorist leader Ante Pavelić.[1]

When Pavelić and his coterie took over the reins of government, their priority, indeed their obsession, was the elimination of Serbs from NDH territory.[2] Considering that there were some two million Serbs in the NDH, it is perhaps not surprising that this task seemed to take up almost all the Ustashas' energy, sometimes even to the dismay and amazement of their German and Italian allies. There is some dispute about the number of Serbs ultimately massacred by the NDH during the war years, but most historians cite a figure of close to one million.[3] Genocide was, however, merely one part of the Ustasha plan. For, as the Catholic Church (which played a leading ideological role in NDH affairs) taught, the purgation of the external source of sin could achieve nothing if it was not accompanied by an internal purification. Thus, the elimination of the Serbs had to be accompanied by a new affirmation of Croatian national identity. The nurturing of Croatian national consciousness in the citizens of the NDH was the job of the novelist Mile Budak, the NDH minister of religion and education. He was in charge both of drumming up support for the new regime among creative artists and inculcating Croatian nationalist views among the youth. It was he who "ensured that the young were taught to honour the medieval Kingdom of Croatia, whose red-and-white chequerboard emblem now appeared on the flags of the NDH and the sleeves of Ustasha troopers."[4]

In other areas of the former kingdom, separatist nationalism was less encouraged than in the NDH. Certainly, it was to the advantage of any occupier to exploit existing animosities among the various national groups under its control. At the same time, encouraging nationalist feeling ran the risk of awakening desires for autonomy that the occupying regimes had no desire to whet. Ultimately during the war, outside of the NDH it was only in Serbia that an avowedly nationalist group (the Chetniks under the command of Draža Mihailović) garnered substantial support, and it did so outside of official channels.[5] Unlike Pavelić, whose only interest was the creation of an ethnically pure Croatia, Mihailović retained some feeling for the Yugoslav concept. His vision, however, was of a monarchy consisting of ethnically pure enclaves, including, most importantly, one for the Serbs that would have comprised all of Serbia, Montenegro, Bosnia-Herzegovina, Srem, Banat, and Bačka. Since many of these territories were inhabited in part by other national groups, it would be necessary, according to Mihailović's plan, to cleanse them of unwanted elements. Although in their attempts to carry this plan out his men sometimes engaged in large-scale killings, it appears that, at least for Mihailović, cleansing implied exile rather than murder.[6] What is more, unlike Pavelić and his Ustashas, Mihailović and his men did not have the resources of a nominally independent state to advance a coherent nationalist ideology. Rather, they took advantage of existing Serbian nationalist feeling among the peasants of central Serbia.

The Communist-led government that came to power in the aftermath of World War II was well aware of the savage intertribal fighting that had claimed at least one-half of the total casualties sustained among Yugoslavs. They believed, and probably correctly, that the roots of this fighting lay in the failure of interwar Yugoslavia, particularly the constant conflict between Serbs and non-Serbs that had been its most characteristic and tragic feature. In the political arena, there had certainly been ample cause for resentment, as the Belgrade government had undoubtedly, sometimes with malice aforethought, sometimes not, slighted Yugoslavia's non-Serbian citizens. In the cultural arena, the situation had been far less dire, but there remained a deep-held suspicion on the part of many non-Serbs that Yugoslav nation building, particularly state-sanctioned Yugoslav nation building, had in fact been nothing more than an attempt to Serbianize the country. As we have seen, this was not necessarily the case. Nevertheless, it became an article of faith in postwar Yugoslavia that any and all overt unitarism was actually disguised hegemonism, and it was a cornerstone of official state policy that no further attempts at forced unitarism would be made.

Tito and his followers were not about to repeat the mistakes of the royal administration, but neither were they prepared to give up control over the country as a whole. Their political solution was the paper creation of a federal system (as enshrined in the 1946 Constitution) in which equal rights were vested in six national republics (Croatia, Slovenia, Montenegro, Macedonia, Bosnia-Herzegovina, and Serbia, with the latter including the autonomous province of Vojvodina and the autonomous region of Kosovo-Metohija). At the same time, central control was assured by reserving true political power in the country for the fully centralized Communist party. Thus, as one historian put it succinctly: "A study of the formal constitutional provisions does not convey the reality of Yugoslav society in the early post-war years. Just as the autonomy of the republics and the communes was severely circumscribed by the centralised nature of the administrative hierarchy, so the structure of government was controlled by the Communist Party."[7]

Regarding the "national question" the new government trod a fine line. Before the war, the Communist party of Yugoslavia had been a strong supporter of unitarist Yugoslavism, even before such a policy had officially been embraced by the government.[8] And though the Communists' attitude toward unitarism wavered during the 1930s, they never really abandoned it.[9] However, the Yugoslavism envisioned by the Communists was, at least theoretically, quite different from that which had been proposed by most other interwar unitarists. As we have seen in the previous chapter, interwar unitarism was based fundamentally on a racial principle: the three constituent Yugoslav peoples were seen as one, and differences between them were ultimately inessential. The goal of the majority of the unitarists, therefore, was to effect a synthesis of the separate national cultures into a new Yugoslav culture, thereby recreating a unified Yugoslav people and nation. The Communists, on the other hand, "maintained that the creation of a new supranational 'universal' culture was fully compatible with the flourishing of individual 'national cultures' in a particular multiethnic country."[10] Such a supranational culture went beyond the national to the ideological, and it would overarch and connect the national cultures rather than eliminate them. As such it was potentially sympathetic to the supranational strategies that had arisen during the interwar years as a challenge to the vision of a unified multicultural Yugoslavia.

During World War II, of course, rather little could be done to establish a supranational organization. Although the central committee of the Yugoslav Communist party continued to function during the war, the partisan groups that did the bulk of the fighting were organized at the local, rather than the national, level. This policy was dictated by the conditions of German, Italian, Bulgarian, and Hungarian occupation, which made reliable communications with any center difficult and at times impossible. It was also an effective strategy to rally members of the various nationalities, many of whom were suspicious of integrationist tendencies.[11] Nevertheless, the Communists always envisioned the creation of a single postwar state, rather than a collection of independent Yugoslav nations. Their slogan, during and after the war, embodied this dualism; they fought for "the brotherhood and unity of the peoples of Yugoslavia."

This locution was meant to be a replacement of the concept of the "three-named people" that had dominated the royal government's attitude toward the national question, and it had a number of advantages. First of all, it could be interpreted as being more inclusive because the "peoples of Yugoslavia" were clearly a more diverse group than the Slovenes, Serbs, and Croats, who had been the only recognized source for Yugoslavs between the wars. Certainly, the national idea had now expanded to include Macedonians (officially recognized for the first time as a separate South Slavic people), and by the early 1960s it expanded further with the recognition of the Bosnian Moslems as a national group. Even non-Slavic groups were theoretically included, although the retention of the country's name called this into question. Second, the plural "peoples" rather than "people" implied a recognition of and tolerance for diversity. No longer was the goal of the country to be the recreation of a unified ethnos. Rather, any unity would have to be created on some other basis, at least theoretically.

Examined closely, however, "brotherhood and unity" was no less problematic a formula than the Trinitarian one it superseded. After all, unless brotherhood and unity are understood to refer to separate things, the slogan is an oxymoron. Unity, if it could be achieved, would result in full agreement and synthesis, whereas brotherhood, although it certainly emphasizes closeness, implies difference and potential disagreements of all kinds. In addition, and in this respect there was little difference between the interwar and postwar formulations, the citizens of the country were still viewed solely as members of a given nation. The state was understood to be constituted by agreements among the nations, rather than as an aggregate of individuals, each one of which had, in theory, a direct contractual relation to the state. In this context, personal and cultural realization was conceived as possible only within a national envelope. To be sure, the envelopes were now more numerous, but the country was still oriented toward communitarian rather than individual values. This would prove a major problem in the 1960s, when federal structures weakened.

Throughout most of the 1950s, the authorities tried to make it appear that the centrifugal force of brotherhood and the centripetal force of unity were in equilibrium, but this balance was more apparent than real. Particularly in the years after the split with Stalin, when Yugoslavia felt itself to be entirely surrounded by hostile states, unity was the far more important element and the central government tended to control all significant activities. What is more, even in the cultural sphere the expectation was that some kind of homogenization would eventually occur, even if it was not being forced and even if it did not require the elimination of the national cultures.[12] Indeed, such an outcome was in keeping with the general principles of Tito and the men surrounding him, who had, from the very beginning, "felt that Yugoslavia would be unified, solid, that one needed to respect languages, cultural differences, and all specificities which exist, but that they are not essential, and that they can't undermine the whole and the vitality of the country."[13] Nevertheless, and this is crucial, the maintenance of central control was made a great deal easier by the presence of an attractive new national formula that helped convince Yugoslavia's citizens that the government was not merely replaying prewar unitarism.

As a matter of practice the two prongs of the brotherhood and unity formula were understood to apply to different objects, and the objects to which they referred changed frequently depending on the context. During the war and until the 1948 split with Stalin, brotherhood was generally understood to refer to the "fraternal struggle" of the various nations of Yugoslavia to free themselves from fascist invaders and internal traitors. But this brotherly struggle was always seen as having been subsumed by an essential unity that derived, in theory, from the partisans' shared belief in communist ideals and the fact that they worked under the overall ideological umbrella of Tito's party (even if ties had frequently been quite tenuous during the war). The story of the war in this interpretation was, one might say, the postwar Yugoslav creation myth. It became the theme for a huge number of central texts that were designed, among other things, to define a new version of Yugoslavism.

Starting in the mid-1950s, however, the war began to recede from the collective memory, or, at the very least, it could not be counted on to provide an ideological underpinning for both poles of brotherhood and unity forever. The concept of worker self-management, which was introduced in 1950, became the second great Yugoslav myth: insofar as it explained how Yugoslavs would work, on their own, after the Tito-Stalin split, it can be seen as a kind of debased expulsion from paradise myth. Because worker self-management was billed as a decentralizing tendency, it automatically fit onto the former pole of the brotherhood and unity equation.[14] It was balanced, on the latter side, by the revolutionary struggle (which was now interpreted as having been primarily a unity with separate national contributions muted or ignored), as well as by such centralizing forces as the Communist party (renamed the League of Communists in 1952), the Yugoslav army (which inherited the unity mantle of the partisan fighters), and of course Tito himself.

The ways in which this balancing act were perceived can perhaps best be seen in the following quote from 1961: "Our peoples, who are building socialism, are imbued with the idea and feeling of the need to know and respect things of cultural, artistic, and historical value of the Yugoslav peoples, and have a great need for mutual cultural rapprochement. That feeling is strengthened by the great achievements of unity and brotherhood as the foundation of Yugoslav patriotism."[15] In order to show what progress had been made on this front, this commentator pointed to such all-Yugoslav events as the Yugoslav book fair, the Pula film festival, the Belgrade festival of short films, and the unified programs for radio and television. He also cited the *NIN*[16] award for best Yugoslav novel. He concluded by saying "Our ideal is that the culture of each Yugoslav people, while retaining its own characteristics, should simultaneously become the culture of all the others in a dynamic, united totality."

This dialectic balancing act between separate national and supranational cultures, however, was inherently unstable. As self-management took hold, it "resulted in a kind of social integration, but not into Yugoslav society. Integration was into the local community, nation, or at least into a particular federal unit."[17] This, conceivably, could have been tolerated had the Communists themselves remained unified. But as republican-based groups of Communists asserted their authority, they almost inevitably came to nationalism as opposed to supranationalism. It is possible, of course, that true democratization introduced at this point would have blunted the power of republican-based collectives and led to a much more stable Yugoslavia. But this was a step farther than anyone in the central ruling elite was prepared to go. In any case, we will see what the results of the breakdown of balance between unity and brotherhood were in the next chapter. For now, however, I would like to examine how the vision of a nonnational Yugoslav culture of brotherhood and unity was articulated from the immediate postwar years until the early 1960s.

Education, Language, and Nationalism: 1945–1962

Like all Communist states, Yugoslavia placed a great deal of emphasis on education. A literate population was vital if the kinds of mobilization and propaganda efforts needed to transform the country were to be successful. Education was seen as a tool and a weapon, and the government hoped to make it as universal and uniform as possible. In the first place, this required extending the education system to cover a much greater percentage of the country and eliminate educational discrimination. A comparison of statistical data before and after the war gives an indication of how much was achieved in this area.[18] At the primary school level in 1937–38, for example, children from the more developed Sava (which contained most of Croatia with the exception of the coast), Drava (covering most of Slovenia), and Danube (including the northern parts of Serbia and Vojvodina) *banovinas* (provinces) plus the immediate region around Belgrade comprised 50 percent of pupils although these regions accounted for only 39 percent of the population of school-age children in the country. On the other hand, schooling for children from the Drina (central Bosnia), the Littoral (Dalmatia), and Vrbas (northern and eastern Bosnia as well as the Krajina) banovinas lagged far behind; they provided less than 10 percent of the country's pupils although they made up some 28 percent of its population. At the university level, Catholic students (presumably almost all Croats and Slovenes) took up a bit over 45 percent of the places, whereas Serbs (Orthodox students minus a few Russians) took up a bit under 44 percent. Moslem students made up less than 0.5 percent, although the population of Yugoslavia was 14 percent Moslem at this time.[19]

By the 1952–53 school year, discrimination by region had been all but eliminated, at least in terms of raw numbers of schools and of children in school. Thus Serbia (including Vojvodina and Kosovo) had almost 38 percent of the nation's schools and 41 percent of the students, followed by Croatia with 23 percent of students and 23 percent of the schools, Bosnia-Herzegovina with 19 percent of the students and 14 percent of the schools, and Slovenia with 9 percent of the students and about 9 percent of the schools. This compares to almost identical population percentages for these groups in the country as a whole. In higher education, however, students from Serbia (this group would have also included reasonably large numbers of Hungarian students from Vojvodina) seem to have done better compared with prewar totals. They made up more than 50 percent of students at universities in 1952–53, whereas Croats made up 23 percent. Bosnia-Herzegovina was still woefully underrepresented, with only about 1 percent of students at the university level coming from there. This reflected their lower level of prewar education, one imagines, and indeed the percentage of university students from that republic rose as time went on.[20]

In the interwar period the Yugoslav Ministry of Education had approved educational plans for the entire country (although these were modified, particularly in the lower grades, for Slovenian students). Despite this, however, schools appear to have had a great deal of flexibility in the application of these plans, and, at least in Slovenia, the school literature readers, for example, contained almost exclusively Slovenian writers.[21] After World War II, responsibility for education was at least in principle devolved to the republics (indeed, after 1948 there was no Federal Ministry of Education at all), each of which promulgated its own educational plan. But, as was the case in all other areas, republican freedom was severely circumscribed, particularly in the years surrounding the Tito-Stalin break. The balancing act between central and republican control can be followed most easily by an examination of the program guides that were published periodically by the education ministries of all of the Yugoslav republics.

The first published programs (for grades 1–4) appeared not in 1945 but in 1947. The two-year delay was understandable, considering the extent to which the educational infrastructure of the country had suffered during the years of occupation. In each of the plans pride of place was given to instilling in the students general goals such as "love and respect for their homeland and its peoples," as well as "an appreciation for the principles of brotherhood and unity." The latter formulation was, as we have noted, the most popular catchphrase in the postwar period. Many elements of the curriculum were more or less uniform, including the total number of hours in school (twenty hours per week in first grade, rising to twenty-six in fourth) as well as the basic subjects to be taken—language, history, geography, natural science, mathematics, drawing, singing, and physical education.

Nevertheless, a careful examination of the plans reveals significant differences of emphasis in the various republics; these are most apparent in the treatment of history, interwar history in particular. In Croatia, for example, teachers were given a detailed blueprint and were supposed to treat

Old Yugoslavia and its founding. Our peoples during the First World War, their struggles for freedom from foreign yokes, their unification as the only path to independence, and the construction of a unified state; the dissatisfaction of the masses with the monarchical and centralizing state order (the Vidovdan Constitution); the struggle of the Croatian and other oppressed peoples, the excitation of national and religious hatred by the ruling classes; the murder in the parliament [of Stjepan Radić] and the institution of dictatorship.[22]

The plan from Bosnia and Herzegovina implied that a bit less attention should be paid to the interwar problems of Yugoslavia, or at least it gave teachers a wider latitude in their treatment of them: "The founding of the Kingdom of the Serbs, Croats, and Slovenes. The Vidovdan Constitution and the situation in 1921. The situation from 1921 to 1929; the situation from 1929 to 1941."[23] The amazing contrast, however, is between the Croatian plan and its Serbian counterpart. In the latter, teachers were left entirely to their own devices regarding the treatment of interwar history. They were told to deal with "the founding of Yugoslavia . . . Yugoslavia from 1918–1941," and that was all.[24] Of course, this does not necessarily mean that in Croatian schools children learned in great detail the fact that Serbian attempts at political unitarism had been a major problem in interwar Yugoslavia. Nor does it necessarily mean that Serbian children did not learn about this. However, there is good reason to suspect that children educated in various Yugoslav schools would not have had an identical view of the vital question of what their country had been like before the Communist era.

The differences in educational plans, evidence perhaps of a bit too much brotherhood and not enough unity, troubled the central authorities, and they convened a conference in Belgrade in early 1948 to do something to rectify the situation.[25] Conference participants agreed that three basic theses, couched in customary Communist jargon, should lie at the foundation of any curriculum:

(1) it is necessary to institute a broad and organized struggle for the elevation of teaching and for the proper ideological and political education of school-aged youth. The basis of ideological and political education is Yugoslav patriotism, which means the building of socialism in our homeland, fraternity among the Yugoslav peoples, pride in the achievements of the War of National Liberation, the fulfillment of the five-year plan, and the struggle for a democratic world all over the globe. (2) Teachers must be the most active fighters against all falsifications and superstitions, against mistakes and the seduction of youth by anti-intellectual, mystical, and idealistic trends in society and nature. (3) Teaching must be based on the scholarly foundations of Marxism-Leninism.[26]

In the aftermath of this conference, republican education plans were rewritten in 1948 for the 1949 school year. The new plans were far more similar to each other than had previously been the case. If we look, for example, at the sections dealing with interwar Yugoslav history in the programs for older classes, we find that they are now identical in the Serbian and Croatian versions—closer to the 1947 Croatian variant, but not as detailed—and that the Slovenian and Macedonian plans provide a close translation.[27]

Of all aspects of education, the language and literature curriculum was considered particularly important and was given significantly more time than any other subject. It was supposed, "through the ideational richness and emotional strength of literary works . . . to build in students a scientific outlook on the world, life, and society, and to prepare them for the fulfillment of all objectives in the building of socialism in our country, developing in them a fighting spirit, stamina, decisiveness, self-reliance, and self-conscious patriotism."[28] What this jargon meant in practice for the students who had to learn in Yugoslav schools can be seen from the fervent writing of one educational authority who attended the conference at which the above principles were promulgated: "Our readers should speak not only about the war for national liberation, but also about the industrialization and electrification of our land, they should show examples of heroism in the workplace, the unbreakable brotherhood and unity of our peoples, the democratic spirit of our peoples government, the role of the Peoples Front and the Communist Party, the leading individuals from among our people, the patriotism and peace-loving nature of our peoples."[29]

Given the importance placed on the literature curriculum, it is not surprising that energetic efforts were made by the cultural authorities to eliminate ideologically untrustworthy or otherwise dubious writers from the textbooks, anthologies, and histories of literature that were quickly published to take the place of prewar editions. Among those dethroned from the pantheon of Yugoslav literature were the majority of the most talented interwar writers, including Miloš Crnjanski, Tin Ujević, Stanislav Vinaver, and Jovan Dučić.[30] Religion, the great bugbear of Communist governments, was also eliminated: "In Slovenian textbooks, for example, texts and pictures relating to Christian teachings (the text 'The Virgin Mary Smiles,' pictures of the nativity, etc.) as well as those relating the history of prewar Yugoslavia . . . were removed . . . as were the texts of authors who had published books during the war on occupied territory."[31]

High Communist party officials not only oversaw the educational programs as a whole; they also paid surprisingly careful attention to the individual books that were to be used in the instruction of Yugoslavia's youth. An example of this concern can be seen in an article that was published by the Communist cultural watchdog Radovan Zogović in the party newspaper *Borba* in 1947.[32] Entitled, "A Sample of How Not to Construct 'Samples of Literature,'" it took to task the Croatian Ministry of Education as well as Vice Zaninović, the compiler of an anthology that had been approved for use in Croatian schools. Zogović charged that this anthology contained far too many passages from "decadent" writers (the writers in question were the major figures of the Croatian moderna, one of the most glorious periods of Croatian literature) and did not pay enough attention to the precursors of the Yugoslav version of socialist realism. He ended his article by announcing: "It is shameful that in our country a book like 'Samples of Literature' could appear. And not just appear, but be approved for use in schools for the youth of our new Yugoslavia."[33]

Linguistic policy in the schools of Communist Yugoslavia echoed the attitudes toward literature. As noted earlier, one of the priorities of the NDH government in wartime Croatia had been the inculcation of Croatian nationalism. For Pavelić, the primary carrier of a nation's identity was its language, and the separation of Croatia's cultural (particularly linguistic) heritage from that of Yugoslavia in general and Serbia in particular became of central ideological importance. Mile Budak went so far as to claim that the Serbs had not merely damaged Croatian interests by their political activity but, even more insidiously, by intellectual means: "The Serbs in Yugoslavia distorted and destroyed everything Croatian, and most of all Croatian culture, history, language, and literature . . . on the level of language, they encouraged every kind of barbarism, particularly Turkisms, solely in order to marginalize good Croatian and give the language a Serbian character."[34] This inflammatory claim was absurd, since the Serbianization of Croatian, insofar as it had occurred, was more a product of work done by Croatians of Yugoslav orientation than it was a Serbian conspiracy. But in any case, if Croatian was to be "rescued," radical methods needed to be employed, and much energy was expended during the years of NDH control to "purify" the Croatian language, particularly in the area of lexicon.[35]

Because they had abandoned the claim that the Yugoslavs formed a single nation, the Communist government had no need to prove that the Serbs and Croats were one people. Still, it was obviously vital for Yugoslavia's survival to undo the vitriolically separatist work of the NDH ideologues. One way to accomplish this was by rehabilitating the concept of the linguistic unity of Serbo-Croatian. In the first postwar educational programs for use in schools, the existence of a single Serbo-Croatian language was simply assumed.[36] This was the case in teaching manuals as well.[37] Of perhaps even greater importance was the Novi Sad Agreement on linguistic unity prepared in 1954 and signed by every major Serbian and Croatian writer, linguist, and literary critic. Article 1 of the Agreement read: "The national language of the Serbs, Croats, and Montenegrins is a single language. And thus, the literary language which has developed on its foundation in two major centers, Belgrade and Zagreb, is a unity with two dialects, Ijekavian and Ekavian."[38]

Regarding the other Yugoslav languages, the Communist regime proved more liberal than its predecessor, in part because the republics themselves were given a bit more control of their educational programs. All thought of the possible unification of Slovenian and Serbo-Croatian disappeared, and Macedonian, now recognized as a full-fledged language, became the main language of instruction in Macedonian schools.[39] And though Macedonians and Slovenes were encouraged to learn Serbo-Croatian, which was unquestionably the lingua franca for the country as a whole, instruction began rather late and was given limited time. Indeed, Macedonian school children in the first four grades of elementary school had no Serbo-Croatian at all, whereas students in Slovenia studied a scant one hour per week in the fourth grade rising to two in the fifth and sixth. On the other hand, the official attitude among Serbs and Croats toward the other South Slavic languages was summed up in one of the leading Yugoslav teaching manuals as follows: "The goal is not an active knowledge of these languages, merely a passive understanding."[40] In practice, however, it was a rare Serb or Croat who learned any Slovenian or Macedonian worth talking about, a situation guaranteed by the almost complete lack of original-language texts from these languages in postwar readers.[41]

On the whole, although the formal fact of educational and linguistic decentralization in postwar Yugoslavia might lead one to believe that central control over the educational process had become less intrusive than it had been in the interwar period, in reality such was not the case. Central authorities had ways to make sure that texts and programs in all languages followed the lead of the center when it came to subject matter. Such an approach was entirely in keeping with the Stalinist formula that cultures could be "national in form" provided they were "socialist in content."

Recanonizing the Classics: 1945–1962

The schools were not the only place where the new government's cultural authorities were active. The Yugoslav government believed that cultural works had a major role to play in inculcating the worldview they wished their citizens to acquire. Therefore, works of high culture that could be used to make the kinds of points the regime wanted to emphasize were to be brought to all levels of the population. The question was, which works could be used to reorient the cultural focus of the country from synthetic multiculturalism to supranational internationalism? At first glance, one might have expected that the canonized writers of interwar Yugoslavia would have faired badly. But the Yugoslavs had learned more than governing tactics from their Soviet teachers, and one thing they had come to realize was that with the proper interpretive spin most works of the past could be useful in the Socialist present. As a result, the canon did not have to be changed significantly, it merely needed to be reinterpreted.[42]

The first order of business was to change the way in which the literary history of the country as a whole was understood. As we noted in the previous chapter, it was an article of faith among literary historians in interwar Yugoslavia that a unified national, Yugoslav literature had already come into existence. Such a view did not fit very well with the notion of a Yugoslavia constituted by the union of separate peoples. To rectify this, clichés about "Yugoslav literature [or history]" were generally replaced by "the literature [or history] of the Yugoslav peoples."[43] In this way, at least on the verbal level, the very concept of a unified Yugoslav literature, that darling of interwar cultural theorists, was eliminated.

As usual, however, what was given with one dialectical hand was taken away with the other. Although the idea that Yugoslav culture formed a unity was abandoned, the desire to create a national literary canon only intensified. It was fed, according to Aleksa Djilas, by "outside pressures" that "brought to the fore the need for ideas and policies that would promote integral unity in Yugoslavia."[44] Although this may be true, it is equally true that the recreation of a national canon and its proper interpretation (unity) were inevitable given the new focus on the cultures of the various republics (brotherhood). For whatever reason, however,

the party began to underline especially the deep historical roots of Yugoslav identity and even more to affirm common Yugoslav historical traditions and cultural affinities. It particularly praised 19th-century political and cultural figures who had propagated the Yugoslav idea. Some influential Croatian and Serbian Communist intellectuals even tried to promote a certain romantic revolutionary Yugoslavism and defined the spirit of independence and rebellions as characteristic of the South Slavs.[45]

The latter point is particularly significant because it points up the fact that the Communists were searching for overarching cultural themes (heroism being an old chestnut, as we have already seen) rather than specific forms as a basis for a supranational Yugoslav culture. But after the 1948 split with Stalin pushed Yugoslavia out of the Soviet orbit, a new overarching theme, the idea of Yugoslavia as a mediator between East and West, provided an even better model for a unique supranational unified culture.

In terms of scale, the most intensive effort to create a centralized culture of the peoples of Yugoslavia without repeating the mistakes of the past can be seen in the celebration in 1947 of the one hundredth anniversary of the publication of Njegoš' *The Mountain Wreath*. There were two major stumbling blocks to the creation of a red Njegoš, however. First of all, his work was overtly Serb-oriented. But since this issue had been successfully skirted by their interwar predecessors, postwar Yugoslav critics had home-grown models for dealing with this problem. More worrisome was the fact that he had been one of the central pillars of multicultural Yugoslav culture, as well as a favorite of King Aleksandar. So if Njegoš was to be rehabilitated in the new Communist context, he would clearly have to be freed from the weight of his previous interpretive history as well as his unsavory posthumous associations, all of which required a certain amount of interpretive legerdemain.

One wonders why the Communists bothered, but it must be admitted that in addition to the convenient timing of the jubilee (the first year that the new government had the energy to put on a big cultural show), the work and its author had certain advantages. First of all, he was long dead. As opposed to someone like Meštrović, for example, who had interpreted his own work in a now unacceptably multicultural manner, Njegoš had never suspected that his work would become a supranational Yugoslav symbol. Inconvenient interwar interpretations could be blamed on the ideological mistakes of the period rather than on the author and his work. What is more, Njegoš's ethnic background was felicitous. Since the main lines of cleavage in interwar Yugoslavia had been between Serbs and Croats, it would have been difficult to fete a writer who was one or the other.[46] But as the Montenegrins had never been accused of hegemonic tendencies (even though most of them considered themselves Serbs), Njegoš was someone everyone could accept; and commentators in 1947 made sure to refer to him as a Montenegrin, rather than as a Serbian writer. Finally, the fact that Njegoš had also been a central political figure was of great importance, helping to legitimate the new regime's insistence on a close alliance between politics and culture.[47]

In any event, the June 7 anniversary was celebrated nationwide (the front page of the Croatian newspaper *Vjesnik* on June 9, 1947, for example, displays a portrait of Njegoš with the headline "The celebration of the hundredth anniversary of 'The Mountain Wreath' is a holiday for all the nations of Yugoslavia"), and Njegoš and *The Mountain Wreath* were transformed into precursors of the most up-to-date Communist thought. New editions of *The Mountain Wreath* were published in Serbia, Croatia, and Bosnia-Herzegovina, a new translation appeared in Slovenia, as did the first-ever Macedonian translation (25,000 copies were published in Montenegro alone so that "practically every house in Montenegro will have it").[48]

All the newspapers of Yugoslavia devoted substantial coverage to the event. In *Borba*, the organ of the Communist party of Yugoslavia, four of six columns on the front page for June 8, 1947, were devoted to Njegoš, and his picture was reproduced approximately five times larger than that of Tito and the Romanian prime minister Petru Groze, whose meeting was described in the other two front-page columns. Considering Tito's fondness for oversize pictures of himself, such a layout was indeed a rarity.

As might be expected, however, *Pobeda*, the organ of the Montenegrin "People's Front" contained the most lavish coverage. Seven of the paper's eight pages on June 7 and six of eight on June 11 (the paper was a biweekly) were devoted to the festival. The lead article on June 7, by Niko Pavić, concentrates in one place all of the catchphrases and interpretive moves that were employed at this time to recanonize *The Mountain Wreath* and its creator. After a long summary of some favorite passages, Pavić opines:

For all of these reasons, *The Mountain Wreath* has played a gigantic role in the patriotic and martial upbringing of our younger generations over the past 100 years. This role is no smaller today. Quite the reverse. The War for National Liberation, the most difficult and the most glorious period in the history of our peoples brought it closer to us than it had ever been. Tito's generation embodies, in new conditions and in broader fashion, those very qualities of our people which were the key factor in all their triumphs, those qualities that are sung, with unheard of poetic strength, in *The Mountain Wreath*: self-sacrifice, heroism, the refusal to give in, and the noble hatred of enemies of and traitors to the fatherland, the highest conscience and answerability to the people and history. That is why, during the course of the War of National Liberation, the verses of *The Mountain Wreath* sounded like a password on the lips of our fighters, and they could achieve their heroic feats . . . which enabled the realization of the ideals of national freedom and a better life. That is why when we read *The Mountain Wreath* today we see in its heroes the same qualities we see in the heroes of our war of national liberation. Those same people who perfectly developed and completed the struggle for national liberation, fulfilled the ideals and dreams of the great Njegoš and the heroes of *The Mountain Wreath*. That is why *The Mountain Wreath* is today a true textbook of patriotism for today's and future generations. That is why we celebrate its hundredth anniversary not only as the most important cultural event of the new Yugoslavia, not only as a confirmation of a new attitude toward great people and events from our past, but as a true national holiday.[49]

Of primary importance, of course, is the idea that the partisans of World War II were merely updated versions of the "freedom fighters" Njegoš had described. The uncomfortable fact that Njegoš's work describes, with a fair amount of enthusiasm, the slaughter of a group very similar to that which made up some 12 percent of the nation's population was easily elided by turning what is in *The Mountain Wreath* a homogenous ethno-religious group (Islamicized Slavs) into the more generalized "traitors." Of equal importance is the claim that the simple folk (that is, the workers and peasants who officially made up the backbone of Yugoslav Communist society) both knew and appreciated Njegoš's work. Thus, despite Njegoš's noble background, he was, through his work, an honorary man of the people. It is also noteworthy that the ethic of heroism, such an important component both for Serbianizing unitarist thought as well as Yugoslav multicultural ideology, is preserved intact here.

Commentators vied with each other, finding ever more imaginative ways to provide updated interpretations of Njegoš's great work. The writer of the introduction to the edition of *The Mountain Wreath* published in Sarajevo, Salko Nazečić, had a particularly difficult task in this respect.[50] Considering that a good portion of the book's potential readers in Bosnia-Herzegovina were Islamicized Slavs, it was simply not possible to ignore the fact that the Islamicized Montenegrins were the villains of and victims in Njegoš's epic. Nevertheless, Nazečić found a way to make the book palatable. Njegoš, he claims, was against feudalism and for freedom. At the time the action of the book takes place the Islamicized Slavs were the agents of Turkish feudalism (in this respect, no different than agents of Hungarian or Austrian feudalism among the Croats or Slovenes in other parts of Yugoslavia). As a result, the work can now be read as having nothing to do with ethnicity or religion—rather, it depicts a battle of economic systems. That the feudal representatives happen to be Islamicized Slavs is purely accidental. He then concludes with a virtuosic Stalinist rhetorical flourish: "Many people have, incorrectly, purposely, and in various (always dark and reactionary) ways tried to twist Njegoš's thought, applying it to today's situation—as if in *The Mountain Wreath* Njegoš was defending religious unity in today's conditions!"[51]

The most thoroughgoing reevaluation of *The Mountain Wreath* was provided by the Communist-party culture tsar, Radovan Zogović, in the introduction to the edition published in Belgrade. Like Nazečić, Zogović turns attention away from the ethno-religious background of the work's villains by seeing them as representatives of feudalism. In addition, he uses the popularly anthologized scene of Vojvoda Draško's description of his visit to the Venetians (during which he describes the stark differences between rich and poor and the terrible prisons of Venice) to make the claim that Njegoš was just as much against capitalism, as represented by seventeenth-century Venice (!), as he was against feudalism. What this implied was that he was a kind of protosocialist, an excellent candidate for canonization.

In a move that his Soviet mentors would have found particularly inspired, Zogović insists on Njegoš's realism, although he admits that Njegoš as realist seems a strange concept. Undeterred, however, he goes on to show that Njegoš was actually not merely a realist but a true socialist realist(!) writer. His final peroration employs every trick in the Soviet critical lexicon to redden Njegoš and blacken his interwar interpreters:

Njegoš's realism was closer to new realism [Zogović's term for socialist realism] than to either classical or modern critical realism. Its closeness is revealed in that it is permeated by a kind of martial romanticism, a refusal to submit to the negative sides of life and the world; in that it has positive heroes who, in the conditions of their time, fight for the truth and a beautiful life, for the dignity and happiness of humankind, for the destruction of death; in that his heroes are typical of the environment from which they emerged and which they incarnate; and in the fact that it boils with internal optimism and that noble and great insanity of the bravest of the brave. . . . And this was the poet whom our reactionary critics called a religious mystic, a "good and pious Christian" . . . a pessimist, despairer, etc.[52]

Creating a Culture of Brotherhood and Unity: 1945–1962

Canonization and education were, however, only two parts of a triadic attempt to create a new, supranational Yugoslav culture. Even more important than the preservation and transmission of culture was the creation of new works that would embody a coherent version of Yugoslavism appropriate for the new state. As in all other areas of public life in the immediate postwar period, cultural production was dominated by the dialectic struggle of brotherhood and unity. And, as had been the case elsewhere, no matter how things may have looked on the surface, in the immediate postwar years unity was dominant, pursued with far greater intensity and more far-reaching results than had ever been the case in the interwar Yugoslavia that the Communists never tired of vilifying for its supposedly unitarist policies. Whereas the unitarist interwar government had lacked a definite cultural policy, allowing for a multiplicity of competing cultural models, the Communists attempted to enforce (and more or less succeeded until about 1953) a highly centralized and rigid cultural model. This culture was, however, now defined in Soviet terms and was understood to stand above and outside of any national questions. As opposed to most interwar models of Yugoslav culture (either unitarist or cooperationist), which had shared the belief that a Yugoslav culture could only be built through a synthesis of the separate national cultures, the postwar model strove to ignore questions of national identity altogether. Instead, literature was expected to reflect either the experience of the war years or the reality of the socialist country that was being created.

In the latter case, writers were viewed, in Soviet terms, as engineers of human souls whose task was to depict in an optimistic light all the great changes that were taking place in the country, its electrification, industrialization, and so forth. They were to avoid "formalist" and "decadent" approaches to literature and instead to write about the "great themes of our day" with "a clear and deep understanding of reality, a proper and scientific mode of thought."[53] In order to help young writers succeed in their tasks, a whole series of publications appeared with names such as *Mladost* (Youth), *Mladi borac* (Young Fighter), and *Književne novine* (Literary Newspaper). The standard format of each issue was identical. A poem or group of poems by a neophyte author was presented, and then one or more older critics would criticize the new work. The goal was to create the criteria for a single socialist Yugoslav culture, but the problem was that the critics almost never found anything to applaud in the work they saw. For, unfortunately, when young writers turned to the themes that were expected of them the results were weak and unconvincing, as even the most Soviet-minded critics had to admit.[54] As a result, efforts during the first period of the new Yugoslavia's existence to create a new, unified national culture on the basis of material drawn from everyday life under socialism produced almost no positive results.

The main organs of party control on the local level were the so-called agitprop committees, which "had representatives in every organizational group. Anything of any organizational importance took place under its control."[55] Although such committees were certainly inspired by the Soviet Union, party control through agitprop committees remained in place even after the split with Stalin. The agitprop committees were not disbanded until 1952; the same year saw a major loosening of party control in the cultural sphere in general, as signaled by Miroslav Krleža's epoch-making speech "On Cultural Freedom" at the Third Congress of Yugoslav Writers. There Krleža attacked socialist realism and defended the right of individual writers to describe the world as they saw it. This opened the door to the rehabilitation of modernist writing and ushered in a battle that would last for the rest of the decade between two main cultural groups, the realists (heirs to Cesarec's version of a supranational Yugoslav culture) and the surrealists (legatees of Ujević, Crnjanski, and other interwar modernists).

Even without direct party control, literature and literary criticism in this period showed a strong striving toward unity. Although they disagreed on most other issues, both the surrealists and the realists believed that pluralism in culture was a mistake, and each asserted its own method as the only appropriate one for Yugoslav literature. In debates that recall those of the Soviet Union in the late 1920s, frequent attempts were made to discredit literary foes by recourse to political categories. The modernists were characterized by their enemies as decadent, nihilistic, and overly Western, but they counterattacked by accusing the realists of being petty-bourgeois inheritors of the interwar Yugoslav literary tradition and as closet Stalinists (since their method, the Yugoslav version of socialist realism, clearly derived from Soviet practice). The party generally avoided taking sides in the matter and let the two groups air their mutual gripes relatively openly.[56] It did so presumably because both realism and modernism favored a single Yugoslav culture and conceived of it in supranationalist terms.

When reading accounts of the activities of both main cultural groups in postwar Yugoslavia, one is struck by the fact that although they all talk about a need for a unified Yugoslav socialist culture, there was very little cooperation across national boundaries. In the interwar period, when the emphasis was on the synthesis of separate national cultures, it was common for the editorial boards of major journals to include members from all national groups and from a variety of cultural centers. After the war, however, journals tended to be published in individual cities and were staffed only by members of a single national group. At the time this must not have seemed to be a problem. Cultural issues were no longer linked to nationalism, and, even after the break with Stalin, the old Stalinist claim that culture could be "national in form, socialist in content" seemed convincing.[57] Thus, although Ljubljana journals were staffed only by Slovenes, Zagreb journals by Croats, and Belgrade journals by Serbs, they were all discussing the same cultural problems in the same way. This turned out to be only a temporary phenomenon, however, and the essential lack of cooperation across national boundaries meant that when the project of creating Yugoslav socialist culture was basically abandoned in the 1960s, splits along national lines occurred more quickly and were more extreme than they would have been had there been a tradition of working together.[58]

In the years immediately following the war, through all the cultural infighting, one type of literature stood out as simultaneously popular with readers and able to meet the demands of the cultural authorities for works of a supranational Yugoslav character. These were works that chose as their theme the great founding event of the socialist state, the partisan struggle during the "War for National Liberation." In fact, much literature, some of high quality, devoted to this topic had appeared even during the war itself, meaning that the central categories of the postwar Yugoslav literary myths were already being laid down before the new state was created.[59]

The vast majority of these were poems, most of them in folkloric style. They had the undeniable advantages of brevity, spontaneity, and a connection to a living oral folk tradition familiar to a large number of the partisan fighters. According to one literary historian, these poems expressed "an ethic of obligation—to the creation of freedom and to struggle, to proletarian, socialist, and general human values." These include "a revolutionary attitude, internationalism, brotherhood and unity, Yugoslav social patriotism, as well as individual moral qualities of the fighter and communist: fairness, respect, humility, bravery, humanness, pride, discipline, friendship, etc."[60] What is notable about this list is not necessarily what is included, but rather what is left out: any sense of belonging to a group defined by nationality. The qualities prized in such literature are either those of the individual or of the supranational group, which is generally defined in terms of class. This latter fact is somewhat ironic, because proletarians were by no means the only or even the most important component of the partisans in many regions.

Perhaps the single most influential work of "partisan literature" written during the war was not, however, a book of poems, although it was written by a poet: the Croatian Vladimir Nazor (1876–1949). Nazor's "Yugoslav" credentials stretched far back. Already by the turn of the century the young poet was well known in Yugoslav circles for his Kosovo sonnets (1895–97) and "Kraljević Marko" (1901). These works were among the earliest harbingers of multicultural Yugoslavism. For just as his fellow countryman Meštrović was to do a few years later and in opposition to the romantic generation, Nazor used traditionally Serbian themes but eschewed folk forms, turning instead to the elegant European form of the sonnet. In some respects, Nazor's choice of these themes was even more remarkable than Meštrović's since for the poet, who hailed from the Italianate island of Brač, the Serbian folk epic did not resonate with childhood memories. Nazor's version of Yugoslavism earned him a monograph written by one of Meštrović's most vocal champions, Milan Marjanović, who called him "the poetic pendant of Meštrović's plasticity."[61]

At the same time, Nazor's brand of Yugoslavism was not unalloyed synthesis. He clearly did not believe that Croatian culture would or would have to disappear as Yugoslav culture was created. And indeed, parallel to his work using traditionally Serbian material (and far more frequently), Nazor created poems and poetic cycles on specifically Croatian themes, including *Hrvatski kraljevi* (Croatian Kings, 1904) and *Hrvatski gradovi* (Croatian Cities, 1902–6). During the interwar years, Nazor did not play a particularly active role in Yugoslav literary politics, although he did continue to publish fairly steadily.[62] Like most Croatian writers, however, Nazor appears eventually to have become disgusted with the Serbophilic policies of the interwar government, and when the NDH first formed he may even have contributed some patriotic Croatian verses to Ustasha-sponsored publications.[63] Nevertheless, he was clearly never a mindless Croatian xenophobe, and when he became convinced that the Communists would defend Croatia in any future Yugoslavia, he threw his lot in with them. Thus it was that in 1943 the decidedly middle-aged poet was spirited out of Zagreb to join with the partisan group commanded by Tito himself. He described his experiences in *S partizanima* (With the Partisans), which was written during 1943 and 1944 and became an instant postwar classic; excerpts from it were a fixture of school reading lists in all the Yugoslav republics. In diary form, Nazor describes everyday life with the partisan fighters, his conversations with Tito—"a man with the face of a young lion"[64]—and his own activities in support of the war effort. The book makes excellent reading, particularly because the exciting battle scenes and hyperbolic descriptions of the heroic partisan soldiers are carefully balanced with self-deprecating descriptions of the aging writer suffering from diseases, aches, pains, and the discomforts of war.

Nazor makes it clear that he considers himself a Croatian but that this clearly does not make him any less a Yugoslav patriot in the eyes of the partisans. As he puts it at one point: "I was listening to a broadcast of the partisan radio station 'Free Yugoslavia.' They praised Strossmayer and his broad Yugoslav ideology. The partisans are not anational dreamers, as their enemies claim. My Croatian-ness is not a problem at all."[65] What is interesting about the above passage is the way that Nazor shows the partisans using the nineteenth-century figure of the Catholic bishop Strossmayer to promote a vision of Yugoslavia while simultaneously avoiding any taint of interwar unitarism. As would later be the case with Njegoš, dead nineteenth-century unitarists were clearly deemed the best cultural allies by the Communists. Even so, Nazor finds it necessary immediately to balance the unity implied by Strossmayer with the brotherhood inherent in his Croatian identification. Of course, it should not be forgotten that the fact that such a prominent Croatian was willing to come to the partisan side when the so-called Independent State of Croatia was flaunting its own claims to defend the Croatian nation was one of the primary reasons the partisans were willing to drag Nazor around with them.

In his descriptions of the partisan leaders, Nazor is careful to note their varied national origins, emphasizing again the extent to which the brotherly struggles of the separate Yugoslav nation are simultaneously a unified effort.[66] Nazor's strongest "ecumenical" statement is his "Message to the Dalmatians," which was broadcast on the partisans' clandestine radio station as a recruiting pitch (and whose text is reproduced in full in the "diary"): "Croatian pride, Croatian defiance, and Croatian heroism have been shown through the ages in the deeds of our fathers and forefathers. . . . Beyond Dalmatia an ever crueler war of partisans versus fascists has erupted and continues to burn. Croatians and Serbs, Catholics, Orthodox, and Moslems, bound together by slavery have risen against the occupier" (91). The way in which the brotherhood of separate nations was seen to be joined with their unity of purpose and goals during the war in *With the Partisans* is further emphasized by the replies to the "message" that Nazor received from various fighting units. Most explicit is from a Serbian brigade: "We, sons of the Serbian people, fighters of the second Serbian proletarian brigade will continue the fight along with the other units of our national liberation army which are the personification of the armed brotherhood and brotherly unity of the peoples of Yugoslavia, a fight that will completely crush the hated occupiers, the age-old enemies of the South Slavs" (102).

Although Nazor's ostensibly nonfictional account proved quite popular both in Yugoslavia and abroad, and although a number of well-regarded diary accounts were published in the postwar period, this genre was not destined to become the primary literary vehicle for a description or interpretation of the meaning of the partisan struggle. That role was reserved for the partisan novel-epic, together with its cinematic counterpart. Some of the best-known novels of this type were by the Serbian writers Dobrica Ćosić (*Daleko je sunce* [*Far Away Is the Sun*, 1950]), Branko Ćopić (*Prolom* [The Breakthrough, 1952]), and Oskar Davičo (*Pesma* [The Poem, 1952]), by the Montenegrin Mihailo Lalić (*Lelejska gora* [The Wailing Mountain, 1957]), and by the Slovenians Ciril Kosmač (*Pomladni dan* [A Day in Spring, 1950]) and Miško Kranjec (*Pisarna* [The Office, 1949, *Pod zvezdo* [Under the Stars, 1950], and *Zemlja se z nami premika* [The Earth Touches Us, 1956]).

Although the plots of these novels vary considerably, they share a number of features: they focus on a small, isolated band of partisans fighting against great odds; the partisans, as a rule, are of a single nation, but they share a universalist outlook in distinction to their enemies (who can either be foreign—Germans, Italians, or Bulgarians—or domestic—Chetniks, Ustashas); the plot itself tends to converge around a single action in which the partisan fighters must overcome insurmountable difficulties before they triumph; along the way a number of the most appealing partisan characters are killed. What is more, women characters act not merely as love objects (although they usually play this traditional role as well), but also as partisan fighters, thereby helping to back up the Communists' claims of equal rights for women. Their excitingly romantic descriptions of real-life situations, their ultimate optimism, and their stylistic neutrality and avoidance of the fantastic connect them to the Soviet socialist realist novel that was their model.[67] Nevertheless, Yugoslav war epics were by no means as formulaic as, say, the Soviet production novel.

An analysis of one such novel—Dobrica Ćosić's *Far Away Is the Sun* —will provide a picture of the central features that allowed the genre to embody the postwar myths of brotherhood and unity in fictional form. I choose Ćosić's novel not for its literary qualities, although it does have a certain attractive rough-edged terseness about it, but because it was one of the few postwar novels to become a fixture on reading lists throughout the Yugoslav republics. Thus, it was a work with which most Yugoslavs born after World War II were familiar and one canonized by the educational authorities as telling the story "in the proper way."[68]

Far Away Is the Sun focuses on a group of Serbian partisans. They are entirely surrounded by German soldiers, Serbs loyal to the regime of General Nedić, and the Chetniks of Draža Mihailović. The central conflict of the novel is not provided by the partisan struggle, however. Rather it is within the partisan company itself. The issue is the tactics to be followed by the group. Should they remain where they are, in the region in which they lived before the war and which they are now defending, or should they, in the face of overwhelming enemy forces, break through the German lines and attempt to join up with other partisan forces elsewhere? This conflict is embodied in the arguments between Gvozden, a party member and a brave fighter from the region, and Comrade Paul, the political commissar assigned to the band from the center. In Gvozden's view, Comrade

Paul and his deputy are willing to abandon the region because they are men "without any ties anywhere, and no families of their own to worry about." To the Communist leaders (and it is obvious that the implied author of the work is on their side), Gvozden's opposition, although understandable, is rooted in particularist sentiment unworthy of a partisan. As Comrade Paul puts it in a discussion with a different member of the band who thinks like Gvozden: "Partisans mustn't have such thoughts. It's only the Chetniks who think about themselves and their homes. And that is why they're not fighting for freedom; but we're Communists and we're fighting for the whole nation."[69]

Here in a nutshell is the immediate postwar balance of brotherhood and unity. Whereas in Nazor's work, motivated by the exigencies of the actual wartime situation, the expression of particular nationalism (in his case Croatian) was permitted as long as it went together with an internationalist outlook, in the postwar period an attachment to Serbian or Croatian nationalism was simply unacceptable; it was viewed as a sign of belonging (objectively at least, to use a favorite Communist term) to the Chetnik or Ustasha cause. Although it is true that all the members of the partisan group are Serbs and therefore members of only one of the brotherly nations, they are simultaneously exemplars of Yugoslav unity, which is seen as more important than their particular origins.

This does not mean, however, that the resolution of the conflict between particularity and universalism within the Yugoslav context was without tragedy. In the scene that plays out the victory of unity (and also, by the way, reprises the triumph of discipline over spontaneity that was the hallmark of the Soviet revolutionary novel)[70] the partisan band recognizes that it must execute Gvozden for his objectively treasonous refusal to accede to Comrade Paul's plan. Although the execution is tragic, it is also the cathartic moment that allows for the recognition that the good will ultimately triumph, unity will defeat particularism, and centralized Communist discipline will conquer all tendencies to spontaneous separatism.

That what was important about the group of Serbs described in Ćosić's novel was their metonymic connection to any and all groups of partisans, whatever their particular national origin, would have been far clearer in the context of Yugoslav culture as a whole. For each separate book or movie describing the partisan struggle could be and was seen as merely part of a kind of unconscious collective work that, in its totality, provided a full picture of the interrelation of brotherhood and unity that characterized the war years. We can see this best, perhaps, if we compare the action of Ćosić's novel to the struggle described in one of the first Yugoslav feature films, the Croatian-made *Slavica*, directed by Vjekoslav Afrić in 1946. This movie depicted the partisan struggle along the Dalmatian coast in somewhat melodramatic fashion. Its exemplary nature, as well as its structural similarity to *Far Away Is the Sun* will be clear from the following comment made by one expert on Yugoslav cinema:

The film "Slavica" is built on a structural model which was to be emulated by most of the other early Partisan films of this period. It is a pattern which begins by affirming Partisan-led local initiatives in specific locales, involving the distinctive nationalities of the region, and builds organically to an affirmation of the epic all-Yugoslav character of its leadership and heroes—with Tito presented as the preeminent heroic unifying symbol—and of the all-Yugoslav character of the Partisan fighting forces, which becomes the essential guarantor of ultimate victory in war, as well as the basis upon which to build a completely new Yugoslavia.[71]

Nor did it take post hoc criticism to bring the lessons of *Slavica* home, as the following contemporary review from a leading Slovene newspaper brings out: "Thus the meaning of the film 'Slavica,' despite its many failings, illustrates the success of our young film industry. In its content it shows the life and struggle of a portion of our people at a time of great crisis in the history of the Yugoslav peoples. This life is depicted truthfully and convincingly. The people who live it are part of the collective of all our nations who fought in the mountains of Slovenia, the forests of Bosnia, or on the shores of the Yugoslav sea."[72]

Although literary works dealing with the partisan struggle were the most obvious venue for the expression of postwar conceptions of brotherhood and unity, they were not the exclusive one. The earliest stories of the Croatian writer Antun Šoljan provide a fascinating example of how the theme was embodied in creative works not about the war. In "Bjeloglavi Pavlići" (The Blond Pavliches, 1953), Šoljan's narrator is a young boy who lives in a village cut off from everyone. Most importantly, there are no "others" of any kind to be seen: "There were other people in the village, but I have long ago forgotten them all, because everyone looked identical, like the houses, like the stalks."[73] The narrator himself, although at first he only dimly realizes this, is made uncomfortable by the uniformity of his fellow villagers, particularly because he himself is unable to be happy acting as

they do. At first, he merely separates himself physically from his compatriots, spending his time daydreaming in the cornfields. Later, however, he
comes to realize that he shares a kind of spiritual kinship with the only people in the area who do not look and act like everyone else, the Pavlich family (a father and six sons), who live a bit beyond the edge of town. Although
they have done nothing to attract attention, the Pavliches are hated by the
entire village. As the narrator puts it when recalling that time: "Then I did
not know why they hated them, but now I know. They hated them because
they were different" (256). This, of course, is precisely what makes them attractive to the narrator, and in the story's culminating scene he sneaks up to
the edge of the Pavlich land to observe and, perhaps, to interact with these
strange beings. Ultimately, however, he is unable to bring himself to make
contact with his attractively exotic neighbors, and he rushes home. His failure becomes particularly poignant because soon after this all the members
of the family die, in quick succession, of some mysterious cause. "I thought
about this for a long time. They had their small other world and they knew
the secret of how to live in it. I had the chance to get to know it and I let it
pass. Had I had a bit more courage, had I had a bit more faith, perhaps they
would have sat me down among them at the table to eat and drink" (257).

It is instructive to compare Šoljan's story with "The Turk" by Dinko
Šimunović (discussed in the previous chapter). In both cases, the grown-up
narrator reminisces about a scene from his boyhood in an isolated Croatian
village. In both cases, outsiders are hated, and in both cases this hatred is
completely unmotivated. The major difference, however, is that in Šimunović's story, hatred of the other is seen as something that can be overcome,
not just by the narrator himself, but by the community (as symbolized by
his mother). In Šoljan's story, even the narrator is unable to get beyond the
prejudices of his world, at the time that the story takes place. Although as
an adult he apparently could do so, his earlier inability has led, symbolically at least, to an irrevocable loss. The recognition of the need for contact
and reconciliation with the other came too late to save the Pavliches (there
is some indication that their death was the result of foul play, poison in the
well perhaps, and the narrator appears to feel that had he befriended the
family he might have saved them) and too late for the narrator to learn
what he could have found out from them. It is not very hard to read into
this story an allegorical depiction of pre- and postwar Yugoslavia. After all,
what happened in Croatia during the war was precisely the slaughter of

others—primarily Serbs, but also Jews and Roma. Their loss cannot be made up for after the fact, of course, but the recognition of the need for an acceptance of otherness is the cornerstone of a new attitude in which brotherhood with the other has become not just the unrealized dream of a powerless boy but officially approved policy.

Despite the postwar belief in the marginality of nationalism and the conviction that particular national traditions had no role to play in the formation of a supranational Yugoslav culture, one important contemporary author nevertheless succeeded in entering the postwar Yugoslav canon even though his work did not ignore national particularities. Alone in a friend's Belgrade apartment, surrounded by the chaos and destruction of World War II, Ivo Andrić had ample time to consider the reasons for the failure of interwar Yugoslavia. He certainly knew intimately the kinds of religious, ethnic, and national differences his country had been unable to overcome. After all, he had been born into a Catholic family in the Bosnian town of Višegrad and had therefore grown up a member of a minority group in the most heterogeneous of the South Slavic lands. There is ample evidence that he himself held unitarist views before, during, and after the first World War. As a young man, he had been a sympathizer of the Young Bosnia movement, and he spent much of the war in Austrian internment, evidently for his Yugoslav views.[74] Even before the proclamation of the Kingdom of the Serbs, Croats, and Slovenes, Andrić had helped to found the unitarist-oriented journal *Književni jug*, to which he had contributed his first "Bosnian" story, "Djerzelez at the Inn."[75] He spent most of the interwar period in the Yugoslav diplomatic corps, eventually rising to the crucial post of ambassador to Berlin just before Germany's declaration of war against his country. The fact that he was entrusted with this and other important posts indicates that he did not oppose the Serb-oriented political policies of the royal government.[76]

During the war, Andrić produced his most famous works, the novels *Na Drini ćuprija* (The Bridge on the Drina) and *Travnička hronika* (Bosnian Chronicle). Published to great acclaim immediately after the war, they were immediately proclaimed classics of Yugoslav literature, and excerpts from them became required reading all over Yugoslavia until the time of its dissolution.[77] The reason Andrić the writer and his central novels could be accepted as emblematic of Yugoslavism in the postwar period is something of a mystery. Not only did the novels flout expectations by dealing forthrightly with contested questions of national identity, they also lacked any connection to the favored themes of the day. Even worse, Andrić himself had never expressed any sympathy for Communism. To explain this mystery, one prominent historian has pointed to the culturopolitical motivations of the Tito regime. A cultural icon was needed (a living equivalent to Njegoš, as it were) and Andrić was chosen precisely for the sort of conformism that had allowed him to rise in the interwar diplomatic corps.[78] Although there may be a grain of truth to this claim, it overlooks the fact that there were compelling literary and cultural aspects of Andrić's work that made it singularly appropriate for canonization in this period. In particular, though the apparent thematics of the novels goes against the grain of contemporary expectations for the expression of brotherhood and unity, on a structural level the works reproduce the paradigm perfectly.[79] What is more, they do so not in the messy present, where, as was typical in Communist societies, today's demigod could became tomorrow's enemy of the people, but in a past that was safely mythologized.

Andrić, of course, did not produce his novels with an eye to becoming postwar Yugoslavia's national novelist any more than Meštrović created his sculpture primarily in order to be a prophet of Yugoslav unity. In both cases, however, the artistic form of the works turned out to articulate powerful views of the nation that at least in part coincided with official nation-building programs. At the same time, as artistic works and not policy plans they expressed these ideas in highly complex ways and, what is more, they expressed quite a lot in addition that was of no interest to nation-building politicians. In the case of Meštrović, the artistic mix of European form with folk themes instantiated the possibility of a multicultural Yugoslav nation. In Andrić's case, his two great Bosnian novels chronicled the difficult interaction of the peoples of Yugoslavia through historical time, while yet holding out hope for a supranational union that might bind them together.

The topic of history in the works of Andrić has become a popular subject in recent years, and much interesting work has been done in sketching out both his methods of using historical material and his general philosophical approach to the subject.[80] But the question of the relationship between Andrić's view of history and his view of Yugoslavia has not been proposed precisely. It is necessary to delineate the basic structure of Andrić's historical conception in order to see how it functioned to create a new vision of the imagined community that Yugoslavia could be.

In a passage from the essay "A Conversation with Goya," which a number of scholars have noted to be crucial for an understanding of Andrić's art, the spirit of Goya observes:

There are several points of human activity around which through all time legends appear, slowly and in fine layers. Long perplexed by what was taking place directly around me, in the latter part of my life I came to a conclusion: that it is useless and wrong to seek for meaning in the insignificant, yet seemingly important events that take place around us. Rather we should seek it in those layers which the centuries have built up around a few of the central legends of humanity.[81]

In this view, the historian is simultaneously Eastern storyteller and Western archeologist. And indeed, if we examine *Bosnian Chronicle* and *The Bridge on the Drina* in tandem, we will see that what they provide is an intricately interlocked series of stories that offer the illusion of a scientific and complete picture of Bosnian (and by extension Yugoslav) history. For now let us hold off discussing the meaning of the particular archeological site that is Yugoslavia for Andrić. Instead, let us turn to the question of the proper approach to the subject as it is expressed in Andrić's fiction. For any given site (actual or metaphorical) allows not for one but three potential methods of excavation. One possibility is to excavate fully one particular layer, to work laterally along a horizontal plane. In this way, the complex synchronic interrelations of various people living at a single time can be revealed. An example of such a dig would be Pompeii, where archeologists have chosen to explore the city as it was on one fateful day in A.D. 79 rather than digging down deeper to discover what may have been on the same site a couple of hundred years earlier.

In the realm of fiction, the classic historical novel represents an analogue to this approach. This is the one that structures Andrić's *Bosnian Chronicle*, which focuses on the Bosnian town of Travnik during a relatively circumscribed period of time: the so-called years of the consuls, 1806–13. Andrić's narrative glance ranges widely, however, to include Travnik insiders from among the Moslems, Orthodox, Roman Catholics, and Jews, as well as outsiders like the Ottoman viziers and the European consular officials and their families. Naturally, in telling his story Andrić occasionally alludes to events that took place earlier. But he does so fleetingly, while concentrating on the intricate political and social climate of the period in question. The result is, in effect, a cross-sectional portrait of

Bosnian life at a particular point in history. If a novelist wished to provide a comprehensive portrait of his nation using this genre, he would need to produce a series of longitudinal slices of this type (that was what Walter Scott attempted in the "Waverley" novels). But achieving full coverage this way is obviously an impossible dream, one that even Scott with all his graphomaniacal energy was unable to accomplish. As opposed to Scott and his imitators, Andrić tried to escape the chronotopic limitations of the historical novel, not by the brute force method of writing more and more of them but rather by attempting an entirely different line of attack on his nation's history in *The Bridge on the Drina*.[82]

For Andrić understood that the historian/archeologist can also and with equal justification choose to explore history diachronically, through a vertical examination of a society's *longue durée*. An example of this type of archeological dig would be the reconstruction of the succession of cities on the site of Troy by Schliemann and his successors. Interestingly enough, although this approach is quite commonly used by archeologists, it had never to my knowledge been realized on an extensive scale in fictional form before. In *The Bridge on the Drina* Andrić boldly extends his temporal focus to cover more than four hundred years. But of course, Andrić's avoidance of the temporal limitations that bind the classic historical novel provides not full creative freedom, but rather a different set of chronotopic constraints: on space and character. To accommodate the book's *longue durée*, Andrić narrows his spatial focus, describing only events that take place on or about the bridge itself. What is more, he does not provide nuanced and detailed portraits of each of the historical periods he covers. Instead, each one is sketched lightly, through a focus on a single, almost anecdotal event or person from a chosen period. The separate sections are related to one another only through their contiguity to the bridge. The resulting fictional structure is analogous to the archeologist's core sample. By digging straight down through all the layers in a specific place we get a deep feeling for the various temporal layers of local development, exactly the opposite effect from the one produced by the broad but temporally shallow approach of the classic historical novel. It is, of course, significant that Andrić wrote his vertically and horizontally oriented treatments of history at the same time, for this implies a realization that the two could and should augment each other. Indeed, one might say that with their two opposing but complementary approaches, *Bosnian Chronicle* and *The Bridge*

on the Drina imply a dialogic attitude to history, even as each seems to assert its own, monologic approach.[83]

There is, however, one drawback that these two methods share; both
are ultimately closed structures, overdetermined as it were, one by time
and the other by space. The same thing can, of course, be said of the two
archeological methods described above. But the archeologist has one more
choice; he can dig into the site at random spots along the vertical and horizontal planes in an attempt to avoid being bound by either the purely synchronic or purely diachronic approach. Such a "random" sampling could
conceivably allow for a recognition of patterns that would otherwise remain hidden. I believe that we can discover in an embryonic state a literary
analogue of this technique in Andrić's unfinished and posthumously published collection entitled *Kuća na osami* (The Isolated House). This work
consists of eleven short stories and is generically unclassifiable, although
historical meditations might be the most appropriate term. The conceit of
the stories is that each one represents the narrator's recreation of the life
and times of a particular individual, whose spirit comes into the writer's
isolated house. Each segment represents a kind of random slice of life related to the others solely by its shared place in the writer's consciousness
and the fact that the spirit had once inhabited the area around Sarajevo. Of
course, the choice of stories is not really random; it is possible to guess at
various reasons for Andrić's inclusion of these particular stories and not
other ones. Nevertheless, especially in comparison to Andrić's more tightly
structured novels, this collection produces an impression of randomness,
of openness.[84] The author limits himself to only a few stories, but the implication is that there could be an infinite number of them.

They offer themselves, waken me, and disturb me. And later, when I am dressed
and sit down to work, characters from these stories and fragments of their conversations, reflections and actions do not cease to beset me, with a mass of clearly delineated detail. Now I have to defend myself from them and hide, grasping as
many details as I can and throwing whatever I can down on to the waiting paper.[85]

As was the case with Andrić's two previously mentioned master-
pieces, this work also suggests, although it cannot achieve, the goal of complete historical coverage. Here, to present a comprehensive picture one
would need the life story of every individual who ever lived in the nation,
just as one would need to examine every possible period in a series of hor-

izontal historical novels or every spatial point in a series of vertically oriented books such as *The Bridge on the Drina*. Taken together, however, the three works I have sketchily discussed here exploit all of the possibilities inherent in the archeological metaphor—they point to, although by definition they cannot encompass, the possibility of a full exposition of every story at every historical moment—a God's-eye view of history as it were. Thus, what Andrić's rich fictional experiments do when taken together is to create in his readers' minds the illusion of a vast depth and breadth of historical coverage, the feeling that the full spectrum of national experience has been tapped.

But what holds these three structures together other than their collective realization of the potentials inherent in the archeological metaphor itself? What allows us to see them as not merely three separate entities, but as a kind of unity illustrating the various ways in which a Yugoslav nation could be imagined? In order to answer these questions we must turn from the chronotopic features that made each work distinctive to the elements that remain constant despite the differences. For we must assume that if some things are found on every level of our archeological site, throughout its breadth and depth, then these must be of central importance to that culture—they may indeed be the distinctive features that define it as a nation.

Since *The Bridge on the Drina* remains Andrić's best-known novel, it might be wise to begin our examination of his expression of postwar Yugoslav ideas of nation building with it. Most who have written on the novel concentrate on the bridge itself as the central "Yugoslav" symbol of the novel, a kind of metonym for the country as a whole.[86] Like Yugoslavia, the bridge is seen as that which connects East with West, partaking of both but being neither. Interestingly, when Andrić wrote his novel, the idea of Yugoslavia as mediator between Eastern and Western traditions was not very well developed. It came into political focus with the country's split from the Soviet Union in 1948 and reached its apogee with Tito's leadership of the nonaligned movement in the 1960s. Andrić's novel, therefore, can be seen as a prefiguration and even a possible inspiration for this national self-image.

As a matter of fact, the bridge is a far more ambiguous and complicated symbol than is generally recognized.[87] We are told by the narrator that the bridge was built in the sixteenth century by the grand vizier,

Mehmed Pasha Sokoli, who had been taken to Istanbul from his home village in Bosnia as a young boy, converted to Islam, and had then risen by dint of his talent to the highest posts in the Ottoman Empire. Like all such people, he is characterized by a yawning chasm between his origins, which he does not clearly remember, and his present condition, a chasm instantiated for him in the roaring Drina River at whose banks he was separated from his family and over whose churning waters he was ferried, never to see his home again. He builds the bridge in the hope that by linking the banks of the river, he will be able to close the psychological wounds that tear him apart, "the same black pain which cut into his breast with that special, well-known childhood pang which was clearly distinguishable from all the ills and pains that life later brought back to him."[88] In fact, however, the vizier's attempt at bridge-building therapy succeeds only for a short time: when the bridge is completed the black pain does seem to disappear, but it reappears soon after in the person of an unknown dervish who murders Mehmed Pasha, thereby cutting off forever the bridge's creator from his creation.

The bridge remains an ambiguous presence throughout the novel. Most important, it continues to link and not to link simultaneously. Although it lies squarely on the road that connects Bosnia to Serbia, it never spans the gap between them for the simple reason that it is not on the border. When it is first constructed the land on both sides of the river belongs to the Ottoman Empire. And even after the Serbian revolts of the early nineteenth century it remains firmly planted in Ottoman territory. This does not change until after 1878 when the Ottomans are replaced by Austrians, but now the latter occupy both river banks. The bridge's failure as an international boundary is echoed on the local level, for it does not connect the local people either. Indeed, we see that each community has its own set of legends, its own customs, and its own attitude toward the bridge.

With this in mind, let us return now to the specific details of the archeological site that is Bosnia as it is presented in the novels, for they can help us recognize the peculiar historical dialectic of the nation as Andrić imagined it. A couple of passages taken from *Bosnian Chronicle* should help. In the first, des Fossés, the young French vice-consul, and a character who clearly has the narrator's sympathy, describes a local archeological find in a conversation with his bored and unappreciative superior, Daville:[89]

To a depth of some dozen feet you could see, like geological layers, one on top of the other, the traces of former roads that had passed through this same valley. At the bottom were heavy paving stones, the remains of a Roman road. Six feet above them were the remnants of a medieval cobbled way and, finally, the gravel surface of the Turkish road where we walk today. So, in a chance cross section, I was shown 2,000 years of human history, and in them three epochs, each of which buried the other.[90]

A bit later in the novel, the Levantine doctor Cologna makes a further discovery, which underlies the importance of the archeological approach for understanding Bosnian history. He describes it to des Fossés, the only person in Travnik capable of appreciating the find:

When you make your way through the bazaar, stop by the Yeni mosque. There is a high wall round the whole grounds. Inside, under huge trees, there are some graves. No one knows any longer whose they are. The people know that once, before the arrival of the Turks, this mosque was the Church of St. Catherine. . . . And if you look a little more closely at the stone in that ancient wall, you will see that it comes from Roman ruins and tombstones. And on a stone built into the wall of that mosque you can clearly read the steady, regular Roman letters of a fragmented inscription: "Marco Flavio . . . optimo . . . " And deep beneath that, in the invisible foundations, lie large blocks of red granite, the remains of a far older cult, a former temple of the god Mithras. (265)

In both cases, we note the dizzying array of civilizations that have dominated the region—what is more, by the time Andrić's public was reading the novel, this list had been augmented a few more times. Nevertheless, it is significant that for all the changes, the site des Fossés discovers was and remains a road. One civilization built directly on top of the other, changing the surface forms, but leaving inner relationships intact. Thus, depending on how one chooses to interpret the find, it could either be seen as an example of radical discontinuity or of remarkable continuity. The same holds for Cologna's discovery. The site he describes went from being a pagan altar, to a Roman ritual place, to a church, to a mosque. Again, the dominant civilization changed but the meaning of the place remained the same.

Despite the evidence surrounding them, the residents of Travnik at the beginning of the nineteenth century (Moslem, Christian, and Jewish) all choose to interpret the world as static. The rich local Moslems, for example, see themselves as outside the historical process, a force for permanence in a world that is constantly seeking something new. Their historical wisdom is summed up by the influential and wealthy Hamdi-beg: "We're on our own ground here, and anyone else who comes in is a stranger and won't be able to hold out for long. . . . Many people have come here intending to stay, but so far we've seen the back of all of them" (3). The outside world can offer them nothing but change, and change, in their view, is always for the worse. Therefore, history, at least history as a record of so-called important people, dates, and events, is useless. All they ask for is that "God preserve us from glory, important visitors, and major events" (7).

But it is not only the local Moslems who view history with suspicion and pretend that change does not occur. The attitude of Travnik's Jews is strikingly similar. Toward the end of the novel the wealthiest of them, Salomon Atijas, offers to lend money to the departing French consul, Daville, in recognition of the consul's humane conduct toward the Jews. Daville knows that the vizier recently boasted to have extorted all of the Jews' money, so he expresses amazement that there is anything left to lend. Salomon's answer is imbued with the hard-won wisdom of a people whose historical consciousness lies deep within an insular tradition:

The vizier is really a severe, a severe and hard gentleman. But he has only to deal with the Jews once, while we have endured dozens and dozens of viziers. Viziers are replaced and leave. . . . The viziers go, forgetting what they did and how they behaved, new ones come and each starts all over again. But we remain, we remember, we record everything that we have suffered, how we defended ourselves, and we pass this dearly bought experience on from father to son. (421)

At the same time, Andrić calls the adequacy of this antihistorical view into question in his novel. In the prologue he describes the local beys and their conviction that Travnik is immune to change. At the end of the novel, Hamdi-beg pronounces the townspeople's last word on the eight-year incursion of history: "The consuls will clear out of Travnik. People will refer to them for another year or so. The children will play consuls and khavazes on the river bank, riding on sticks, and then they too will be forgotten as though they had never existed. And everything will be as it always has been, by God's will" (432). Since these are the last words spoken in the novel it might appear that the local population was correct. In fact, however, Hamdi-beg's pronouncement does not mark the absolute ending of the work. Immediately after the last lines of the novel proper we read, "In Belgrade, April 1942."[91] This final statement, in the voice of the author, both indicates the temporal distance separating the author from the period described, and shows how incorrect the beys (and the rest of the towns-people) ultimately were. As Andrić's readers certainly knew, history even-tually caught up with Travnik. The Napoleonic upheaval marked the be-ginning of the end of the Turkish way of life in Bosnia, and the insular tra-ditions of the Bosnians proved to be no match for the forces of change. Nevertheless, the evidence of the archeological site reminds us that at an-other level, the local inhabitants might not have been entirely incorrect. For though external forces may and do change, we do not know how or whether these changes are registered by the local population. Ultimately, we cannot learn this in the framework of a historical novel, for it can only show perceptions at a specific time. If we wish to explore how change and stasis work themselves out over time, we must turn instead to a book whose concern is society's *longue durée.*

In *The Bridge on the Drina* the tension between stasis and change is, not surprisingly, filtered through varying attitudes toward the bridge itself, for, as the narrator tells us, "the story of the foundation and destiny of the bridge is at the same time the story of the life of the town and of its people, from generation to generation" (21). Nevertheless, the implied history of the town itself is by no means limited to the time frame of the novel, long as it may be. As was the case in *Bosnian Chronicle*, archeology reveals the inevitability of change: "On the right bank of the river, on the crest of a precipitous hill, where now there are ruins, rose the well preserved Old Fortress, with widespread fortifications dating from the time of the flower-ing of the Bosnian kingdom" (22). But despite the visible ruins of the once-mighty fortress that stare them daily in the face, reminding them of the transitory existence of even stone things, the townspeople (and the narra-tor as well, it would seem) imagine the bridge as a structure outside of time. Rather than perceiving the bridge as a product of man, everyone chooses to see it as a fact of nature, a part of the landscape: "And the sig-nificance and substance of its existence were, so to speak, in its perma-nence. Its shining line in the composition of the town did not change, any more than the outlines of the mountains against the sky" (71).

The inhabitants of Višegrad, as if infected by the permanence of the bridge, seem equally immune to change, despite the various governments and empires that nominally control their destiny. For example, one of the biggest jolts in the town's existence should have been the cession of Bosnia to the Austro-Hungarian Empire, but as the narrator notes with a tinge of irony, "Thus the great change in the life of the town beside the bridge took place without sacrifices other than the martyrdom of Alihodja. After a few days life went on again as before and seemed essentially unchanged" (134). As opposed to the characters, however, the narrator realizes that no change does not really mean no change; it simply means that people choose not to notice how different things are:

Those same people, who in their own homes maintained the old order in every detail and did not even dream of changing anything, became for the most part easily reconciled to the changes in the town and after a longer or shorter period of wonder and grumbling accepted them. Naturally here, as always and everywhere in similar circumstances, the new life meant in actual fact a mingling of the old and the new. Old ideas and old values clashed with the new ones, merged with them or existed side by side, as if waiting to see which would outlive which. (136)

Ultimately, in Višegrad as in Travnik and Sarajevo, and as in Andrić's own Yugoslavia, the only truly permanent force was the constant interchange between the different peoples who lived on this same, contested territory. This is what makes up the country's peculiar historical value. And these interrelationships are complicated, irrational, and maddeningly permanent. The imagined community of Yugoslavia can only exist by including these competing, inimical, yet closely related groups, and it is ultimately the passion of their static yet ever-evolving relationships that appears in all of Andrić's work, cutting across the chronotopic lines of his fictions.

Andrić puts the raw and dangerous side of this relationship most starkly in a work that is not, strictly speaking, historical—the novel *The Woman from Sarajevo*:

Adherents of the three main faiths, they hate each other, from birth to death, senselessly and profoundly, carrying that hatred even into the afterlife, which they imagine as glory and triumph for themselves, and shame and defeat for their infidel neighbor. They are born, grow and die in this hatred, this truly physical revulsion for their neighbor of different faith, frequently their whole life passes without their having an opportunity to express their hatred in its full force and horror; but whenever the established order of things is shaken by some important event, and reason and the law are suspended for a few hours or days, then this mob, or rather a section of it, finding at last an adequate motive, overflows into the town, which is otherwise known for the polished cordiality of its social life and its polite speech.[92]

But lest one think that riot was the only type of interaction Andrić could imagine, one should recall his description in *The Bridge on the Drina* of Višegrad during one of the great floods: "Turks, Christians and Jews mingled together. The force of the elements and the weight of the common misfortune brought all these men together and bridged, at least for this one evening, the gulf that divided one faith from the other" (77).

Always each group believes that its way of doing things at a particular time and place is as permanent and as "natural" as the Višegrad bridge. But as all of Andrić's historical narratives show, the only permanent thing is their constant conflict, interaction, and interrelationship. No matter how much they may hate each other, no matter how much they may wish to shut themselves off from the various others who surround them, this proves to be impossible. Just as pagan civilization was folded into Roman, as Roman ways were incorporated by the Bosnian or Serbian kingdoms, as the Slavs became part of the Turkish Empire, so Andrić imagined a Yugoslav nation that would be unified through its common legacy of change and stasis. Perhaps individuals would not recognize the truth of their situation, but this truth would be there. Hatred and rivalry would always play important roles, as would cooperation and intermingling. So it had been at every depth and across every width of the archeological site that was Yugoslavia. So it was in the very language Andrić employed, with its extravagant Turkisms and frequently used German terms grafted onto an artificially unified Serbo-Croatian. Recognizing the full difficulty of the situation, Andrić could still imagine a nation created from its history, one in which Cologna's prayer toward the end of *Bosnian Chronicle* might apply: Having described the different archeological layers underneath the mosque, Cologna adds: "You understand, it is all connected, one thing with another, and it is only apparently lost and forgotten, scattered, haphazard. It is all moving, even without realizing it, towards the same goal, like converging rays towards a distant, unknown focus. You should not forget that it is expressly written in the Koran: 'Perhaps one day God will reconcile you and your opponents and establish friendship between you'"(266).

At the same time, although the characters do not recognize it, there is one additional level of overarching truth in the novels. It is provided by the voice and position of the narrator. In the majority of fiction writing, the narrative perspective is either from the inside (some form of first-person narration) or from the outside (third-person). Andrić, however, manages to blur the line between these types of narration, often by presenting his stories through an inclusive first-person plural narrator.[93] For Andrić's narrator in all three historical imaginings is a part of the land and people he describes, the sum total of the Yugoslav historical process, even as he stands outside their lives.

In *The Bridge on the Drina*, for example, though the narrator carefully places himself within the polis of Višegrad, he tries to avoid identifying himself with any single group. The life of Višegrad, the separate lives of its Turkish and Christian inhabitants in their various interrelationships over almost four hundred years are fathomable only because the narrator is one of them. They pass before his eyes less as subjects for description, and more as fellow citizens with a shared destiny.

How many Viziers or rich men are there in the world who could indulge their joys or their cares, their moods or their delights in such a spot? Few, very few. But how many of *our* townsmen have, in the course of centuries and the passage of generations, sat here in the dawn or twilight or evening hours and unconsciously measured the whole starry vault above! Many and many of *us* have sat there, head in hands, leaning on the well-cut smooth stone, watching the eternal play of light on the mountains and the clouds in the sky, and have unravelled the threads of *our* small-town destinies. (20, emphasis mine)

By extension, any Yugoslav reader of Andrić could have felt part of the polis imagined here, for though Višegrad may have been unique, the kinds of people and relationships described in *The Bridge on the Drina* were undoubtedly well known to most of the country's inhabitants.

In *Bosnian Chronicle* the narrator is not quite as closely identified with the inhabitants of Travnik as is the narrator of *The Bridge on the Drina* with the population of Višegrad. Nevertheless, he is not entirely an outsider, as his comment on the riots in town suggests: "This is the typical pattern of the beginning, progress and end of riots in our towns" (143). Once again, the group of people included by the "we" here is far larger than the inhabitants of Travnik itself. It could theoretically include any of Andrić's readers who had come across anything like this, and that certainly included a good portion of Yugoslavia's residents.

Equally important, however, is the narrator's emphasis on his connection to the townspeople (both lifelong and temporary) in his role as chronicler, the synthesizer and ultimate repository of the collective memory that organizes the life of the town. Each group and character in the novel is dominated by a particular historical consciousness, beginning in the first lines of the novel's prologue with the Turks who gather at the cafe Lutvo's: "Not even the oldest people can remember Lutvo, its first proprietor . . . but everyone goes to Lutvo's for coffee and his name is still recalled and mentioned while so many sultans, viziers, and beys have been long forgotten" (1). The narrator is a supra-individual storyteller, the modern-day incarnation of the guslar, perhaps, and it should not be forgotten that guslari were to be found among both Christians and Moslems.

In *The Isolated House* history can exist only insofar as the narrating voice is included, because historical significance in this work is defined in terms of a character's success in capturing the narrator's attention, engaging his sympathetic ear. Thus, Andrić begins the story "Ljubavi" (Loves) in *The Isolated House* as follows:

It is not just separate individuals or groups who appear before my house or descend on my room, requesting something of me, taking up my time and changing the direction of my thoughts. Entire regions or cities, streets and apartments fly in, like light airy visions wafted on memory, and they all want to discover their final form, their proper meaning and explanation here in my manuscript.[94]

Even more important, it is the narrator who illustrates the possibility of knowing truth from falsehood, thereby ensuring the very possibility of the reconciliation of varying, seemingly contradictory points of view. We can see this best if we examine the narrator's role at the beginning of *The Bridge on the Drina*. In the very first chapter, three sets of legends that circulated in the town concerning the bridge are recounted. In each case the legends explain some feature of the bridge itself or the land around it. The first set tells of a pair of twins who were immured in the bridge's piers during its construction in order to appease the "vila" (witch or spirit) who continually prevented the bridge from being completed, and about a black Arab who is said to live in the central pier.[95] The second set concerns a series of depressions in the stone cliffs near the bridge: "The children who fished for tiddlers all day in the summer along these stony banks knew that these were the hoofprints of ancient days and long dead warriors. . . . Only for the Serbian children these were the prints of the hooves of Šarac, the horse of Kraljević Marko. . . . But the Turkish children knew that it had not been Kraljević Marko, nor could it have been (for whence could a bastard Christian dog have had such strength or such a horse!) but Djerzelez Ali on his winged charger." Most importantly, the narrator goes on to note that "they did not even squabble about this, so convinced were both sides in their own belief. And there was never an instance of any one of them being able to convince another, or that any one had changed his belief" (17). Here we see one more example of the ambiguous nature of the linkage provided by the bridge, for it simultaneously connects (insofar as it provides a subject of discussion for both sides) and separates (as there can be no agreement on what a given phenomenon means). The final group of myths has to do with the origins of a tumulus not far from the bridge. The Serbs believe it is the grave of the hero Radisav, who stirred the people to revolt against the bridge and whom the vizier only overcame with great difficulty. The Moslems, on the other hand, counter with the conviction that this is the tomb of a spiritual leader who had defended the spot against an infidel army.

At this point these appear to be hopelessly conflicting stories, and we suspect that there is not nor could there be any way to discover which, if any, are true. But Andrić's narrator does not leave it at this. A bit later, the novel revisits a number of these legends, explaining what the true basis for them was and telling us which version is more correct. The narrator starts his reprise with the assertion that "the common people easily make up fables and spread them quickly, wherein reality is strangely and inextricably mixed and interwoven with legend" (36). And it is precisely this interweaving of stories that gives Andrić's best novels their charm and power. But in the fabric of his work, exuberant storytelling is usually balanced by an overarching narrative voice, as is the case here. First the narrator explains how the legend of the children immured in the bridge came about. While the bridge was being constructed, it turns out, a half-witted local woman gave birth to still-born twins. She could not understand what happened to the babies, and in order to get rid of her, the villagers told her that they had been taken away by the Turks and walled into the bridge. A bit later we discover that whereas the story of the twins has no factual basis, the story of the black Arab in the central pillar does. When the pillar was being constructed, the master builder's assistant, a young African man, was crushed and killed by an enormous stone. The lower half of his body remained entombed in the bridge, thereby providing the basis for the legend (63).

The point, of course, is not whether one or another story is claimed to have a basis in fact. What is important is that whereas the townspeople who live around the bridge do not have access to the truth, whatever it may be, the narrator does. Their stories can be reconciled, and the truth can be known and expressed in narrative. Thus it is crucial to the message of the novel that Andrić's narrator not be a skeptic as to the possibility of knowing the truth, for if the novel is to come to a Yugoslav position various points of view must be weighed and sifted, and the reader needs to know where the truth lies. If the belief that finding the truth is possible were to disappear, the result would be a very different kind of narrative and a different kind of imagined nation.

In the course of the novel we come to see that each of the separate groups that inhabits Bosnia shares its historical space with other nations, and in that lies their brotherhood and their unity. It is ultimately the paradoxical existence of an overarching truth that links people and groups who think they share no common ground that becomes Andrić's central nation-building message. As opposed to his interwar predecessors, Andrić does not claim that difference can be reconciled through synthesis; rather it can only be overcome by stepping outside and above it, by viewing it from the position of a nonnational but sympathetic observer.

In the final analysis, we can say that Andrić's novels provide a unique vision of a supranational point of view that overarches but does not eliminate the views of the various Bosnian nations. In this it echoes perfectly the basic belief of Yugoslavia's Communist political leaders, for whom "the creation of a new supranational 'universal' culture was fully compatible with the flourishing of individual 'national cultures' in a particular multiethnic country,"[96] although it expresses this view in a far richer and more nuanced way than they ever did. Clearly, any national unity Andrić might have imagined for his country could not have been based on fully shared social, religious, ethnic, or political bases since none of these existed. Instead, it is founded on a shared attitude toward the particularities of the national history, a shared worldview across time, space, and ethnic groups in which stasis is conceived of as the norm despite all outward appearances to the contrary and in which change, when it occurs, is assimilated in such a way as to be folded back into a new stasis. The unifying feature in Bosnian and Yugoslav history that Andrić's novels uncover (or, perhaps, create) is the paradox that on a territory that has been characterized both vertically and horizontally by a continuous and radical mix of civilizations and influences, the inhabitants are convinced that nothing ever changes. The tension, or dialectic if you will, between constant change and the constant denial of change drives Andrić's historical narratives and forms a basis for shared nationhood. It goes without saying that the resulting cultural and national richness cannot be perceived by any individual or group within this society, nor can it be fully understood by an outsider. And it is this fact of national culture that helps to explain why Andrić's narrator must be both inside and outside his narratives simultaneously. He must be inside to understand the feeling of solidity and permanence that colors the perceptions of his countrymen, yet he must be outside in order to perceive that the only true permanence rests in the inevitability of change.

The Precipitous Rise and Calamitous
Fall of Multinational Yugoslavia

The Slow Slide Toward Cultural Fission: 1956–1963

The concept of a unified Yugoslav culture based not on a synthesis of the various national cultures but rather on socialist, specifically Yugoslav socialist, values was not without its detractors, even in the heady days of national liberation that immediately followed World War II. In particular, Slovenian cultural leaders were disturbed by centralizing tendencies, which they suspected were merely a mask for a reimposition of the prewar cultural and political status quo. Thus, the Slovenian critic Drago Šega, in response to an initiative for the creation of a "single unified Yugoslav evaluative criterion in our literature" sponsored by the Yugoslav Writers' Association in 1956, complained that the phrase smacked of the interwar desire for "the integration of Yugoslav literature" and "eventual Yugoslav integration."[1] Slovenian critics noted as well that most visions of a Yugoslav literary culture assumed the existence of a single literary language, thereby relegating Slovenian (not to mention Macedonian, Albanian, and other "minority" languages) to the margins. Eventually, even the highest echelons of the Communist party came to believe that a centralized culture would not work, and by 1962–63 Tito "abandoned the idea of Yugoslav integration. . . . He then tried to give greater rein to the federalist tendencies inside the Party and the state."[2] As opposed to the first fifteen postwar years, when in the Titoist formula of "brotherhood and unity" the latter concept had been stressed, the former concept now took pride of place. This turn toward true federalism, as opposed to the pretense thereof, which had been characteristic of Yugoslavia in the immediately preceding years, was reflected in the new constitution of 1963. Among other things, this document affirmed the right of secession to the "peoples of Yugoslavia" (an article that had been absent in the 1953 Yugoslav constitution), and it gave the republics "the right to engage in cooperative ventures among themselves without any role being played by the federal government."[3]

Cultural policy changed to meet the new decentralized vision of Yugoslavia as well. Significantly, for the first time in its history as a state, Yugoslavia gave up the goal of creating some form of unified culture for all its citizens, embracing instead what could be called a multinational self-image. Instead of seeing national cultural particularities as something to be overcome by one means or another, Yugoslav leaders decided to embrace cultural difference and use it as a sign of strength. The multinational vision became an important part of Yugoslavia's external self-advertisement as well. For example, in a report prepared for UNESCO, the section entitled "Cultural Development of the Peoples and Nationalities" began with the statement: "The right of every people and nationality in Yugoslavia to free development and their own cultural identity plays an extremely important part in the life of the country."[4] Note, however, that this formulation implies that there can be no culture other than a nation-based one; groups defined in some other way and, even more importantly, individuals do not have any explicit right to cultural development. This view, as we will see, proved quite dangerous, for it practically guaranteed the strengthening of separate, nationally oriented cultural blocs within Yugoslav society. At the same time, it would be wrong to think that with its appearance the multinational cultural model simply supplanted earlier views. Supranational visions of Yugoslav culture remained strong in Yugoslav society, and it would be best to characterize their interaction as a competition, one in which particularist views eventually triumphed. It was the gradual victory of cultural particularism that laid the crucial groundwork for the ultimate political collapse of Yugoslavia.

Throughout the 1960s and into the 1970s, as the power of the separate republics grew steadily the federal government lost influence. And although the devolution of power to the republics was conceived as a way to minimize nationalist tensions in Yugoslavia—by assuaging the fears of

Croats, Slovenes, Macedonians and others that centralization was merely Serbian hegemony in sheep's clothing—it did just the opposite. Indeed, as Sabrina Ramet has shown, internal Yugoslav relations in this period came to resemble not the interactions of, say, the American states, but rather those of competing countries always ready to "provoke a crisis rather than forego an opportunity to increase [their own] capabilities."[5] By encouraging each of the republics to look after its own interests first, the federal policy ensured that interrepublican cooperation would suffer. There had, of course, always been this potential inherent in the federal arrangements by which Yugoslavia was governed in the postwar period. But the monolithic and centralized nature of the Communist party (and later the League of Yugoslav Communists) was such that particularist tendencies could be and were minimized.

Three events in the sphere of culture marked the change from the relatively unificatory 1950s to the separatist trends of the 1960s. The first of these, what might be called the last hurrah for the dream of a single Yugoslav culture, was the award of the Nobel Prize for literature in October 1961 to Ivo Andrić. The second was the polemic between the Serbian writer Dobrica Ćosić and the Slovenian critic Dušan Pirjevec on the subject of nationalism, and the third was the publication of Miroslav Krleža's *Zastave* (Banners), which appeared between 1962 and 1968.

Andrić was supported for the Nobel award by the Yugoslav government, and his recognition was treated both by Andrić (at least publicly) and by the press as a triumph not so much for him as for Yugoslav culture as a whole. The writer, for example, was quoted as saying: "I think that the award goes first of all to my country. . . . The world has turned its attention to Yugoslav literature. More than 400 works by Yugoslav writers have appeared since 1945 in various countries of the world. The honor that has been given to me encompasses all of Yugoslavia."[6] Interviews published in the communist party daily *Borba* with writers and political figures from all parts of the country all emphasized that the award was to be understood as extending to Yugoslav culture as a whole. The official line was expressed best perhaps by the Macedonian politician Krste Crvenkovski: "Finally, our culture and first of all our literature has received the greatest international recognition. . . . The award of the Nobel Prize for literature to Ivo Andrić is a symbol of the high value both of his work and of the culture from which he emerged, in which he works and which he enriches. I am

more than convinced that throughout the world people will look differently at all the other cultural achievements of our peoples after the award
for the writer Ivo Andrić."[7]

Nevertheless, the Nobel award, that apotheosis of Yugoslavism triumphant, was received against a background of increasing tension between competing visions of the future of culture in Yugoslavia. The writer
Dobrica Ćosić, last seen on these pages as the author of one of the most
popular partisan novels, was at the center of these discussions. In a January
1961 article, he railed against the specter of "vampire nationalisms" and
claimed there would always be obstacles to significant inter-national
(within Yugoslavia that is) mixing "as long as the Republics existed."[8] This
statement provoked a caustic response from the Slovenian critic Dušan
Pirjevec, who accused Ćosić of noticing separatist nationalisms but of ignoring tendencies toward a restoration of a form of forced unitarism that
would inevitably have Serbian hegemonic overtones.[9] In Ćosić's long re-
joinder, an article entitled "O savremenom nesavremenom nacionalizmu"
(On Modern Unmodern Nationalism), the author strenuously denied the
charges that he was in favor of a forced unitarist culture or of great-Serbian
nationalism; rather, he claimed that his view was absolutely in keeping
with the founding ideals of the postwar state, which saw the separate republics not as ends in themselves, but as means toward the creation of a
single socialist Yugoslav culture.[10] According to one historian who has had
ample access to the archival material relating to this polemic, Ćosić's position was supported by conservative Serbian political heavyweights Jovan
Veselinov, Aleksandar Ranković, as well as by Tito himself, whereas Pirjevec's theses had the approval, and even benefited from emendations
made by Boris Kraigher, the most powerful political figure in Slovenia.[11]
If this is true, the Ćosić-Pirjevec debate can be seen as a kind of culturopolitical proxy fight. It reopened the Pandora's box to which discussion
of nationalism had been confined, and that box proved impossible to
close, despite the happy Yugoslav rhetoric that surrounded the Nobel
award to Andrić.

The third major cultural event of this period was the publication of
Miroslav Krleža's epic novel *Zastave* (Banners), which appeared in install-
ments in the new Zagreb journal *Forum*. Krleža can be seen in many ways
as Andrić's antipode in Yugoslav culture—they form the same kind of unbreakable and fascinating pair as Dostoevsky and Tolstoy in Russian liter-

ature. A towering intellectual figure who had already made a literary name for himself during World War I, Krleža was a protean writer who produced major work in every conceivable genre. As was noted earlier, he was a convinced Marxist from just after World War I and had been a bitter critic of bourgeois Yugoslavia, but he himself had been severely criticized in Communist circles for his refusal to submit to party discipline in literature. After the break with Stalin and the decision to allow for greater freedom in Yugoslav literature, Krleža emerged as a key figure. Indeed, it was his epochal speech at the 1952 Congress of Yugoslav Writers that signaled a new era of comparative freedom in Yugoslav literature. Throughout the 1950s, he held a succession of important posts, most critically as the editor of the Yugoslav Lexicographical Institute, and was a constant advisor on cultural affairs to Tito himself.

But although he continued to write prolifically in nonfictional genres, Krleža had published no new prose fiction since 1939. Thus, the appearance in 1962, first of the long-awaited third volume of his novel *Banket u Blitvi* (The Banquet at Blitva) and then of the first and part of the second volume of *Banners* (the rest of volume two, all of volume three, and part of volume four appeared in 1964, followed by the rest of volume four in 1965 and volume five in 1968) created a gigantic literary sensation. The first parts of *Banners* were well received, and they garnered the nation's biggest independent literary award, the *NIN* prize for best Serbo-Croatian novel for 1962. Although there is no proof that Krleža's decision to resume publishing fiction was related to Andrić's receipt of the Nobel Prize, it is hard to avoid suspecting that the proud Croatian chose just this time, at least in part, to compete with Andrić. In any case, as we will see, Krleža's theme in *Banners* marks a clear, albeit indirect, challenge to unitary Yugoslav thought.

Krleža's novel belongs to the fathers and sons genre. Set between the years 1910 and 1922, it follows the fortunes of Kamilo Emerički, Senior and Junior. Throughout the novel, the son is on the side of principle and individual and national freedom, whereas the father defends the side of law and order and is always ready to serve whoever is in power.[12] Krleža's choice of setting was, in and of itself, a significant gesture. By concentrating on the World War I period, Krleža opened the possibility for fictional treatment not of the relatively uncomplicated (at least from an ideological point of view) theme of the partisan struggle, but rather of the far more vexed issues surrounding the creation of the first Yugoslav state. The Emerički family belongs to the old Hungarianized Croatian aristocracy. At the beginning of the novel, Kamilo Senior holds a high administrative post in the Croatian-Hungarian government and believes that the Union of 1868 was the salvation of Croatia. His son, on the contrary, is at a very young age already militantly anti-Hungarian and pro-Yugoslav. Together with his friend Joachim Deák (they are about fifteen years old at the beginning of the novel), he plans to blow up a Hungarian building in Zagreb. Joachim is caught, Emerički Junior's name comes up, and his father exiles him to school in Hungary. There he gets in trouble for refusing to sing the Hungarian hymn and is eventually packed off to Vienna, where he becomes a leader in the Yugoslav student movement before the war.

Krleža's sprawling work is also a bildungsroman of sorts, in that it allows us to watch the growth and development of Emerički the younger. We follow him as he makes a number of clandestine trips to Serbia, but the Serbian-Bulgarian war of 1913 sours him on the idea of Yugoslav unity, at least as it is carried out by the Serbs. Before World War I begins, Kamilo is drafted and almost loses his life on maneuvers. Later in the war he is again almost killed on the front lines in Poland. By the end of the war, after the senseless fighting and killing, he has completely lost his "nationalist" ideals and becomes a Communist lawyer in Belgrade.[13] His father, on the other hand, switches loyalty and becomes a Yugoslav patriot, allowing their endless ideological battles to continue.

What is significant about the novel in the context of Yugoslav culture in the early 1960s is its illustration of one man's disillusionment with the Yugoslav ideal. And although that disillusionment is with the past rather than the present incarnation of Yugoslavia, it is reasonable to believe that, particularly in the context of the Ćosić-Pirjevec debate, many people could have seen connections between the two. By bringing up forcefully the question of what Croatia gained by joining with Serbia (and indeed of whether it gained anything at all), Krleža's novel helped to lay the foundations for a whole series of debates in Croatia regarding the relation of Croatian to Yugoslav culture. What is more, by using the World War I period as a kind of foil to that of World War II, Krleža provided a cultural template for a whole group of mostly Serbian novels of anti-Yugoslav bent that would appear in the late 1970s and early 1980s.

Education, Language, and Nationalism:
The 1950s and 1960s

The effects of the new cultural policies became apparent not merely in works of literature and literary criticism, but also in the more quotidian areas of linguistic and literary education. It will be recalled that in the late 1940s, the central authorities acted quickly to ensure that "unity" rather than "brotherhood" would dominate in the educational sphere. Through the 1950s, however, the central government paid increasingly less concern to this area, and a comparison of the educational plans published in the late 1940s with those of 1960 shows that the republics had already taken advantage of this to produce programs that were beginning to exhibit marked tendencies toward separation. Most of the curriculum remained similar to be sure, but, for example, in the teaching of history each republic had begun to slant coverage so that events unique to it got a bit more space. In the Slovenian program things had gone so far that the life of Boris Kidrič received more attention than did that of Tito.[14]

The most striking difference was in the teaching of language and literature, however, still, as always, considered the pillar of the curriculum. The Ministry of Education of Serbia, for example, provided a full list of texts for use in grades 5–8.[15] Except for texts devoted to Tito and the war (which were supranational by definition), the Serbian program included almost no Croatian authors (the exceptions being excerpts from Šenoa's *Peasant Revolt* in sixth grade and excerpts from Mažuranić's *The Death of Smail-Aga Čengić* in seventh). Of the Illyrians, only a bit of Preradović was provided. Dubrovnik literature of the Renaissance was ignored entirely, as was Croatian realism, moderna, and Krleža. Little was provided from Slovenian, although that literature was probably better represented than Croatian, with excerpts from Cankar, Levstik, and Gregorčič (all in translation, by the way).

The Croatian school program for 1964 was practically a mirror image of the Serbian. The complete list of texts published for use in grades 5–8 was heavily weighted in favor of Croatian authors, with secondary importance given to world and Slovenian literature. Fifth grade students were expected to read oral epic songs, Croatian folk tales, stories by the Slovenians Cankar, Voranc, and Levstik, poems by the Montenegrin Mitrov Ljubiša, and texts by Pushkin and Swift. The sixth-grade program was almost entirely composed of foreign authors—Tolstoy, Gorky, Homer. The Croatians, Šenoa and Ante Kovačić were included, as was the Bosnian Serb Petar Kočić, but there were no other Yugoslav writers. The seventh grade saw the Croatians Ivan Kozarac, Vladimir Nazor, Vjenceslav Novak and Evgenij Kumičić. Serbs included Sterija Popovic, Branislav Nušić, and Desanka Maksimović. Finally, the eighth grade program gave students Mažuranić, Šenoa, Dinko Šimunović, Dragutin Tadijanović, Nazor, August Cesarec, Slavko Kolar, Dragutin Domjanić, Ivan Goran Kovačić, and Vesna Parun. Serbs were represented only by Andrić, Milovan Glišić, Laza Lazarović, and Svetolik Ranković, and Slovenes by Ivan Cankar.[16]

The Macedonian program mandated a reading list almost identical to the one given to Serbian children, although it did add many Macedonian writers.[17] This meant that students whose native language was Macedonian got a fairly good feeling for Serbian literature as well as the rudiments of Croatian and Slovenian literature. They also studied Serbo-Croatian for two hours per week from grades 4 to 8. On the other hand, students in the Republic of Macedonia whose native language was Albanian or Turkish were not taught Serbo-Croatian at all (only Macedonian, three hours per week from the third to eighth grades). They read a tiny amount of Yugoslav literature in Macedonian translation but would have been almost complete strangers to general Serbo-Croat Yugoslav culture. Slovenians also would not have known very much about the culture of the other peoples of Yugoslavia. As opposed to the Macedonians, Slovenes concentrated almost all their students' attention on Slovene writers. Only the most famous Serbo-Croatian writers were to be taught (Vuk, Njegoš, Mažuranić, Zmaj, A. Kovačić, Nušić, Nazor, Andrić, Ćopić, Ćosić), "and other important ones if time allows."[18]

Readers from this period also give some indication of how far apart the various republican educational programs had been allowed to grow. If we take the reader that was used for the eighth and final grade of basic schools in Serbia, we find that in some respects it is quite similar to the readers of the 1930s.[19] But there are many subtle differences. Most important, writers were now strictly classified as Serbian, Croatian, Macedonian, or Slovenian. The lone exception was Ivo Andrić. Although his text was printed in Cyrillic, he was simply called one of "our best contemporary authors." Poetic texts from Slovenian and Macedonian were generally provided in the original (prose excerpts were given in translation), although there were fewer of them by percentage, as well as far fewer Croatian texts than there were in prewar readers. Texts with a strong Yugoslav integrationist message from classical authors were rarely present. What is more, even the ones that were, such as Branko Radičević's "Kolo" were given in excerpts that did not emphasize their all-Yugoslav character.[20] Also present were some Serbian patriotic poems, such as "Srbija se budi" (Serbia Awakes) by Desanka Maksimović, that would have certainly been excluded from prewar readers.

The reader that was to be used in Bosnia in the same grade was extremely different from the Serbian one, indicating how loose centralization had become by this point. It was organized chronologically and thematically rather than by the nationality of the authors and contained different texts (although with some repetition of classics). In addition, a far higher percentage of the reader was taken from foreign, especially Russian literature. There were a few texts from Slovenian (all in Serbo-Croatian translation) and none from Macedonian.[21] This format may reflect the greater importance of Yugoslavism for the mixed republic of Bosnia and Herzegovina as compared with Serbia. The Croatian reader of this period was relatively similar to the Bosnian, although it contained a significantly higher percentage of Croatian authors.[22]

Toward the Collapse of Supranational Yugoslavism in Literature

The short stories of Antun Šoljan provide an excellent literary embodiment of the gradual loss of faith in the supranational Yugoslav project that took place during these years in Croatia. I discussed Šoljan's short story "The Blond Pavliches" in the previous chapter. In that story the narrator's lack of ability to make contact with the Pavlich family served as an allegory for the situation in prewar Yugoslavia, but at least his belated recognition of the need for contacts with the "other" provided grounds for hope in the present. In "Specijalni izaslanici" (Special Envoys, 1957) Šoljan returns to the theme of selves and others. Here, a narrator and his friend find themselves in a bar in an unfamiliar part of their city. Their situation vis-à-vis the bar's regulars is, however, explicitly equated to that of a meeting between people of different nations: "The two of us were sitting in a corner by the window thinking our own thoughts. We were a small but completely independent unit and no one had the right to enter our space, which belongs to us by some higher law. For we were aliens here, foreigners from another land."[23] Lingering a bit longer, however, the narrator and his friend desire ever more fervently to interact with the people who surround them. They observe the strange customs of the locals carefully and are attracted in particular by a group that includes some evidently unattached women. They, too, have attracted attention, and the waiter eventually comes over to their table to say that the women they have been admiring have sent some flowers. It would appear now that all obstacles to "international" contact have been removed. Not only have the foreigners been tolerated, they have been encouraged to join in the mating habits of the locals.

Nevertheless, the story concludes most unexpectedly. The narrator and his friend stand up and face the women, who also stand. But the inevitable meeting that would have overcome the barriers that previously separated individuals on the "false" basis of group identity, the meeting that would have provided a microcosm of ideal Yugoslav development and that undoubtedly would have been depicted had the story been written even five years earlier, does not occur. Instead, the story ends with the following lines: "Everyone stood and waited. . . . We could do nothing. We are special envoys who have been forbidden to make contact, to accept a foreign way of life, or to fraternize. There is nothing we can do. You must understand, dear people, we can't do anything. We stood amongst the dumbfounded people with our hands up, waiting" (278). The despair is palpable, even as it is unclear why, precisely, the young men were unable to integrate themselves. At the beginning of the story, we are told that they chose to come here and did so without the knowledge or consent of their own group. Thus, their appeal to some unnamed people who sent them and gave them orders not to fraternize appears to be nothing more than an excuse to cover their own inhibitions. Šoljan is now saying that it is simply not possible to cross the boundaries that separate nations, much as such crossings are desirable and even necessary (as in "The Blond Pavliches"). Thus, Šoljan presents the impossibility of the realization of the Yugoslav ideal in the tragic key befitting a man who has had, but lost, an ideal.[24] In this he can be seen as emblematic of the culture at large.

An equally telling cultural expression of the gradual decay of supranational ideals can be found in the remarkable novel *Drviš i smrt* (Death and the Dervish) by the Bosnian Moslem author Meša Selimović. First published in 1966, this stream of consciousness novel about the tribulations and temptations of Ahmed Nuruddin, the leader of an order of Sarajevo dervishes sometime during the period of Ottoman rule, owes much to the French existentialist tradition. It brilliantly dissects the mind of an individual in a personal and psychological crisis brought on simultaneously by outside circumstances and his own moral weakness. The plot of the novel is simple but devastating. Nuruddin is unwilling to dirty himself with everyday affairs and uses his position to isolate himself entirely from public life. He succeeds until his brother is arbitrarily arrested. In his attempts to free his brother, Nuruddin becomes entangled in the Byzantine wiles of the Ottoman power system and befriends Hassan, a man whose extended family is close to the levers of power but who has himself rejected the system. Nuruddin's brother is eventually killed, and in order to find justice and revenge himself on those who killed him, Nuruddin allows himself to be coopted into that same system, becoming the highest official in the local organs of justice. At first he believes that his rigorous personal honesty and sense of honor will allow him to control the system, but it eventually swallows him up, forcing him to betray his only friend, Hassan, before itself killing him.

Although on the surface the novel appears to have little to do with Selimović's contemporary Yugoslavia, readers had no trouble recognizing its allegorical depiction of the immediate postwar political situation. The total control achieved by the use of spies, the paternalistic attitude of the authorities, and the aura of fear that surrounds life in all its aspects all echo most uncomfortably the practices of the vanguard Communist party and the realities of postwar Yugoslav life.

Even more significant, the novel implicitly repudiates the vision of contested multicultural Bosnia that had been typical for the novels and stories of Ivo Andrić. It should be recalled that Moslem as a national category had appeared for the first time on the Yugoslav census in 1961. In earlier Yugoslav literature and ideology, Bosnia, with its culturally mixed population, was frequently seen as a microcosm of Yugoslavia as a whole, but this is not the case here. For in the world of this novel, to be Bosnian is to be Moslem. No other cultural groups are depicted, so there is no potential for even the appearance of the kind of supranational authorial synthesis that

Andrić provides. And the consciousness of this group, as recounted by Hassan, by far the most appealing character in the novel, is horribly distorted. He calls Bosnians

The most complicated people on the face of the earth. . . . Until yesterday we were what we want to forget today. But we haven't become anything else. We've stopped halfway on the path, dumbfounded. We have nowhere to go anymore. We've been torn away from our roots, but haven't become anything else. . . . With a vague sense of shame because of our apostasy, we don't want to look back, and have nowhere to look ahead of us. Therefore we try to hold back time, afraid of any outcome at all. We are despised both by our kinsmen and by newcomers, and we defend ourselves with pride and hatred.[25]

It was, perhaps, a similar self-hating view that eventually led Selimović to abandon Sarajevo and to identify himself as a Serbian writer.[26] And insofar as *Death and the Dervish* describes a Bosnia cut off from any outside cultural influences, it contributes to the sense that Yugoslavia is not a country in which various national cultures can interact, but rather a series of separate enclaves, each of which is hermetically sealed to outside influences.[27]

Ethnic Nationalisms Reappear: Language and Education, 1968–1983

The void left by the gradual collapse of a belief in any form of Yugoslav culture was quickly filled by national-based cultural formations that tended to appear before the expression of political nationalism. That is to say, the centrifugal effects of the abandonment of central control were felt first in culture as, for the first time in modern Yugoslav history, significant portions of the cultural elites gave up on the Yugoslav project. Indeed, in certain crucial cases, most notably Croatia in the late 1960s and Serbia in the early 1980s, it would not be an exaggeration to say that nationalist political movements rose on the back of cultural ones rather than the other way around.

Be this as it may, by the late 1960s central authority was being openly defied in one area of the country after another, with nationalist flare-ups in the Albanian Kosovo region, in Bosnia-Herzegovina, and, most ominously, in Croatia, where matters reached crisis proportions. After all, though few thought that the Albanians or Bosnian Moslems had the potential to destroy the country, full-scale tension between Serbs and Croats manifestly did. In the course of the late 1960s a number of issues had come together to fuel nationalist sentiment in Croatia—these included the belief that economic planning initiated in Belgrade was skimming the profits made by the lucrative Croatian tourist industry and fears that Croatian territory and the Croatian language were being Serbianized.[28] Croatian nationalist sentiment found its strongest expression, however, among intellectual and cultural figures, particularly those grouped around the major Croatian cultural society *Matica hrvatska*.

One of the most significant cultural attempts to foster Croatian national feeling was the publication of the "Declaration Concerning the Name and the Position of the Croatian Literary Language" in March 1967. This document was a direct repudiation of the 1954 Novi Sad Agreement on the Serbo-Croatian language, which had been signed by leading Serbian and Croatian intellectuals in more unificatory days, and it illustrated how far the country had moved from the ideals of the initial postwar period. Equally important, in demanding recognition of the Croatian literary language as an independent entity, it undermined the only remaining historical connection to the original Yugoslav movements of the nineteenth century. For it was the choice to strive for a unified Serbo-Croatian literary language that had provided the underpinnings to the Illyrian movement. And, however relations between Serbs and Croats may have fluctuated in the ensuing years, the goal of an integrated literary language had remained intact (with the notable exception of the World War II period). By opening the door to full linguistic separation, the Croatian cultural nationalists thus called all other types of Serb-Croat cooperation into question.[29]

In the literary arena, the leading Croatian publications did everything possible to stress the autochthonous nature of Croatian culture: "The emphasis was on things Croatian and on the revival of Croatian national consciousness."[30] It was no coincidence that *Matica hrvatska* began its ambitious publication of a series of books entitled "Five Centuries of Croatian Literature." The aim was undoubtedly to raise Croatian national pride at the imposing sight of several yards worth of national literature. Thus, the Croatian revival was spearheaded by cultural figures rather than Croatian politicians, who until early 1970 were divided on this issue.[31] Their division was in sharp contrast to the unanimity displayed in Croatian cultural circles of this period.

Few Croatian intellectuals hid their support of separatist ethnic national feelings at this time. A particularly strident presentation of Croatian intellectual opinion can be seen in the proceedings of a conference that was held in Zagreb in 1970.[32] Attended by most of Croatia's leading intellectuals, the conference amounted to a full-scale attack on the previous school program for the teaching of literature and a call to arms to use literature and culture to create specifically Croatian citizens. "The duty of Croatian schools is to make available to the Croatian student, the future Croatian intellectual, the basic works of value of Croatian literary culture and of Croatian culture in general."[33] This required the separation of Croatian literature from the "literatures of the Yugoslav nations," a sharp reduction in the number of Serbian writers being taught (in this respect, Croatian intellectuals hoped to bring their education program in line with that of the Slovenians, who were admired for basically all but ignoring the literatures of the other Yugoslav peoples), as well as the elimination of any attempt at demonstrating that such a concept as a unified Yugoslav literature had ever existed.

Although Croatian separatism was officially crushed in December 1971, its suppression was handled in a fashion that was to be expected in a country in which the role of politics was overvalued and that of culture undervalued. Tito's decision was to remove the Croatian party leadership, and tens of thousands of Croats were eventually punished in one way or another for their support of Croatian nationalism. At the same time, "Tito moved to undercut the popular bases of the Croatian nationalists by granting many of the nationalist demands,"[34] particularly in the cultural sphere. Most dangerously, little or nothing was done to change the nationalist orientation in the Croatian schools. If we look, for example, at the educational plan published for the Croatian schools in 1974,[35] we find some amazing things considering the fact that Croatian nationalism had supposedly been decisively blocked only three years earlier. Programs provided for all schools in Croatia by the republican Ministry of Education had been mandatory until 1968. From 1968 until 1974, schools had basically been allowed to do whatever they wanted provided they offered the required minimum number of hours in each subject. The new 1974 plan was, however, described as "normative" according to the appended note signed by Dr. Pero Šimleša, president of the Educational Council of Croatia. It was also extremely specific.

The differences between this plan and the ones printed in the 1960s and late 1940s were immense. Most important was a turn in the overall philosophical direction of education from a focus on Yugoslavia and brotherhood and unity to one in which belonging to one's own nation in the context of the various Yugoslav republics was emphasized. That is, as Yugoslav sociologists would later put it, there was a turn from an emphasis on salient Yugoslav identity (that is, primary affiliation with Yugoslavia) to divided Yugoslav identity (split Yugoslav and particularist identity). Since it was ideologically possible to combine divided loyalty with straightforward nationalism (though it seemed impossible to combine salient loyalty with this), this was a dangerous tack, and one that would yield disastrous fruits when this generation of children came to full maturity.

The change in policy can be most strongly seen when we look at the stated goals of literary and linguistic education (this area was obviously considered the single most important and was given twice the number of hours devoted to any other subject). Along with the usual desires to develop a love for reading and culture in general and to train students in Marxism, we find that literary education was supposed to "develop a feeling of belonging to one's own nation, its culture, literary heritage, and language" as well as "develop a recognition of the common interests and goals of the Yugoslav socialist community."[36] In case there was any doubt about which nation was one's own, the assigned readings and the various amounts of time devoted to them make everything clear. First, Croatian literature was always examined separately, whereas the literature of "the other peoples of Yugoslavia" was lumped together. At least five times more Croatian writers than Serbian ones were treated, even in periods when Croatian literature was relatively weaker. Standbys of the old school program, such as Ćosić's partisan novel *Far Away Is the Sun*, were not even on the recommended list, although some less-Serbian partisan novels by non-Croats were included (works by the Montenegrin Mihailo Lalić and the Serb Oskar Davičo, for example). The same emphasis can be found in the treatment of history topics; Croatian history was treated as separate and distinct from that of the "other Yugoslav peoples." Indeed, for all intents and purposes the program here was one of full-scale, or almost full-scale, Croatian nationalism. And second, although the language taught was said to be "Croatian or Serbian," no provision in this normative program was made for schools in majority Serb districts.

A similar nationalist-inspired turnabout can also be seen in the Macedonian education plan for 1974.[37] Whereas in earlier periods Macedonian students had read a bit of Macedonian literature supplemented by large quantities of world and Serbian (and to a lesser extent Croatian) literature in Macedonian translation, they were now given far larger quantities of original Macedonian and rather little of the literature of the other Yugoslav peoples. In the section on the romantic period, for example, five class hours were supposed to be devoted to Pushkin, Lermontov, and Byron, nine hours to Vuk, Zmaj, Njegoš, Mažuranić and Prešeren, and fourteen hours to the almost nonexistent Macedonian romantic tradition. The mid-nineteenth- and early-twentieth-century sections are equally extreme; here we have three hours for Poe, Baudelaire, and Rilke, eight hours for Mayakovsky, Gorky, Jack London, and Upton Sinclair, five hours for all of twentieth-century Yugoslav literature, and twenty-one hours for Macedonian writers. Nor was the lack of breadth made up for in the Serbo-Croatian classes that were held for the upper classes four hours per week. Here they merely read in the original the same works they had read in Macedonian (thus guaranteeing that Macedonian children would not actually need to learn Serbo-Croatian). Although the purpose of literary education was not expressly defined, as it was in Croatia, as leading to a love for and appreciation of one's own nation, the program could not help but accomplish that goal to some extent.

By the 1980s, it was an article of faith among the Yugoslav republics that no federal control or even recommendations in the field of education were to be tolerated. The extent to which this was true can be seen in the debates that raged in Slovenia during the spring and summer of 1983, after the federal government had proposed a core curriculum to ensure that students in the various republics had at least some fund of common knowledge. Although the core was never laid out in detail, it was envisioned as covering primarily the natural and social science curricula. In the more sensitive areas of language and literature, it was proposed that the core mandate approximately 50 percent of the literary texts to be taught in elementary schools, leaving the remaining 50 percent to be chosen freely by the educational authorities of the individual republics. These measures were proposed after long interparty debate, and they drew support from many republican groups even in Slovenia. For many had come to realize that the utter lack of interrepublican coordination regarding educational plans had produced serious problems, particularly for students whose parents might move from one republic to another. When the plans for a core curriculum were made public, however, a scandal ensued, with opposition coming primarily from the Slovenian Writers' Association, which held a long and angry conversation on the subject in May 1983.

As one listens to the audio tapes in which one Slovenian writer after another comes to the microphone to denounce the core, it becomes obvious that from their point of view, no central Yugoslav authority existed.[38] If the Slovenes chose to teach a few writers from the other republics, well and good, but any shared directives on what to teach, even if agreed upon for practical reasons by their own republican educational ministry, were deemed an unacceptable infringement on Slovenian sovereignty. Whatever merit the program may have had (and it is amusing that most of those denouncing the proposals admitted that they had not read them), it is seen as one more example of hegemonic Serbian centralism. "Today they want a core curriculum. Tomorrow, 'for practical reasons,' they will want us to give up our language," thundered the writer Ivan Mrak. Given these attitudes toward the central government and the idea of a shared culture it is hard to see how Yugoslavia could have survived, even had the most able and compromising political leaders emerged after the death of Tito.

Overlapping Views of the Nation: Sociological Perplexity

The confusion engendered among the public at large in the wake of the gradual move from official endorsement of a supranational unitarist cultural policy to a multinational one can be seen clearly in the responses of randomly sampled Yugoslav citizens to a roundtable on the subject of Yugoslav social patriotism sponsored by the Belgrade weekly *NIN* in the summer of 1969.[39] The first set of answers to be published were from Sarajevo. They give an excellent feeling for the variety of ways in which more or less normal Yugoslavs understood the relationship between nationalism and supranationalism in this transitional period. One of the first respondents, a former partisan, insisted that the experience of the war in Bosnia-Herzegovina should be seen as paradigmatic because Bosnia-Herzegovina is multinational and therefore a microcosm of Yugoslavia as a whole. In his partisan unit in 1941, "the majority were Serbs, although there were Moslems as well. But it is interesting that at the head of the unit we had, and we even joked about it, Vajner, Štajner, and Fliker." The former was a Croat, the latter two Jews. "We were all united in the struggle for freedom."[40] This respondent, clearly, is still using an older paradigm in which loyalty to the abstract ideals of freedom (as defined by the communist-led partisans) trumped any separate national identities, and his view of Bosnia as a patchwork of separate national identities that can come together in moments of crisis is closer to Andrić's than to Selimović's. Many other respondents from Sarajevo echoed these views.

There was general agreement that Yugoslavism in 1969 meant something very different from the interwar concept, because now it was a class-based idea that could coincide with more traditional national affiliation (that is, the "unity" of Communism could balance the "brotherhood" of separate national identities). A number of participants noted that the concept of "Yugoslav social patriotism" had never been defined (rather surprising since it was one of the ideological slogans on which the postwar country was based), and most found this unfortunate. One said it had to do with "how one worked rather than how one thought," that it meant "knowing and caring what was going on in all parts of the country." Other participants took a different, less theoretical tack and described specific instances of cooperation and exchanges among Yugoslav youth in order to show that there was indeed a feeling of the whole in the younger generation.

A later issue (July 20) printed answers from Vojvodina. Respondents there tended to point to some different aspects of Yugoslav life as central to the concept of "social patriotism," including equality before the law and the right of each nation to cultural self-determination. Most who stressed the latter, however, still expressed conviction that a Yugoslav nation was being built slowly and on the basis of mutual belief in the same ideals, this despite the fact that such a policy had been officially abandoned for the previous five years. The answer of one young boy, Petko Koprivica, which was published under the telling heading "The Confusion of a Student," is particularly interesting. He says quite openly that in his opinion the separate but equal policies that existed by this point in Yugoslavia—including education in the mother tongue, as well as radio and television programs in minority languages—were spreading hatred and intolerance rather than equality. Uninfluenced by the remnants of postwar Yugoslavism that prevented his elders from seeing that the new policies were gradually driving the country apart, he recognized that the newfound strength of the separate parts was inexorably weakening the whole. The solution he proposed, however, harked back to the most unacceptable interwar proposals for cultural unitarism, including a single Yugoslav language and one Academy of Sciences. This throwback to interwar unitarism might indeed have been a mark of confusion (and it certainly provided evidence that not all students absorbed what they were being taught in school), but it also revealed what the authorities were loath to admit: that there were serious problems with the way in which the new multinational programs were working.

Such blatant comments were rare, of course, but minor deviations from official views were frequent. In particular, one sees a remarkable number of respondents who call themselves Yugoslavs and reject any national affiliation; that is, it appears that even in 1969, many people still considered that the policies that had been pursued until the early 1960s were the most appropriate for the country. The most strident exponent of this view was one Josip Zuparić from Zagreb (in the July 27 issue), who went out of his way to say that he and many other like-minded Croatians were working for the greatest possible integration with Serbs, particularly in the area of language. He specifically criticized the elites whom he saw as responsible for whipping up separatist tendencies in society, lambasting especially those scholars who contributed to *Hrvatski književni list* (Croatian Literary Magazine) for hating everything Serb and Yugoslav, and claimed that normal people like him, who used words from the various areas of the country, reflected the reality of Serbo-Croatian better than the specialists who claimed that it was really two languages. The split between the intelligentsia, which was rapidly becoming nationalized in this period, and more average Yugoslav citizens can be sensed by comparing Zuparić's comments with those of Božin Pavlovski from Macedonia (director and editor-in-chief of the publishing house Misla), who stated bluntly in the August 31 issue: "Among literatures and literati, a feeling of Yugoslavness does not exist."[41]

In general, the lower a person's level of education, the greater the chance that he or she would express integrationist views of some kind. In some cases, particularly among the Serbian workers interviewed on August 10, what could be called openly hegemonic thoughts were broached, although they appeared only in a context of complaints that the country was falling apart into separate and hostile regions. Workers tended to blame republican authorities for this and called for, among other things, the elimination of republican boundaries, a common school program, and even the use of a single language for the entire country.

Complaints about this series of articles were voiced by Bora Pavlović in the Communist party daily *Borba* on September 6 and republished in *NIN* on September 7 under the title "Jugoslovenstvo ili antijugoslovenstvo" (Yugoslavism or Anti-Yugoslavism). Pavlović took *NIN* to task for allowing people to say anything they wanted, up to and including the expression of separatist views on the one hand and overly unitarist ones on the other. In a word, what *NIN* had done was to show the wide variety of thought that existed in Yugoslavia on this subject at the time, something the central government would have preferred to ignore. Eventually *NIN* was forced to publish (September 21, 1969), with its editorial tail between its legs, the reprimand it received from the self-identified "Communist" journalists of *Politika*. This was followed on September 28, October 5, and October 12 by the publication of the official word on the subject: "The Communist Party of Yugoslavia and the National Question" by the Slovene Janko Pleterski.

Perhaps surprisingly, if the evidence of rising republican nationalism is taken into account, the Serbian backlash one might have expected had not yet developed at this point. Indeed, a survey completed in Serbian schools in December 1971 by the distinguished Yugoslav psychologists Drs. Nikola Rot and Nenad Havelka indicates that, at least for younger Serbs, separatist nationalism was not yet an issue.[42] Although the authors of the survey do not remark on this in their narrative description of it, 1971 was a particularly interesting year to undertake such a survey, for it would have been difficult for high school students in Serbia not to have known about the nationalist unrest in neighboring Croatia, which was coming to a head precisely at this time. How this news might have affected their own views on nationalism is not clear, however. It is possible that they would have been more inclined to oppose it, since nationalism had specifically been recognized as a danger to the Yugoslav Federal State. On the other hand, the fact that Croatian students were in the forefront of nationalist unrest might have encouraged Serbian students so inclined to develop their own nationalist programs. In any case, as the authors of the survey did not ask specifically about attitudes to Croatian nationalism, we can only speculate as to the effect that immediate current events might have had on the responses.

In the capital city of Belgrade as well as in the Shumadian regional center Kragujevac, 790 high school students were surveyed. Students were chosen at random from two types of schools (vocational and traditional academic) and demographic information was collected in addition to their answers to specific questions regarding nationalism. Although both surveys took place in cities and 86 percent of gymnasium pupils were of urban origin, only 56 percent of the vocational school ones were, so the survey covered a reasonably representative sample of the Serbian population. The opinions of respondents were solicited to several series of questions. The first related to their attitude toward nationalism in general. Five basic categories were available, with questions designed to elicit both positive and negative scaled responses. The five overall categories were (1) ethnocentrism; (2) national idealization (or salient national attachment, as the authors called it): emphasizing the significance of any national attachment and, therefore, one's own; (3) divided national attachment: simultaneous attachment to one's own nation and to humankind and cooperation with other nations; (4) attachment to humanity: emphasizing the priority of attachment to the general human community over narrow national importance; (5) the absence of national attachment: denying the importance and value of any national attachment.[43] For all intents and purposes number 3 is what was taught in Yugoslav schools as part of the values program, whereas numbers 1 (especially) and 5 were considered negative. For this part of the survey, no specific national attachment was required. Respondents were asked general questions about the importance of "the nation," which they could interpret however they wanted.

The second part of the survey attempted to focus specifically on attitudes to nation and nationalism in Yugoslavia. Here three basic categories were used: (1) salient Yugoslav attachment: attachment to Yugoslavia as a whole is more important than attachment to one's own nation; (2) divided Yugoslav attachment: attachment to the Yugoslav community and to one's own nation are of equal importance; (3) limited Yugoslav attachment: giving priority to attachment to one's own national group over attachment to Yugoslavia as a whole. The authors then asked questions using a modified version of a scale invented by E. S. Bogardus in 1925 to measure social distance from various other national groups—they investigated attitudes toward Slovenes, Macedonians, Croats, Austrians, Germans, Russians, Blacks, Americans (U.S.), English, and Bulgarians. Finally, they investigated the "authoritarian syndrome" as defined and studied by Adorno, by looking at attitudes toward the supposed binary pairs of autocracy/democracy, socialism/capitalism, atheism/religiosity, sexual equality/male dominance. This section is the most problematic in that terms such as *democracy* and *socialism* are defined in a fairly meaningless Yugoslav context.

The results of the survey are striking. In fact, one could say that had nationalist politicians like Slobodan Milošević read the results (and it is certainly possible that they did), they could have found a blueprint of the groups on whose support they could count and the themes needed to rally that support. In category number 1, when asked about nationalism in general, divided national attachment (number 3) led the pack, relatively closely followed by categories 4 and 2, with 5 and 1 trailing far behind. My guess is that in this rather abstract area students simply did not recognize what was at stake and followed the formulas that had been given them in school. Even here, however, among various surveyed groups there are strong statistical differences that point to more important underlying differences. For example, vocational school pupils (the less well-educated, and, in a highly tracked society, usually the less intelligent) had a much higher attachment to category 1 than did students in academic programs. What is more, it was found that "residence in towns is in a negative correlation with nationalistic and in a positive correlation with an internationalistic orientation. The father's education, if it does not exceed the level of primary school, is in positive correlation with acceptance of national attachment to one's own nation, but in negative correlation with acceptance of divided attachment. When the father has a higher education then the correlations are in an opposite direction."[44]

When we turn to specifically Yugoslav attachment, things get more interesting. Divided and salient responses were pronounced, with only about 20 percent of respondents admitting to a limited (that is, solely Serbian) attachment. At the same time, the authors found no correlation between those who answered positively to questions meant to show attachment to divided and salient nationality. To them, this indicated that "these two forms of attachment have a certain independence." Equally important, they noticed that "a positive, low, but statistically significant correlation exists between divided and limited Yugoslav attachment."[45] This indicates that those people who exhibited divided attachment could in theory be pulled toward limited attachment in the right conditions, since those types of views overlap in certain ways, whereas those who exhibited salient attachment were probably immovable. Thus, the large group of respondents who exhibited divided national attachment were in fact a swing group whose members, if they could be mobilized to support one part of their identity, could potentially be turned into limited nationalists.

When we examine background and schooling, we find that gymnasium pupils exhibited a slightly higher than average degree of salient Yugoslav attachment, whereas vocational school pupils had a much higher than average degree of limited Yugoslav attachment. What this indicates, of course, is that a nationalist-oriented party would have done well to concentrate on the less-well-educated, more rural segments of the populace, something that all the nationalist parties in the former Yugoslavia would eventually do. Indeed, it has been suggested that the Yugoslav wars of the 1990s were less between ethnic and national groups than they were between country and city.[46]

As far as distance from certain nations goes, results here were quite curious. Most striking were highly positive attitudes toward Macedonians and Slovenians, positive attitudes toward the English, Americans, and Russians, acceptable attitudes toward Blacks and Croatians, and dismal attitudes toward Germans, Austrians, and Bulgarians. In general, people from the provinces showed greater distaste for strangers than did Belgraders, girls greater distaste than boys. Of particular interest is the fact that in the Kragujevac region support for Croatians was quite low, particularly in vocational schools, the same as for Blacks, although still above Germans and Austrians and Bulgarians. The general dislike of the latter groups can be easily explained by the fact that they were World War I and World War II enemies who always appeared as bad guys in popular media presentations. The greater distaste for Croatians than for Slovenians and Macedonians certainly indicates which group it made sense to fight when Yugoslavia broke up. Unfortunately, no questions were asked about Moslems or Albanians. As far as authoritarianism goes, again we find some curious things. The authors felt that the mean authoritarianism score was "very high"[47] and that it was highest among boys in vocational schools and girls in general. The authoritarianism score of those from villages and from poorer educational backgrounds was higher than that of those from towns.

Taken together, the results of this survey clearly indicate that an autocratic party with strong ties to the church and to traditional values would be able to garner significant support for a program based on Serbian nationalism, particularly in the countryside, the provinces, and among the lumpen-workers of Belgrade. Anti-Croat, anti-German propaganda would work as well. And what do we see here other than the basic ideology of Milošević's party and its program? Indeed, the success of Milošević in Serbia was guaranteed precisely when he discovered the formulas that tapped into the chauvinistic side of the silent majority of Serbs, who, before Milošević, almost certainly would have been found to have had a divided national attachment. The rise of a political movement to exploit these feelings was, however, far in the future.

There was one other curious fact uncovered by the survey. When students were asked about their own nationality, *64 percent responded Serb and 32 percent Yugoslav. Among gymnasium pupils, the figure was 53 percent Serb and 41 percent Yugoslav, with the rest as others.*[48] These are astounding figures, and they demand some explanation. After all, in the 1971 census, only 273,077 people declared themselves as Yugoslav (or something like 2 percent of the population). One possible explanation would be that the students surveyed felt pressured, either overtly or merely by the nature of the survey, into declaring themselves Yugoslav. The problem with this answer is (1) there is no evidence that it is true (the survey was scrupulously designed to make it impossible to tell what answers the surveyors wanted, although students were certainly aware that strong nationalist sentiments were officially frowned upon); (2) the survey was anonymous; and (3) there was and had never been any official pressure not to identify oneself as a Serb, Croat, Macedonian, and so forth on demographic forms in postwar Yugoslavia.[49] We are left to consider the possibility that large percentages of young students did indeed see themselves as Yugoslavs first and foremost. If we take into account that on the 1981 census, when many of these students would have been old enough to have been asked questions separately from their parents, some 12 percent of the country declared themselves to be Yugoslav, we might well come to the conclusion that the surveyors were in fact detecting the beginnings of a sharp rise in supranationalist sentiment, particularly in the best-educated strata of the country. Such a conclusion tallies with the personal recollections of many foreigners, who found that young people from Belgrade or Zagreb were as likely to identify themselves as Yugoslavs as anything else in this period.

What this indicates is that Yugoslav supranationalist sentiment, at least in Serbia, was becoming stronger at this time, in tandem with a strengthening of separatist national identification. Such a conclusion dovetails with the findings of other surveys. "It is interesting that [during the early 1970s] survey research also revealed that the majority of young people supported the notion of nurturing a more 'unified Yugoslav nation.'"[50] This conclusion shows what a tragic mistake the Yugoslav government made when it responded to the separatist problem by jailing political leaders but allowing separatism to flourish in the cultural sphere. By the early 1970s, there was a strong cadre of Serbs who would, when they reached political maturity, have supported the deepening and broadening of the Yugoslav concept. These people, however, never got a chance. The economic crisis of the late 1970s forced many of them into immigration and blunted the initiative of those who remained. And by the 1980s, a new generation had appeared, one effectively educated in separatism. It was primarily from the ranks of these young people that the soldiers of the most recent Balkan wars were drawn. And they were led, not by the generation that grew up on "soft" Yugoslavism from the mid-1950s to the 1970s, but by a group who had come of age during or just after the ethnic slaughter that had riven the country during World War II.

The Serbian Cultural Backlash

What occurred in Yugoslavia from the early 1970s on, and what prepared the ground for the eventual rise of a Serbian nationalist political movement, was the cultural polarization of the country. On the one hand, one group of the population became, if anything, more attached to some form of the Yugoslav solution, whereas a larger group, particularly in Serbia, but also in Slovenia and to a lesser extent in Macedonia and Croatia, began to espouse and publicize more and more strident particularist nationalist views. In a series of literary and publicistic works, these nationalist-oriented intellectuals took advantage of the new climate to initiate a gradual delegitimization of the supranational policies that had guided cultural life in Yugoslavia until the early 1960s. Although it was a change in the political climate that created an opening for such moves, the actual work of dismantling Yugoslav unity was carried out primarily in the cultural arena.

Nowhere was this trend more obvious than in Serbia. The first major genre to register the new state of affairs was the war novel. This was no accident, for the partisan novel had been one of the central genres for the propagation of post–World War II supranational Yugoslav identity. Partisan literature by such writers as Vladimir Nazor, Branko Ćopić, Dobrica Ćosić, and Ivan Goran Kovačić had been among the few postwar works to be included in school readers, and many of these authors enjoyed a large audience of low- and middle-brow readers. Perhaps the best author to examine as a way of measuring the gradual reappearance of Serbian national sentiment in culture is Dobrica Ćosić. As mentioned in the previous chapter, Ćosić was the writer of one of the most popular and influential of the partisan novels, *Far Away Is the Sun*. We have also seen that in the early 1960s, Ćosić played a central role in bringing discussions of nationalism back to center stage in Yugoslavia. Although in his publicistic articles Ćosić continually denied that his Yugoslavism was tainted by interwar Serbian hegemonistic tendencies, his opponents were not reassured by the subject matter he treated in the novels he published after *Far Away Is the Sun*. In *Koreni* (Roots, 1954) and *Deobe* (Divisions, 1961), Ćosić provided a vast panorama of Serbian life from the mid–nineteenth century through World War II. And although he never appears overtly sympathetic to Serbian nationalist ideals in these novels, his deep love for traditional Serbian ways comes through clearly, as does his attempt to build a new myth of Serbian culture.

By the late 1960s, however, Ćosić's cultural politics became overtly Serbophilic. Indeed, by 1968, he was kicked out of the Communist party for his outspoken criticism of the official policy in Kosovo. He claimed (with truth), that Serbs and Montenegrins were being pushed by the Albanian majority to emigrate from Kosovo and that the party had failed to take account of the "chauvinist bent and nationalist psychosis among the members of the Skipetar [Albanian] nationality."[51] Although this new phase in Ćosić's career might lead one to believe that the critics who had lambasted his earlier Yugoslavism as nothing more than a mask for Serbian hegemony had been correct, I am not inclined to think so. Although he had undoubtedly always had a soft spot in his heart for a certain populist romanticism, there is no reason to disbelieve his strenuous denials when he had been attacked for Serbian nationalism.[52] Instead, I believe that by the late 1960s Ćosić came to recognize that the government had indeed truly abandoned its earlier Yugoslav policy in favor of a multinational federalism. This betrayal, as Ćosić must have seen it, completely changed the political and national equation in Yugoslavia and led him to the conviction that the Serbs would have to assert their own national rights if they did not wish to become second-class citizens in their own country.[53]

Despite his loss of party position, Ćosić remained a vocal figure on the Serbian cultural and political scene through the 1970s and 1980s. In particular, he became notorious as the main author of a draft "Memorandum" sponsored by the Serbian Academy of Arts and Sciences devoted to the crisis of Yugoslavia. Although the "Memorandum" was ostensibly written to find a way to preserve the integrity of Yugoslavia, its authors spent most of the document proving that Tito's Yugoslavia had discriminated against Serbs in a variety of ways, supposedly permitting Serbia's economic subjugation to Croatia and Slovenia, as well as the "genocide" perpetrated by the Albanians against the Serbs of Kosovo.[54] After the final collapse of Yugoslavia, Ćosić was rewarded for his early embrace of the Serbian cause with his election to the presidency of the rump Yugoslavia on June 15, 1992.

The gradual shift in Ćosić's views regarding the national question in Yugoslavia can be traced in his fictional work as well. Here, they move from the realm of abstract political and social theorizing and/or active propaganda (areas in which Ćosić is less than perfectly trained) to the more subtle but more effective mode of fictional discourse. As we recall, *Far Away Is the Sun* was unambiguous in its condemnation of separatist nationalist movements (both Serbian and Croatian), whose adherents were equated with the German and Italian invaders. The Communists were presented as the only force concerned with more than local problems, although national and ethnic diversity in the partisan ranks was not depicted. Rather, the national question was simply passed over and implicitly made to seem irrelevant. Such a position was in keeping with the overall artistic and cultural policies of postwar Yugoslavia.

A comparison of *Far Away Is the Sun* with the four-volume epic *Vreme smrti* (A Time of Death) illustrates how Ćosić's perspective on the Yugoslav situation shifted in the course of some twenty years.[55] In terms of literary technique, the writer evolved rather little from the early 1950s to the mid-1970s. We find many of the same basic building blocks—war and the exploration of the psychology of people who are caught up in it. The sweeping epic tone is the same as well, as are the effective renderings of taut battlefield reality. What has shifted, however, is the subject matter and the extent of the conversations that fill the time between the shooting. Whereas these were relatively brief and quite closely related to the action in *Far Away Is the Sun*, in *A Time of Death* they are expansive and they digress from the immediate concerns of battle to cover a much broader sweep of characters, situations, and events. The primary overt reason for this is a shift in focus, from a concentration on a small band of partisan fighters interested only in survival under extreme wartime conditions in *Far Away Is the Sun* to a panorama of Serbian life, military and political, during the crucial years of World War I in *A Time of Death*.

In the latter novels, Ćosić focuses on a father and son, Vukašin and Ivan Katić. Katić the elder had been a rising star in Pašić's radical party, but broke with Pašić and is now an opposition leader. His son is a young university student who, like so many others of his age, volunteers for the Serbian army at the outset of the war, despite his deep unsuitability for military life. Although battle descriptions take up a great deal of narrative space, they are present merely to motivate a series of strategically placed discussions among the main characters devoted to whether or not South Slavic unity should occur and if so, how. They pit Vukašin Katić, his son, his son's idealistic colleagues, and the long-suffering Dr. Radić (all of whom believe in the desirability of South Slavic unification) against a group of characters who believe that unity is either undesirable or impossible. These discussions are the raison d'être for the novel as a whole, and they serve, ultimately, as a first step toward discrediting the myths of brotherhood and unity on which the postwar Yugoslav state rested.

Ćosić's narrative technique is quite skillful, and he brings these debates to life without the heavy-handedness one might expect in what is, in its essence, a novel bent on undermining the supranational consensus that had underpinned the entire war novel genre in postwar Yugoslavia. Indeed, it is at first not obvious which set of characters Ćosić actually supports. As one reads further, however, it becomes clear that although Ćosić is not entirely unsympathetic to the Katićs' pro-Yugoslav arguments, the force of events and the way they are presented impels the reader to see the Katićs as utopian dreamers who are unable to recognize a reality that is staring them in the face: there can be no Yugoslav unity because the differences separating Serbs and Croats are too large (these are the main ethnic groups Ćosić explores, but considering that Serbs and Croats were the largest and, in many respects, the closest, if they cannot overcome their differences it should be clear that others will certainly not be able to do so).

Two conversations that appear toward the end of the third volume of *A Time of Death* serve to illustrate both how Ćosić presents his arguments and what impression they make on the reader. The first is between the hard-boiled but sympathetic Dr. Radić (a self-sacrificing physician whose efforts to control the typhus epidemic that more than anything else defeated the Serbian war effort in 1915 are chronicled in detail) and Father Božidar (the name means "God's gift"), an equally sympathetic Serbian Orthodox priest. Radić begins by expressing his fear that Serbia will lose the war. Father Božidar counters:

"What I'm afraid of, my boy, is that we'll win the war as planned by Pašić and our politicians, by professors and their students. Have you read in the newspapers about us uniting with the Croats and Slovenes? I mean that declaration of the Assembly about the creation of a large state consisting of Serbs, Croats, and Slovenes? Three separate faiths, estranged by fire and sword, and divided by blood— but now they're to be combined in a single state! What louse or reptile shot this poison—this death-dealing sickness—into Serbian heads? I often ask myself this when I'm alone, Doctor, I ask it aloud. What kind of union can we have with the Catholics? After all the crimes committed by those brothers of ours in Austrian uniform, can anyone in his right mind believe in unity and peace with them? Why are you silent? You educated people are heading straight for the precipice, but why push this unhappy nation over it, too?"

"I'm not a politician, Father. I hate politics, maybe even more than you do. The one thing I approve of in the politics of both government and Opposition is the unification of all those unhappy people. I think it's better for us to be together, because then at least the Austrians and Russians won't be able to set one group against another. If we're going to be bruised and smother, at least we'll be doing it to ourselves."[56]

The first thing one notices in this discussion is the relative weakness of Dr. Radić's position. Against the facts, contemporary and historical, presented by Father Božidar (which Radić does not bother even to contest), the doctor can offer only faint hope. Perhaps when all are together and outsiders no longer have a chance to influence them, they will be better off. Even here, however, Radić leaves open the possibility that fratricidal struggles will continue (something that did indeed transpire, as the reader knows).

Against this vague hope we have the fact of two different religions (Father Božidar does not even consider the Moslems in his equation, but readers easily might have) as well as the fact that in World War I Croatian soldiers played a significant role in the attacking Austro-Hungarian army. Again, although the context is World War I and not World War II here, Serbian readers in the 1970s would have undoubtedly recalled the Ustasha terror during the latter war (a subject that was more or less taboo in Tito-era literature or history) and thus question the basis for contemporary as well as historical brotherhood and unity. Even more insidious is Father Božidar's identification of Yugoslavism with the educated—politicians and intellectuals. The implication is that such talk was and is worthless utopianism, merely an intellectual fantasy that was imposed on the people, whose good common sense allowed them to see that Yugoslav unity, cultural or political, was an impossible dream. Ironically, as we noted above, in the period the novel was written the truth was exactly the opposite. Surveys showed that it was precisely the common people who were in favor of various forms of Yugoslavism, whereas the intellectuals were more and more opposed.

The same theme is hammered home in a conversation between Vukašin Katić and General Mišić that takes place just before Katić is to head off to Paris to promote Yugoslav union among the allies. Mišić asks whether the supporters of Yugoslav unity are aware that almost half of the Austro-Hungarian army attacking them is made up of Croats. He claims that there is a gulf between Serbs and Croats, unbridgeable because the two do not know or understand each other. Vukašin objects: "The Italians who were united under Cavour didn't know each other, nor did the Germans united by Bismarck. Even their languages were less similar. But we speak the *same* language, Živojin!" Mišić replies, "Do we indeed? Only individuals and nations on an equal footing speak the same language. A free people and a subject people do not speak the same languages even when they understand each other. The Croats, to their own misfortune, are a subject people" (379). It is significant that Mišić does not deny the truth of Katić's claims. However, he wants to stress something else, a fundamental psychological incompatibility between Serbs and Croats that derives from the differences in their political condition. That Mišić's position is undermined by the fact that the vast majority of Serbs had escaped Ottoman rule less than one hundred years before goes unremarked by Katić, and the fact that he does not mention it might legitimately be seen as Ćosić's way of stacking the deck in Mišić's favor.

Whatever their views on the desirability of South Slavic unification, what all the characters in the novel share is a basic belief that the Serbs are a special people, chosen by God and marked by a love and an ability to suffer for freedom. This basic worldview is shared by the narrator as well, who in a historical aside à la Tolstoy claims: "A long time ago the powerful Austro-Hungarian Empire resolved to crush the small nation of Serbia, a freedom-loving democratic country."[57] Serbia's qualities, according to General Mišić (who is undoubtedly the character in the novel with whom Ćosić sympathizes most closely), are hereditary and reside not in intellectuals but rather in the peasants who have worked hard and endured much.[58] What is more, Serbia suffers not just for itself, but for all of its allies and even its enemies. "At Valjevo we gave our lives for Paris and the French; on the Kolubara we defended the Dardenelles for the English; at Milovac we shed our blood for the Russians and the Ukraine. And on Baćinac we've perished at the hands of our Croatian brothers, giving our lives for their freedom."[59]

The ideas expressed in *A Time of Death* were by no means confined to Ćosić's fiction. By the late 1970s the Serbian war novel, traditionally a primary vehicle for the dissemination of a Yugoslav worldview, was just as likely to express nationalist feelings. Something of the same set of beliefs and ideas that inspired Ćosić's epic appears for example in the popular *Knjiga o Milutinu* (A Book About Milutin, 1985) by Danko Popović. Popović's novel won the prestigious Isidora Sekulić prize in 1985 and went through at least nine editions in the first year after its publication. The majority of the novel consists of a monologue by the title character. Imprisoned after World War II as a kulak, although merely the owner of a small farm, he tells his life story in a thick peasant dialect. He recounts the death of his father and brothers in the Balkan Wars, his experiences as a soldier during World War I, the hard lot of his life as a farmer in interwar Yugoslavia, and his efforts to save his son, who is eventually killed during World War II. The novel ends with a short section in which a prison comrade describes Milutin's death.

Like Ćosić's epic, however, *A Book About Milutin* is nothing more than a pretext on which to string a litany of complaints and questions, most of which have to do with Serbia's alleged tendencies to sacrifice its own interests for the sake of others and the ungratefulness of those for whose sake the sacrifices were made. Milutin's suspicions about the wisdom of the Yugoslav idea date from before the beginning of World War I, and, as was the case in Ćosić's work, Milutin's common-sense opposition to unification is shown to be opposed by intellectuals—in this case, the village teacher. After hearing about the "heroic" assassination of Franz Ferdinand, our hero says: "It just don't seem right to me. I don't like this empty heroing of them Bosnians, killing off princes and their wives, and afterwards hiding their asses so our peasants have to pay the piper, ain't that it? . . . But the teacher just went on. There, he goes, in Bosnia and the other places where our brothers, the Southern Slavs, live the uprising has all but burst into flames up. 'From your mouth to God's ears, teach'—and I go out into the fields, but I don't believe in no Slavs. . . . I hear, our brothers, but my brother already died for some 'our brother.'"[60]

Milutin's rambling monologue provides plenty of fictional ammunition for the standard Serbian anti-Yugoslav claim: that the other South Slavic nations are happy to allow the Serbs to do their fighting for them, something that the naive and idealistic Serbs have continually done to their own detriment.[61] Furthermore, the latter part of the novel brings to the surface an even more inflammatory issue; the behavior of the Croatian Ustashas during World War II. "Well in those days, my boys, refugees came to our village. . . . I remember that one day Lazar and Vasilij came. They had taken in refugees and had heard what was happening to the Serbs in Croatia. They told me, but I didn't want to hear. Don't you guys tell me this, I say. Pašić and Prince Aleksandar, Colonel Garašanin and Mladen should hear this. It's they built this big country—I don't want to hear about this, I want to forget!"[62]

There is no doubt that the Communists' decision to sweep under the rug in the name of unity and brotherhood the crimes committed both by the Ustashas and the Chetniks was a major error. The belief that wartime wounds would close if they were ignored turned out not to be true. When the issue finally became a permissible subject in Serbian fiction, it was used as a specific weapon in the arsenal of Serbian nationalism. This is not to say that literary works, even relatively popular ones, were the sole weapon used to undermine the stability of Yugoslavia—clearly many factors, including political malaise and economic disaster played their part in destroying the country. What works of fiction did, however, was to nurture the belief that the naturally good, kind-hearted, and self-sacrificing Serbs had been taken advantage of, and this belief, together with reminders of the perfidy of other national groups during the war, helped to create an intellectual and political climate in which continued coexistence became impossible.

That at least some readers recognized the message lying just below the plot surface of novels like Popović's can be seen from reviewers' comments. The following, which was reproduced as a blurb on the inside jacket of a later edition of the novel (a sure sign that its message was one the author or at least the publishers wished to underscore), makes this clear. "Two structural, thematic lines intertwine in the novel: the first is the portrait of the protagonist Milutin, while the second, concerned with crucial problems, opens up to analysis our entire historical behavior for the past two centuries: Was it necessary, in such an idealistic and naive fashion, to jump in and fight in every battle to the point of physical exhaustion, or would it have been better to temper our national romanticism and idealism by rational and pragmatic means, taking into account our true strength?"[63] Like the novel itself, the blurb expresses in coded form the national self-conception of the Serbs as the sacrificial victims of Yugoslavism, which ultimately provided the moral and cultural justification for the policies that were followed by Slobodan Milošević a few years later.

Perhaps the most complex treatment of the problem of inter–South Slavic national relationships in a novel of this period, however, is to be found not in the narratives discussed above, but in a work set entirely during and after World War II: *Nož* (The Knife, 1983) by Vuk Drašković.[64] This novel can be seen as a kind of *Mountain Wreath* redux, although no overt reference to that work is made. Still, the plot, which features a massacre of Orthodox Christians by Moslems, as well as a central concern with questions of identity, particularly the question of religion versus ethnicity (that is, the recognition of the fact that these people are all of the same ethnic background but are separated by religion, which overlays and may override these connections), harks back to Njegoš's great work. Characterizing the book overall is quite difficult, but a preliminary comment is in order. Drašković was very careful not to write a book that would seem patently offensive or inflammatory. As opposed to *A Book About Milutin* and like Ćosić's *Time of Death*, he attempts to balance a pro-Serbian mes-

sage with other voices. Indeed, the Moslem Sikter Efendij is his most authoritative spokesman in the book, a voice of balance and reason. Nevertheless, it becomes clear in the course of the novel that though the Serbs
were not the only victims during the war, they were the unavenged. What
is more, they are consistently shown as responding to attacks by others,
rather than initiating them.

The narrative fabric of the work is somewhat complicated. The narration of the main text is, for the most part, in regular type and takes place
in 1963. Sections in italics relate the dreams or memories of various characters, all of which relate to actions that took place during World War II in
Bosnia and, primarily, Herzegovina. The plot itself is exceptionally far-
fetched, replete with an outrageous number of coincidences, yet they are
necessary to allow Drašković to explore simultaneously the accidental nature of identity creation, while still acknowledging its paradoxical strength.

The book begins with a horrifying scene of a massacre by the Moslem
Osmanoviches of their Orthodox Serbian neighbors the Yugoviches. The
massacre takes place on Orthodox Christmas Day, January 7, 1942. The
choice of day is significant, not merely because the Yugoviches are not prepared to defend themselves during their celebration, but because this is the
very day on which the Orthodox Montenegrins massacre their Moslem kin
in *The Mountain Wreath*. The symbolic connection of the events in the
novel to Serbia's epic past is further strengthened by the family name, Yugovich, which is taken directly from the sung poem and whose root meaning (*yug* = south) indicates an allegorical connection to the whole idea of
South Slavic unity. The massacre is horrible both because it is described in
surgically gory detail, but also because the Osmanoviches and Yugoviches
had been, we are told, *kumi* (the term is perhaps best translated as "blood
brothers") in the interwar period—that is, they got along well and were
seen by all as models of how the cycle of conflict between Serbs and
Moslems could be broken.

During the massacre, one of the Osmanoviches, Hussein, is disem-
boweled by a woman he is raping. All of the Yugoviches are brutally murdered, except for a newborn child. As they are about to kill him, the *hodža*
proclaims that he should be brought back to the Osmanovich village to be
brought up Moslem (in imitation of the Ottoman-era practice of taking
Christian children and Islamicizing them). As they return to their village,
the Osmanoviches are met by another party of Moslem raiders who are

carrying with them another newborn child, a Moslem boy whose family was killed by Chetniks. Both of these children are given to Hussein's wife, Rabija, but she is told they are both Moslem orphans. She names one, the Christian-born boy, Alija, the other Selim. The next day Chetniks attack the Osmanovich village in revenge and kill most of the men who knew the truth about the children. Rabija hides but can save only her own child, Farudin, and one of the orphans (Alija). The other is taken by the Chetniks, never to be seen again.

After the war, Alija is brought up in his all-Moslem village, told by his foster mother that he is an orphan from an unknown Moslem family, and raised to hate all Serbs. Cut to the early 1960s. Alija, now a college student in Sarajevo, desires to discover his true identity. His mother, of course, can tell him nothing but what she knows; he was brought to her as a war orphan, and she can't understand why he wants to know more.

Parallel to this story we have another narration, about a Moslem shopkeeper in Trieste named Atif Tanović (a.k.a. Sabahudin Muratović). Atif had been a small shopkeeper in Sarajevo before the war. When the war began the local Ustasha leaders told him that he was to get the shop and goods of a local Serbian merchant, his neighbor and good acquaintance Djordje Vilenjak. What they did not tell him was that to receive the store he would have to slit the throats of Djordje and all his family. Although Atif is not happy about this, greed and fear for his own safety triumph, and he agrees. As the war is ending, Atif escapes along with many other Ustashas. On the way, he meets up with a man who, it turns out, was the sole survivor from the Osmanovich group that had murdered the Yugoviches. They tell each other the stories of their earlier life, and that very day, the Osmanovich is killed. Atif, however reaches the Italian border, but on the night before he is to cross over to safety, he is burned in a fire and his documents disappear. He pays off the Ustasha officers he is with to get new identity papers, and with the money he managed to stash away he opens a store in Trieste. Fast forward to 1963 again. A young Moslem man named Hamdija appears at the store and asks for help in getting to Germany to work as a *Gastarbeiter*. Atif tells him that this is a bad idea and ultimately allows Hamdija to stay with him and work.

Meanwhile, back in Sarajevo, at the urging of his Serbian girlfriend, Alija tries to place an ad in the newspaper in the hope of locating people who might have knowledge of a lost Moslem wartime baby. The newspaper refuses to print the advertisement but instead decides to write an article about his plight. Somehow the newspaper with this article appears in Trieste and Atif sees it. This gets him reminiscing, and he tells Hamdija the story he heard from the Osmanovich but asks him not to tell it to anyone else. During a trip to Switzerland, however, Hamdija sends a cryptic note to Alija revealing certain details. Alija brings the note to Sikter Efendij, a lonely man of his village who, during the war, had been one of the few who refused to go along with the Ustashas. Prompted by the note, Sikter tells Alija reams of stories, the most important of which is about the Osmanovich family, which it turns out had once been a Christian one. His ancestor's wife was threatened by a Moslem and so the ancestor went to Istanbul, converted to Islam, and eventually returned. Even more interesting, Sikter tells Alija that the Osmanoviches and Yugoviches had not only been friends in the interwar period but they were, in fact, two branches of the same family. Sikter tries to mute Alija's hatred of Serbs, and asks Alija to see whether any papers were preserved in the Osmanovich village. When these are retrieved, Sikter, who had guessed much, reveals from birthmarks that Alija was the Christian boy, the Yugovich. This is a huge blow to Alija's sense of personal identity, for he has been brought up to hate Serbs, the putative murderers of his parents. And although Sikter tries to explain that all Bosnian and Herzegovinian Moslems are in fact Serbs, and that ethnicity and religion do not have to be identical, Alija is devastated. In despair, Alija dreams of murdering his foster mother and all the remaining Osmanoviches even though he finds seeing himself as a Serb extremely difficult. It is in these scenes that the novel's central political message appears, for Alija begins to see that his village and the surrounding area are filled with former Ustashas who have gone unpunished for their wartime atrocities.

Meanwhile, the narrative returns to Trieste, where we have a scene in which two friends of Hamdija's appear, supposedly because they are going to take him to Australia. In fact, they are here to confront Atif with his past. And now we discover that Hamdija, too, is not who he seems to be. He turns out to be a Vilenjak who has disguised himself as a Moslem to see what Atif is and to avenge the murders. He is, therefore, the mirror image of Alija, although the twist is that Hamdija has chosen voluntarily to take on a Moslem identity for a time. His uncle, one of the prospective Australian emigrants, had been a British officer who was present when Atif changed his name and who has devoted his life to tracking down Ustashas. Having allowed Atif to live in Trieste for many years, he now hopes to exact revenge. The three men force Atif to write a will leaving everything to Hamdija, who is then supposed to kill the shopkeeper. But, unlike Alija, who now dreams only of murdering the entire Osmanovich family that brought him up, and unlike Atif himself, who had murdered the Vilenjaks in cold blood, Hamdija is able to break the cycle of violence. Having worked for Atif for many months, he has come to love the old man, and despite the prodding of his uncle, he refuses to kill Atif.

In the last scenes of the novel, Hamdija appears in Sarajevo to help Alija clear up the final mysteries. He brings with him a manuscript entitled *Nož*, in which he proposes the knife as a symbol of South Slavic identity. For this novel, of course, it is the knife's double-edgedness that is of central interest. Alija identifies himself as a Moslem who hates Serbs, although he is in fact a Serb, albeit an unwitting one. And, as the novel points out, this true of all the other Yugoslav Moslems at some generational remove. Drašković appears thus to be deepening and echoing Andrić's observations about the paradoxical similarity and difference between the separate Bosnian groups, saying that their very kinship, seen metaphorically as the proximity of the two sides of a knife blade, is what makes possible great connection and empathy *and* the most horrifying and violent enmity. One might say that he is bringing Freud's observation of the narcissism of small differences from the individual to the social level.

These three novels of the late 1970s and early 1980s brought up the questions of Croatian wartime guilt and claims of disproportionate Serbian suffering in the creation of Yugoslavia. This was the first public forum for a discussion that would, by the middle of the 1980s, spill over into the political life of the country as well.[65] Thus, just as it had in the nineteenth century, Yugoslav culture led, rather than followed political developments. Now, however, the process went in the reverse direction from an imperative toward synthesis to one of fission. Undoubtedly, the novels we have been discussing initiated a process by which the outlook of a good portion of the Serbian population moved from one of divided Yugoslav identity to one of limited Serbian identity over the course of the 1980s.

Although these novels found readers from various backgrounds and classes in Serbia, their primary target audience was the mass of low- and middle-brow readers. And though these types of readers would prove to be important footsoldiers in the war against the Yugoslav idea, they would need to be guided by members of the Serbian elite. Among the educated elites, who had traditionally been the most convinced believers in some version of Yugoslavism, there were naturally individuals who believed that their own and the national self-interest would be best served by the disintegration of the Yugoslav idea. Many others, however, needed to be convinced of this, and unsophisticated novels dealing with Yugoslavia's historical problems solely on a thematic level would not serve. To change their minds what was needed was a new worldview to replace the romantic cum modernist synthetic ideal on which Yugoslavism had always been based. Enter Milorad Pavić's celebrated novel, *The Dictionary of the Khazars.*[66]

Insofar as it problematizes the basis for Yugoslav existence, *The Dictionary of the Khazars* does not operate primarily at the level of plot—indeed, on the surface, the novel does not seem to be directly related to problems of nation building or nation breaking at all. Rather, using some fairly basic, but no less effective for that, postmodern narrative devices, Pavić endeavors to introduce to a Yugoslav context precisely the ideas that Jean-François Lyotard describes as fundamental to the belief structure of postmodernism in general—that grand narratives of synthesis have no legitimacy and that they can be replaced only by various "language games," each of which possesses "an irreducible singularity" and "its own delimited and delimitable rules."[67] Let us turn to the novel to illustrate the point.

On the surface, *The Dictionary of the Khazars* is an extremely complicated text. It purports to be a reconstruction of a book about the Khazars that was initially printed in 1691 and subsequently destroyed. We are given this information in an "author's" introduction that precedes the text of the dictionary proper. The main text of the work consists of three sections (presented in the form of alphabetically ordered encyclopedia-style entries) that present parallel Christian, Moslem, and Jewish versions relating to the question of how the Khazars changed their religion sometime in the ninth century A.D. as well as narratives about the efforts of certain people to investigate (or perhaps recreate) the events of the ninth century in subsequent periods. Because the "plot" elements of the novel are contained in the discrete entries, it is possible to read the *Dictionary* in any order one wishes, an aspect of the novel that was appreciated by Western critics who were quick to provide it with a genealogy that included Cortazar and Pynchon. The quotations that appeared as blurbs on the book's U.S.

jacket cover illustrate the initial reaction of Western readers quite well. "All its delights . . . the structural novelty and the comic inventiveness of the imagery . . . [are] an ebullient and generous celebration of the reading experience" (*The New York Times Book Review*).

In fact, as is all too frequently the case with such novels, on closer examination the structure of Pavić's work proves more a gimmick than a true innovation, because no matter what order you choose to read the work in, the story remains the same. And it is this story, or rather its philosophical implications, that interests us. Ultimately, the plot of the *Dictionary* is that of a mystery novel, with two complementary mysteries—to which religion did the Khazars convert? and why at regular intervals do symbolic representatives of each of three religions come together in an attempt to solve the first problem? The twist, we discover, is that there is and can be no answer to the first mystery and that the second contains its own—why do death and destruction haunt every attempt to reconstruct part one?

Let us begin with a consideration of the first problem—when and to what religion did the Khazars convert? But first of all, why the Khazars? The Khazars were a rather mysterious tribe that lived in the steppes north of the Black Sea and disappeared from recorded history (in which they had played only a vague role to begin with) sometime around the eleventh century. According to the best available historical information they (or at least some portion of them) converted at some point in their history to Judaism, and these legends of a religious conversion presumably led Pavić to choose the Khazars as his central image.[68] However, the idea of a contest to determine to which of the monotheistic religions a nation should convert is by no means unique to the Khazars; it appears in its most detailed form in the *Primary Chronicle* of Rus'. The entry for the year 986 (6494 according to the Russian Church calendar) describes a delegation of Volga Bulgars who appear before the Rus'sian Kagan Vladimir and attempt to convert him to Islam. In the entries that follow we read of delegations of Christians from Rome, a Jewish delegation of Khazars(!), and finally one from Byzantium. In the entry for 987, Vladimir sends out his own fact-finding missions to each of the religions and, finally, in 988, decides to convert his land to Orthodoxy.

Pavić thus retains the polemic between religions found in detail in the Rus'sian chronicle, but moves it to an earlier period and to a people who left no historical record of their own. The latter shift is most likely

motivated by Pavić's desire to replace the certainty of the Rus'sians' conversion with uncertainty, one that is heightened by presenting the story of
the conversion of the Khazars not through the purported records of the
Khazars themselves, but rather from the competing points of view of those
who attempted to do the converting. And, when we compare the Christian, Moslem, and Jewish accounts, what becomes apparent is that the
novel does not allow us to know which religion the Khazars actually chose.
This is because each religion is convinced that it was the chosen one. Thus,
in the Hebrew account under the heading "Khazar Polemic" we find: "Hebrew sources cite this as the key event in the Khazars' conversion to Judaism. . . . it all took place under the reign of Kaghan Bulan, at the invitation
of an angel, right after the capture of Ardabil (around 731). It was then, if
this source is to be believed, that a debate on religions was conducted at the
court of the Khazar kaghan. Since the Jewish envoy bested the Greek and
Arab representatives, the Khazars adopted Judaism under Kaghan Bulan's
successor, Obadiah" (260). This passage exemplifies the carefully produced
vagueness of Pavić's historical presentation—even when strong claims are
made they are almost immediately undercut or placed into doubt. Nevertheless, it would seem from this account that one thing is beyond doubt:
the Khazars converted to Judaism.

Let us compare this entry with that to be found in the Moslem version of the *Dictionary.* Under the heading "Khazar Polemic" we read: "Al-
Bakri notes that the Khazars adopted Islam before other religions, and that
this was in the year 737 after Isa [Jesus]. Whether the conversion to Islam
coincided with the polemic is a different question. It obviously did not.
Thus, the year of the polemic remains unknown, but its essence is clear.
Under strong pressure to adopt one of the three religions—Islam, Christianity, or Judaism—the kaghan summoned to his court three learned
men—a Jew who had been expelled from the caliphate, a Greek theolo-
gist from the university in Constantinople, and one of the Arab interpreters of the Koran" (150). The entry ends with the information that after
the Arab's successful presentation, "the kaghan embraced Farabi Ibn Kora,
and that put an end to it all. He adopted Islam, doffed his shoes, prayed to
Allah" (153).

The Christian version of the story itself contains two variants. Again
we hear of a polemic and we are told: "The kaghan then turned away from
the Jew and again found the most acceptable arguments to be those of

Constantine the Philosopher. He and his chief aides converted to Christianity. . . . According to another source, the kaghan, having accepted Constantine's reasons, quite unexpectedly decided to go to war against the Greeks instead of adopting their faith. . . . He attacked them from Kherson and when he had victoriously completed his campaign he asked the Greek emperor for a Greek princess to take as his wife. The emperor set only one condition—that the Khazar kaghan convert to Christianity. To the great surprise of Constantinople, the kaghan accepted the terms"[69] (83).

The point, quite obviously, is that in the universe of this novel there can be no answer to the first mystery, for each religion is entirely convinced that the Khazars accepted each religion's own tenets. Pavić provides no Archimedean point from which to judge the accuracy of any claim, and no grand truth can be found by sifting the evidence provided by the separate narratives. All we have (and, apparently, all we ever can have) is a series of incompatible microtruths. To put the novel's plot structure in the terms used by Lyotard, there can be no metanarrative, only local language games.

In the context of Yugoslavia, such a radically relativized vision of historical truth was quite obviously problematic, for it implied that no agreement or mutual understanding could be reached among peoples who begin from different starting points. This, to put it mildly, was precisely the situation that obtained in the country as a whole. Pavić was most certainly aware of the danger of such implications, for they had been pointed out explicitly by Danilo Kiš, who had identified relativism as the philosophical corollary to particularist nationalism a decade before the publication of the *Dictionary*. "Nationalism lives by relativism. There are no general values—aesthetic, ethical, etc. Only relative ones. And it is principally in this sense that nationalism is reactionary. *All* that matters is to be better than my brother or half-brother, the rest is no concern of mine."[70]

From what has been said to this point, it might appear that Pavić's novel should simply fall apart. The centrifugal force of three separate narratives that describe the impossibility of any reconciliation should lead to three separate, incompatible novels. That it does not can be attributed to the presence of equally strong centripetal forces, which glue the work together. These forces are present most obviously in the sections of the novel devoted to events not directly surrounding the Khazars' conversion. As it turns out, the *Dictionary* is built on an overtly cyclical pattern and the bulk of the entries deal not with Khazars themselves, but with those who tried to solve the Khazar mystery in two different periods: at the ends of the seventeenth and twentieth centuries. Each of these periods is marked by the same event: one representative from each of the religions who claimed to have converted the Khazars becomes himself possessed by a desire to discover everything that can be known about them.[71] He recognizes the impossibility of discovering the truth on his own, and this recognition leads him to intuit the existence of fellow sufferers from the other religions. In an attempt to fit the separate pieces of the Khazar puzzle together, they search for each other through a complicated series of scholarly actions and dreams. Ultimately, the three individuals representative of their religions succeed in coming together, but when they do, instead of discovering the truth they seek, all are destroyed.[72] The desire for synthesis, therefore, is seen as a utopian and foolhardy quest; for when it is achieved, synthesis leads not to perfect knowledge, but rather to immediate death and destruction.

The death of a few characters is by no means the only baneful effect caused by metanarratives of synthesis. It is also encoded in the very texts that have attempted to record the story of the Khazars—most prominently the so-called Daubmannus dictionary of 1691, the work on which this novel is said to be based (it is a "second, reconstructed and revised, edition")—and it extends to all those readers, actual and implied, who have or will read the work. "In 1692 the Inquisition destroyed all copies of the Daubmannus edition, and the only ones to remain in circulation were the poisoned copy of the book, which had escaped the censors' notice, and the auxiliary copy with its silver lock, which accompanied it. Insubordinates and infidels who ventured to read the proscribed dictionary risked the threat of death. Whoever opened the book soon grew numb, stuck on his own heart as on a pin. Indeed, the reader would die on the ninth page" (6). And although the narrator assures the contemporary reader that such a fate does not await him, this assurance is vitiated by the epigraph to the work as a whole: "Here lies the reader who will never open this book. He is here forever dead."

If the whole attempt to recreate the story of the Khazars was nothing more than an elaborate and limited fictional mystery, the novel's Yugoslav readers (as well as outsiders) might well have been able to ignore its broader implications. But Pavić makes it difficult to do this by his indications that the novel is meant to function not merely as a complicated hoax, but rather as an allegorical replacement for any attempt to reach perfect truth.[73] This can be seen most obviously in the "Story of Adam Cadmon," a text that is interpolated into the life of Samuel Cohen. "The Khazars saw letters in people's dreams, and in them they looked for primordial man, for Adam Cadmon, who was both man and woman and before eternity" (224).[74] The Khazars, as a result, possessed a kind of perfect knowledge that was lost after their conversion and disappearance. Consequently, the quest to discover the lost secrets of the Khazars is neither more nor less than an attempt to fuse earthly and heavenly knowledge through the recreation of perfectly transparent language, for "the letters of language already contain hell and heaven, the past and the future." This is, of course, a utopian project that lay at the root of much modernist artistic practice—for example, the suprematism of Kazimir Malevich and the transsense language of the Russian futurists. In this novel, however, the punishment for human presumption to divine understanding is immediate death. As a result, the *Dictionary* does not merely express the postmodernist contention that separate language games are incommensurable, it also implicitly claims that any attempt to combine them, to form an overarching metanarrative, leads inevitably to disaster.

An indication of how destabilizing such a philosophical position must have been in the context of Yugoslav literary culture can be found by comparing Pavić's *Dictionary* to Ivo Andrić's celebrated novel *The Bridge on the Drina*. Like the *Dictionary*, Andrić's novel covers a long period of time (some five hundred years of Bosnian history) and is informed by cyclical repetitions. More to the point, Andrić also shows that every Bosnian group views historical experience in its own way and that these views are frequently at variance with those of the others with whom their lives are intertwined. The narrator's description of how the Moslem and Christian townspeople interpret a barrow by the side of the bridge is exemplary: "That tumulus was the end and frontier of all the children's games around the bridge. That was the spot which at one time was called Radisav's tomb. They used to tell that he was some sort of Serbian hero, a man of power. . . . The Turks in the town, on the other hand, have long told that on that spot a certain dervish, by name Sheik Turhanija, died as a martyr to the faith."[75] Thus, as in Pavić's novel we appear to have irreconcilable claims, but in this work the narrator enters the text to explain the origins of these stories and to tell the reader the truth. First, he explains why such variants arise: "The common people remember and tell of what they are able to grasp and what they are able to transform into legend."[76] It is the narrator's job to separate fact from fancy, to explain to us some twenty pages later, for example, that Radisav was indeed a real person; he was not a hero of superhuman strength and ability, but a cunning Serbian peasant who sabotaged the bridge while it was under construction and was eventually caught and executed in the cruelest of fashions. Thus, the narrator, standing outside of his own text, illustrates that the seemingly irreconcilable positions of "the common folk" can be overcome by the knowledge that history provides. If this is so, then there is undoubtedly hope that knowledge and enlightenment can overcome the differences that separate the groups that make up Bosnia, and, by extension, Yugoslavia.

In sum, the central features of Andrić's novel are (1) a cyclical view of time; (2) a recognition that what characterizes Yugoslavia at any moment in time is difference, but difference heightened by the unavoidability of intercourse among seemingly irreconcilably opposed groups; and (3) that difference is potentially surmountable on a mundane level through the actions of people in the world and in literary texts through the ability of the storyteller to know the truth and to unify the world through his work. And it is on this basis that Andrić constructs an imagined community of Yugoslavia. Coming back to Pavić's *Dictionary of the Khazars*, we see that it reproduces parts 1 and 2 of Andrić's "Yugoslav" equation, while completely rejecting the possibility of part 3 (which is, precisely the part in which a Yugoslavia is imagined despite all the problems caused, particularly, by part 2). Where Andrić ultimately asserted the hope that despite difficulties, difference can be bridged and history demystified, Pavić's *Dictionary* implies precisely the opposite. Pavić's novel can, therefore, be seen as a parodic reworking of the central themes and devices of Andrić's masterpiece, an anti-Yugoslav novel in the same subtle and powerful ways that Andrić's novel was pro-Yugoslav. Considering that Andrić, at least from the time of his receipt of the Nobel Prize for literature, had generally been viewed as a kind of unofficial Yugoslavian national writer and that *The Bridge on the Drina* was rated his most important work, a metonym for Yugoslav literature as a whole and a central statement of the country's cultural identity, Pavić's challenge to Andrić's legacy was quite significant.

Of course, it might well be asked at this point, even given that Pavić's novel encodes an ideological position that implies the unviability of the very philosophical bases on which Yugoslavia rested, what proof is there that it had any direct or indirect role in the destabilization of the country? Naturally, Pavić's novel was not held aloft by Serbian soldiers in battle, nor was it quoted copiously by the ideologues of nationalism. Nevertheless, there is evidence that it had important effects, particularly on the thinking of Serbian elites.

Most obviously, it had a major effect on Pavić's own thinking. When the novel was published, its author was a respected but relatively obscure professor of literature at the university in Novi Sad. When asked by some obviously puzzled journalist to explain the *Dictionary*, Pavić pointed to his novel's universality, claiming that it was about "how a nation looks when it stands between great ideologies but does not belong to any of them."[77] In the context of the time, most Yugoslav readers would probably have felt that the "nation" to which Pavić was referring was Yugoslavia, not Serbia. Following this line of reasoning, they would have seen the book as an attempt to revisit one of the central post-1948 Yugoslav obsessions: the possibility of finding a unique place for itself as a land between, but not part of, East and West (refigured in the postwar period as the capitalist countries of NATO and the Soviet Union and its Warsaw Pact allies).

By the 1990s, however, Pavić's interpretation of his work had changed dramatically. One can see this clearly from an article published in the 1992 *Village Voice Literary Supplement*. The article's author (who appears to have derived his interpretation of the *Dictionary* solely from conversations with Pavić) notes: "In the global praise for the book (it is being translated into 26 languages), its political implications tying the fate of the no-longer-existent Khazars to that of the Serbs have gone largely unremarked."[78] As evidence for the inevitability of the Khazar-Serb equation, he quotes Pavić, who claims: "I am a Khazar too because the fate of my family was very similar and in the end we went back to our original religion."[79] Perhaps not surprisingly, by this time Pavić had become increasingly identified with the Serbian nationalist movement, playing an important role in providing intellectual support for the Milošević regime through his activities in the Serbian Academy of Sciences.[80] Indeed, one can only view the collaboration of the erudite, highbrow Pavić and the decidedly lowbrow nationalist Dobrica Ćosić as a real-world example of postmodern practice.

That the *Dictionary* could well have had an influence on Serbian intellectual elites in general can be inferred from the broad popularity of

Pavić's novel, which has been far and away the best-received work of fiction published in Serbia in the past fifteen years. Upon publication, it easily won the *NIN* prize (considered the most prestigious literary award in Yugoslavia) for the best novel in Serbo-Croatian for the year 1984. And an indication that the novel has retained its influential position can be seen in the fact that in a poll to choose the best novel of the ten years from 1982 to 1992 conducted by the respected Serbian publishing house Dereta, *The Dictionary of the Khazars* topped both the readers' and the critics' lists (only one other book even managed to make both lists).[81]

This is not to say, of course, that readers and critics necessarily understood the novel as I have interpreted it. But there are indications that its subversive potential was recognized in Yugoslavia from the beginning, as can be seen from a review published in the leading Slovenian cultural organ *Naši razgledi* (Our Views).[82] The review's author, the Croatian critic Zvonko Kovač, concerned himself entirely with the literary qualities of the novel, which he praised highly. But in the final two paragraphs he turned to the inevitable national question. "Others will speak more about ideologies and their power to establish false identities, particularities, and peoples. I need just mention that a specific Khazar national association is being embraced almost euphorically by a Serbian culture that is sensitized to nationalism; and we shouldn't forget about this external factor when discussing the value of this book."[83] As far as Kovač was concerned, such readings are illegitimate, for they ignore what he saw as the basis of Pavić's *Dictionary*: "its exaggeratedly ironic rejection of the importation of any actuality in its reception." That is, Kovač denied the possibility that the book could be read as a description of any real society. Nevertheless, he continued prophetically, "other nations will read the history of the lost Khazars through their own paranoid visions of the future."[84]

Ultimately then, there is no doubt that Pavić's *Dictionary* could have been and in some cases was read by Yugoslavs both as a specific warning against Serbian assimilation into Yugoslavia and as an attack on the very bases on which the country was constructed. And there is a great deal of theoretical and practical research indicating that the behavior of elite groups is crucial to the crystallization of nationalist thinking in a population at large.[85] Of course, as we noted before, in the context of Yugoslavia in the 1980s, high literary attacks on the country's foundations were seconded by lower- and middle-brow attacks on the substance of the myths of brotherhood and unity. The resulting two-pronged assault played a central role in delegitimizing the very concept of Yugoslavia. Given this cultural context, when economic and political malaise gripped the country in this period, dissolution was probably inevitable.

From Culture Wars to Civil Wars

In order to gauge how far the cultural attitude to the national question shifted in the course of the 1980s, it is instructive to compare the ideology of some of the novels examined above to a series of books that was published at the very end of the decade, just before the breakup of the country. Slobodan Selenić's 1989 novel *Timor mortis*, for example, presents the Croatian massacres of Serbs during the war not as an isolated tragic incident, but as the culmination of a long-term pattern, thereby confirming and deepening the fears that had been raised by the earlier novels and ultimately encouraging the kind of seemingly irrational aggressive behavior by Serbs in mixed Serb-Croat regions that was so characteristic of the 1991 war. Before looking more closely at Selenić's novel, however, I would like to discuss an earlier work of his, because a comparison of the two will show that Selenić, like Dobrica Ćosić and Antun Šoljan, followed an evolutionary path that inexorably led away from a belief in Yugoslavism, however ambivalent or complex, and toward particularist nationalism.

Selenić published his *Prijatelji sa Kosančićevog venca 7* (Friends from 7 Kosančić's Crown St.) in 1980. The book was an immense hit with Yugoslav readers and critics, winning the country's most prestigious literary award, the *NIN* prize, in 1981, as well as a citation as the most-read book in Serbia for the same year. The novel tells a story that is clearly meant to be particular and allegorical at the same time. A middle-aged engineer named Istref sits in his study reading a manuscript sent him by the Serbian Vladan Hadžislavković. The time is the late 1970s. The manuscript itself describes Belgrade just after World War II from the idiosyncratic point of view of Vladan. Interpolated chapters, however, allow Istref to review Vladan's point of view and make his corrections, so that to a certain extent we see the story from both sides. The prehistory of both Istref and Vladan is provided by a narrator, who makes it apparent that they are meant as allegorical representatives of their people. Istref comes from an Albanian family in Kosovo that has lost all its male representatives save Istref, who is too young to kill, to a blood feud. The orphaned Istref is brought up in Kosovo according to strict Islamic tradition, but immediately after the war he makes his way to Belgrade. There he lives at first with other Albanians, all of whom feel very strongly their separation from the surrounding world.[86]

Then one day Istref accidentally meets the Vladan, the decadent scion of a degenerate old Serbian family. Vladan more or less adopts the youth, bringing him to live in what has remained of the family home (the rest has been unofficially nationalized after the war). The story breaks for a long description of the Hadžislavković family, which had been involved in much of recent Serbian history, particularly the nineteenth-century insurrections against the Turks. Their house itself was built by a fairly traditional Serbian ancestor, but it combines Turkish and European styles; it is thus a symbol of one Serbian (and, more broadly, Yugoslav) cultural self-view—a bridge between East and West.

The actual relationship between the two protagonists appears to be quite complicated. At first, Istref looks up to Vladan as to his better. Vladan has been to school in England and knows everything, whereas Istref, who grew up in squalor in Kosovo, knows nothing but a few Albanian books, the Koran, and most of *How the Steel Was Tempered.* But as time goes on the tables begin to turn. Istref works like a madman, by day as a laborer and in the evenings as a student, and begins to progress. Vladan can do nothing but sit at home lamenting his family's lost past. He hates everything about the new Communist Yugoslavia, of course, whereas Istref gradually befriends the group that has taken up squatters' rights in the rest of Vladan's house—this group consists of a veritable Yugoslav U.N., which sings Communist songs and is actively engaged in building socialism.

Vladan's attempts to keep control of Istref become ever more futile. At first, they have English tea every evening. Vladan holds Istref's hand (the homoerotic overtones are obvious) and tells him the story of his family. Istref eventually refuses to have his hand held, then refuses to come to Vladan's room to drink tea. Vladan begins to come to Istref's room but realizes that he is losing his younger friend. To avoid this, he affects Albanian costume, learns how to play Albanian instruments and translates with Istref Albanian heroic songs. The pull of the present and bright future, however, turns out to be too strong. Istref starts spending more and more time with the agitator Mirčetić. The latter despises Vladan. One day he basically attacks Vladan, and Istref must defend his old friend. This is the moment when they realize that defender has become defended and vice versa. The true denouement comes when Istref starts to have sex with a woman. This infuriates Vladan. He breaks in on them and Istref beats him up. During the following month Vladan suffers until he pulls off his big revenge, the pathetic massacre of two pigs that were being kept by the Yugoslav squatters in the yard. After this he decamps to his aunt's house.

There are two possible ways to read the novel: either it depicts a Serbian attempt at self-renewal through the introduction of Albanian wildness, or it shows Serbia's civilizing mission vis-à-vis other Yugoslav peoples (a mission for which they get no real credit, simply decaying further in the process, whereas the others, like Istref, become modern and civilized). In either case it is a transparent allegory for the Yugoslavization of Serbia. It does not assert, by the way, that this is a bad thing—after all, Hadžislavković is clearly decadent and renewal of some kind is badly needed, but the book shows how this Serbian family is overwhelmed by outsiders, of their own choosing and not. At the same time, it illustrates the domestication of the Albanian outsider. Istref becomes a perfect Yugoslav citizen through the influence of Serbia and Communism (in the person of Pavel Korchagin, the hero of the Soviet socialist realist novel *How the Steel Was Tempered*). In this sense the allegory is that of the civilizing myth. If the Serbs are willing to disappear, they can create perfect Yugoslav citizens. Ultimately, from the text itself, there is no way to decide which reading to prefer.

In an interview in *NIN* just after winning their award, Selenić responded coyly when asked what he wanted readers to get out of his book. Nevertheless, the implication of his response is that, at least in his opinion, a proper reading of the novel would encompass both points of view:

I would not want readers to understand the book exclusively as a story of a single instance. I think that the whole work should be a kind of parable with a different meaning. That is to say, it is not only about a young Albanian and a decadent Belgrader. I wish it to be understood as a story about the meeting of two civilizations, two religions, two worldviews that are not merely characteristic of 1945 but, it seems to me, of the historical repetition of a certain rhythm. I think this is a typical relationship characteristic for a change of civilization that is historically necessary from time to time.[87]

Ambiguity and understatedness are, however, completely absent in *Timor mortis*, which is set in the period during and just after World War II. Structurally, the later novel employs the same format that Selenić had used in *Friends*. The narrator, Dragan Radosavljević, a young medical student, tells retrospectively the story of his wartime friendship with one Stojan Blagojević, a man who was one hundred years old at the beginning of the war. A Serb from the Austro-Hungarian Empire, Stojan had lived in Belgrade since 1903. In the course of his long life, he was both at the center and the periphery of Yugoslav political life. On the first day of the war, the narrator's parents are both killed in the Nazi air raids, and he finds Stojan at the site of the ruined bomb shelter that became his parents' tomb. As it happens, he and Stojan live in the same building, one that is soon mostly taken over by the invading Germans. Dragan and Stojan adopt each other, for all intents and purposes, and spend the war in the same apartment after Dragan's is requisitioned. Along the way we come to know Biljana, the dancer-prostitute who lives next door and with whom the narrator eventually falls in love, as well as Stojan's long-lost niece whose family is almost entirely murdered by the Ustashas.

The novel itself combines the narrator's recollections of wartime Belgrade with his reconstruction of Stojan's life, a reconstruction based on Stojan's own tales, his journals, and some "historical" research. As is the case with many postmodernist historical novels, Selenić's presents itself as a hybrid of literature and history, for the narrator claims to be using real historical documents in order to discover the truth about Stojan's life and times. The question of the actual historical veracity of the documents cited is unimportant, however. What is crucial is the ability of a novel of this sort to seem factually based, while nevertheless enjoying all the freedom of fictional narration.

As a vehicle for Serbian cultural nationalism, this novel goes much farther than the works of Ćosić and Popović discussed above. In those novels, Serbs were seen as positive figures who fought for the benefit of their Yugoslav brethren. Although in Ćosić's novel the fact that Croats had fought willingly for the Austrians against the Serbs was noted, and in Popović's the Ustasha massacres were touched on, neither of them dwelt on Croatian enmity. Both can be seen as attempts to raise Serbian self-esteem and self-consciousness rather than as novels whose central feature is to recall interethnic hatred and call for revenge.

Selenić's novel not only provides graphic descriptions of Croatian atrocities against Serbs during World War II (a subject that by the time of the novel's publication had become discussable), it presents these massacres not as incidents that arose against the background of Serb-Croat enmity during the interwar years, but rather as part of a longstanding, illogical historical animus characteristic of Croats in general. Selenić leads the reader to this conclusion by his clever juxtaposition of Stojan's historical experience with wartime descriptions. Thus, on the one hand, we have a description of life for the Serbs in the Austro-Hungarian Empire as seen through the relationship of Stojan, a Serbian who believed that his best interests were served by the Magyarone parties (he was an enemy of Yugoslavia, by the way, because he always thought that Serbs and Croats could not live together), and his wife (a virulent Serb patriot who believed that the Croats were out to destroy the Habsburg Serbs, culturally at least, by folding them into the Croatian nation). On the other, we have a short description of Ustasha atrocities as recounted by Stojan's niece and a friend of hers. These are clearly meant to be seen as a modern-day continuation of a policy that had already existed in the nineteenth century. Croats, the novel implies, desire and have always desired nothing less than the complete disappearance of the Serbs in their midst, a fact that makes coexistence with them out of the question.

In the same year that Selenić's *Timor mortis* presented Serbian readers with a fictional description of Croat perfidy, a novel by Vojislav Lubarda painted precisely the same picture of Serbian-Moslem relations in Bosnia. This novel, *Vaznesenje* (The Ascension) was the winner of *NIN*'s best novel award in 1990 and is set in the imaginary Bosnian town of Čaršija with the bulk of the action taking place during World War I. It is narrated, however, by the grandson of the central character some time after World War II. The World War I story centers on events in the town just after the news of Franz Ferdinand's assassination has been received. Jovo Lukarda (the barely modified name of the author encourages the reader to believe that the story is based on actual events—an old Tolstoyan trick—which it may or may not be), the leading Serb citizen of the town, founder of the church that was built after the Austro-Hungarian arrival in 1878, goes into town to see what is happening. He is arrested in the courtyard of his friend, Salihbeg Kulaš, a Turk (that is, a Bosnian Moslem) with whom Jovo has spent hundreds of hours in defiance of the mutual distrust and hatred of Bosnian Moslems and Serbs. The eighty-five-year-old Salihbeg, we discover later, has nothing to do with the arrest, for he has been confined to his bed. It was instigated instead by Salihbeg's son-in-law, who has always hated Serbs in general and Jovo in particular. Salihbeg, however, feels that his honor has been forever stained by the arrest of his friend. He cannot save his friend and eventually takes poison and poisons the son-in-law who is guilty of betraying Jovo. Jovo, naturally, feels he has been betrayed by the only Moslem he ever trusted at all, and although we readers discover that Salihbeg was not at fault, Jovo's family never finds this out.

Meanwhile, Jovo has been beaten up badly in prison under the watchful eye of Lajos the Hungarian in the absence of Čaršija's commandant, Krišković. Lajos, it turns out, has for years been shadowing Jovo by paying off his servant Milisav Bojat. Eventually, Lajos encourages Jovo to ask Krišković for permission to go and pray in the church, knowing that the newly empowered Moslem corps that have been armed by the Austrians against the Serbs will do him in. In a climactic scene, Jovo is lynched, and the priest, Father Jauković, has his tongue cut out and either jumps or is pushed to his death from the church tower. In flashbacks, we also get the story of the strange friendship between Salihbeg and Jovo (strange because neither understands the other) and the story of Salihbeg's family and inter-Turk rivalries.

On a second plane of action we follow the Serbian Second Army after the breakthrough on the Salonika front, particularly the thoughts of Vojvoda Stepa (the army's commander, a kind of Kutuzov figure in Lubarda's novel), Mitroslav Šuka (whose brother Milisav remained in Čaršija as a kind of outlaw preying on Turks and Serbs alike), and Obrad Jauković, son of the murdered priest. We watch as they hack through Bulgarian armies on their way to Čaršija, which they liberate. In the climactic scene, instead of getting the revenge he thought he desired, young Jauković (who was a priest before he became a soldier), at the request of the heroic fatherly Vojvoda, calls for reconciliation between the Serbs and the Turks. But this reaching out is stained by the murder of Mitroslav by a fanatic Moslem.

The novel's third level consists of events between 1939 and 1941. The narrator's father and the second Father Jauković are best friends (as were Jovo and the first priest), and we are encouraged to see that during World War II a rerun of the massacres of World War I will take place. This is despite the fact that the narrator's father is well-prepared for the outbreak of war. Nevertheless, the narration ends with the father and two relatives, heavily armed, heading for the town as war is about to be declared. It is clear that they will fall victim to Moslem gangs, in an eternal return of Moslem animus against the Serbs.

The narration is quite complicated. Much of it is filtered through the mind of the post–World War II grandson (who intimates that he was with the Communist partisans), some through the stories of his grandmother, the wife of Jovo, who has her own horror stories to tell of how she was treated during the war (she was imprisoned by the Austrians as an accessory to the "crimes" of her husband—consorting with Serbs such as Apis, Princip, and others), and through interior monologues of Salihbeg. The language, particularly in scenes with Bosnian Moslems is filled with Turkisms, much more than the language Andrić or Selimović used, almost to the point of incomprehensibility for a non-Bosnian reader.

The overall ideological point of the novel, however, is transparent: it endeavors to show that the Bosnian Moslems have always hated the Serbs and that they massacre them every time they get a chance, whereas the Serbs are good people, always ready to forgive and forget, to their detriment. The Serbs alone created Yugoslavia, which was a huge mistake since it forced them to live with people who hated them. There are, of course, some evil Serbs just as there are some good Moslems, but for the most part Moslems are nasty and scheming, whereas Serbs are saintly and wonderful. In the logic of Lubarda's novel, Bosnia, which had always been seen as a microcosm of Yugoslavia, is not an example of the potentials of multiculturalism, but rather as a site of unalloyed hatred and disaster.

It is no coincidence that *Timor mortis* and *Vaznesenje* were published in the same year and that they were both quite popular. In addition to their literary qualities—their authors are effective storytellers who have full control over their material—they tapped into rising Serbian nationalism and so represent a logical outgrowth of the Serbian cultural and political situation. At the same time, by spreading the message that Serbs were not merely naive and self-sacrificing, but that the people for whom they had sacrificed themselves had always been the Serbs' greatest enemies, ready and indeed happy to stab them in the back at the slightest provocation, they helped to create an atmosphere in which the indiscriminate massacre of Moslems and Croats could be seen as an act of self-defense rather than one of aggression.

The novels described above, show a clear thematic progression from attempts to boost Serbian national esteem coupled with a questioning of the possibility of Serb-Croat or Serb-Moslem cooperation to depictions of Croatian and Moslem anti-Serb animus. This chapter has, through an analysis of cultural politics and exemplary cultural texts, attempted to show how Yugoslavia went from being a country with a poorly articulated but vitally important supranational policy to an ungovernable group of squabbling republics in less than thirty years. Federal policies encouraged, indeed almost guaranteed, a revival of nationalism both in the political and the cultural spheres. By leaning toward "brotherhood" and away from "unity," the governing Communist party encouraged citizens of Yugoslavia to see themselves first and foremost as members of a specific national group. The establishment of a "separate but equal" cultural policy allowed certain members of the cultural and political elites to ally themselves with preexisting nationalist undercurrents, destabilizing the compromise that had been in effect since the end of the war. Although it was believed that giving the various nations more autonomy would reduce centrifugal tensions in the country, this did not happen. Rather, the separate nations of Yugoslavia simply demanded more and more autonomy at the expense of a rapidly weakening center. Cultural and particularly educational policies were revised to pay more attention to the specific contributions of the national group that constituted the majority in each republic. As the various minorities demanded and received greater recognition, autonomy, and rights, the Serbian plurality felt increasingly threatened. Ultimately, a number of their elite cultural figures decided to pursue a strategy similar to the one that had worked so well for the smaller nations—a boosting of national pride at the expense of supranational institutions. The situation that had obtained in prewar Yugoslavia was now reversed. Then, Serbian attempts at political hegemony had produced nationalist reactions among Croats and Macedonians. Now, Croatian, Slovenian, Albanian, and Macedonian separatist nationalism elicited a violent Serbian reaction. This time, however, no invasion from the outside was necessary to make the country fall apart, and it appears that there will be no postwar reconciliation to put it back together.

Conclusion

Danilo Kiš, who has with reason been called the last Yugoslav writer,[1] specialized in the subject of death. His greatest work returns again and again to the theme, in general in his *Encyclopedia of the Dead,* and also in its most striking twentieth-century European manifestations: the Holocaust in *Hourglass* and the Stalinist purges in *A Tomb for Boris Davidovich.* His subspecialty was the cenotaph, which stands to reason because many of the bodies he described had disappeared without a trace: "The ancient Greeks had an admirable custom: for anyone who perished by fire, was swallowed by a volcano, buried by lava, torn to pieces by beasts, devoured by sharks, or whose corpse was scattered by vultures in the desert, they build so-called cenotaphs, or empty tombs, in their homelands."[2] It is perhaps a bitter irony that his own death in 1989 prevented him from producing a final cenotaph to an idea and a country that has, it would appear, disappeared irrevocably from the face of the earth, its corpse entirely consumed by rapacious particularist nationalisms.

Insofar as it has attempted to show how the idea of Yugoslavia was born, developed, and died, this book is itself a cenotaph, albeit a far less eloquent one than Kiš might have written. In my analysis, I have attempted to accomplish two tasks. The first has been to show that there was in fact something to destroy in Yugoslavia. Given the image spread by the popular press and by nationalist groups in the former Yugoslavia of a country "seething with ancient hatreds" that was "entirely artificial" and "lacking in popular support," such a corrective seems necessary, if only as a memorial for a lost ideal and the men and women who held it.

As we have seen, the Yugoslav national idea was much more similar to the Italian or the German than it was to national concepts created on the basis of political expediency, like the Soviet, or geographical accident, like many postcolonialist African variants. Although it is possible in hindsight to see why the Yugoslav experiment did not succeed, it would be an error to think that its failure was inevitable. Specific choices made by groups and individuals at various times destroyed it, but different choices could have been made. Certainly, the fact that Yugoslav national consciousness had to be nurtured in its citizens is not in itself grounds for thinking that the idea was doomed from the outset. "We have made Italy," said D'Azeglio, "now we must make Italians."[3] And make Italians they have, even though the separate Italian regions in the 1870s were at least as divided as those of Yugoslavia—by language, economics, and historical and cultural traditions. Yugoslavs were made as well, in substantial numbers, and the catastrophic results of the country's breakdown might lead one to believe that had even more been created the South Slavs would have been better off.

The second goal was to delineate how the Yugoslav idea developed over time—to write its cultural history, as it were. This proved to be necessary because I found it impossible to understand why Yugoslavia collapsed without knowing why it had come to exist in the first place, and, to my surprise, no one had ever traced the development of the notion in a comprehensive fashion. As we have seen in Chapter 1, the initial burst of Yugoslav national identification was predicated on the assumption, admittedly not shared by all, that the South Slavs were a single ethnic group and should be joined in a nation-state possessing a unified language and culture. During the 1830s and 1840s, under the influence of German romantic ideas of nationhood, this culture was built on a collectivistic model and oriented to Serbian norms. After a hiatus in nation-building efforts during the period that stretched from approximately the 1860s to the 1890s, new efforts at creating a single national culture were undertaken. The South Slavs were still understood to be a single ethnic group, but their diversity was better appreciated, and it was expected that their future multicultural national culture would reflect that diversity, because it would draw on elements chosen from the various South Slavic groups. In the short run, it was believed, this synthetic culture would serve to link the separate "tribal" cultures, but in the long run it would probably supersede them. It was on this cultural basis that the first Yugoslav state was formed in the aftermath of World War I.

After World War II, Yugoslavia was reconstituted as a multinational state (for the country was now officially conceived as a union of particular national groups), and its multiethnic character was also officially recognized for the first time. Nevertheless, the striving for a single collectivistic national culture did not cease, even as the foundations on which such a culture was to be built were completely reconstructed. On the basis of the Stalinist formula ("national in form, socialist in content"), the Yugoslav Communists tried to create a supranational culture that would overarch rather than link the separate national cultures. These latter were to be marginalized if not outright persecuted, and it was expected that they would eventually wither away. Finally, in the period after 1963, Yugoslavia changed cultural course again. The project of creating a single national culture, which had in one form or another linked every previous Yugoslav project, was definitively abandoned. In its place "the right of every people and nationality in Yugoslavia to free development and their own cultural identity" became the central tenet of cultural life.

It has been the argument of this book that the abandonment of attempts at cultural nation building on the part both of political and cultural elites created the conditions for the collapse of the Yugoslav state. In foregrounding cultural processes, I am disagreeing with the emphasis of other accounts of Yugoslavia's failure, which have placed the blame primarily on political and economic factors. This is not to say I believe that cultural analysis alone can explain Yugoslavia's demise. Such a claim would clearly be simplistic. But Yugoslavia's political and economic malaise in the 1980s, real as it was, would not have led to the disappearance of the country had a robust vision of the Yugoslav nation been in place. It will be countered by some that though this may be true, such a vision never appealed to the population at large. To this I would respond that (1) the cultural works I have analyzed illustrate that a variety of acceptable Yugoslav views did undoubtedly exist, and (2) the studies I have cited in Chapter 4 reveal that substantial numbers of the country's citizens felt significant attachment to the Yugoslav idea in the mid-1960s and even into the 1970s. Had efforts at nation building been strengthened rather than given up, the results might have been quite different.

As it was, however, the 1970s and 1980s saw a confluence of centrifu-gal factors against which no effective centripetal force in Yugoslavia could stand. Most important, because the collectivistic basis of nationhood re-mained even after attempts to create a single national culture were aban-doned, Yugoslav citizens were unable to satisfy their desire for national identification in purely political structures (particularly since these were es-sentially empty of content in Communist Yugoslavia). Instead, they in-creasingly sought and found their identity in collectivistically oriented par-ticularist nationalisms. As Sabrina Ramet has chronicled, already by the early 1970s interrepublican relations in Yugoslavia had come to look more like those among sovereign states in a balance-of-power system rather than as among partners with a single goal.[4] At first these maneuverings were confined to the political elite. But by the mid-1980s populist nationalist politics trickled down to a population that had been sensitized to particu-larist thought by the cultural processes that have been detailed in Chapter 4 of this book. By the late 1980s, all semblance of an effective Yugoslav po-litical center had disappeared. Simultaneously, the increasingly dire eco-nomic situation of the country exacerbated antagonisms between republics and helped to pull the country apart.[5] Changing external conditions, too, contributed to centrifugal pressures on Yugoslavia. We have already spoken about the basic postmodern preference for particularity and its suspicion of synthesizing narratives. To this were added the demise of the Soviet Union, which eliminated external security threats in the region and therefore made size a less important criterion for viability, and the success of the European Union, whose willingness to integrate smaller and poorer states into its economic sphere has made a large internal market seem increasingly unnecessary.

In effect, then, by the early 1990s conditions were perfect for the breakup of Yugoslavia. Given an internal situation characterized by dimin-ishing belief in the Yugoslav idea, a moribund political system, and dire eco-nomic conditions, and external circumstances that appeared to make smaller states increasingly viable, the elites of Yugoslavia threw their full weight behind the particularist nationalisms that had always existed side-by-side with the Yugoslav idea. The results, as no one who reads newspapers or watches television can fail to have seen, were utterly disastrous. Yugosla-via ruptured violently. In its place appeared a series of uninational or would-be uninational states, only one of which, Slovenia, has answered its citizens' hopes for a better future. In the other successor states, collectivistic particular nationalisms that had no place for members of other groups (substantial quantities of whom lived on the territory of each of these new states) took firm hold, and the achievement of nationally pure states became the guiding obsession.[6] The dream of a unified South Slavic nation, what one Slovenian has called "a many-colored carpet that allowed me to maintain contact with lands that were dramatically different from the baroque Central European town where I grew up yet still be part of the same country"[7] was definitively smashed, first by the brutal Serb-Croat conflict and then by the even more brutal triangular wars in Bosnia and Herzegovina.

For an outside observer, it is hard to see what has been gained by the dismemberment of Yugoslavia. Perhaps if one is a true Croatian or Serbian nationalist it is possible to convince oneself that the sacrifices—political, economic, and moral—have been worth it, but most others would probably agree that the ravaged economies, the millions of refugees, the thousands of rapes and murders, and the incalculable psychic damage sustained by both the victims and the victors was a high price to pay for the creation of five independent South Slavic states. This is particularly true given the fact that so little has actually changed in the new countries, for in great measure the new is merely a repackaged but far less creative version of the old, as Dubravka Ugrešić has eloquently noted: "They claimed that Yugoslavia was a gigantic lie. The Great Manipulators and their well-equipped teams (composed of writers, journalists, sociologists, psychiatrists, philosophers, political scientists, colleagues, and even generals!) began to take the gigantic lie apart. . . . They threw ideological formulae out of the dictionary ('brotherhood and unity,' 'socialism,' 'titoism,' etc.) and took down the old symbols (hammer and sickle, red star, Yugoslav flag, national anthem, and Tito's busts). The Great Manipulators and their teams created a new dictionary of ideological formulae: 'democracy,' 'national sovereignty,' 'europeanization,' etc. The Great Manipulators had taken apart the old system and built a new one of the identical parts."[8] Be that as it may, however, no use was found for one element of the former system: the Yugoslav idea, born in the heady days of romantic national awakening, revived and refined a number of times in the twentieth century, appears definitively to have completed its life cycle.

Should the case of Yugoslavia be considered paradigmatic? And if so, what warnings or lessons can other nations of the world take from the Yugoslav experience? These are questions that many observers must have asked themselves and some have written about. To answer even the first question, however, we need to ask a few more. Was Yugoslavia's disintegration the result of a unique concatenation of internal and external circumstances? If so, the Yugoslav catastrophe may be a gruesome and fascinating spectacle, but one of little paradigmatic interest. Or can the catastrophe be blamed on a series of miscalculations and mistakes by successive generations of Yugoslav leaders, mistakes that could have been averted? If this is the case, the collapse of Yugoslavia could conceivably provide valuable lessons in what not to do. Or, finally, is it inevitable that, in the post–cold war world, groups that harbor the potential for nationalist aspirations will develop them at the expense of larger entities? If this is so, then Yugoslavia may indeed be a paradigm, the first in a long line of states that will fission, perhaps violently, into their potential constituent parts.

Perhaps not surprisingly, each of these positions has found its partisans. In many Western countries there has been a tendency to minimize the generalizability of the Yugoslav experience. The minimalists bracket Yugoslavia by viewing its collapse narrowly either as the result of unique local conditions and historical traditions or as an example of atavistic "tribal" barbarism that may still exist in certain parts of the world but has, it is implied, disappeared among civilized nations. Given this, we should merely sigh and thank our lucky stars that our societies are different and therefore immune to the kind of out-of-control violence that has gripped the Balkans. On the other hand, there are maximalists who view the dismemberment of Yugoslavia as merely a fanfare heralding the general collapse of civilization as we know it. This claim has been advanced most globally by the sociologist Stjepan G. Meštrović (the grandson, ironically enough, of Ivan Meštrović) in his book *The Balkanization of the West.* There Meštrović denies that Yugoslavia's collapse was caused by local conditions; rather it was the consequence of a postmodern rebellion against the master narrative of the Enlightenment—characterized specifically by the coupling of particularist nationalism with religious fundamentalism. Although this rebellion initially broke out in those economically and spiritually weakened countries in which Communism had held sway, it is only a matter of time, asserts Meštrović, before its corrosive influence eats away at the advanced societies of the West, for they are equally dependent on Enlightenment metanarratives for their existence. Indeed, for Meštrović, the handwriting is already on the wall: "American society still has a long way to go before it reaches the pitch of Balkanization in the former Yugoslavia, yet the existing divisiveness is already tinged with considerable hostility. For example, the celebration of the Super Bowl victory by the American football team, the Dallas Cowboys, in January 1993 resulted in some ugly rioting on the streets of Dallas, Texas. In some instances, African Americans pulled Caucasian Americans out of their cars and beat them up; as revenge for slavery, they claimed. Dallas is not Sarajevo, and it may never become Sarajevo exactly, but disturbing similarities exist already."[9]

It is, of course, incontrovertible that specific local structural features encouraged Yugoslavia to develop and collapse as it did. These have been the focus of the bulk of the best historical scholarship devoted to the topic, and I have tried to detail some of the less-well-known cultural bases for them in this book. What is more, as I endeavored to show in Chapter 4 (and has also been demonstrated by scholars treating Yugoslavia in more conventionally political and economic terms), it is possible to identify specific mistakes made by Yugoslav political leaders that encouraged the collapse of the country. Nevertheless, I do not think that either of these explanations (or both of them taken together) is sufficient to account fully for Yugoslavia's demise as a state and as an ideal. That is to say, I do think that what happened in Yugoslavia has implications for other parts of the world as well. Still, although I am clearly sympathetic to the claim that broad cultural changes related to postmodern thinking played a significant role in destroying Yugoslavia, I am not necessarily ready to agree with Meštrović's apocalyptic prognostications because I do not believe that all nations are equally vulnerable to "Balkanization."

If we wish to predict whether the processes that destroyed Yugoslavia will have the same effect elsewhere, we need to ask not just how Yugoslavia came to be but what sort of nation and state the Yugoslavs formed in comparison to other states and nations. One way to do this is to compare Yugoslavia with other states on the basis of what could be called the three "multis" that can potentially be present in any state: multinationalism, multiethnicism, and multiculturalism. It is common among students of nationalism to distinguish between the former two, whereas the last category is often ignored. The standard distinction is based on the attitude of a given state's citizens toward questions of national identity as well as on the structure of the state itself. In a multiethnic state, citizens are drawn from a number of genetically distinct backgrounds (in some cases the distinction is marked obviously by such factors as skin color, but in many others it may be unrecognizable, at least on the surface), and, no matter what religion they practice or language they speak, all imagine themselves as belonging to a single nation.[10] Multinational states, on the other hand, are created of a number of nations, each with its own territory and practices. These nations are considered the constituent actors in the multinational state. Individuals identify primarily not with the state but rather with their own nation.

I believe, however, that in order to understand the experience of Yugoslavia it is important to recognize a third category—the multicultural state. A multicultural state includes citizens from differing cultures but possesses a unifying culture that each of its component groups recognizes as its own because each has made recognizable contributions to it. The presence of a multicultural culture says nothing about the ethnic or national composition of a given state. Thus the United States or Australia are multiethnic but uninational countries each of which has a multicultural culture. Canada is a multiethnic and multinational country with a multicultural culture. Albania is another multicultural country, but it is uniethnic and uninational.[11] On the other hand, France is a highly unicultural and uninational country but not a uniethnic one, for people who believe themselves to be culturally and nationally French can in theory and do in fact come from many different ethnic stocks including Celtic (Bretons), Berber, and Arabic (at least those immigrants who have chosen to embrace French culture).

In order to appreciate the ways in which these "multis" can coexist as well as to trace what happened in Yugoslavia, let us trace schematically their potential interactions. The accompanying table shows all the possible permutations of multinationalism, multiethnicity, and multiculturalism. They are arranged (theoretically) from the most stable to the least stable configurations.[12]

If we recast our summary of Yugoslav developments in the above terms, we see that in the course of its existence its organizing structures traced a path descending the entire length of the chart. As was described in Chapters 1 and 2, the initial burst of Yugoslav nationalism was predi-

TABLE I
National, Ethnic, and Cultural Ideals, by Level of Stability

Type	National	Ethnic	Cultural	Example
		MORE STABLE		
1	–	–	–	Sweden, Poland
2	–	+	–	France
		LESS STABLE		
3	–	–	+	Albania
4	+	–	–	No such state exists[a]
5	–	+	+	Sri Lanka, United States
		UNSTABLE		
6	+	–	+	Lebanon
7	+	+	–	USSR[b]
8	+	+	+	China, India

KEY: + = multi–; – = uni–.

[a] Because national difference can be imagined on either ethnic or cultural grounds, the absence of difference in both these areas would seem to make the creation of a multinational state from a group so constituted impossible.

[b] This is not to say that the USSR ever actually achieved a single national culture. Such was the goal and the ideal, however.

cated on the assumption that the South Slavs formed a single ethnos which should possess a single national culture. Thus, the ideal was a uninational, unicultural, and uniethnic Yugoslav nation. This does not mean that the Yugoslavs ever achieved this ideal; simply, that is how the future South Slavic state was imagined. By the turn of the nineteenth century, however, a modified view had appeared, according to which the Yugoslavs were a single ethnic group that hoped to live in a uninational state. It would not, however, be a unicultural country, for its culture would reflect contributions of each of the "tribal" groups that made it up. This was the basis on which the first Yugoslav state was founded. After World War II, the reconstituted Yugoslavia saw itself as a multinational, multiethnic state, but the striving for a unified culture did not stop. Thus, Yugoslavia became in theory a state of type 7. And finally, in the period after 1963, Yugoslavia changed course again. Abandoning the project of creating a national culture of any kind, Yugoslavia reconfigured itself as a state of type 8.

When Yugoslavia broke up, then, it was a multinational, multicultural, multiethnic state, and we might theorize that it is precisely with states of this type that it should be compared. Indeed, there are many such states in the world, many of which are having a difficult time surviving. Rwanda and Burundi, to take two examples from postcolonialist Africa, are states of this type. Both of them tried to instill a uninational consciousness in their citizens, but neither has succeeded, and violent conflicts in both between Tutsi and Hutu call their long-term survival prospects into question. The case of Nigeria, eloquently described by Wole Soyinka, is even more instructive. As happened in Yugoslavia, Nigeria did succeed in creating a sense of nationhood in at least some of its citizens. In Soyinka's view, this was attested to by the elections of June 1993 in which Moshood Abiola won substantial quantities of votes in all parts of the country from various ethnic and religious groups. The elections were annulled after a few weeks, however, and when that happened, as Soyinka puts it, "the military committed the most treasonable act of larceny of all time: it violently robbed the Nigerian people of their nationhood!"[13] The result of this robbery may ultimately well be the destruction of Nigeria, for even Soyinka, who calls himself an "incorrigible idealist" in regards to the national question (33), recognizes that its future is in serious doubt.

At the same time, not every multinational, multicultural, and multiethnic nation is in the same degree of danger. India, for example, seems on the surface to be fairly similar to Yugoslavia. It is a large and exceedingly diverse state containing citizens of many religions, ethnic groups, and backgrounds, some of whom dislike each other intensely. It has been frequently and perhaps increasingly ill-governed, and its economic performance has hardly been stellar. And yet, despite continuous threats to its national integrity, India seems likely to survive.[14] Why? Clearly this is not the place to engage in anything more than speculation on the subject, but the answer seems to me to be connected to the fact that the chart above ignores one crucial factor—the basic type of nationalism (either collectivistic or individualistic) characteristic for a given society.

That there is a direct correlation between collectivistic thinking and particularist nationalism was apparent to Danilo Kiš in the early 1970s. Already at that time Kiš laid the responsibility for separatist nationalism in Yugoslavia at the door of the basic collectivistic mind-set that had been characteristic of South Slavic national thought from the beginning and that had been further emphasized by the two most baneful ideologies of the twentieth century, fascism and communism: "Oppressed by ideologies, on the margin of social changes, crammed and lost between antagonistic ideologies, unequal to individual rebellion because it is denied to him, the individual finds himself in a quandary, a vacuum. . . . The nationalist is a frustrated individualist, nationalism is the frustrated (collective) expression of this kind of individualism, at once ideology and anti-ideology."[15]

In Yugoslavia, this frustration, one that had been fanned by years of particularist cultural expression, was what the leaders of the separate republics tapped into and what ultimately led to the disasters we have recently witnessed. India, as a former British colony whose national idea was borrowed from its one-time masters, is built on a basically individualistic-libertarian base. This encourages Indians of all backgrounds to identify not so much with the nation as a unique collective but rather to see themselves as sovereign individuals whose national identity is rooted in democratic institutions and ideas, even when these exist in sometimes distorted forms. As a result, India has been able to find a third way between the Scylla of hegemonic national centralization and the Charybdis of total decentralization.[16] This is obviously not the only reason for India's relative success, but it unquestionably bears further investigation. If this hypothesis is true, it hints that despite the centrifugal pressures active in the world today countries such as India can survive, but that they would do well to strengthen their individualistic bases by cultural and political means and to avoid policies that would encourage their citizens to think in collectivistic terms. For them, the Yugoslav debacle is not a death sentence, as Meštrović would have it, but it is a warning.

And what, if anything, does the experience of Yugoslavia have to do with the contemporary situation in the United States? At first glance, it appears that the United States is so unlike Yugoslavia in crucial respects that comparisons, though possible, are meaningless. After all, as opposed to a country whose unity had to be created from among distinct groups of people living on or around territories that had traditionally belonged to them, the land of the United States belonged to no one but the Native Americans, whose virtual disappearance, by disease and violent conquest, created the conditions for settlement almost entirely by immigration. Whereas Yugoslavia inherited the cultures of the various empires that had ruled it and had to mediate them, the United States threw off its colonial burden relatively easily. It was free to invent new solutions for new problems. Each new group that arrived in the United States shed the vast majority of its traditions, assimilating to a new uninational ideology based on the individualistic-libertarian model.[17]

Even more important, the United States has been able to create a thriving multicultural culture, one that connects the various subcultures (regional, ethnic, religious, and generational) that exist under the umbrella of American culture. That culture is not identical to the culture of any one of the groups that have settled the country, which is not to say that it has drawn from each of them equally. But the sum of American culture is greater than any of its separate parts. American culture as a whole includes at least some elements drawn from each of the cultures that live or have lived in U.S. society. Again, the cultural contributions of a given group may not be proportionally appropriate; unquestionably the English heritage dominates American culture far out of proportion to the number of Americans of English descent. But American society has worked well in part because American culture has traditionally been sufficiently permeable and flexible to allow for, if not encourage, influences from all of its subcultures, even the most recent arrivals, and as a result each subculture feels that it can contribute something of value to the culture of society as a whole. When I speak of cultural influences here, I have in mind a very broad array of possibilities, ranging from contributions to the language—American English—to literature, music, art, cuisine, and fashion. The third important tradition that marks American culture as a national culture is that it includes some elements unique to it. It is not merely the sum of its parts. The cultural interaction that has been so characteristic in the United States has produced new formations that subsequently can and do spread through society as a whole. An excellent example of such a formation is jazz, derived as it is from the amalgamation of a number of separate cultural traditions. Ultimately, it became part of the society's culture while not belonging wholly to any of the individual cultures that make up American society. Finally, American culture has been marked by an ability to develop and evolve to reflect changes in the cultures that make it up or to reflect the practices of any new cultures that might appear, either by processes of immigration or even military conquest. We might call this the principle of unfinalizability.

The success of American society has not been, however, solely a function of healthy vertical relations between the ever-changing national culture and the separate subcultures from which it is drawn. It is also predicated on healthy horizontal relationships between the various subcultures themselves. By this, I mean that the various national or ethnic cultures have traditionally been open to cooperation with and interpenetration by the other cultural groups inhabiting the same territory. This does not mean that there is not and has not been resistance. Each generation of immigrants, as it has become accepted into American culture, has tended to resist interpenetration by the next groups to arrive. But nevertheless, interpenetration has always occurred. It is thus not only true that, say, Russian Jews were Americanized within a generation, or even that American culture as a whole was enriched by the Russian Jewish stream. It is also true that other American subcultures were changed by the appearance of Russian Jews on American soil. And the same could be said for any other immigrant group of sufficient size. In this respect, it should be noted that American society, both on the level of its horizontal and vertical cultural relationships has not merely been tolerant. For tolerance only implies being willing to let others do what they want as long as it does not interfere with what you want to do, whereas traditionally in the United States groups have been willing and able to learn from each other and to change or adapt at least some of their cultural practices under the influence of their neighbors.

There is, of course, at least one major group whose experience does not fit with this picture: African Americans.[18] They arrived not as immigrants, but as slaves, and there has been a consistent unwillingness on the part of American society (however understood) to treat African Americans as other groups have been treated. Nevertheless, even in this case, African American culture has undoubtedly penetrated all levels of American national culture, and it has enriched the subcultures of many immigrant groups. What is more, the fact that despite centuries of intolerance a sizable portion of African Americans continues to believe in general American cultural ideals illustrates the powerful hold that these ideals continue to have in the culture of the United States.

Nevertheless, certain trends in U.S. society that have become increasingly more visible in the past two decades lead one to fear that even though the starting points and the historical experiences of the United States and Yugoslavia were vastly different, a process of convergent cultural evolution is bringing them too close for comfort. The most obvious way in which the United States is becoming more like Yugoslavia is in what appears to be a slow slide toward a consideration of itself not as a uninational but as a multinational country coupled with an increasing tendency to collectivistic thinking. The basis for potential national separation in the

United States is not, as it was in Yugoslavia, cultural or religious, but rather racial. The idea that Americans are first and foremost Americans and should self-identify as such is being slowly replaced by what is sometimes called a multicultural view (I would call it a multinational one), which sees Americans as belonging to five official races: white, black, Hispanic, Asian, and Native American. In this society, people are believed to have place and value not as individuals, but as members of their specific racial group. This trend is encouraged by large and small government policies ranging from preference based on race to the requirement to check off a racial box on many forms. Such policies have also spilled over into the private sector, where race-based typing has become the norm on job applications and other forms.

One way to see the extent to which problems of ethnicity in Yugoslavia and race in the United States are analogous is to compare the debates surrounding the addition of the category "Yugoslav" to census forms in postwar Yugoslavia to those presently raging around proposals to add a "multiracial" category to the upcoming U.S. census. The choice of "Yugoslav" first appeared on the 1961 census forms but appears to have drawn little comment and less support.[19] A decade later, the census coincided with a time of heightened nationalist feeling, and at that time the category drew criticism from many quarters. Scandal was averted, however, at least in part because the number of people checking "Yugoslav" actually dropped significantly. But in 1981, when more than 5 percent of the population declared themselves Yugoslav, eyebrows were raised throughout the country. In particular, Dušan Bilandžić, a member of the Croatian central committee, complained that the choice of "Yugoslav" had lead to the "disappearance of 30,000 Croats in Vojvodina."[20] Bilandžić's fear was that the "Yugoslav" category, were it to continue to grow, would call into question the entire basis of Yugoslav cultural and political policies, which were predicated on a person having a single national identification. Specifically, a "loss" of Croats would mean fewer people to support Croat politicians and a diminution of their power base within the multinational state. Considering that the intermarriage rate in Yugoslavia was by this point well over 10 percent, such fears on the part of politicians were not completely unjustified. Of course, had the category been eliminated, it is not clear what people who felt themselves to be Yugoslav would have done, although the large-scale emigration of South Slavs of mixed descent in the

1990s indicates their difficulties when forced to choose one nationality or the other.[21]

Given how frequently Americans are now required to identify themselves by race, a "multiracial" category on census forms would seem inevitable, particularly since interracial marriages have been becoming more and more common in the past two decades (although they are, as a percentage, still relatively rare). The category is being opposed, nevertheless, by "some of the nation's leading civil rights organizations as an unnecessary and expensive move that would *deplete the ranks of blacks and other racial minorities and curtail their political power*" (emphasis mine).[22] As in Yugoslavia, a question of identity, which is presumably a matter of personal choice, is being challenged on the basis of its inconvenience for the leaders of certain collectivities, particularly ones that benefit (in the short-term at least) from separatism. According to one spokesman for such interests: "This multi-racial hocus-pocus pleases only a relatively few individuals, and for everyone else, it's dangerous."[23] As long as "everyone else" is considered to be precisely these leaders, the spokesman is correct. One answer to the whole problem would be to stop fostering such distinctions in the first place, but this will probably prove difficult to accomplish.

On the cultural front, we see a parallel process in claims that American culture as such either does not exist at all or that if it does it should not because it has systematically marginalized nonmainstream voices. Policies that encourage the abandonment of what I call multicultural culture in favor of what is often called multicultural (but what I would call multinational) culture are most evident and have been discussed most frequently in the area of higher education. At their best, "multicultural" programs promote a recognition of the heterogeneous unity of American culture. Too frequently, however, they function to separate the interwoven strands of the culture by creating separate special-interest departments—African-American studies, Asian-American studies, Women's studies, Chicano studies. This is not the place to revisit the entire question of the academic culture wars, but I would like simply to note that the problem is not, as some would have it, with the legitimacy of courses like these as such. Rather, what is wrong are two related beliefs they implicitly encourage: the first is, in the words of Mikhail Epstein, "that every ethnic, sexual, or class culture is perfect in itself";[24] and the second is that these various subcultures have nothing in common, that they have been impermeable to cross-fertilization. Ultimately, on this view, American culture is merely the sum of its separate, unrelated parts. Thus, they typically appeal to and are directed to members of those groups, not the student body in general, thereby encouraging a vicious cycle of separation.

What is even more disquieting, and also reminiscent of Yugoslavia, has been the response that radical multiculturalist and separatist-inclined policies have elicited in the United States. The backlash against such views has not always taken the form of liberal defenses of the melting-pot ideal.[25] Rather, a too common response appears to be the promulgation, wittingly or not, of equally separatist programs by the "non-ethnic" Americans who still make up the majority of the population. At their most extreme, these ideas underlie the vitriolic rhetoric (and the violent acts) of various self-appointed militias. Nevertheless, although in the wake of the bombing of a federal building in Oklahoma City these groups and their policies have received the lion's share of attention, this is not where the real problem lies. In any society there will be marginal groups dedicated to hate and destruction. What is crucial is whether or not their actions are perceived to be beyond the pale by the rest of society. If they are, such groups remain relatively powerless and, though unpleasant, not dangerous to society as a whole. If, on the other hand, their activities and thought are perceived of as being merely the end of a continuum, the radical but in some sense logical outcome of a way of thinking shared by much of the population at large, the society in question has a major problem.[26]

This was precisely what occurred in Serbia beginning in the early 1970s. As we have argued, Serbs did not begin to kill their neighbors in the early 1990s because they had always hated them (although they may well have in some cases). They did so because the cultural ties that had bound them to their neighbors were undermined by a slow process of elite-led backlash against federalist policies. In this new cultural climate it came to seem reasonable and even morally defensible to move from dislike of difference to active attempts to destroy it. The relatively small minority who had always wanted to kill their neighbors were encouraged to do so by demagogic leaders who rode to power on the antagonisms that had been nurtured in popular and elite culture, but these leaders did not and could not have created the conditions for ethnic strife by themselves. And the silent majority, who would have loudly disapproved of such actions a decade before, had come to see them as, at the very least, not entirely unreasonable.

Given this scenario, what seems most worrisome in the United States is not the presence of small, hate-filled nativist groups, but rather the gradual rise of what could be called weak white separatist theory, which, if it continues unchecked, has the potential to do precisely what it did in Serbia: encourage a large portion of the population that is susceptible to such pressures to abandon the basic cultural ideals they now hold, albeit inchoately. What I have in mind are a series of responses to so-called multiculturalism, most of them originating on the right, that tend toward the weakening of the American ideal. These include, but are not limited to, advocacy for a voucher system to pay for private schooling,[27] educational initiatives that would codify American culture and thereby make it less welcoming to contributions from new, particularly Asian, African, and Latin American, immigrants,[28] and the appearance of gated communities all over the United States.

The disappearance of a traditional liberal response to issues surrounding multiculturalism in the political arena can easily be seen in the rhetoric surrounding education employed in the 1996 presidential campaign. Republican candidate Bob Dole claimed that the public schools in the United States have been "a model to the world, where people of all classes and all races and all creeds were brought together."[29] Although one may legitimately question whether this statement reflects the truth about the history of public education in the United States, it undoubtedly does reflect one of the central myths of U.S. culture. Dole charged that the Democrats, by supporting educational theories based on "politically correct nonsense," are destroying the public school system, presumably because such theories encourage divisiveness. But rather than countering with strong proposals to ensure the continuation of the great tradition he invoked, Dole endorsed the creation of a school voucher system. And as Michael Lind puts it: "the privatization of American education, unless accompanied by strict government controls over the content of the curricula [extremely unlikely, since it is precisely the controls of various governmental bodies the voucher program attempts to circumvent] . . . would probably accelerate the fissuring of the American population into hostile tribes living in radically separate mental universes."[30] Thus we see indications of the same tendency we observed in Yugoslavia. When the largest ethnic group feels itself threatened by policies that promote the separation of minority groups from the supranational ideal, its response is to separate itself rather than to pursue policies consistent with the once-dominant supranational ideals.

It has frequently been noted by American cultural commentators that separatist rhetoric, though quite loud, is confined to a relatively narrow group of self-styled spokespeople, political and cultural. The vast majority of immigrants (as well as the majority of members of minority groups already in the United States) continue to believe in melting-pot ideology. This is generally held to be a good sign, and I think that it is. However, the Yugoslav experience shows that it does not necessarily take much time for particularist advocates to go from isolated voices crying in the wilderness to the majority, particularly if their viewpoints have already become enshrined in the school curricula. Dobrica Ćosić was almost alone and unsupported in his attempts to raise Serbian national consciousness in the late 1960s. By 1992 he was president of the republic.

Human beings in any society have a tendency to fear and dislike others who look, think, and act differently. It is almost certainly easier to avoid internal conflict in a society that is ethnically, racially and/or religiously more rather than less homogenous, and as a result those countries that contain strikingly heterogeneous populations will always be at greater risk of dissolution. But the success of such heterogeneous countries as Australia and the United States has unquestionably come, at least to a great extent, from their combination of an individualistic nationalism with a flexible multicultural culture. It is therefore hard to justify policies whose net results would be the weakening of either of these. In the collapse of Yugoslavia we can see, in exaggerated and speeded up form, not only the results of the failure of nation-building policies but a formula by which they can happen. First, smaller groups are encouraged to move away from the national culture because that culture is perceived as being too closely connected with the largest group in the population. After a certain period of time, members of the largest group begin to feel aggrieved as more power devolves to smaller groups. Instead of pushing for a more multicultural (in my terminology) culture for a single nation, they press instead for their own cultural and political "rights" and tend to take up increasingly intolerant positions.[31] The result is cultural conflict, which is made far worse if the society's national view is a collectivistic one.[32] If the political situation is propitious, it proves relatively easy to turn cultural disagreement into something far more serious than academic conflict.

It is clear that the United States is very far from being Yugoslavia. Americans are still highly individualistic in their basic mentality, and despite efforts from the left and right American culture remains resolutely multicultural. But at the same time, it needs to be recognized that American multiculturalists, government-sponsored initiatives that force people to identify on the basis of racial categories, and some of the conservative response to both of these are slowly making the United States look more like Yugoslavia. Indeed, in some respects I think that we can see Yugoslavia as an example of what might happen if what has been erroneously called the multicultural paradigm (and the backlash against it), which has dominated American thinking for the past few decades, is not replaced by a revised version of the melting-pot theory. If this is true, the very survival of the United States may depend on its ability to defuse the pressures that ultimately destroyed Yugoslavia. By recognizing where Yugoslavia went wrong Americans may be able to head off their own failure, thereby ensuring that the United States' future does not look like Yugoslavia's present.

REFERENCE MATTER

Notes

1. Although in the 1981 census only some 5 percent of Yugoslavia's citizens declared "Yugoslav" as their primary allegiance, other measures found substantial support for the concept. Thus, "in 1966 sixty percent of a large Yugoslav sample proclaimed readiness to accept members of other nationalities in friendship or even marriage and revealed declining attachment to region, dialect and customs. Most people questioned expressed satisfaction with national relations" (MacKenzie, 453). And, in a survey conducted in 1971, when Serbian high school students were asked about their own nationality 64 percent responded Serb and 32 percent Yugoslav. Among students in an academically oriented school the figure was 53 percent Serb and 41 percent Yugoslav, with the rest as others. And of those responding Serb, only some 20 percent were found to lack any sense of Yugoslav indentity. See Rot and Havelka, 113–18.

2. For a succinct discussion of the differences between nation and state, see Gellner, 1–7.

3. Sandel, 146.

4. Swift, 35–36.

5. Greenfeld, 7. For another view, see Anderson, 16.

6. This problematizes Anderson's "imagined community," by the way, because his formula implies and his subsequent analysis emphasizes the independent imagining of the members of a given nation, downplaying the coercive side of the issue.

7. Brass, 16.

8. Barthes, 142–43.

9. This quotation is taken from what has been undoubtedly the most influential theoretical work on nationalism published in the past quarter century; Benedict Anderson, *Imagined Communities: Reflections on the Origin and Spread of Nationalism*, 13.

10. Soyinka, 129. It may well be that Soyinka puts this too categorically. In 1917, for example, when both the tsarist and imperial Russian governments failed,

the Communists succeeded precisely by trampling on most of Russia's traditional cultural values, placing their political agenda first.

11. Walicki, 77. Emphasis mine.   12. Greenfeld, 348–49.

13. Greenfeld, 10–11.   14. Ugrešić, "Balkan Blues," 10.

15. Anyone wishing for a more detailed survey should consult Barbara and Charles Jelavich, 3–37; Lampe, chapter 1; and Sugar, 63–110, 168–83.

16. Of these groups, only the Bulgarians were not ethnically Slavic. They were descendents of a Turkic tribe that had migrated to the Western shores of the Black Sea in the seventh century. In the course of the next few centuries, however, the Turkic Bulgars were culturally and linguistically Slavicized.

17. The Croatian kingdom was an exception in this regard, for despite its incorporation into the Kingdom of Hungary in 1102, some of its political institutions survived more or less intact into the modern period.

18. Whenever possible I have tried to analyze literary works that have been translated into English. In most cases, these also happen to be written by the best-known and most influential South Slavic writers. When translations are not available, I have provided plot summaries of the works in question.

19. Perhaps the most influential single work of this sort is Robert Kaplan's *Balkan Ghosts: A Journey Through History.*

20. Misha Glenny puts it succinctly: "Mass killing in the Balkans has always taken place in times of political and constitutional crisis whose origins are thoroughly modern. Specifically, they have been caused by the steady degeneration of both the Ottoman and the Austro-Hungarian Empires in the nineteenth century and the political consequences of imperial collapse in the twentieth century" ("Why the Balkans Are So Violent," 36).

21. This claim is usefully exploded by Predrag Matvejević in his spirited defense of the Yugoslav idea: "That unhappy 'Versailles' Yugoslavia is in great measure the source of our contradictions, both individual and collective. First of all, it is not actually 'Versailles.' We ourselves wanted it, and the best among us had given a great deal for her without regard to the decision of the Versailles Conference. . . . Of course, the great powers, France in particular, had their fingers in the pie, but without the definite will of the Yugoslav peoples which was already manifested to the world with the actions of Princip, there would have never been such a state" (196–97). Translation is mine, as are all further unattributed translations.

22. Žižek, "Caught in Another's Dream in Bosnia," in *Why Bosnia?*, 239.

23. Taylor, 7.

24. In this conclusion, I differ strongly from most other scholars who have analyzed Yugoslavia's breakdown. They have generally placed the blame on too much centralism and have claimed that federalism, applied earlier and more broadly, would have saved Yugoslavia. I, on the other hand, see no evidence that federalism applied earlier would not have merely hastened the dissolution of the country. To my mind, it was not centralism that was at fault, but the wrong kind of central-

ism, one that emphasized political and economic cooperation without providing a sufficiently strong central culture.

25. Gellner, 45.

CHAPTER I

1. The exception was Hungary, where native gentry had managed to remain in power but were no less invested in the existing hierarchy than their German-speaking peers.

2. In this focus, the thought of German theoreticians, particularly Johann Gottfried von Herder was decisive. As Liah Greenfeld puts it in her discussion of German nationalism: "German nationalism, like any other, symbolically elevated the masses and profoundly changed the nature of status hierarchy in German society. In its veneration of the people, specifically the peasantry, the virtuous *Volk*, gloriously indifferent to the march of unnatural civilization and faithfully upholding its pristine purity, German nationalism, in fact, far surpassed its Western counterparts" (369).

3. Quoted in Taylor, 29.

4. It is this tradition also that helps explain the high political position attained in our own day by such writers as Václav Havel, Arpad Göncz, and Jozsef Antal.

5. For a solid summary of the political situation of the empire in this period, see Taylor.

6. Of course, these uninational movements themselves had to reach some kind of consensus as to which peasant practices and dialects would become characteristic for the national tradition, for there were larger or smaller differences present in each of the above-mentioned groups.

7. Most early plans for South Slavic unity included the Bulgarians as well, but the Bulgarians themselves showed little interest in combining culturally or politically with their South Slavic brothers, and separate Bulgarian nationalism was already triumphant by the mid-1870s. The final nail in the coffin of a potential pan–South Slavic union including Bulgaria was the so-called Second Balkan War (1913) fought primarily between Serbia and Bulgaria. For a succinct account of the founding of Bulgaria, see Barbara and Charles Jelavich, chapter 11.

8. As M. H. Abrams has noted, romantic ideologies strongly opposed the analytic tendencies that had been in the ascendancy during the previous cultural period, which were criticized precisely for their inability to grasp the whole. See Abrams, 303–11.

9. I am, of course, aware that I am using these national terms anachronistically here. In the period we are discussing, a feeling of national solidarity was completely lacking in most of these groups, who would have imagined their identity in other terms.

10. Anderson, 123.

11. For a detailed discussion of this literary language, see Albin, 483–91.

12. For a summary of Kopitar's life and work, see Cooper, 45–51.

13. For a competent source on Gaj's life and work, see Despalatović.

14. The names of the dialects derive from the ways in which each expressed the word "what."

15. "In the academic year 1828–29 Gaj and Demeter became increasingly involved in the problems of the Croatian literary language. They assumed at this time that modern Croatian would be based upon the kajkavski dialect" (Despalatović, 44).

16. Despalatović, 81.

17. Reprinted in *Antologija ilirskog pokreta*, 47.

18. Quoted in Jonke, 47.

19. The other points on which they agreed were more minor matters of grammar and orthography.

20. Indeed, it is interesting that the changes that would have been required to switch to the dialect proposed were quite minor in comparison to the changes that Gaj and his followers had already agreed to some years before. That is to say that, in terms of linguistic requirements, the creation of a unified language from existing Serbian and Croatian should have been easier, at least on paper, than the creation of a single and unified Croatian literary language had been.

21. Franolic, 32.

22. The Yugoslav Academy remained in Zagreb for the entire period of Yugoslavia's existence as a unified state. Indeed, it was perhaps the only prestigious national institution that was not headquartered in Belgrade. During the existence of the so-called Independent State of Croatia during World War II, the academy's name was changed to the Croatian Academy of Arts and Sciences, but after the war it was rechristened with its original name. In 1991 the name was again changed to the Croatian Academy of Arts and Sciences.

23. Jonke, 52.

24. There has been, over the years, quite a bit of controversy as to whether the Vuk-Daničić approach was indeed a fair, reasonable, and intelligent compromise. Croatian linguists, especially in periods of heightened Croatian national feeling, have attacked the academy *Dictionary* for failing to include Croatian dialectical forms from Kajkavian and Čakavian, for its rejection of many modern loan words, as well as an overreliance on forms taken from folk poetry (see, for example, the discussion in Franolic, 29–40). On the other hand, certain Serbian-oriented writers have decried the loss of the Slaveno-Serbian high style and tradition (perhaps the most eloquent expression of this view is in *Za i protiv Vuka* by the Bosnian Meša Selimović, esp. chapter 8). Although both of these criticisms are justified to an extent, there is no question that, for Daničić at least, the approach of the *Dictionary* represented a reasonable compromise between Serb and Croat desires and

practices. Clearly, it did provide the basis for a usable unified language for as long as that was desired.

25. For a general survey of efforts to bring Serbian and Croatian closer together in the second half of the nineteenth century, see Herrity, 162–75.

26. The proposal appeared in his article "Istočno ili južno narečje" published in the leading Serbian journal *Srpski književni glasnik* in response to a survey of leading cultural figures. Like many of his predecessors, Skerlić pointed to language and literature as the basis for a Serb-Croat union which, he felt, was both desirable and inevitable. "In the first half of the nineteenth century, amidst the Serbo-Croatian people who had hitherto lived regionally divided, a strong movement toward unification and unity appeared. The great success in this direction was the disappearance of local literatures and the concentration of the cultural and literary life of our nation in two centers: Belgrade (at first in Novi Sad) and Zagreb. Particularly important was that the Serbs and Croats developed a single literary language. . . . National unity follows its natural course, and this process of strengthening, even if it goes more slowly than it should, can be stopped by nothing" (quoted in Novak, 655). Other participants expressed the need for a compromise even more forcefully: "Ekavian and the Latin alphabet are the elements of a compromise formula (the most practical one) for the achievement of full literary unity between Serbs and Croats" (Josip Smodlak, quoted in Novak, 673). Fran Ilešič, the head of the most important Slovene cultural society, Matica slovenska, was also in favor of the switch to Ekavian, claiming that it would be seen by Slovenes as a step toward compromise with them as well (because they also spoke Ekavian). See Novak, 667.

27. de Bray, 315. The final joint statement of belief in the existence of a unified Serbo-Croatian was the so-called Novi Sad Agreement signed in 1954 by almost every major Yugoslav writer and linguist. For a text of this agreement and list of signatories, see *Pravopis hrvatskosrpskoga književnog jezika*, 7–10.

28. Tomšič, 18.

29. Cooper, 47.

30. Prešeren was identified as the national poet of Slovenia in an 1838 article by France Malavašič. See Cooper, 58.

31. For a summary of later arguments in this vein, see Vidmar, 60–77.

32. Anderson, 43.

33. These collections were expanded to four volumes in the "Leipzig" edition of 1823–33. The definitive edition of Vuk's collection appeared in Vienna in four volumes between 1841 and 1863.

34. In fact, South Slavic oral poetry had been introduced to Germany even before Vuk's collection appeared. The poem "The Wife of Asan Aga" had been published by the Italian Alberto Fortis as early as 1774 and was translated by Goethe soon afterward. Nevertheless, it was not until Vuk's edition appeared that the full richness of the South Slavic oral tradition was appreciated.

35. Quoted in Cooper, 57. Carniola is one of the main regions of Slovenia.

36. For more on this, see Merhar, 66–67.

37. The diction of sung poetry also provided a good part of the basis for a unified Serbo-Croatian language. One of Djura Daničić's fundamental sources for the linguistic material on which he based the Yugoslav Academy's Croatian-Serbian *Dictionary*, for example, was the oral tradition. See Čubelić, 313–27.

38. For an excellent discussion in English on the South Slavic oral tradition in general (and the oral epic in particular), see Koljević.

39. It appears that the oldest South Slavic oral tradition employed poetic lines of longer length, the so-called *bugarštica*. In any case, the earliest recorded examples of South Slavic epic songs (dating from the sixteenth century) employ this poetic line. However, it appears that already by this time the bugarštica was being supplanted by the decasyllabic line.

40. Serbo-Croatian text from Karadžić, vol. 2, 214. English translation from *Marko the Prince*, 17.

41. *Marko the Prince*, 18.

42. Serbo-Croatian text from Karadžić, 220. English translation from *Marko the Prince*, 24.

43. From his commentary in *Marko the Prince*, 30. English translation from *Marko the Prince*, 46. In this translation the poem is called "Prince Marko Knows His Father's Sword."

44. Serbo-Croatian text from Karadžić, vol. 2, 248.

45. Letter of May 5, 1845. Published in *Gradja za povijest književnosti hrvatske*, vol. 1, 115.

46. Preradović, 141–42.

47. Mažuranić's work has been translated into English several times, most recently as *Smail-Aga Čengić's Death* in a Yugoslav-published journal called *The Bridge* (trans. Charles A. Ward, no. 17 (1969): 5–34).

48. It is true that some of the sections of Preradović's Marko Kraljević play employ the deseterac, but the overall form is that of romantic drama, rather than folk song.

49. In all fairness, however, it should be noted that the elegance, terseness, and sonic quality of Mažuranić's verse line recalls not so much folk poetry as the techniques of the Croatian Renaissance poets (particularly that of Ivan Gundulić, for whose uncompleted epic *Osman* Mažuranić wrote two cantos in 1844). Thus, it is possible to say that by combining the verse techniques of the oral epic and the Croatian Renaissance, Mažuranić showed the way for a "Yugoslav" culture that would synthesize the most productive elements of the mostly Serbian popular cultural tradition with the mightiest achievements of Croatian high culture. In this sense, his work is a predecessor to that of Meštrović.

50. Njegoš, 1. Further references to *The Mountain Wreath* are taken from this bilingual edition. Page numbers will be noted in the main text.

51. Actually, there is quite a bit of controversy surrounding the question of whether the central event described in *The Mountain Wreath* (the destruction of the Montenegrin converts to Islam) ever occurred. Most commentators seem to feel that if such a violent process happened at all, it was over a long period of time and in disorganized fashion, rather than in the way Njegoš portrays it.

52. According to the sung poetry describing the events surrounding the Battle of Kosovo, before the battle Vuk Branković had accused Obilić of being a traitor. On the day of the battle, however, Obilić proved his loyalty by killing the Turkish sultan, and Branković turned out to be a traitor to Serbdom.

53. The most telling recent example of this was the famous speech of Slobodan Milošević at Kosovo on April 27, 1987. "In his address to the assembled Slavs, he [Milošević] spoke of the injustice and humiliation they were suffering; of their ancestral land; of the proud warrior spirit of their forefathers; of their duty to their descendants. The speech was aimed at the people's emotions: listening to the speech, Pavlović saw 'an idea turned into a dogma, the Kosovo myth becoming reality'" (Magaš, 201).

54. The original of this line literally means "the way a soup is put together in a pot."

55. The Abbot Stefan appears to be, in many respects, modeled on Pushkin's monk Pimen from *Boris Godunov*. Like Pimen, Stefan has traveled much and seen much, and again like Pimen, his words lead directly to the actions of others. This is only one of a number of potential connections to Pushkin's drama (others include the prominent role played by the "folk," the specific comic touch of an illiterate being forced to read, and the more general role of the paralyzed leader).

56. Selenić, *Timor mortis*, 246.

57. Skerlić, 235. Skerlić (1877–1914) was an extraordinarily prolific literary critic, who also played a very visible role on the cultural-political scene in the immediate prewar period.

58. Ivo Vojnović (1857–1929) hailed from an old noble Dubrovnik family. He was a prolific writer of stories and dramas and is best known for his modernist inflected *Dubrovačka trilogija* (Dubrovnik Trilogy), a trilogy of one-act plays.

59. For details on the controversy surrounding the choice of a site for Meštrović's work at the 1911 exposition, see Marjanović, "Genij jugoslovenstva Ivan Meštrović i njegov hram." The temple itself was never completed, although drawings and the wooden model survive.

60. Strajnić, "Umetnost Meštrovića," 115–16.

61. Meštrović, "Zamisao Kosovskog hrama," 447–48.

62. Krleža, *Zastave*, vol. 2, 159.

63. *Almanah srpskih i hrvatskih pjesnika i pripovijedača*, 8.

64. Rogel, 89.

65. Podlimbarski, 234.

66. I do not know for certain that the journal was closed by the exigencies of

the war, but only two issues, March and May 1914, appeared. The latter issue contains a memorial to Skerlić who died in mid-May, so it is likely that the journal did not actually appear until the very end of the month. Given the general situation, a July/August issue would almost certainly have been banned had the editor not decided to close up shop on his own.

67. *Glas juga* 1, no. 1 (Mar. 1914): 3.

68. For a more detailed treatment of South Slavic culture during World War I, see my article "The South Slavic Lands During World War I: Culture and Nationalism."

69. The only Slovene-oriented cultural groups that were allowed to operate more or less freely in the first few years of the war were clerical groups that supported the monarchy. For a detailed discussion of Slovene cultural life during the war, see Matič, 1994.

70. An example of the latter was the newspaper *Tedenske slike* (The Week in Pictures), which began to appear in Ljubljana just as the war commenced. It advertised itself as a "completely loyal, patriotic, openly Austrophilic paper" (no. 1 [Aug. 12, 1914]: 13).

71. The group also published a series of four pamphlets entitled *The Southern Slav Library*, which were distributed in English and French. The fourth pamphlet, entitled "Southern Slav Culture" made this claim: "In former epochs Jugoslav literature was represented by a series of provincial schools. . . . From the end of the eighteenth century, however, they began to be drawn together, to tend toward unity; they expanded on broadly national lines, and finally became one great indivisible *Jugoslav literature*" (15). This view of the history of South Slavic literature would become completely standard in the interwar years.

72. Ćurčin, "Prefatory Note," v. The Croatian poet Tin Ujević was equally lavish in his praise. See "Meštrovićeva izložba i jugoslovenska intuicija," Ujević, vol. 6, 258–66.

73. Seton-Watson, 59.

74. See, for example, *Jugoslovanski glasnik* (Niš), 1915, or *Prosveta Almanah za godinu 1918*. The latter was compiled in 1917 by Pero Slepčević and published in Geneva while the war was still going on. The almanac is filled with secessionist-style woodcuts, reproductions of Meštrović sculpture, and lots of Yugoslav integrationist propaganda.

75. Information about editions of *Smail-Aga Čengić* was taken from an edition of the work edited by Davor Kapetanić and published in Zagreb in 1968.

76. Unsigned feuilleton, *Savremenik* 12, no. 7, (Oct. 1917): 318.

77. *Tedenske slike*, Mar. 27, 1918, 2.

78. *Književni jug* 1, no. 6 (Mar. 16, 1918): 209.

79. Loboda, 181.

80. *Slovenski narod*, Sept. 2, 1918, 1.

CHAPTER 2

1. Tkalčić, 263–64.

2. Bogumil Vošnjak, 104. Although Vošnjak's book is written in Serbo-Croatian, he was a Slovenian by birth.

3. "The Southern Slav Programme," 3.

4. Cvijić, *Balkansko poluostrvo*, 347–60. Cvijić's book, originally written in French, was supported by the Serbian government as part of its campaign to convince the allies of the wisdom of a postwar Yugoslav state. The role of the Serbian government in subsidizing this and other, similar scholarly works is discussed extensively in Trgovčević.

5. Trifunovska, 159; emphasis mine.

6. It is unclear exactly where and when this formula was invented. In the prewar period the belief that Serbs and Croats were a single nation was widespread (see, for example, the forceful use of this formula by Adam Pribićević in his defense of the Serbs accused of treason in Zagreb in 1909 [Novak, 545]). I have not found the three-named people usage before the war, however.

7. Recognized minorities included Germans (505,790), Magyars (467,658), Albanians (439,657), Romanians (231,068), Turks (150,322), Czechs and Slovaks (115,532), Ruthenes (25,615), Russians (20,568), Poles (14,764), Italians (12,553). Figures provided in Darby et al., 165.

8. In practice, minority groups were treated variously in the kingdom. Germans and Hungarians had elementary schools in their own languages from 1918, as did Romanians a bit later. Albanians and Turks, however, had no schools of their own. In part this situation was merely a continuation of the prewar educational picture, but it is clear that the Yugoslav government was in no hurry to provide education to minorities in the southern part of the country.

9. If these groups are separated, one sees that the actual population breakdown was as follows: Serbs (39 percent), Croats (24 percent), Slovenes (8.5 percent), Bosnian Moslems (6 percent), Macedonians (4.5 percent), other minorities (18 percent). These percentages are derived from the population figures estimated by Banac, *The National Question*, 49–53.

10. Trifunovska, 190. For a detailed summary of the Macedonian question in this period, see Banac, *The National Question*, 307–28.

11. Such attitudes had a basis in the late-nineteenth-century ideology of certain Serbs and Croats. For details on this, see Banac, *The National Question*, 362–65.

12. For an extremely forceful statement on the subject of Moslem assimilationism, see Muradbegović. Muradbegović argues that the Yugoslav Moslems are an essential part of the nation, "the purest and best-preserved type of our race" (108). He goes on to say, however, that "the Moslems must purge their culture by means

of occidental civilization, for oriental forms are not only not ideal, but are actually foreign to its character" (115). The journal *Nova Evropa* devoted two entire numbers to the question of Yugoslav Islam (3, no. 4 [1921] and 11, no. 10 [1930]).

13. In fact, although the political policies of the postwar government are usually seen as pro-Serb, it would be more accurate to characterize them as anti-Habsburg. For they discriminated as much against Serbian former citizens of the Austro-Hungarian Empire as against Croats and Slovenes. An example can be seen in the country's tax system, which "favored Serbia" and was "unfair not only to the Croats and Slovenes, but also to the Serbs outside Serbia proper" (Banac, *The National Question*, 224–25).

14. Banac, *The National Question*, 116.

15. For example, in 1915, Pašić was induced to support the Entente's gift of large portions of Croatian and Slovenian territory to Italy (as a reward to the Italians for joining the Entente) by the promise that Serbia would be allowed to control adjacent territories—most importantly Bosnia-Herzegovina and Slavonia—not given to Italy in a postwar treaty.

16. The committee published a four-volume set of pamphlets in 1915–16 entitled *The Southern Slav Library*, which was widely distributed in English and French.

17. Quoted in Banac, *The National Question*, 123.

18. Of the leading parties in the parliamentary elections of 1920, the powerful Radicals "were an almost exclusively Serb party" (Banac, *The National Question*, 156). The Democrats, who were in principle an all-Yugoslav party and who received the largest share of the popular vote, "did very badly for a party that considered itself above Yugoslavia's national divisions. Only 41.48% of its votes came from the former Austro-Hungarian territories, and almost two-fifths of that was in areas of Serb concentration" (ibid., 175). In Croatia, on the other hand, the leading party was Stjepan Radić's Croatian Peasant Party, which had almost no backing outside of Croatia. The only real exception to this trend was the Agrarians, but they were more a coalition of separate national peasant parties than an actual political party. The Communists, who should theoretically have appealed to voters in all areas of the country, in fact had a large following only "among the nationally disaffected" (ibid., 329), primarily in Montenegro and Macedonia.

19. Ibid., 404.

20. L., "Priča o polugi," 289–90.

21. See Perovšek, 121–34.

22. These quotations are taken from the "Pohorska Declaration" of 1935 as quoted in Jurij Perovšek, "Slovenci in Jugoslavija v tridesetih letih" (unpublished paper).

23. Rebecca West, 85–86.

24. A typical expression of this feeling can be found in Kluić, 133: "The first task in the creation of a nation is this: let there be one basic thought of our ideol-

ogy whether it be God or the Devil, Serbia or Croatia, Tsar Lazar or Petar Svačić, but the main thing is that there be a single thought, a single conscious and unconscious philosophical worldview, a single ethic from Maribor to Dževdželie from the Adriatic to Džerdapa. One cannot have a nation while one part of the people views the world from the point of view of European rationalism while another part still squints through the mysticism of the East." The obvious preference for some form of European thought here clearly shows that this author, along with many other unitarists, did not view the various Yugoslav cultures as equal. What is more, his view appears to be not synthetic but rather assimilationist (that is, one of the preexisting cultures should be the basis for the nation's culture). Nevertheless, his prejudices should not obscure the call for some form of unification.

25. As will be seen in my more detailed description of the interwar cultural scene below, my analysis differs sharply from that of Banac in *The National Question in Yugoslavia* (202–8). In great measure this is because, in my view, Banac is not sufficiently attuned to the variety of models that were proposed for a unified Yugoslav culture. Thus, he recognizes that many Croat intellectuals turned away from the type of synthesis that had been proposed by Meštrović in the prewar period, but he does not see that their criticisms contained different models for a synthetic culture.

26. "The state must unify the legal system for practical reasons, but it is not necessary for higher cultural reasons, to 'create' some kind of uniform 'culture' that would be raised on the ruins of today's cultural differences. Because these differences, that energy and variety of cultures, are, in our opinion, a great advantage and a factor of actual creative strength" (Borko, 16).

27. A tendency to pay lip service to Yugoslavism without actually including very much non-Serbian material appears to have been fairly common in Belgrade journals. For example, in his editor's introduction to the first number of a journal entitled *Prilozi za književnost, jezik, istoriju i folklor* (Contributions in Literature, Language, History, and Folklore), which began publication in 1921, Pavle Popović claimed that the journal would treat "our domestic, national, Yugoslav humanistic sciences" and that all were invited to publish their work "in the Cyrillic or Latin alphabets, in Serbo-Croatian or Slovenian." Nevertheless, on the thirty-seven-member editorial board there were exactly two Croatians and one Slovenian. And the articles published in the 1920s were heavily oriented toward Serbian themes.

28. *Savremenik* 12, no. 3 (June 1917): 119–24. The sets and costumes for this opera, reproduced in *Savremenik*, were by the noted Yugoslav-oriented artist Tomislav Krizman.

29. *Književni jug* 1, no. 2 (Jan. 15, 1918): 51. Šantić (1868–1924) a Serb from the Herzegovinian capital Mostar, was well known in the prewar period for his "patriotic" poetry devoted to the need for freedom from Austro-Hungarian domination. In the immediate postwar period, he published a number of poems of a strongly multiculturalist bent.

30. Nor were these publications unique in Zagreb. Another example was the journal *Narodna starina*, which appeared in Zagreb beginning in 1922 and was published more or less regularly into the mid-1930s (the final issue was, in fact, in 1939). Edited by Josip Matasović (who continued his duties even after being appointed to a chair in Skoplje), the journal was devoted to "the cultural history and ethnography of the Southern Slavs" (from the inside cover of vol. 1, no. 1), and it published a wide range of articles contributed from all over Yugoslavia.

31. *Jugoslavenska njiva* 10, no. 1 (Jan. 1, 1926): 1.

32. Tkalčić, 263.

33. Among others on the editorial board were Jovan Cvijić, Ivan Meštrović, and Milan Rakić. Contributions were promised from Ivo Andrić, Miloš Crnjanski, Jovan Dučić, the Slavist Vatroslav Jagić, Miroslav Krleža, Tin Ujević, and Ivo Vojnović, to name just a few.

34. Cankar, 322.

35. Emphasis mine. Quoted in Zečević, 352.

36. See Zečević, 360–69, as well as Dolenc, 23–40 and passim.

37. Andrić's speech on this topic was published in full in the journal *Jugoslavenska njiva* 3, no. 24 (1919): 373–75.

38. *Naš jezik* 1, no. 1 (1930): 1.

39. Quoted in Nećak, 99.

40. Vidmar himself was not opposed to Yugoslavism. Indeed, in the course of his long career he did much to promote a knowledge of Slovenian culture among Serbs and Croats and vice versa. He was, however, convinced that Yugoslavia could flourish as a multinational, rather than a multicultural culture. *The Cultural Problem of Slovenia* had become a bibliographical rarity before it was republished in the flush of Slovenian independence—edited with an introduction by Aleš Debeljak (Ljubljana: Cankarjeva izložba, 1995). It is ironic that, having now achieved not only full cultural autonomy but also national independence, the Slovenes are discovering that those "Yugoslavs" who claimed that there were too few Slovenes to support a modern language and culture were right to a certain extent. Because the market is so small and translation costs so high, translations of all but the most popular technical materials are prohibitively expensive. As a result, most Slovenes must now read the majority of such works in the original in English or German.

41. See Dolenc, 23–40.

42. *Slovenska čitanka za četrti razred srednjih šol,* ed. Josip Wester (Ljubljana, 1922).

43. Bartulović, 353.

44. Cvijić, "Osnovi jugoslovenske civilizacije," 216.

45. Zubović, 151. A bit later in the same article, Zubović makes his eugenic point quite clearly: "There is no true unity without blood ties, without a mixing of the various Yugoslav elements. Such a mixing is necessary in order to soften and eliminate sharp differences, of blood and territory. That is why it must be com-

plete, and cross all boundaries, of tribe and belief, of class, of region, and of terrain. It is the basis for the laws of modern eugenics, according to which the mixing of various but nevertheless close elements creates physically capable types" (152).

46. Dvorniković's cited methodological sources are impressively broad and include Freud, Jung, and Dilthey, in addition to many Nazi favorites. And although much of Dvorniković's methodology smacks of the worst Nazi racial theories, he claims to have nothing but scorn for the uses to which racially based characterological theorizing was put in the Third Reich. Indeed, he officially rejects national chauvinism, claiming that there is no hierarchy of races, but he still manages to let readers know that in addition to its prototypical warlike qualities, the Dinaric race is "despite its cultural backwardness, one of the most naturally gifted peoples of Europe" (609). In addition, he carefully quotes the research of another scholar to prove that "in the comparison of the Serbo-Croatian cranium with that of the other nations of Europe, Asia, and Africa, it is clear that Serbs and Croats lead all other peoples in brain size" (612).

47. Dvorniković includes the Bulgarians in the Turanian group, by the way, claiming that although they were Slavicized linguistically and culturally, their essential racial character is defined by the Turkic origins of the original Volga Bulgars. While this theory may not hold ethnological water, it does have the advantage of removing the Bulgarians from the Dinaric racial picture. The Yugoslavs for Dvorniković then can include only those Slavs who live in Yugoslavia.

48. Krklec, 138

49. Barac, "Književno jedinstvo." Barac (1894–1955) was probably the best-known Croatian literary historian of the twentieth century. In addition to monographs on many preeminent Croatian writers of the nineteenth and twentieth centuries, he wrote a textbook, translated as *A History of Yugoslav Literature*, which is the best available overview of South Slavic literature in English.

50. In particular, Barac attacked the view of Jovan Skerlić, who, despite his personal Yugoslav leanings, had expressed the belief, in his *Istorija nove srpske književnosti* (1914), that the literatures of the various South Slavic people were best treated and understood separately.

51. Pavle Popović, *Jugoslovenska književnost (Književnost Srba, Hrvata i Slovenaca)*. Popović (1868–1939) was one of the most influential Serbian literary critics in the period from just before World War I to just before World War II. Popović was born in Belgrade and was professor of Serbian literature at the University of Belgrade. He was also the secretary of the *Srpska književna zadruga* (Serbian Literary Society) from 1911 to 1920, its vice president from 1920 to 28, and president from 1928 to 1937. Thus, his views carried enormous weight in the literary world.

52. Pavle Popović, "Jugoslovenska književnost kao celina," 22.

53. Kršić, 144–45. See also in this regard Nikola Andrić. Andrić was the president of the League of Croatian Writers at the time, so his words were significant.

54. Kršić, 147.

55. *Antologija savremene jugoslavenske lirike*, 5. In their introduction, the editors claim that they made their choices on aesthetic grounds and that "in this anthology the majority of the poems derive from the eternal springs of poetry, to which poets always return" (3). The anthology avoids overtly patriotic or nationalistic poems for the most part, although a number are devoted to the Balkan wars and a couple are relatively well-known Yugoslav patriotic ones, including in particular Aleksa Šantić's "Novo pokolenje," which had originally been published in the first number of *Književni jug*, and Anton Aškerc's (Slovene) poem called "Na Kale-Mejdanu," which ends with the Blokian lines

> Tako smo, Evropa, te čuvali mi
> Pred narodov divjih udari;
> Tako, ah, potratili mlade smo dni
> Mi jugoslavenski—barbari.

> Thus it was, Europe, that we guarded you
> From the blows of wild peoples;
> Thus, alas, we spent our youth
> We, the Yugoslav barbarians.

56. In this respect, postwar textbooks were substantially different from those that had existed in the prewar period. In his fundamental study, *South Slavic Nationalisms—Textbooks and Yugoslav Union Before 1914*, Charles Jelavich makes it quite clear that prewar textbooks were not written with the idea of Yugoslav unity in mind at all and that they therefore did not serve to prepare their readers to live in the state that was created after the war: "An analysis of the textbooks makes one point very clear: none of the books—Serbian, Croatian, or Slovenian—even remotely conveyed the type of information and enthusiasm about South Slav unity or Yugoslavism that was being expounded by intellectuals, university students, and a few politicians in the decade before the war" (272).

In Jelavich's subsequent article entitled "Education, Textbooks, and South Slav Nationalisms in the Interwar Era," he claims that interwar textbooks did not differ significantly from their predecessors. I disagree with his analysis for a number of reasons. First of all, Jelavich appears to expect too much from textbooks. Where it would be possible to see gradual progress, he concentrates on those places where none was made. More important, however, is his strange idea of what an acceptable Yugoslav message might have been in this period. Thus, for example, he complains that readers from the 1920s included the national hymns of the Serbs, Croats, and Slovenes, rather than only a Yugoslav hymn. But, as we have seen, most visions of a synthetic Yugoslav culture included a recognition of its diversity, so there is nothing subversive about this. Finally, the reasons for our differing conclusions, I suspect, lie in the fact that Jelavich concentrates his attention on readers for the lower grades, while I looked primarily at those designed for high schools. I did so because it is the opinions of elites that tend to affect the country as a whole, and the higher grades were where these elites were trained. What Jelavich's work may illustrate is a split between what elites and normal children in the first Yugoslavia were taught, a split that was amplified by the fact that in many of Yugoslavia's poorest regions, education was almost nonexistent.

57. The extent to which unitarism was official policy of the Ministry of Education by the 1930s can be seen from the published educational program for the kingdom. For example: "Geography lessons in conjunction with history and the national language develop a feeling for the unity of our people and state" (*Učni načrt za osnovne šole v Kraljevini Jugoslaviji* [Ljubljana, 1933; with approval of the Ministry of Education, Belgrade], 6). The only(!) stated purpose of history lessons in this document is "making students aware of the past of the Yugoslav people and raising them in the spirit of the nation" (7).

58. *Čitanka za srednje škole*, comp. Asa Prodanović, 4 vols. Belgrade, 1928. In vol. 2, for example, we find thirty-three authors identified as coming from Serbia, fifteen from Croatia, seven from Slovenia, nine from Bosnia or Herzegovina, and two from Montenegro. In addition, there are seven from Dalmatia, and fifteen from Old Serbia (i.e., Kosovo region), Slavonia, Srem, Bačka, and Banat.

59. At the same time, it is worth noting that the kinds of blatantly chauvinistic (i.e., Serbian, Croatian, or Slovenian nationalistic) texts that Jelavich found so prominently represented in the prewar readers are absent here.

60. *Istorija jugoslovenske književnosti sa teorijom i primerima za III i IV razred gradjanskih škola*, 107. This book was published with a stamp of ministerial approval for use in schools.

61. From the article entitled "Kako je postao dobrovoljački odred u Rusiji," by Č, 359, one of a whole series of articles on the volunteer movement in this issue.

62. Vitomir F. Jelenc, "From the Memoirs of a Jugoslav Volunteer," in *Slovenska čitanka za četrti razred srednjih šol*, ed. Josip Wester (Ljubljana, 1922), 26–27. Another reader provides the following information on the volunteer movement: "During the time of our desperate fights against the Germans and Hungarians, Serbs, Croats, and Slovenes from Austria came to our aid. Of course there could not be many of them. But when the enemy overran Serbia, our brother Serbs, Croats, and Slovenes who live in America quickly came to our aid in large numbers. More than 10,000 volunteers came from far-away America to the Solon front. Thus, of the Serbs, Croats, and Slovenes a Yugoslav division was formed." *Čitanka za IV razred osnovne škole u kraljevini Jugoslaviji*, ed. Mih. Jović, 5th ed. (Belgrade, 1931), 173.

63. *Nova Evropa* 11, no. 16 (1927): 497.

64. Dvorniković, 358 and 425. Miroslav Krleža, one of whose greatest talents was deflating myths of all kinds, provides an excellent picture of the strength of this particular myth in his novel *Zastave* (Banners).

65. Ibid., 358.

66. *Primeri nove književnosti*, 139.

67. It is, for example, the only passage provided in *Istorija jugoslovenske književnosti sa teorijom i primerima za III i IV razred gradjanskih škola*. It is the featured passage in *Primeri nove književnosti*. The other, shorter, excerpts presented there are similarly "harmless." One finds the same tendency, by the way, in post–World War II readers. "Vojvoda Draško Visits the Venetians" is, for example, the only extended passage present in *Čitanka za VIII razred osnovne škole* ed. Bojin Dramusić and Radojka Radulović 8th ed. (Sarajevo, 1960; with approval of the Ministry of Education, BiH); the other passages given are all aphoristic statements that give no idea of the theme of the work as a whole. The same is true for *Naš put u jezik i književnost (Priručnik za drugi stupanj osnovnog obrazovanja odraslih)*, ed. Stojadin Stojanović (Belgrade, 1970).

68. Njegoš, *Izabrana pisma*, 152.

69. Ibid., 173.

70. Škerović, 3.

71. Prodanović, 562.

72. Njegoš, *The Mountain Wreath*, 23.

73. Ivo Andrić, *Sabrana djela*, vol. 13, 16.

74. Njegoš had asked to be buried on Lovćen, one of the highest points in Montenegro. However, after he died, Montenegrin authorities feared that the body would not be safe in this unguarded and unguardable spot, and he was instead buried on the grounds of the Cetinje monastery. His body was soon transferred to Lovćen, however (in 1854), where it remained until 1916, when the Austrians exhumed Njegoš and brought his remains back to Cetinje. For an extensive consideration of these events, see Durković-Jakšić.

75. Vrhovac, 3.

76. Even the daily newspaper *Jutro* in far-off Slovenia, gave the event quite a bit of space. Readers were given daily bulletins on the trip of the king and queen to Cetinje (they passed through the Kosovo region on the way, visiting Dečani and Peć). On September 22, the paper carried a long article on Njegoš and his significance, noting that he was "a great Illyrian, a great Yugoslav, and prophet of today's freedom" (5).

77. Quoted in Durković-Jakšić, 260.

78. Vrhovac, 3.

79. Bogdanović, 577.

80. Štedimlija, 122–23.

81. Dvorniković, 545.

82. L., "Novo jugoslovenstvo," 81. The same view was stated even more forcefully in the journal's lead article of August 21, 1924: "We cannot allow people to say to us again: 'From the last Balkan war and even before, twelve full years and more, you have been preaching continually about some kind of Yugoslavdom, postulating some new person, some Yugoslav type, but you have never showed clearly either what you want or how you will do it. How will you win us over and convince us?'—Starting from our basic ideas, we must give a clear picture of our Yugoslav person, the Yugoslav family" (Zubović, 145).

83. Quoted in Vošnjak, 49–50.

84. Silvije Strahimir Kranjčević (1865–1908) was the greatest Croatian lyric poet of the second half of the nineteenth century. His nationalist poetry is highly rhetorical and frequently Croatian-oriented. Nevertheless, his poetry was quite influential in Yugoslav circles, particularly such pan-Slavic works as "Slavenska lipa" (The Slavic Linden), from 1897.

85. In particular, beginning in the last years of the war, Meštrović began to produce significant numbers of religious works that by their nature alluded solely to Western traditions. The sculptor was also internationally respected and produced many works on commission, like his monumental *Native American on Horseback*, which stands in Chicago, which lacked any connection to Yugoslavia.

86. Although most of Meštrović's most rabid supporters were Croats, he had many Serbian admirers as well, including King Aleksandar. For Serbian praise of the artist, see Kordić.

87. Of these, only the last was completed as the sculptor had envisioned. The victory monument was originally planned as a commemoration of the Serbian victory in the First and Second Balkan Wars and was erected only in part (for more on this, see below). The Njegoš project was never built at all, although an impressive preliminary drawing was completed (as shown in Figure 4, page 110). In addition, the sculptor did complete a plaster study for a sculptural monument to Njegoš in 1932 (see the frontispiece). A granite version of this monument, completed in 1958 by Andrija Krstulović, now stands in the Njegoš mausoleum on Mt. Lovćen.

88. *Nova Evropa* 27, no. 10 (1934): 338.

89. Anderson, 17.

90. Meštrović's recollection of the events surrounding this commission is related in his usual off-hand style in his memoirs: "In the Fall the King asked me to come and see him. This time it was due to 'artistic' affairs. He told me that in imitation of the French everyone had begun paying homage to the graves of 'unknown soldiers' and that here all foreign delegations were going to the base of Avala, where some peasants had erected an ugly headstone and given it the name 'tomb of the unknown soldier' because they had found there the skeleton of some buried soldier wearing Serbian boots. He was embarrassed by this poor grave and what is more he owed a debt to fallen warriors. So he asked me to make a plan for a suitable tomb for an unknown soldier" (*Spomini*, 293–94).

91. Vojnović, 25–26.

92. In the view of many Meštrović supporters, it was the originality of Meštrović's art that separated it from the works of any of his predecessors. For the clearest statement of this view, see Strajnić, *Ivan Meštrović*, 18.

93. *Književnik* 1, no. 3 (1928): 79.

94. This was the view of the young, pre-Communist Moše Pijade as well as that of Krleža. For an unsympathetic summary of their arguments, see Milan

Ćurčin, "Na pedeseti dan rodjenja Ivana Meštrovića," *Nova Evropa* 26, no. 8 (1933): 323. Krleža, with his usual razor-edged wit, managed to get in some excellent digs against the leaders of the Meštrović cult: "Snobs, English ladies, and Herr Doctor Milan Ćurčin, editor of *Nova Evropa* think of Meštrović in the style of the introduction to an exhibition catalogue: he is the heaven-inspired genius who has come to earth to unite the Serbs and Croats. He is for them a prophet, and an artist only insofar as he is a prophet" (*Književnik* 1, no. 3 (1928): 83–84).

95. In the spring of 1927 the Belgrade newspaper *Vreme* published a series of articles devoted to this subject under the title "What Do Our Literati and Artists Think of Meštrović's 'Victory'?" See also the lengthy discussion on the subject in *Nova Evropa 16*, no. 1 (July 11, 1927): 2–9.

96. "Srpska mistika—Meštrović," *Pravda* (Belgrade) nos. 121–24 (Apr. 30–May 3, 1932): 17.

97. By the way, the newspaper in which this was published was by no means a hyper-Serb nationalist one. The same issue contains a series of articles devoted to contemporary Slovenian culture, for example, aimed at allowing Serbs to get to know the Slovenes better. But it is not a Yugoslav paper as Meštrović and his friends would have understood it in that it does not expect that these people will ever become one.

98. Cesarec, "Vidovdan slijepih miševa," 100.

99. *Politika*, May 20, 1927, 1.

100. "Pred Meštrovićevim 'Hristom,'" 37.

101. For a detailed description of the variety of attempts to use oral poetic motives as the basis for a modern literature in Serbia, see Mitrović, 43–68. Mitrović traces the origins of this movement to the work of Lazarević in the late 1880s through the 1920s.

102. Mitrović, 60.

103. Andrić, *Sabrana djela*, vol. 8, 9–10.

104. Other writers of this period to incorporate a Moslem perspective or a Moslem concern in their work included the Jewish writer Isak Samokovlija and Herzegovinian Moslem Alija Nametak. The question of Andrić's own attitude to Yugoslav Moslems is ambiguous. Certainly he described them frequently in his stories and novels set in Bosnia. But his doctoral dissertation, *The Development of Spiritual Life in Bosnia under the Influence of Turkish Rule*, written in 1924, has nothing good to say about the influence of Moslem culture in Yugoslavia. I take up this issue in more detail in Chapters 3 and 4.

105. Šimunović, 435.

106. Ibid., 436.

107. Ibid., 437–38.

108. Nazor, "Dinku Šimunoviću, mjesto nekrologa," 429.

109. Miloš Crnjanski, "Objašnjene Sumatre," quoted in Stefanović and Stanisavljević, 189.

110. Quoted in "Kronologija Tina Ujevića" compiled by Dragutin Tadijanović in Ujević, *Sabrana djela*, vol. 17, 506–7.

111. Others who could profitably be discussed in these terms include the Croatian Antun Šimić, the Serbians Miloš Crnjanski and Marko Ristić or the Slovenian Oton Zupančič.

112. Kadić, 44.

113. Quoted in the notes to Ujević, *Sabrana djela*, vol. 1, 243. Ujević's hostility to the heroic cultural model can be seen in his comments on Meštrović's *Victory*: "Today, in the age of tanks, cannons, bombs, poison gas and airplanes, one cannot get away with emphasizing physical strength." Quoted in an interview on the subject in Ujević, *Sabrana djela*, vol. 14, 618.

114. Ibid., vol. 1, 176.

115. In a discussion of Miloš Crnjanski in the context of avant-garde poetry, Zdenko Lešić identifies four features shared by the poets of the postwar avant-garde. These are "(1) a new poetic sensibility (usually followed by a new faith); (2) the introduction of new poetic rhythms (usually realised by free verse); (3) the break up of the usual syntagmatic order in the linguistic discourse; and (4) a critical attitude towards all traditional poetic forms" (Lešić, 14).

116. The following description, by the Serbian Jewish poet Stanislav Vinaver, gives some idea of Ujević's modus vivendi in those days: "During the day he usually sleeps, frequently in some ravine. . . . At night Tin roams, usually from one cafe to another. He visits various groups, speaks about any topic, and in his banter there is more wisdom than in the entire repertoire of our best-known and most-authoritative giants. Tin drinks enormous quantities, screams horribly, never changes his clothes or bathes." Quoted in Ujević, *Sabrana djela*, vol. 17, 508.

117. The willingness of the editors of such Belgrade journals as *Progres*, *Misao*, *Vreme*, and *Putevi* to publish Ujević's poetry illustrates not only their good taste, but the cosmopolitan nature of the Belgrade literary scene in the 1920s and 1930s.

118. See his 1940 article "Tin Ujević traži katedru na sveučilištu" in Ujević, *Sabrana djela*, vol. 7, 251–55 for the most extreme statement of this belief.

119. Indeed, the major book on Krleža in English, by Ralph Bogert, is entitled *The Writer as Naysayer: Miroslav Krleža and the Aesthetic of Interwar Central Europe*.

120. Krleža, *The Return of Philip Latinowicz*, 31–32.

121. Ibid., 68.

122. Ibid., 58.

123. Krleža's debt to Dostoevsky is a topic worthy of a separate investigation. In this novel, other Dostoevskian elements include constant philosophical digressions and a frequent use of public scandal scenes. Krleža's Dostoevskian orientation helps explain his rivalry within Yugoslav literature with Ivo Andrić, who is generally Tolstoyan in approach.

124. Lasić, 325.

125. Cesarec, *Pjesme, novele, zapisi, eseji, i putopisi*, vol. 1, 44.

126. Vladimir Popović, "August Cesarec," in Cesarec, *Pjesme, novele, zapisi, eseji, i putopisi,* vol. 1, 32.

CHAPTER 3

1. The Ustashas were a fascist group that evolved out of the prewar Croatian Frankist Party of Right. The party's leader, Ante Pavelić, lived as an emigré from 1929. Supported by Mussolini and Admiral Horthy, they planned the successful assassination of King Aleksandar in 1934. They were installed as rulers of the NDH by the Germans. For more background, see Lampe, 170–73 and 203–6.

2. Jews and Roma were also to be liquidated, but they were clearly of less importance to Pavelić.

3. The actual numbers of wartime casualties, as well as the guilt for their deaths, have been a subject of ongoing controversy. For a good summary of views on the subject, see Bogosavljević, xi–xvi.

4. Richard West, 80–81.

5. See Singleton, 187–90, for a summary of the history and activity of the Chetniks.

6. See Richard West, 118–19 for a description of Mihailović's Chetnik ideology.

7. Singleton, 211.

8. "In the early 1920s, unitarist Yugoslavism was not official policy, even though the country was being governed in a centralist way. Unitarist Yugoslavism was to be introduced only after the establishment of the royal dictatorship in 1929. Communists, however, were unitarists from the very foundation of Yugoslavia" (Djilas, 61). The basis for their belief in unitarism was, of course, Marxist theory, which predicted that nations would eventually disappear, their place taken by international working-class solidarity. Hence, anything that could be done to hasten the disappearance of nationalism was to the good.

9. The waverings were the result of the Stalinist revision of Marx's views of nationalism. Stalin recognized that national cultures were still quite important, and in his typically pragmatic fashion decreed that this was not a problem for the Soviet Union (and, by extension, for Yugoslavia) as long as culture was "national in form, socialist in content."

10. Cohen, 22.

11. Banac goes so far as to assert that the success of the Communists was due solely to their embracing the "clear identity of the constituent parts." He says, "They did not win the war under the banner of Yugoslav unitarism; they won under the banner of the national liberation of Slovenia, Croatia, Serbia, Macedonia, and so on" (*Why Bosnia?* 141).

12. "During the 1950s, 'Yugoslav' was touted sometimes as an ethnic/national category in its own right, sometimes as a supranational category. This Yugoslavism (*jugoslovenstvo*) campaign reached its culmination at the Seventh Congress of the

LCY in 1958. Although the party program adopted on that occasion denied the intention of assimilating the composite groups into a homogeneous Yugoslav nation, the concept of 'Yugoslav culture' endorsed by the congress implied an expectation of homogenization" (Ramet, *Nationalism and Federalism*, 50).

13. Milovan Djilas, "Novi tok istorije," *Socijalizam* 33, nos. 1–4 (1990): 37. Quoted in Cohen, 24.

14. To be sure, in the 1950s worker self-management was quite carefully circumscribed. But I am interested not so much in the reality of power relations in Yugoslavia as in the mythology.

15. Veselinov, 2.

16. The *NIN* literary awards are one of the best ways to track changes in literary politics and cultural taste in Yugoslavia. This Belgrade-based journal was founded in 1951 as the first weekly in postwar Yugoslavia. It made a claim to cover the entire country as well as the world in political, historical, and cultural spheres, and, for much of its existence, it was respected for its independent stance and high journalistic quality. The *NIN* awards for best novel started in 1955 for the best novel written in 1954. At first, in keeping with the unificatory ideals of the time, the jury considered not just novels in Serbo-Croatian but also in Slovenian and Macedonian. Claiming an inability to follow carefully the entire literary spectrum in the non–Serbo-Croatian-speaking republics, the journal soon gave up this practice and awarded the prize, which quickly became the single most prestigious one for new fiction in Yugoslavia, to the best new novel in Serbo-Croatian. The first winner was Dobrica Ćosić for *Koreni* (Roots). Among the significant recipients in subsequent years were Miroslav Krleža for *Zastave* (Banners, 1964), Meša Selimović for *Drviš i smrt* (Death and the Dervish, 1967), Slobodan Selenić for *Prijatelji sa Kosančićevog venca 7* (Friends from 7 Kosančić's Crown St., 1981), and Milorad Pavić for *Hazarski rečnik* (The Dictionary of the Khazars, 1985). By the late 1980s, the journal, like so much of the Serbian media, had gone unabashedly over to the nationalist side.

17. Sekelj, 240.

18. It should be noted, by the way, that contrary to popular belief, educational discrimination in the prewar period had not been in favor of Serbs and against Croats and Slovenes; rather, it had favored selected areas in which members of all three of these groups lived against all the other citizens of Yugoslavia.

19. These figures indicate that in the area of education the interwar state did not practice Serbophilia. Rather, Croats and Slovenes were overrepresented in higher education at the expense of the Moslem population.

20. The sources for this information are *Statistički godišnjak, 1938–39* (Belgrade, 1939) and *Statistički godišnjak FNRJ, 1954* (Belgrade, 1954).

21. The primary reason schools appear to have been left on their own was that the Ministry of Education in prewar Yugoslavia was a revolving-door position. So many different and conflicting educational plans were promulgated that schools

were in effect able to do what they wanted. For a thorough discussion of education policy in Slovenia in the prewar period, see Dolenc, 23–42 and 212–29.

22. *Nastavni plan i program za osnovne škole u narodnoj republici Hrvatskoj* (Zagreb, 1947), 35.

23. *Nastavni plan i program za osnovne škole narodne republike Bosne i Hercegovine* (Sarajevo, 1947), 6.

24. *Nastavni plan i program za osnovne škole* (Belgrade, 1947), 13.

25. As we are told in the introduction to a Slovene educational plan: "In order to come to some agreement on education programs for the peoples republics of Yugoslavia . . . in particular so that they would have a proper ideological orientation, in 1948 a conference on schools and education was convened by the Federal Peoples Republic of Yugoslavia Ministry for Education of the peoples republics in order to set up a plan for an education program for general gymnasia" (*Učni načrt za gimnazije, nižje gimnazije in višje razrede sedemletk* [Ljubljana, 1948], 3).

26. *Učni načrt za osnovne šole, nižje razrede sedemletk in višje osnovne šole* (Ljubljana, 1948), 5.

27. See *Nastavni plan i program za sedmogodišnje škole* (Zagreb, 1948), 26; *Nastavni plan i program za više osnovne škole* (Belgrade, 1948), 21; *Učni načrt za gimnazije, nižje gimnazije in višje razrede sedemletk* (Ljubljana, 1948), 80; and *Nastaven plan i programa za osnovnite učilišta* (Skopje, 1948): 23.

28. *Osnova nastava u FNRJ* (Belgrade, 1948), 110. The continuing centrality of literary education in Yugoslavia can be felt in the claim, made more than a decade later, by a prominent Yugoslav educator that literature was "in the greatest sense the companion of mankind's evolution, as well as a portrait, a documentation of social development" (Pavlović, 121).

29. Kosta Grubačić, introduction to *Osnova nastava u FNRJ* (Belgrade, 1948), 4.

30. There were a number of different reasons why a given author might be deemed unacceptable. Generally, however, the problem was either an overly strong concern with formal experimentation or unitarist political views. Of the writers mentioned above, the first three were unacceptably modernist in orientation, and the last had became a virulent Serbian nationalist during the war. For a fairly full list of such "blacklisted" writers, see Dimić, 67–71. In most cases, these writers reappeared in school programs by the late 1950s or early 1960s.

31. Gabrič, "Slovenska agitpropovska," 514.

32. This article was then produced as a pamphlet, in both the Cyrillic and Latin alphabets, and circulated throughout the country. The Cyrillic edition alone numbered 10,000 copies. See Peković, 44.

33. Ibid., 5.

34. Quoted in Samardžija, 57. In general, this book provides an excellent discussion of linguistic developments in the NDH.

35. Perhaps not surprisingly, this same task has been energetically prosecuted in Croatia since its attainment of independence in 1991. The results have often

been somewhat comical, particularly when it happens that major political leaders find themselves unable to speak the new official language of the country.

36. See *Nastavni plan i program za osnovne škole u narodnoj republici Hrvatskoj* (Zagreb, 1947); *Nastavni plan i program za osnovne škole narodne republike Bosne i Hercegovine* (Sarajevo, 1947); and *Nastavni plan i program za osnovne škole* (Belgrade, 1947).

37. See, for example, Pavlović. Pavlović had been active in writing interwar textbooks as well, so the fact that he was chosen to do so in the postwar period indicates the essential continuity between interwar and postwar ideas about Serbo-Croatian.

38. The full text of the agreement as well as a list of its signatories is included in *Pravopis hrvatskosrpskoga književnog jezika*, 7–10.

39. What is more, in districts where a large proportion of pupils spoke a language other than Serbo-Croatian, Macedonian, or Slovenian, another language could be the primary language of instruction. In Serbia, Croatia, Bosnia and Herzegovina, and Montenegro, instruction in Serbo-Croatian was also required. But in Macedonia and Slovenia, pupils in minority language schools learned only their own and the republic's language, meaning that Albanians in Macedonia never officially learned Serbo-Croatian, although their Macedonian peers did.

40. Pavlović, 212.

41. This was quite a change from the interwar period during which centrally published readers contained a far larger percentage of Slovene texts in the original (although none from "nonexistent" Macedonian, of course).

42. There were exceptions, of course, and they included those writers who were overly "formalist" (i.e., experimental), as well as those who were overtly in favor of separatist nationalism. The former made their way back into the canon by the 1950s, as part of a general cultural loosening in the wake of destalinization. Many overt nationalists, most notably the notorious Mile Budak, never made it back into the canon during the existence of Yugoslavia.

43. One can still find many books published in the postwar period that use the older forms, particularly "Yugoslav literature." See *Novija jugoslavenska poezija* (Zagreb, 1962) and *Jugoslovenska poezija* (Belgrade, 1949). In both these anthologies, poems are ordered more or less chronologically rather than by the nationality of the writer, and texts are given in the original languages and alphabets. By the mid-1960s, however, such usage was extremely rare. The extent to which the nomenclatural change was carried out can be seen easily in the card catalogue of the National and University Library in Ljubljana, Slovenia. Sometime in the mid-1960s, all the prewar cards under the subject heading "Yugoslav literature" (Jugoslovanska književnost) were removed and librarians penciled in "Yugoslav literatures" (Jugoslovanske književnosti) in their place. In other, less politicized areas of cultural endeavor, however, the term remained in use far longer. Thus, in the series called "Art on the Territory of Yugoslavia," which was jointly published in

the early 1980s by Jugoslavia (Belgrade), Spektar (Zagreb), and Prva književna komuna (Mostar), the term "Yugoslav art" is used quite frequently, and I have not found that anyone objected to it. The same is true with such terms as "Yugoslav theater," "Yugoslav music," and, sometimes, "Yugoslav film."

The question of whether there was or was not a single Yugoslav culture continued to be debated right through the 1960s. In his book *Contemporary Yugoslav Literature: A Sociopolitical Approach*, Sveta Lukić claimed that Yugoslav literature was an organic whole, but he felt constrained to point out that, if asked their opinion on the subject, "the vast majority of writers, cultural workers and ideologues throughout Yugoslavia would reply in the negative" (24).

44. Djilas, 175.

45. Ibid. In a footnote, Djilas points specifically to Gaj, Njegoš, Strossmayer, Svetozar Marković, and Dositej Obradović as models.

46. It is interesting in this regard to contrast the treatment of the hundredth anniversary of *The Mountain Wreath* with the hundredth anniversary of Ivan Mažuranić's *The Death of Smail-Aga Čengić*, which took place a year earlier. Despite the fact that, in many respects, Mažuranić's work might have been a better national symbol than Njegoš's, the earlier anniversary received almost no play in the Yugoslav press and was celebrated with nothing more than a new edition of the work in Croatia and a commentary by Antun Barac. One finds a one-column note to this effect in the journal *Naša književnost* ([Belgrade] 1, no. 3 [Mar. 1946]: 458) and nothing at all in the other major literary journal, *Republika* (Zagreb). Even given the fact that the reconstruction of the country was a top priority at this time, this seems somewhat meager.

47. The fact that Njegoš had been a religious in addition to a political leader was, of course, somewhat inconvenient. But Communist-era commentators were always careful to play down this aspect of his life, noting the fact that he was not doctrinaire and that he usually wore civilian clothes.

48. *Pobeda* (Montenegro), June 7, 1947, 4.

49. Niko Pavić, untitled, *Pobeda*, June 7, 1947, 1.

50. Nazečić was the vice minister of culture of the Republic of Bosnia-Herzegovina at this time.

51. S. Nazečić, introduction to Petar Petrović Njegoš, *Gorski vijenac* (Sarajevo, 1947), 15.

52. Zogović, introduction to P. P. Njegoš, *Gorski vijenac* (Belgrade, 1947), 32. This edition is printed in the Latin alphabet, by the way, presumably as part of a strategy to de-Serbianize Njegoš.

53. Zoran Mišić, quoted in Peković, 42.

54. For a summary of the interrelationship of new literary production and criticism in this period, see Peković, 35–60. For a discussion of the situation in Slovenia, see also Gabrič, *Socialistična kulturna revolucija*, esp. 310–16, and "Slovenska agitpropovska kulturna politika," 470–655.

55. Gabrič, "Slovenska agitpropovska kulturna politika," 503.

56. For a very detailed account of the battles in literary criticism in this period, see Peković.

57. Although I have not found this formula used precisely in postwar Yugoslavia, the following quote by a leading Albanian critic, Hasan Mekuli, shows that it was present in spirit at least. After noting that there had been about one hundred postwar works originating in Yugoslavia in Albanian, Mekuli says: "Because of its ties to the language, and to the traditions, because of its local color, this literature is Albanian, but it is Yugoslav in content because it is created in a new socialist community and carries the seal of the new era" (cited in Lukić, 25).

58. In the immediate postwar period, such central organs as the Yugoslav Writers' Union played key roles in fostering some sense of community among various national writers. By the end of the 1950s, however, the Yugoslav Writers' Union, like most other central authorities, had lost much influence, and the separate republican unions became far more powerful.

59. For a survey of some of the major wartime works in Serbo-Croatian, see Bandić. For a collection of such poems with commentary from Slovenia, see *Partizanske pesmi*, ed. Josip Ribičič (Ljubljana, 1968).

60. Bandić, 82.

61. Marjanović, *Vladimir Nazor*, 10.

62. That in this period he still thought of himself as someone in the "Yugoslav" rather than the "Croatian" camp can be seen from the obituary he wrote for Dinko Šimunović in *Nova Evropa*. There, he approvingly called his dead colleague a "nationalist," which in the context of Šimunović's work and the journal, meant a supporter of Yugoslav unitarism (Nazor, "Dinku Šimunoviću, mjesto nekrologa," 429).

63. According to Hubert Butler, "I am told that the great poet Nazor was induced at the beginning to write praises of the new régime, but though I found many articles in the Occupation papers praising his work, I could not find anything written by him" (228).

64. Nazor, *S partizanima*, 16.

65. Ibid., 50.

66. "Dr. Ribar [a Croat] is here with his closest associates: the Moslem Nurija, Dr. Simon Kotoranin, the Orthodox priest Vlada—a soldier whose carriage and visage are like King Agamemnon's—and the Montenegrin Comrade Milutin" (ibid., 73).

67. The Yugoslav version of socialist realism as such was only imposed between 1945 and 1952, and it was never imposed with as much uniformity as it had been in the Soviet Union. Particularly in Slovenia, in the works of Kosmač and Kocbek it was practically absent, at least stylistically. Nevertheless, its shadow hung over the war novel for many years after its disappearance as doctrine.

68. The novel was also known through its adaptation as a popular film in 1953.

69. Ćosić, *Far Away Is the Sun*, 79.

70. Comrade Paul, who is described as a "man of inflexible will" is clearly modeled directly on the central heroes of Soviet socialist realist novels. In particular, his attitude (as well as some of his methods) reprise the role of the political commissar Fedor Klychkov in Dmitry Furmanov's 1923 novel *Chapaev*.

71. Goulding, 19–20.

72. Stiglič.

73. Šoljan, vol. 2, 252.

74. His first major literary work, the prose poem *Ex Ponto* was mostly written during this period of internment, and in its lyrical melancholy it stands as one of the great literary monuments to World War I.

75. Andrić also provided work to the unitarist *Jugoslavenska njiva*. His "Crveni listovi" was published there in 1919 (3, no. 20: 324).

76. Andrić's own national identity is a matter of some controversy. Given his upbringing as a subject of the Habsburgs as well as his Catholicism, a self-identification as a Croatian was natural. And indeed, Andrić's first published work appeared in the celebrated 1914 collection *Young Croatian Lyrics*. Nevertheless, most of his literary work focused on Bosnia, and he appears later in life to have self-identified first as a Serb and later, especially around the time he won the Nobel Prize, as a Yugoslav. In the early 1980s, as nationalist passions in Yugoslavia rose, Andrić was posthumously claimed by each of the separate national groups. See, for example, a characteristic article by Radivoj Cvetićanin, "Andrić je naš," *NIN*, Jan. 6, 1980, 29. Cvetićanin's article is in response to the claim by an unnamed Bosnian that Andrić should be considered a writer of Bosnia-Herzegovina. He admits the possibility that a writer could belong to more than one republic's literature, but then, as proof that such is not the case with Andrić, he goes on to cite a 1942 letter in which the author referred to himself as a Serbian writer.

77. In one of the first postwar reviews, the critic Petar Lasta characterized the novels as follows: "These two books of calm observation seem to be balm to the wounds that have lacerated our land and peoples in our day" (131).

78. This claim is made by Ivo Banac in an interview published in the collection *Why Bosnia?* 164.

79. As early as the 1960s, some Moslems objected to Andrić's canonization as the Yugoslav writer par excellence, claiming that his novels showed only caricatured versions of Moslems. They buttressed their position by reference to Andrić's doctoral dissertation in which he evaluated the influence of Turkish rule on Bosnia in entirely negative terms. "What is decisive is the fact that at the most critical juncture in its spiritual development, with its spiritual powers still in ferment, Bosnia was conquered by an Asiatic military people whose social institutions and customs spelled the negation of any and all Christian culture and whose religion—begotten under other skies and social circumstances and quite incapable of adaptation—shackled the life, the spirit, and the mind in Bosnia, disfiguring it

and molding it into an exceptional case" (Andrić, *Development*, 17). For a recent discussion of this controversy, see Muhsin Rizvić, Bosanski muslimani u Andrićevu svijetu," *Sveske zadužbine Ive Andrića* 13 (1997): 159–78.

80. Most notably, one should mention the volume entitled *Reflets de l'histoire Européen dans l'oeuvre d'Ivo Andrić.* I will be referring to some of the separate contributions to this book below.

81. Original in Andrić, *Sabrana djela*, vol. 12, 23.

82. It should be noted, incidentally, that later in life Andrić returned to the longitudinal approach in his unfinished final novel, *Omer-paša Latas.*

83. For a detailed discussion of how dialogic approaches to history can come from the juxtaposition of monologic works by the same author, see Wachtel, *An Obsession with History.*

84. It is possible that the open structure of *The Isolated House* represents a conscious attempt by Andrić to retrieve something of the openness that had characterized his earliest works, *Ex Ponto* and *Nemiri*, but that had largely been lost in his middle period. For a discussion of the differences between Andrić's early and middle periods in this context, see Gordana Crnković, "*Ex Ponto* and *Unrest*: Victimization and 'Eternal Art,'" in *Ivo Andrić*, 63–81.

85. Ivo Andrić, *Sabrana djela*, vol. 14, 12. Translation from Hawkesworth, 114.

86. Such a view was perhaps best expressed in an obituary for Andrić written by the Slovenian novelist Ivan Potrč: "Thus, Andrić did not merely write "The Bridge on the Drina." He built, is building, and will continue to build bridges between our peoples and nationalities" (*Delo*, Mar. 14, 1975, 1).

87. For a stimulating discussion on the function of the bridge itself in this novel, see Dragan Kujundžić, "Ivo Andrić and the Sarcophagus of History," in *Ivo Andrić*, 103–22.

88. Ivo Andrić, *Na Drini ćuprija* in *Sabrana djela*, vol. 1, 26. In English as *The Bridge on the Drina*, trans. Lovett Edwards (Chicago, 1977), 26. Further references to the novel will be made in the main text by reference to page numbers in the English translation.

89. The belief that des Fossés is a character with whom Andrić has a great deal of sympathy is accepted (for good reason, I think) by most scholars. For only one example, see Nedeljković's own article from his collection: "Le véritable messager d'Andrić dans *La Chronique de Travnik* est le jeune Français Chaumette des Fossés" (*Reflets de l'histoire*, 206).

90. Ivo Andrić, *Travnička hronika* in *Sabrana djela*, vol. 2, 148. In English as *Bosnian Chronicle*, trans. Celia Hawkesworth and Bogdan Rakić (London, 1996), 113–14. Further references to the novel will be made in the main text by reference to page numbers in the English translation.

91. Ivo Andrić, *Sabrana djela*, vol. 2, 533. The English translation leaves this out for some inexplicable reason.

92. Ivo Andrić, *Sabrana djela*, vol. 3, 86. Translation in Hawkesworth, 165.

93. He may have learned this technique from Tolstoy, who uses it from time to time in *War and Peace*, most notably on the first pages when describing the discourse of Prince Vasilii: "He spoke in that elaborately choice French, in which our forefathers not only spoke but thought" (Tolstoy, 1). For a more nuanced study of the first person plural voice in Andrić, see Ronelle Alexander, "Narrative Voice and Listener's Choice in the Prose of Ivo Andrić," in *Ivo Andrić*, 200–230.

94. Ivo Andrić, *Sabrana djela*, vol. 14, 104.

95. Yugoslav readers would have recognized the former as a transposition of a legend taken from the oral epic song entitled "Zidanje Skadra" (The Building of Skadar).

96. Cohen, 22.

CHAPTER 4

1. Quoted in Gabrič, *Socialistična kulturna revolucija*, 322.

2. "Separating History from Myth: An Interview with Ivo Banac," in *Why Bosnia?* 141. Ramet, on the other hand, sees the key date for this change in course as December 1964 at the Eighth Congress of the League of Yugoslav Communists. "This was unquestionably a turning point both for Yugoslav nationalities policy and for interrepublican relations. Henceforth it was no longer assumed that Yugoslavia's nations were in the process of disintegration and Yugoslav socialist patriotism was clearly disjointed from Yugoslavism" (*Federalism and Nationalism*, 51). Regardless of the exact date, however, it is clear that the early 1960s marked a gradual turn from an emphasis on unity to one on brotherhood.

3. Ramet, *Federalism and Nationalism*, 73.

4. Majstorovic, 29.

5. Ramet, *Federalism and Nationalism*, 14.

6. *Primorski dnevnik*, Oct. 27, 1961, 1. *Borba* reported his statement a bit differently in its account on the same day: "I know that only one person can receive this award, but the honor given extends to the whole country, for its great struggles in all fields of human activity, particularly in the field of culture" (5).

7. *Borba*, Oct. 27, 1961, 5. Ironically, Crvenkovski later became one of the most outspoken proponents of the policy of separation.

8. Ćosić's article appeared in *Telegram* (no. 39, Jan. 10, 1961). Quoted in Peković, 301.

9. Pirjevec's article appeared in the Slovenian periodical *Naša sodobnost* no. 3 (1961).

10. Dobrica Ćosić, "O savremenom nesavremenom nacionalizmu," *Sabrana dela*, vol. 8, 17–46. He made an even stronger statement against Serbian nationalism in 1965, in a speech entitled "O civilizaciji, naciji, i drugom" (reprinted in *Sabrana dela*, vol. 8, 186–200).

11. Gabrič, *Socialistična kulturna revolucija*, 345.

12. The story is spiced by Kamilo's endless romance with a Hungarian modernist woman poet, with the adventures of Joachim, who is at one point thrown into a Serbian jail for two years, as well as with many other subplots. Unfortunately, however, Krleža was not really a great novelist at this point in his career. He is a master psychologist who learned a lot from Dostoevsky, and he is a spectacular satirical writer able to destroy completely the pretensions of both the Austro-Hungarian and the Yugoslav type. He can also paint individual portraits brilliantly. What he could not or would not do, however, is tell a story, so that *Banners* ultimately seems more like a collection of talking heads and ideological positions than a novel.

13. It is worth noting that Emerički Junior is a transparently autobiographical character, and, therefore, that his development, if not his exact career path are meant to register Krleža's own.

14. *Predmetnik in učni načrt za osnovne šole* (Ljubljana, 1962), 10.

15. *Nastavni plan i program za osnovu školu u narodnoj republici Serbiji* (Belgrade, 1960), 119–22.

16. The program was published in *Prosvjetni vjesnik* (Zagreb) 17, no. 5 (Aug. 17, 1964): 46–47.

17. *Nastavni planovi i programi za osnovnite učilišta vo NR Makedonija* (Skoplje, 1960).

18. *Predmetnik in učni načrt za osnovne šole* (Ljubljana, 1962), 24.

19. *Čitanka za VIII razred osnovne škole*, ed. Radmilo Dimitrijević, Dimitrije Vučenov, 7th ed. (Belgrade, 1960; with approval of the Ministry of Education, Serbia, 1958).

20. The only exception, however, is quite egregious, a "folk song" entitled "Titovo kolo" (Tito's Round Dance), given in the Latin alphabet:

Lijepo ti je druga Tita kolo:
takvo kolo ko ga ne bi voló?

Igraju ga mladi partizani,
partizani kô vitki jablani.

Na glavi im crven-zvijezda blista,
prek' ramena visi puška čista.

A iz grudi pjesma im se vije:
Maršal Tito, naše najmilije!

Ti si voda roda ponosnoga,
slovenačkog, srpskog, hrvatskoga.

Crnogorci, gordi Makedonci,
pa Bosanci, zatim Hercegovci . . .

You are beautiful, Comrade Tito's round dance:
Who would not love such a round dance?

It is being performed by young partisans,
Partisans like supple apple trees.

On their brows the red star shines,
Across their shoulders hangs a clean gun.

And a song bubbles up from their throats:
Marshal Tito, our beloved!

You are the leader of a proud people,
of Slovenes, Serbs, and Croats.

Montenegrins, proud Macedonians,
Bosnians and Herzegovinians . . .

From *Čitanka za VIII razred osnovne škole*, ed. Radmilo Dimitrijević, Dimitrije Vučenov, 7th ed. (Belgrade, 1960; with approval of the Ministry of Education, Serbia, 1958).

21. *Čitanka za VIII razred osnovne škole*, ed. Bojin Dramušić and Radojka Radulović, 8th ed. (Sarajevo, 1960; with approval of the Ministry of Education, BiH).

22. *Čitanka za VIII razred osnovne škole*, ed. Tvrtko Čubelić, 6th ed. (Zagreb, 1960; with approval of the Ministry of Education, Croatia).

23. Šoljan, vol. 2, 268.

24. The story "Turneja" (The Tour) provides further evidence, if more is needed, of Šoljan's ambivalence toward what he clearly saw as the failure of the culturo-ideological project that marked the first years of postwar Yugoslavia. In this story he describes a choir of idealists who traveled the length and breadth of Yugoslavia. The harmonic combination of their voices provides an apt symbol for the Yugoslav project. The story ends with their final concert, attended by almost no one, which takes place fittingly enough by a cemetery. After this, the group breaks up, leaving only bittersweet memories in the narrator's mind.

25. Selimović, *Death and the Dervish*, 408. The remarkable extent to which Hassan's description of Bosnians echoes Chaadaev's characterization of Russians in his "First Philosophical Letter" of 1829 is an indication that such feelings are typical for any group under intense pressure to Westernize.

26. That Hassan's views echo those of the author can be seen from his comments in an interview published in the journal *NIN* (Feb. 5, 1967, 8) after Selimović had won their award for the best Serbo-Croatian novel of 1966. "Q: What role do Bosnia and the phenomenon of Bosnianism play in your artistic vision and particularly in the novel 'Death and the Dervish'? A: Bosnia is my great eternal love and simultaneously my deepest hate. I have tried to leave her several times, but I always remained. . . . Rarely has anyone been more painfully and dramati-

cally defined by history as the Bosnian. A great deal has collected over the centuries in these people: a feeling of their own undefinedness, guilt for the deeds of others, a difficult history, fear of the future, a desire for the good and for humanitarian ideals that would apply to all people regardless of any limitations (this is the famous *merkhamet*, a broad openness before all people, a yearning for a single universal humanism as a defense against all sectarianisms), and frequent disappointments that have bred hatred."

27. Selimović, however, rejected the categorization of his novel as a work of Bosnian literature in the same *NIN* interview: "Without taking into account national origins and particularities, a novel and a literature in general can only be Yugoslav, then European, perhaps even world . . . and that is not only a result of the greater number of linkages in today's world and evaluative criteria which tend toward generalization, but more because ideas and the soul cannot be regional."

28. For a balanced description of the Croatian situation at this time, see Ramet, *Nationalism and Federalism*, 98–107. For a more detailed but strongly Croatian-biased evaluation, see Cuvalo, 104–25.

29. For more detail on the relationship between linguistics and particularist nationalism in this period, see Greenberg, 402–9.

30. Raditsa, 464.

31. See Ramet, *Nationalism and Federalism*, 109.

32. The conference proceedings were published as *Mjesto i položaj hrvatske književnosti u nastavnim programima za škole drugog stupnja i za gimnazije.*

33. *Mjesto i položaj*, 31; from the speech of Ivo Frangeš.

34. Ramet, *Nationalism and Federalism*, 131.

35. *Osnove nastavnog plana i programa za sredno-školsko obrazovanje u SR Hrvatskoj* (Zagreb, 1974).

36. Ibid., 26.

37. As published in *Srednoobrazovanie: Nastavni planovi i programi za podgotvitelniot period* (Skopje, 1973).

38. Audiocassette tapes of this meeting, which took place at Cankarjev dom in Ljubljana on May 3 and 4, 1983, are kept in the archive of the Slovenian Writers' Association.

39. The series, under the general heading "The Yugoslav: Who Is He?" first appeared on June 29, 1969, 32, and thereafter it ran weekly on pp. 6–7 until October.

40. Finci, 6.

41. This split was confirmed by large public opinion surveys. "In 1966 sixty percent of a large Yugoslav sample proclaimed readiness to accept members of other nationalities in friendship or even marriage and revealed declining attachment to region, dialect and customs. Most people questioned expressed satisfaction with national relations" (MacKenzie, 453).

42. The results were published in 1973 in a book entitled *Nacionalna vezanost i vrednosti kod srednjo-školske omladine* (National Affiliation and Values Among

Secondary-School Youth). From the careful description of their work as well as from the stature of the surveyors, it is clear that this was a serious study conducted to world standards.

43. Rot and Havelka, 262.

44. Ibid., 268.

45. Ibid., 269.

46. See the excellent essay on this topic by Bogdan Bogdanović entitled "The City and Death."

47. Rot and Havelka, 273.

48. Ibid., 113–18.

49. It is not entirely clear what Serbian respondents meant by a declaration of Yugoslav identity. It has been noted by many writers that Serbs were more comfortable with the Yugoslav concept as it existed than were other groups, primarily because it was to their advantage. Whereas this may have been true of members of older generations, it is not clear whether fifteen year olds would really have recognized this fact.

50. Cohen, 32. As his source, Cohen cites Liljana Baćević, "Medjunacionalni odnosi" in *Istraživački projekat CDI: Jugosloveni o društvenoj krizi* (Belgrade, 1989), 72–96, and Ivan Šiber, "Javno mnjenje i nacionalno pitanje," in Gavro Lončar, *Socializam i nacionalno pitanje* (Zagreb, 1970).

51. Quoted in Ivo Banac, "Yugoslavia: The Fearful Asymmetry of War," 148.

52. In his article "Two 'Nonconformists' Who Revitalized the Serbian Nation," Nicholas J. Miller makes an analogous point, not just about Ćosić, but about a number of men of his generation who followed a similar path from idealism to Serbian nationalism.

53. Undoubtedly, because of the way Yugoslavia was divided, Serbs had the most to lose were the country to break up on republican lines. As opposed to other national groups, most of which lived overwhelmingly on the territory of their republic, Serbs were spread over many republics, forming sizable minorities in Croatia and Bosnia-Herzegovina. Thus, Serbs could all live in the same country only were Yugoslavia to continue to exist, unless of course they attempted to secede with their territories in the event of a breakup. The latter is precisely what happened in the early 1990s.

54. *Memorandum Srpske akademije nauka i umetnosti.* Ćosić was not the sole author of this draft, and it is not even entirely clear how much of a role he played in its preparation, but its obsessive concern with the Kosovo question marks his hand, and he is generally given credit (or blame) for the Memorandum's overall thrust. The Memorandum itself was not officially published at this time, but leaked copies circulated broadly.

55. The epic was published in Yugoslavia in the late 1970s. When it appeared in English, only the second volume was called *A Time of Death.* The epic as a whole was entitled *This Land, This Time,* and it appeared between 1978 and 1983.

56. Ćosić, *Reach to Eternity*, 344.   57. Ćosić, *Into the Battle*, 99.
58. Ćosić, *A Time of Death*, 82.   59. Ibid., 125.
60. Danko Popović, 6–7.

61. See, for example, Milutin's complaints about the Macedonians (41), and about the Croats and Slovenes (43).

62. Ibid., 79.

63. Zoran Gluščević, quoted on jacket of Danko Popović.

64. The novel was published in Belgrade by Zapis. Drašković is known today for his political role in Serbia, particularly as a leader of the opposition against Slobodan Milošević. He made his name, however, as a novelist.

65. For a good general discussion of the economic and political background to this period, see Lampe, 325–38.

66. Pavić's novel was initially published in Serbia in 1984 as *Hazarski rečnik*. All further quotations from the novel will be given in the main text by reference to the English-language edition.

67. Jean-François Lyotard defined the postmodern most succinctly in his essay "The Postmodern Condition": "Simplifying to the extreme, I define postmodern as incredulity to metanarratives. . . . To the obsolescence of the metanarrative apparatus of legitimation corresponds, most notably, the crisis of metaphysical philosophy and of the university institution which in the past relied on it. The narrative function is losing its functors, its great hero, its great dangers, its great voyages, its great goal. It is being dispersed in clouds of narrative language elements. . . . There are many different language games—a heterogeneity of elements. They only give rise to institutions in patches—local determinism" (xxiv).

68. The most extensive account of the Khazars can be found in Dunlop. This book, by the way, is mentioned as a source by Pavić, and the novelist clearly borrowed some of its stylistic peculiarities in addition to drawing on its factual content.

69. This latter story is also borrowed from an account in the Rus'sian *Primary Chronicle*, by the way.

70. Danilo Kiš, "On Nationalism," in *Why Bosnia?* 127–28. This text was originally published in 1973 and widely commented on in Yugoslavia. Kiš's own work is an excellent illustration of the fact that postmodern literary technique and the type of thinking characteristic of Pavić's novel do not necessarily have to go together. Kiš's novel *A Tomb for Boris Davidovich*, for example, uses an obviously Borghesian narrative voice not for the purposes of abstract literary game playing, but rather as a means to explore the truth about Stalinism.

71. In the sixteenth century, these characters are Avram Brankovich, Yusuf Masudi, and Samuel Cohen. In the twentieth, they are Dr. Isailo Suk, Dr. Abu Kabir Muawia, and Dr. Dorothea Schultz. The following short narrative, taken from testimony regarding the life of Avram Brankovich, illustrates how Pavić sets up the quest for knowledge undertaken by his characters: "He does not believe that he is the only person interested in the Khazars, or that in the past no one outside the

circle of the Christian missionaries who left behind information on the Khazars, no one from St. Cyril to the present day, studied them. . . . He presumes that aside from Christian sources on the Khazars, there also exist extensive Arab and Jewish sources on the same question and people, but something is preventing the individuals working on this from meeting and collecting their knowledge, which, if only it could be pooled, would provide a clear and complete picture of everything concerning this question" (47).

72. Thus, for example, at the moment Brankovich is pierced by a Turkish lance on the battlefield he looks up and sees Samuel Cohen. "That same instant, the pale young man collapsed into his own shadow, as though felled by Brankovich's look" (57). Masudi, who was watching the affair, is executed the next day.

73. In this respect, it is interesting to compare Pavić's novel with *La disparition* (1969) by the French postmodernist novelist Georges Perec, which it superficially resembles. In Perec's work, the key to the mystery plot is the absent letter *e*. "It's a detective novel or at least a whodunit, with this twist: E done it, but we mustn't ever say that. We can't. When the characters get close to E, they get written out of the plot (maimed, shredded, fed to the carp)" (Kincaid, 3). The difference between the novels is not merely that a plot about the impossibility of finding answers in France is merely clever and amusing, but in Yugoslavia it helped encourage people to shoot their neighbors. The point is not the plot alone, but the fact that the reader of Perec's novel is allowed to see it as just a plot, whereas Pavić's reader is led to see the plot as an allegorical attack on the bases of Yugoslav society.

74. Of course, the myth that at some prehistoric time distinctions between man and woman did not exist is common to many cultures as are desires to return to that time. Perhaps the most famous description of this myth is in Plato's *Symposium*.

75. Ivo Andrić, *The Bridge on the Drina*, 18.

76. Ibid., 27.

77. *NIN*, Jan. 20, 1985, 8.

78. Kalfus, 22. Kalfus overstates his case here, for as early as 1988 Vasa Mihailovich had pointed out the novel's political implications. Indeed, the subtitle to his review of the novel reads: "The Zany Political Culture of Pavić's Khazaria Closely Parallels the Predicament of the Serbian Minority Within Present-Day Yugoslavia" (378).

79. Kalfus, 23.

80. For a thorough and scathing description of the role the Serbian Academy of Sciences played in whipping up public support for nationalist policies between 1986 and 1992, as well as numerous references to Pavić's active participation, see Milosavljević.

81. This information was printed on the flyleaf of David Albahari's novel *Tsink*, which made the critics' list.

82. Kovač, 188.

83. Ibid.

84. Ibid.

85. For the most convincing statement of this case, see Brass.

86. Selenić, *Prijatelji*, 28.

87. *NIN*, Jan. 25, 1981, 28.

CONCLUSION

1. Ugrešić, *Kultura*, 52. Kiš, the son of a Serbian mother and a Hungarian Jewish father, grew up in Subotica, on the Hungarian border. He received his education in Belgrade and was known as both a novelist and a translator of French literature. Kiš's fictional work generally avoids Yugoslav characters and settings. However, he is a Yugoslav writer par excellence in his ability to adapt a wide variety of Western literary trends to local cultural conditions, and particularly in his ability to observe critically both East and West.

2. Kiš, *Tomb*, 74.

3. Quoted in Hobsbawm, 267.

4. Ramet, *Nationalism and Federalism.*

5. For more on this see Ramet, *Nationalism*, 136–75, and Woodward, *Socialist Unemployment.*

6. Of course, the situation in each of the successor states was not the same. This, however, is not the place to discuss the particularities of the post-Yugoslav conflicts, which have been treated at length in any number of studies.

7. Debeljak, 35.

8. Ugrešić, *Kultura laži*, 50.

9. Stjepan Meštrović, 108–9.

10. This concept of "all" is, of course, a fiction. Clearly it is never the case that everyone in a given state structure feels the same degree of loyalty toward it, or even any loyalty at all. What is being spoken of, however, is the way the "imagined community" of the state is understood to function. In this respect, exceptions are allowed, but they are nothing more than exceptions.

11. "The Albanians were one nationality and spoke dialects of the same language. They were, however, divided into two main groups, the Gegs and the Tosks, and had three religions: Muslim, Orthodox, and Catholic" (Barbara and Charles Jelavich, 222). And, one might add, despite the efforts of the Hoxha regime to eliminate Albanian multiculturalism, it has persisted even until today.

12. When I say "uni-" in this context, it does not exclude the possibility that minority ethnic, cultural, or national groups are present in a given country. But they are precisely minorities, whose presence is tolerated but who are not considered fully part of the country. This could be true even in countries such as Estonia and Latvia, which consider themselves fully "uni-" despite the presence of a Russian minority approaching 50 percent.

Although there is no state that incarnates the configuration multinational, uniethnic, unicultural (see Table 1), it does reflect the position of groups like the Kurds, Uighirs, or Maya, who have no state of their own but live spread over a number of other states, despite being ethnically and culturally the same on all or both sides of a border. Or at least it did characterize such groups when they were as yet untouched by the nationalist desire for their own state, i.e., when various members of this ethnos were loyal citizens of more than one country. In the present age, however, such groups are ripe candidates for developing their own nationalism and for breaking off, or attempting to break off, from the states in which they live.

13. Soyinka, 9.

14. "In 1947, it was very difficult to see how a seething mass of hungry and mostly illiterate people could keep this nation together. But now, the country's survival is taken for granted. You hardly hear anybody questioning it anymore" (M. J. Akbar, as quoted in *The New York Times* [national edition], Aug. 24, 1997, A6).

15. Kiš, "On Nationalism," in *Why Bosnia?* 126–28.

16. For an analysis of India in these terms, see Chadda. For various other views on the national question in India, see Brass, as well as *Ethnonationalism: Indian Experience*.

17. There are, of course, many who would dispute the uninational character of the United States. But I agree with Michael Lind, who says, "An extrapolitical American nation exists today, and has existed in one form or another for hundreds of years. Most Americans, of all races, are born and acculturated into the American nation; most immigrants and their descendants will be assimilated into it. . . . Not only does the transracial American majority constitute a single nation, but that majority is deeply nationalist in its sentiments" (5–6).

18. Native Americans are, of course, an even more problematic case, but one too complex to discuss here.

19. A bit more than 300,000 people (around 2 percent of the population) declared themselves as Yugoslavs in 1961.

20. My entire discussion of the questions surrounding the "Yugoslav" category is derived from Ramet, *Nationalism*, 51–54.

21. In this regard, by the way, it is interesting to note that a "Yugoslav" branch of the PEN club (there had been Slovenian, Croatian, and Serbian PEN clubs for many years) was formed only in 1992 in Amsterdam, by a group of writers who were unable to find a self-identity in any of the new countries of the former Yugoslavia.

22. *New York Times*, July 6, 1996, 1.

23. Ibid., 7.

24. Epstein, 303.

25. Some notable exceptions are the book of Michael Lind mentioned above,

as well as Arthur Schlesinger, Jr., *The Disuniting of America* (New York, 1992), and E. D. Hirsch, *Cultural Literacy* (Boston, 1987).

26. It is precisely in these conditions that a demagogic leader can lead a society into a genocidal fury. For what has happened in such societies is that the basest impulses, held by almost all to some extent, are encouraged to bubble to the surface.

27. Advocates of school voucher programs come in a variety of stripes, of course, and many are motivated by a sincere and in many instances well-founded belief that the public schools are not working. Nevertheless, under the voucher systems most typically proposed the big winners would be religiously oriented schools, many of which would be dominated by people not known for their willingness to work with those who think, look, or act differently.

28. I have in mind efforts by people to vulgarize and turn into prescriptive and unchanging cultural dogma the well-meaning and perhaps necessary attempts by educators such as E. D. Hirsch and Allan Bloom to describe American culture. Hirsch at least is aware that educational reform efforts do not always produce the results intended. Describing the intentions of the John Dewey–inspired report entitled *The Cardinal Principles of Secondary Education* (1918), Hirsch comments: "They could not have been expected to foresee that, when their principles were actually put into effect in institutional settings, humaneness would be difficult to preserve" (Hirsch, 122). But he is curiously blithe regarding what he recognizes to be the dangers inherent in his list-based method of defining the content of American culture: "How can I deny that such misuse of the list is not only a danger but a near certainty? . . . Won't the whole project end up just as a large-scale crib sheet for general-knowledge tests? . . . Maybe, but that won't be the only result" (143).

29. Quoted in *The New York Times* (national edition), July 18, 1996, A10.

30. Lind, 253.

31. As we have noted, this process tends to be driven by intellectual elites, and in the West at least the intelligentsia has a strong tendency to dislike individualism (equating it with the dreaded "bourgeois subject").

32. Although he does not speak of Yugoslavia in particular, Thomas Sowell's analysis of the results of affirmative action programs echoes my analysis of the path by which Yugoslavia gradually dissolved from the 1960s on:

> 1. Preferential programs, even when explicitly and repeatedly defined as "temporary," have tended not only to persist but also to expand in scope, either embracing more groups or spreading to wider realms for the same groups, or both. . . . [Yugoslavia saw the spread of national "rights-based" policies from the republics to the autonomous regions, and in the United States the spread has been from groups that have historically suffered discrimination to others that have not.]

2. Within the groups designated by government as recipients of preferential treatment, the benefits have usually gone disproportionately to those members already more fortunate.

3. Group polarization has tended to increase in the wake of preferential programs, with non-preferred groups reacting adversely, in ways ranging from political backlash to mob violence and civil war. (Sowell, 15–16)

Works Cited

Abrams, M. H. *The Mirror and the Lamp: Romantic Theory and the Critical Tradition.* New York, 1953.

Albahari, David. *Tsink.* Belgrade, 1995.

Albin, A. "The Creation of the Slaveno-Srbski Literary Language." *Slavonic and East European Review* 48, no. 113 (Oct. 1970): 393–413.

Aleksić, Radomir, et al., eds. *Pravopis hrvatskosrpskoga književnog jezika.* Zagreb/Belgrade, 1960.

Ali, Rabia, and Lawrence Lifshultz, eds. *Why Bosnia?* Stony Creek, Conn., 1993.

Anderson, Benedict. *Imagined Communities: Reflections on the Origin and Spread of Nationalism.* London, 1983.

Andrić, Ivo. *The Bridge on the Drina.* Trans. Lovett Edwards. Chicago, 1977.

———. *The Development of Spiritual Life in Bosnia Under the Influence of Turkish Rule.* Ed. and trans. Želimir B. Juričić and John F. Loud. Durham, N.C., 1990.

———. *Sabrana djela.* 17 vols. Sarajevo, 1984.

Andrić, Nikola. "Jedan narod treba i jednu književnost." *Jugoslavenska njiva* 3, no. 24 (1919): 373–75.

Banac, Ivo. "The Fearful Asymmetry of War: The Causes and Consequences of Yugoslavia's Demise." *Daedelus* 121, no. 2 (Spring 1992): 141–74.

———. *The National Question in Yugoslavia.* Ithaca, N.Y., 1984.

Banac, Ivo, and Katherine Verdery, eds. *National Character and National Ideology in Interwar Europe.* New Haven, 1995.

Bandić, M. I. *Cvet i steg: književnost narodnooslobodilačke borbe.* Belgrade, 1975.

Barac, Antun. "Književno jedinstvo." *Književni jug* 3, no. 7 (1919): 333–34.

Barthes, Roland. *Mythologies.* Trans. Annette Lavers. New York, 1972.

Bartulović, Niko. "Politička sloboda i kultura." *Književni jug* 2, nos. 10–12 (1918): 353–58.

———. "Zadaci vremena." *Književni jug* 1, no. 1 (1918).

Behnschnitt, Wolf Dieter. *Nationalismus bei Serben und Kroaten, 1830–1914.* Munich, 1980.

Bogdanović, Bogdan. "The City and Death." In *Balkan Blues,* ed. Joanna Labon. Evanston, Ill., 1995.

Bogdanović, Milan. "Vratimo Njegoša literaturi." *Srpski književni glasnik*, 2nd ser., 16, no. 7 (1925): 577–79.

Bogert, Ralph. *The Writer as Naysayer: Miroslav Krleža and the Aesthetic of Interwar Central Europe.* Columbus, Ohio, 1990.

Bogosavljević, Srdjan. "Drugi svetski rat—žrtve u Jugoslaviji." *Republika* (Belgrade) 7, no. 117 (1995): I–XXX.

Borko, B. "Jedna kultura i jedna psiha?" *Nova Evropa* 17, no. 1 (1928): 13–17.

Brass, Paul R. *Ethnicity and Nationalism: Theory and Comparison.* New Delhi, 1991.

Butler, Hubert. *The Sub-Prefect Should Have Held His Tongue and Other Essays.* London, 1990.

Č. "Kako je postao dobrovoljački odred u Rusiji." *Nova Evropa* 16, nos. 10–11 (1927): 359–68.

Caney, Simon, et al., eds. *National Rights, International Obligations.* Boulder, Colo., 1996.

Cankar, Ivan. "Slovenci in Jugoslovani." In *Ivan Cankar, Izbrano delo*, vol. 1. Ljubljana, 1967.

Cesarec, August. *Pjesme, novele, zapisi, eseji, i putopisi.* 2 vols. Zagreb, 1966.

———. "Vidovdan slijepih miševa." In *August Cesarec: Rasprave, članci, polemike.* Zagreb, 1971.

Chadda, Maya. *Ethnicity, Security, and Separatism in India.* New York, 1997.

Cohen, Lenard J. *Broken Bonds: Yugoslavia's Disintegration and Balkan Politics in Transition.* 2nd ed. Boulder, Colo., 1995.

Connor, Walker. *Ethnonationalism.* Princeton, N.J., 1994.

Cooper, Henry Ronald, Jr. *France Prešeren.* Boston, 1981.

Ćosić, Dobrica. *Far Away Is the Sun.* Trans. Muriel Heppell and Milica Mihajlović. Belgrade, 1963.

———. *Into the Battle.* Trans. Muriel Heppell. New York, 1983.

———. *Reach to Eternity.* Trans. Muriel Heppell. New York, 1980.

———. *Sabrana dela.* 8 vols. Belgrade, 1966.

———. *A Time of Death.* Trans. Muriel Heppell. New York, 1978.

Crnjanski, Miloš. *Sabrana dela.* 10 vols. Belgrade, 1966.

Čubelić, Tvrtko. "Djuro Daničić—Istraživač narodne književnosti." In *Zbornik o Djuri Daničiću*, ed. Josip Torbarina and Antonije Isaković. Zagreb/Belgrade, 1981.

Ćurčin, Milan. "Pred Meštrovićevim 'Hristom.'" *Nova Evropa* 31, no. 2 (1938): 33–38.

———. "Prefatory Note." In *Ivan Meštrović: A Monograph.* London, 1919.

———, ed. *Almanah srpskih i hrvatskih pjesnika i pripovijedača.* Belgrade/Zagreb, 1910.

Cuvalo, Ante. *The Croatian National Movement, 1966–1972.* New York, 1990.

Cvijić, Jovan. *Balkansko poluostrvo i južnoslovenske zemlje.* Belgrade, 1966.

———. "Osnovi jugoslovenske civilizacije." *Nova Evropa* 6, no. 7 (1926): 213–18.

Darby, H. C., R. W. Seton-Watson, Phyllis Auty, R. G. D. Laffan, and Stephen Clissold. *A Short History of Yugoslavia.* Cambridge, Eng., 1966.

Deanović, Mirko, and Ante Petravić, eds. *Antologija savremene jugoslavenske lirike.* Split, 1922.

Debeljak, Aleš. *Twilight of the Idols.* New York, 1994.

de Bray, R. G. A. *Guide to the Slavonic Languages.* New York, 1951.

Despalatović, Elinor Murray. *Ljudevit Gaj and the Illyrian Movement.* Boulder, Colo., 1975.

Dimić, Ljubodar. *Agitprop kultura.* Belgrade, 1988.

Djilas, Aleksa. *The Contested Country: Yugoslav Unity and Communist Revolution, 1919–1953.* Cambridge, Mass., 1991.

Djordjevic, Dimitrije, ed. *The Creation of Yugoslavia.* Santa Barbara, Calif., 1980.

Dolenc, Erwin. *Kulturni boj. Slovenska kulturna politika v Kraljevini SHS: 1918–1929.* Ljubljana, 1996.

Domanjić, Radoje. *Satire.* Novi Sad, 1960.

Drašković, Vuk. *Nož.* Belgrade, 1983.

Dunlop, D. M. *The History of the Jewish Khazars.* Princeton, N.J., 1954.

Durković-Jakšić, Ljubomir. *Njegoš i Lovćen.* Belgrade, 1971.

Dvorniković, Vladimir. *Karakterologija jugoslovena.* Belgrade, 1939.

Epstein, Mikhail. *After the Future: The Paradoxes of Postmodernism & Contemporary Russian Culture.* Amherst, Mass., 1995.

Finci, Moni. "Pouke revolucije." *NIN*, July 6, 1969, 6–7.

Franolic, Branko. *A Short History of Literary Croatian.* Paris, 1980.

Gabrič, Aleš. "Slovenska agitpropovska kulturna politika, 1945–1952." *Borec* 43, nos. 7–9 (1991): 471–655.

———. *Socialistična kulturna revolucija.* Ljubljana, 1995.

Gellner, Ernest. *Nations and Nationalism.* Ithaca, N.Y., 1983.

Ghosh, Arun, and Radharaman Chakrabarti, eds. *Ethnonationalism: Indian Experience.* Calcutta, 1991.

Glenny, Misha. *The Fall of Yugoslavia.* New York, 1993.

———. "Why the Balkans Are So Violent." *New York Review of Books* 43, no. 14 (Sept. 19, 1996): 34–39.

Greenberg, Robert D. "The Politics of Dialects Among Serbs, Croats, and Muslims in the Former Yugoslavia." *East European Politics and Societies* 10, no. 3 (Fall 1996): 393–415.

Greenfeld, Liah. *Nationalism: Five Roads to Modernity.* Cambridge, Mass., 1992.

Goulding, Daniel J. *Liberated Cinema: The Yugoslav Experience.* Bloomington, Ind., 1985.

Hawkesworth, Celia. *Ivo Andrić: Bridge Between East and West.* London, 1984.

Herrity, Peter. "The Problematic Nature of the Standardisation of the Serbo-Croatian Literary Language in the Second Half of the Nineteenth Century." In *Language Planning in Yugoslavia*, ed. Ranko Bugarski and Celia Hawkesworth. Columbus, Ohio, 1992.

Hirsch, E. D. *Cultural Literacy*. Boston, 1987.

Hobsbawm, Eric. "Mass-Producing Traditions: Europe 1870–1914." In *The Invention of Tradition*, ed. Eric Hobsbawm and Terence Ranger. Cambridge, Eng., 1983.

Jelavich, Barbara, and Charles Jelavich. *The Establishment of the Balkan National States, 1804–1920*. Seattle, 1977.

Jelavich, Charles. "Education, Textbooks, and South Slav Nationalisms in the Interwar Era." In *Allgemeinbildung als Modernisierungsfaktor*, ed. Peter Brüne. Berlin, 1994.

———. *South Slavic Nationalisms—Textbooks and Yugoslav Union Before 1914*. Columbus, Ohio, 1990.

Jonke, Ljudevit. "Daničićev prilog normi i kodifikacija hrvatskoga književnog jezika." In *Zbornik o Djuri Daničiću*, ed. Josip Torbarina and Antonije Isaković. Zagreb/Belgrade, 1981.

Kadić, Ante. *Contemporary Croatian Literature*. The Hague, 1960.

Kalfus, Ken. "Milorad Pavić." *Village Voice Literary Supplement*, Mar. 1992, 22–23.

Kaplan, Robert. *Balkan Ghosts: A Journey Through History*. New York, 1993.

Karadžić, Vuk Stefanović. *Srpske narodne pjesme*. 4 vols. Ed. Vladan Nedić. Belgrade, 1976.

Kincaid, James R. "Read My Lipograms." *New York Times Book Review*, Mar. 12, 1995, 3, 30.

Kiš, Danilo. *A Tomb for Boris Davidovich*. New York, 1978.

Kluić, Stevo. "Duhovno ujedinjenje ili duhovni preporod." *Nova Evropa* 19, no. 5 (1929): 132–35.

Koljević, Svetozar. *The Epic in the Making*. Oxford, 1980.

Kordić, Siniša. *Umetnost i neumetnost*. Belgrade, 1924.

Kovač, Zvonko. "Raširjena asociativnost proze." *Naši razgledi*, Mar. 22, 1985, 188.

Kranjčević, Silvije Strahimir. *Pjesme*. Belgrade, 1968.

Krklec, Gustav. "Naša kulturna politika." In *Kalendar-almanah Prosveta*. Belgrade, 1925.

Krleža, Miroslav. *Izabrana dela*. 15 vols. Belgrade, 1966.

———. *The Return of Philip Latinowicz*. London, 1959.

———. *Zastave*. 4 vols. Zagreb, 1967.

Kršić, Jovan. "Literatura Serbohrvata i Slovenaca kao celina." *Nova Evropa* 9, no. 5 (1924): 141–49.

L. "Novo jugoslovenstvo." *Nova Evropa* 2, no. 3 (1921): 81–83.

———. "Priča o polugi." *Nova Evropa* 1, no. 9 (1920): 289–90.

Lampe, John. *Yugoslavia as History: Twice There Was a Country.* Cambridge, Eng., 1996.

Lasić, Stanko. *Mladi Krleža i njegovi kritičari (1914–1924).* Zagreb, 1993.

Lasta, Petar. "Kronike Ive Andrića." *Republika,* no. 1 (Oct./Nov. 1945): 131–35.

Lešić, Zdenko. "The Avantgarde Nature and Artistic Range of Crnjanski's Poetry." In *Miloš Crnjanski and Modern Serbian Literature,* ed. David Norris. Nottingham, 1988.

Lind, Michael. *The Next American Nation.* New York, 1995.

Loboda, Anton. "Za kulturno zedinjenje Jugoslovanov." *Književni jug* 1, no. 5 (1918): 297–98.

Lubarda, Vojislav. *Vaznesenje.* Belgrade, 1989.

Lukić, Sveta. *Contemporary Yugoslav Literature: A Sociopolitical Approach.* Urbana, Ill., 1972.

Lyotard, Jean-François. *The Postmodern Condition: A Report on Knowledge.* Trans. Geoff Bennington and Brian Massumi. Minneapolis, 1984.

MacKenzie, David. "The Background: Yugoslavia Since 1964." *Nationalism in the USSR and Eastern Europe in the Era of Brezhnev and Kosygin.* Ed. George W. Simmonds. Detroit, 1977.

Magaš, Branka. *The Destruction of Yugoslavia: Tracking the Break-up 1980–92.* London, 1993.

Majstorovic, Stevan. *Cultural Policy in Yugoslavia.* Paris, 1972.

Mamuzić, Ilija, ed. *Antologija ilirskog pokreta.* Belgrade, 1958.

Marjanović, Milan. "Genij jugoslovenstva Ivan Meštrović i njegov hram." In *Jugoslovenska biblioteka,* vol. 1. New York, 1915.

———. *Vladimir Nazor kao nacionalni pjesnik.* Zagreb, 1923.

Marko the Prince. Trans. Anne Pennington and Peter Levi. London, 1984.

Matič, Dragan. "Kulturni utrip Ljubljane v sezonah 1913/14–1917/18." Master's thesis, Dept. of History, University of Ljubljana, 1994.

Matvejević, Predrag. *Jugoslavenstvo danas: Pitanja kulture.* Belgrade, 1984.

Memorandum Srpske akademije nauka i umetnosti. Unpublished manuscript. Belgrade, 1986.

Merhar, Boris. "Ljudska pesem." In *Zgodovina Slovenskega slovstva,* vol. 1, ed. Lino Legiša and Alfonz Gspan. Ljubljana, 1956.

Meštrović, Ivan. *Spomini.* Ljubljana, 1971.

———. "Zamisao Kosovskog hrama." *Nova Evropa* 1, no. 13 (1920): 447–48.

Meštrović, Stjepan G. *The Balkanization of the West.* London, 1994.

———, ed. *Genocide After Emotion: The Postemotional Balkan War.* London, 1996.

Mihailovich, Vasa. "Parable of Nationhood." *The World and I* 3, no. 11 (1988): 378–83.

Miller, Nicholas J. "Two 'Nonconformists' Who Revitalized the Serbian Nation." Unpublished article, n.d.

Milosavljević, Olivera. "Upotreba autoriteta nauke: Javna politička delatnost Srpske akademije nauka i umetnosti." *Republika* (Belgrade) 7, nos. 119–20 (1995): I–XXX.

Mitrović, Marija. "Epsko i bajkovito u procesu radjanja moderne sprske pripovetke." *Književna istorija* 25, no. 89 (1993): 43–68.

Mjesto i položaj hrvatske književnosti u nastavnim programima za škole drugog stupnja i za gimnazije. Rijeka, 1971.

Muradbegović, Ahmed. "Problem jugoslovenske muslimanske izolacije." *Nova Evropa* 3, no. 4 (1921): 107–16.

Nametak, Alija. *Bajram žrtava.* Zagreb, 1931.

Nazor, Vladimir. "Dinku Šimunoviću, mjesto nekrologa." *Nova Evropa* 26, no. 9 (1933): 429.

———. *Priče s ostrva, iz grada i sa planine.* Zagreb, 1927.

———. *S partizanima.* Zagreb, 1968.

Nećak, Dušan. "Revija 'Nova Evropa' in Slovenci." *Zgodovinski časopis* 46, no. 1 (1992): 93–108.

Nedeljković, Dragan, ed. *Reflets de l'histoire Europeen dans l'oeuvre d'Ivo Andrić.* Nancy, 1987.

Njegoš, P. P. "Izabrana pisma." In *P. P. Njegoš: Sabrana dela,* vol. 6. Cetinje/Belgrade, 1977.

———. *The Mountain Wreath.* Trans. Vasa D. Mihailovich. Irvine, Calif., 1986.

Novak, Viktor. *Antologija jugoslovenske misli i narodnog jedinstva (1390–1930).* Belgrade, 1930.

Pavić, Milorad. *Dictionary of the Khazars.* Trans. Christina Pribićević-Zorić. New York, 1989.

Pavlović, Milivoj. *Osnovi metodike nastave srpsohrvatskog jezika i književnosti.* Belgrade, 1961.

Peković, Ratko. *Ni rat ni mir: Panorama književnih polemika 1945–1965.* Belgrade, 1986.

Perovšek, Jurij. "Slovenci in Jugoslavija v tridesetih letih." Unpublished paper, n.d.

———. "Slovenska državna volja v prvem desetletju jugoslovanske krize." In *Slovenci in država.* Ljubljana, 1995.

Pešić, Vesna. "Nacionalni sukobi: Raspad Jugoslavije i rat za nacionalne države." *Republika* (Belgrade) 7, no. 129 (1995): I–XXVIII.

Podlimbarski, Fran Maselj. *Gospodin Franjo.* Ljubljana, 1913.

Poljanec, Franjo, and Blagoje Marčić, eds. *Istorija jugoslovenske književnosti sa teorijom i primerima za III i IV razred gradjanskih škola.* 2nd ed. Belgrade, 1934.

Popović, Danko. *Knjiga o Milutinu.* Belgrade, 1986.

Popović, Pavle. *Jugoslovenska književnost (Književnost Srba, Hrvata i Slovenaca).* Cambridge, Eng., 1919.

———. "Jugoslovenska književnost kao celina." *Glas srpske kraljevske akademije,* 2nd ser., no. 60 (1922).

Prelec, Marko. "The Nationalist Youth Among the Habsburg South Slavs, 1908–1914." Ph.D. diss., Yale University, 1997.

Preradović, Petar. *Pjesnička djela*. Zagreb, 1873.

Prodanović, Jaša M. "Gorski vijenac kao vaspitno delo." *Srpski književni glasnik*, 2nd ser., 16, no. 7 (1925): 558–62.

Raditsa, Bogdan. "Nationalism in Croatia Since 1964." In *Nationalism in the USSR and Eastern Europe in the Era of Brezhnev and Kosygin*, ed. George W. Simmonds. Detroit, 1977.

Ramet, Sabrina. *Balkan Babel: Politics, Culture and Religion in Yugoslavia*. Boulder, Colo., 1992.

———. *Nationalism and Federalism in Yugoslavia, 1962–1991*. Bloomington, Ind., 1992.

Rogel, Carole. *The Slovenes and Yugoslavism: 1890–1914*. Boulder, Colo., 1977.

Rot, Nikola, and Nenad Havelka. *Nacionalna vezanost i vrednosti kod srednjoškolske omladine*. Belgrade, 1973.

Samardžija, Marko. *Hrvatski jezik u Nezavisnoj Državi Hrvatskoj*. Zagreb, 1993.

Samokovlija, Isak. *Sabrana djela*. 3 vols. Sarajevo, 1967.

Sandel, Michael. *Liberalism and the Limits of Justice*. Cambridge, Mass., 1982.

Sekelj, Laslo. *Yugoslavia: The Process of Disintegration*. Boulder, Colo., 1993.

Sekulic, Dusko, Randy Hodson, and Garth Massey. "Who Were the Yugoslavs? Failed Sources of a Common Identity in Yugoslavia." *American Sociological Review* 59 (1994): 83–97.

Selenić, Slobodan. *Prijatelji sa Kosančićevog venca 7*. Belgrade, 1980.

———. *Timor mortis*. Sarajevo, 1989.

Selimović, Meša. *Death and the Dervish*. Evanston, Ill., 1996.

———. *Za i protiv Vuka*. Sarajevo, 1970.

Seton-Watson, R. W. "Meštrović and the Jugoslav Idea." In *Ivan Meštrović: A Monograph*. London, 1919.

Šimunović, Dinko. "Turčin." *Nova Evropa* 26, no. 9 (1933): 435–38.

Singleton, Fred. *A Short History of the Yugoslav Peoples*. Cambridge, Eng., 1985.

Skerlić, Jovan. "Neoslavizam i jugoslovenstvo." In *Sabrana dela Jovana Skerlića*, vol. 7. Belgrade, 1964.

Škerović, Nikola. "Njegoš i Jugoslovenstvo." *Nova Evropa* 11, no. 1 (1925): 1–8.

Šoljan, Antun. *Izabrana djela*. 2 vols. Zagreb, 1987.

The Southern Slav Library. 4 vols. London, 1915–16.

Sowell, Thomas. *Preferential Policies*. New York, 1990.

Soyinka, Wole. *The Open Sore of a Continent*. New York, 1996.

Šrepel, Milivoj, ed. *Gradja za povijest književnosti hrvatske*, vol. 1. Zagreb, 1897.

Štedimlija, S. M. "Sto godina narodne poezije." *Nova Evropa* 28, nos. 4–5 (1935): 120–29.

Stefanović, Dragutin, and Vukašin Stanisavljević. *Pregled Jugoslovenske književnosti*. Belgrade, 1968.

Stiglič, F. "Ob prvem jugoslovanskem umetniškem filmu 'Slavica.'" *Ljudska pravica*, June 9, 1947.

Strajnić, Kosta. *Ivan Meštrović*. Belgrade, 1919.

———. "Umetnost Meštrovića." *Savremenik* 10, nos. 3–4 (Apr. 1915): 113–21.

Sugar, Peter F. *Southeastern Europe Under Ottoman Rule, 1354–1804*. Seattle, 1977.

———, ed. *East European Nationalism in the Twentieth Century*. Washington, D.C., 1995.

Swift, Jonathan. *Gulliver's Travels*. New York, 1971.

Taylor, A. J. P. *The Habsburg Monarchy, 1809–1918*. Chicago, 1976.

Tkalčić, Branko. "Srednja škola kao rasadište jugoslavenske misli." *Jugoslavenska njiva* 3, no. 17 (Apr. 26, 1919): 263–64.

Tolstoy, Leo. *War and Peace*. Trans. Constance Garnett. New York, n.d.

Tomšič, France. "Razvoj Slovenskega knjižnega jezika." In *Zgodovina slovenskega slovstva*, vol. 1., ed. Lino Legiša and Alfonz Gspan. Ljubljana, 1956.

Trgovčević, Ljubinka. *Naučnici Srbije i stvaranje jugoslovenske države, 1914–1920*. Belgrade, 1986.

Trifunovska, Snezana, ed. *Yugoslavia Through Documents*. Dordrecht, 1994.

Ugrešić, Dubravka. "Balkan Blues." In *Balkan Blues: Writing Out of Yugoslavia*, ed. Joanna Labon. Evanston, Ill., 1995.

———. *Kultura laži [antipolitički eseji]*. Zagreb, 1996.

Ujević, Tin. *Sabrana djela*. 17 vols. Zagreb, 1966.

Veselinov, Stanko. "Životno važan put." *NIN*, Jan. 8, 1961.

Vidmar, Josip. *Kulturni problem Slovenstva*. Ljubljana, 1932.

Vojnović, Ivo. "Chords." In *Ivan Meštrović: A Monograph*, ed. Milan Ćurčin. London, 1919.

Vošnjak, Bogumil. *Pobeda Jugoslavije*. Belgrade, 1930.

Vrhovac, P. "Cvetkovanje praha Njegoševa." *Letopis Matice srpske* 306, no. 1 (1925): 3–7.

Vucinich, Wayne S., ed. *Ivo Andrić: The Bridge Still Stands*. Berkeley, Calif., 1995.

Wachtel, Andrew. *An Obsession with History: Russian Writers Confront the Past*. Stanford, Calif., 1994.

———. "The South Slavic Lands During World War I: Culture and Nationalism." In *European Culture in the Great War: The Arts, Entertainment, and Propaganda, 1914–1918*, ed. Aviel Roshwald and Richard Stites. Cambridge, Eng., 1998.

Walicki, Andrzej. *A History of Russian Thought from the Enlightenment to Marxism*. Trans. Hilda Andrews-Rusiecka. Stanford, Calif., 1979.

West, Rebecca. *Black Lamb and Grey Falcon*. London, 1982.

West, Richard. *Tito and the Rise and Fall of Yugoslavia*. New York, 1994.

Woodward, Susan. *Balkan Tragedy: Chaos and Dissolution After the Cold War*. Washington, D.C., 1995.

———. *Socialist Unemployment: The Political Economy of Yugoslavia.* Princeton, N.J., 1995.

Zečević, Momčilo. *Na istorijskoj prekretnici: Slovenci u politici jugoslovenske države 1918–1929.* Belgrade, 1985.

Živanović, Jeremija, ed. *Primeri nove književnosti.* Belgrade, 1921.

Zogović, Radovan. "Primjer kako ne treba praviti 'Primjere književnosti.'" *Borba,* May 8, 1947: 4–5.

Zubović, J. "Jugoslovenski čovek." *Nova Evropa* 10, no. 6 (1924): 145–56.

Index

In this index an "f" after a number indicates a separate reference on the next page, and an "ff" indicates separate references on the next two pages. A continuous discussion over two or more pages is indicated by a span of page numbers, e.g., "57–59." *Passim* is used for a cluster of references in close but not consecutive sequence.

Cultural Memory | *in the Present*

Library of Congress Cataloging-in-Publication Data

Wachtel, Andrew.

  Making a nation, breaking a nation : literature and cultural
politics in Yugoslavia / Andrew Baruch Wachtel.

      p.   cm.

  Includes bibliographical references and index.

  ISBN 0-8047-3180-2 (cloth). — ISBN 0-8047-3181-0 (paper).

  1. Yugoslavia—Cultural policy—History.   2. Nationalism—
Yugoslavia—History.   3. Yugoslavia—Ethnic relations.   4. Yugoslav
literature—Political aspects.   5. Language policy—Yugoslavia—
History.   I. Title.

DR1228.W33   1998

306'.09497—dc21   98-4438

                                                                          CIP

 ⊗ This book is printed on acid-free. recycled paper.

Original printing 1998
Last figure below indicates year of this printing:

07   06   05   04   03   02   01   00   99   98